BORDER *CUATES*

BORDER *CUATES*

A History of the
U.S.-Mexican Twin Cities

By
Milo Kearney
and
Anthony Knopp

Illustrated by
Peter Gawenda

EAKIN PRESS ★ Austin, Texas

FIRST EDITION

Copyright © 1995
By Milo Kearney
and
Anthony Knopp

Published in the United States of America
By Eakin Press
A Division of Sunbelt Media, Inc.
P.O. Drawer 90159 ★ Austin, Texas 78709

ISBN 1-57168-057-8

10   9   8   7   6   5   4   3   2

Library of Congress Cataloging-in-Publication Data:

Kearney, Milo.
    Border cuates : a history of the U.S.-Mexican twin cities / by Milo Kearney
and Anthony Knopp : illustrated by Peter Gawenda.
        p.   cm.
    Includes bibliographical references and index.
    ISBN 1-57168-057-8
    1. Sister cities — Mexican-American Border Region — History. 2. Mexican-American Border Region — History, Local. I. Knopp, Anthony K., 1940– .
II. Title.
F787.K43   1995
972'.1 — dc20   95-17848
                                                                                          CIP

Contents

iv

Acknowledgments

This project is indebted to the Fulbright Program, whose grant to Milo Kearney for lecturing and research at the Instituto Tecnológico in Matamoros, Tamaulipas, during the 1992–1993 academic year allowed the core of this project to be developed. We wish to thank Dr. Juliet García, president of the University of Texas at Brownsville, Dr. Anthony Zavaleta, dean of the College of Liberal Arts, Dr. Peter Gawenda, director of Research and Planning, Dr. Bill Adams, head of the Social Sciences department, Yolanda González, archivist of the Hunter Room of the University of Texas at Brownsville's Oliveira Memorial Library, and Professor Abel González for their help in working out the details of this program. We also appreciate the generous support of Ing. Javier Alonso Banda, director of Matamoros' Instituto Tecnológico, Ing. Leonardo Vargas, the subdirector, and Lic. Patricia García Lerma, head of the Department of Applied Sciences, in making this project a success. The enthusiastic class participation of professors, teachers, students, and members of the town historical societies from both Matamoros and Brownsville was the most important motivating factor. Finally, we would like to express a special thanks for their help on this project to Sean Kearney, Kathleen Kearney, John Kearney, and most of all to Vivian Kearney.

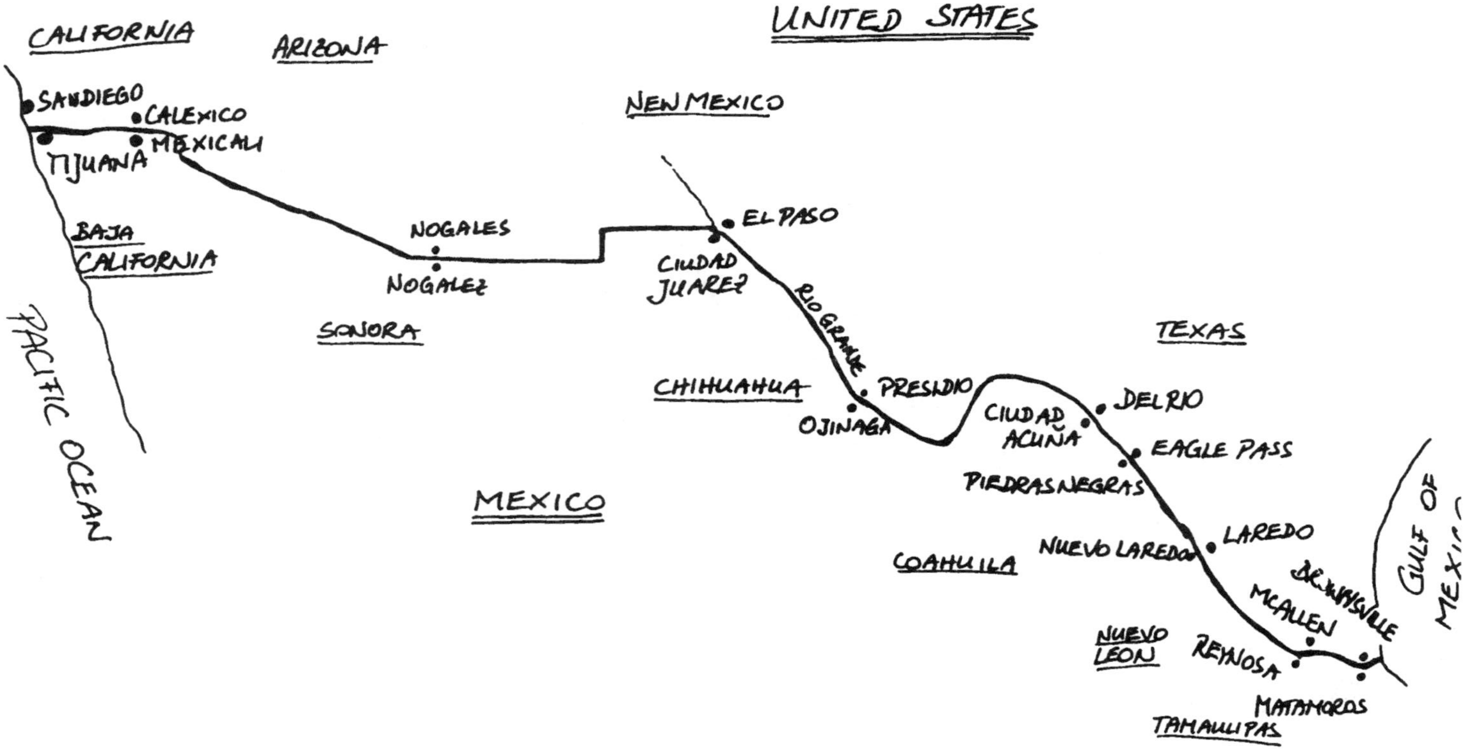
UNITED STATES
CALIFORNIA
ARIZONA
NEW MEXICO
SANDIEGO
CALEXICO
MEXICALI
TIJUANA
BAJA CALIFORNIA
NOGALES
NOGALEZ
SONORA
EL PASO
CIUDAD JUAREZ
RIO GRANDE
CHIHUAHUA
PRESIDIO
OJINAGA
TEXAS
DEL RIO
CIUDAD ACUÑA
EAGLE PASS
PIEDRAS NEGRAS
LAREDO
NUEVO LAREDO
COAHUILA
MCALLEN
REYNOSA
MATAMOROS
NUEVO LEON
TAMAULIPAS
GULF OF MEXI
PACIFIC OCEAN
MEXICO

CHAPTER ONE

Introduction to the Family

The fairy tale of Snow White and Rose Red tells of two sisters who resembled two rose bushes, one with white roses and one with red roses. The sisters were always holding hands and shared everything. When Snow White said, "We never want to separate," Rose Red answered, "So long as we live."[1]

The almost 2,000-mile-long U.S.-Mexican border has given rise to a nearly unique phenomenon in the sister cities which dot its length. San Diego and Tijuana, Calexico and Mexicali, El Paso and Cd. Juárez, Laredo and Nuevo Laredo, McAllen and Reynosa, and Brownsville and Matamoros (along with many lesser sets) are true twins or *cuates* with a shared cultural flavor and economic importance. Yet the two towns in each set are as distinct from each other as Snow White and Rose Red in the fairy tale.

The creation of twin cities is not typical of international borders in general. Until after World War II, borders around the world tended to divide rather than to join their adjacent regions because trade ran mainly between a mother country and its distant colonies in competition with other systems. The linking up of two sizable cities, each significant in its own right, is rare. Most of Canada's major southernmost cities (including Winnipeg and Montreal) are at a significant remove from the border.[2] Cities located on the U.S.-Canadian border have no truly comparable twins (Detroit far outweighing Windsor). Latin America's and Asia's important cities are generally located away from borders. Such large European border

1

cities as Strasbourg, Basel, Konstanz, Görlitz, and Brest have no major twin. The case of Brazzaville and Léopoldville on the border of Zaïre and the Congo is an isolated example in Africa.

The twin city phenomenon has proliferated along the U.S.-Mexican border and here alone due to the geographic isolation of the border zone in the midst of a desert. Thus there has been little incentive for major towns to spring up for some distance both north and south from the border itself, which is a river for half of its length. Only along the U.S.-Mexican border has a developed and a third world country directly met, inviting an exchange of manufactured items for raw materials so that smuggling has brought trade regardless of national agreements. The twin city phenomenon has been perpetuated by the major importance of each of the countries involved, despite the industrial lag of Mexico behind the United States. In size, population, cultural vitality, and national pride, neither society has been able to dwarf the other. The meeting of two such strong cultures and the uneven nature of national and local development have dictated that the advantage for growth has lain alternately first on one side of the border and then on the other.

The story of these twin cities is as distinct from the general history of the border as the life story of human twins is distinct from the history of their family. There are family traits shared by all border towns, but each has its own individuality. Only strangers fail to distinguish one family member from another.

An old bromide to the effect that if you have seen one you have seen them all can be dismissed by noting the general differences between them. The twin city sets fall into an overall symmetrical pattern dictated by the border's location between two oceans. In the highland center is the mother town set of Cd. Juárez and El Paso. This urban location has repeatedly established trends for the other towns. Moving out along the border in both directions from Cd. Juárez and El Paso, passing through various secondary towns, one comes to two more noteworthy sets of originally mining and ranching towns. To the east these are the two Laredos, while to the west these are the two Nogales. Both sets have benefited by lying on main railroad routes between the United States and Mexico. Continuing to move outward along the border in both directions, as one approaches the lower reaches of the two great border river systems — the Rio Grande and the Gila-Colorado — one comes to two great sets of agricultural cities thriving on the combination of good soil and of water from the rivers. These sets are McAllen and Reynosa to the east and Mexicali and Calexico to the west. Finally, at the two end points of the border, lie the two sets of port-influenced towns, namely Matamoros and Brownsville in the east and San Diego and Tijuana in the west. These towns are presently also aspiring to industrial development.

In the chronological order of their emergence into significance, the mother location of Cd. Juárez-El Paso (as Paso del Norte) appeared first, in the mid-seventeenth century; the port cities next with the development of international trade at the turn of the eighteenth to the nineteenth centuries; then the mining and ranching sets, as they were connected to major railroad routes at the end of the nineteenth century; and finally the agricultural sets, thanks to the development of local irrigation systems in the early twentieth century. The symmetrical pattern thus formed suggests a wider variety of experience in the past and a greater hope for a balanced and creative development of the border in the future than is often realized.

The border towns, while long isolated from and unsung by the main societies of the two respective countries, have played a significant role in the destinies of their two nations and seem destined to play an even larger role in the future. Their local interactions exert an impact in the larger relations between the two parent countries. Furthermore, the border towns have repeatedly served as catalysts in the modernization and reformation of Mexican national politics —from the Federalist revolts of the early nineteenth century through the modernist push of the Porfiriato and through the reforms of the Mexican Revolution to the free trade zone talks of our day.

The cliché that the border towns have been mere victims of national policies is inaccurate. At times, they have exerted an impact on the fate of the entire continent. Local influence was at work in the creation of the United States-Mexico border. Activities in these towns helped to catalyze the Mexican-American War. Border town developments also played a role in the entry of the United States into World War I. Most recently, local problems have helped to draw national governments into such experiments as the *bracero* program, PRONAF, the *maquiladora* program, and now the free trade zone talks.

To date, three sets of twin cities have at one time or another held the leadership among them. They are San Diego/Tijuana, El Paso/ Cd. Juárez, and Brownsville/Matamoros. These sets of cities have occupied the three strategic points along the border, namely the main transportation route of the center and the ports at the two ends. Their population figures have reflected their general vigor and leadership in each period. Thanks to its much earlier start, the El Paso/Cd. Juárez area held the lead in population down to the Civil War. The Civil War period then briefly propelled Brownsville/Matamoros to the top place. This position was regained by El Paso/Cd. Juárez in the decade after the war. By 1930, the San Diego/Tijuana set moved to the top spot in population, followed by El Paso/Cd. Juárez. At present, Brownsville/Matamoros has fallen to the fourth set in population. Besides these three sets of towns which have each, at least momentarily, shared the limelight, there are another three sets of towns which have occupied a secondary position. These are Calexico/Mexicali (now the third-largest set), Laredo/Nuevo Laredo, and McAllen/Reynosa. Finally, the tertiary sets of towns include Yuma/Los Algodones (or arguably matched with San Luis Rio Colorado), Nogales/Nogales, Douglas/Agua Prieta, Columbus/Palomas, Presidio/Ojinaga, Del Rio/Cd. Acuña, Eagle Pass/Piedras Negras, Roma/Mier, and Rio Grande City/Camargo. Each of these sets has played a significant role at one point or another. Additionally there are many tiny twin border hamlets.

An overall distinction between the towns along the western end and the eastern end of the border can also be made. The towns to the east have stuck closer to their Mexican parents, their part of the border dipping to the south toward its heart and sharing in Mexico's recent greater poverty. The sets of twins lying to the west, closer to the American parent, have come to be richer and more modern, with San Diego as their most important center of industry and employment.[3]

The family of these twin sister towns has long attracted little interest in the North American neighborhood. The twins have been belittled for their poverty, exploited in their need, and excluded due to their lack of status. However, they have shaped the neighborhood in unsuspected ways, and they may now be in line to receive a major inheritance. It is time for us to get better acquainted with them.

CHAPTER TWO

Youthful Idealism:
The Founding of the Line of Towns

While some may choose to begin the history of the border with the Treaty of Guadalupe Hidalgo at the end of the Mexican-American War, an argument can be made that the history of the border towns should properly commence with their founding. There are several reasons for taking this approach. First, the foundations of the societies and cultures of the towns that antedate the Mexican-American War lie in their pre-1848 history. Second, even before the creation of the U.S.-Mexican border in 1848, the towns along that later line were already border towns by virtue of lying on an exposed border of Mexico with wild Indian territory. The Spanish colony of Texas was too far removed across the Wild Horse Desert to keep the Lower Rio Grande colonies from experiencing a border identity at the edge of Indian territory. Third, isolation by deserts from both Mexico to the south and from the United States to the north characterized these towns before as after the Mexican-American War.

Early Idealism

The moods of families change, so that different children may be born into different environments. Paso del Norte was the first born in the period of youthful idealism. At the heart of this spirit lay a missionary effort to convert the local Indians. The mid-seventeenth century saw a resurgence of the Christian fervor which had typified Spain under Isabel la Católica and again in the Counter-Reformation reign of Felipe II. The preceding period of the early seventeenth

5

century had seen the attention of the Spanish court distracted by the creative delights of the Siglo de Oro. However, the loss of Portugal and the Catalan revolt of the early 1640s had sobered the mood of the government. Felipe IV had experienced a change of mood due to his grief over the deaths of his beloved first wife, Isabel de Borbón, and son, Baltasar Carlos, in 1644 and 1646 respectively. Convinced that God was expressing his disapproval of court frivolities, Felipe turned to fostering a new dedication to God.

The king's change of heart encouraged new missionary commitment in the colonies. Efforts were made to provide better contact between Viceregal Mexico and the Franciscan missions of New Mexico. Attention was drawn to this need by Felipe IV's new correspondent and confidante, María de Agreda, commonly remembered as the blue nun. Abbess of the Concepcionista Convent of the Immaculate Conception in Agreda, on the border of Aragon and Navarre, María was visited by mystic visions, which she described in her book, the *Mística Ciudad de Dios.* Most of all, María was famous for her purported bilocations to New Mexico. While remaining in Spain, her double would miraculously appear in that far-flung province to scold recalcitrant Indians and send them to the missions for baptism or rededication.

It was mainly in this mood of religious idealism that Paso del Norte and the later border towns founded in the following century appeared. "*Lo que nada vale, nada cuesta*" ("Whatever is worthwhile comes at a price"), and the settlers had to accept many dangers and deprivations. There were few amenities of life, provided one survived at all, for the wild Indians took a heavy toll of lives in their attacks. The mood of high-minded commitment was further heightened by a general sharing of the livestock on lands open to all in common. This initial religious idealism was the *sine qua non* for the launching of the border towns. The early Christian settlers themselves would have seen in their survival God's protective blessing over their sacrifice. Even a skeptical point of view might argue that the missionary purpose helped to attract sufficient investment into the area and set a mood of cooperation which allowed the Hispanic and Indian communities to coalesce and cooperate in the face of major problems.

The Oldest Sister is Born

The first of the border towns to be founded is the one that lies right in the middle of the border line — Paso del Norte, now called Cd. Juárez. Its location was a natural place to start, in a fertile valley on the south side of the Rio Grande River next to the lowest, simplest pass across the Rocky Mountains.[1] Several early expeditions had stirred interest in the region, mainly as a passage to New Mexico's fabled Seven Cities of Cíbola. Alvar Núñez Cabeza de Vaca, with the Moorish slave Estebanico and two other companions, had brought reports of rich cities. However, Coronado's expedition to New Mexico had dampened hopes for finding wealth in that direction, leaving the way open for a less materialist settlement.

It was thus Franciscan friars who, in 1581, led the way back through Paso del Norte's valley on their way to convert the Pueblo Indians of New Mexico. The murder of the friars in New Mexico acted as a warning for those who would follow, but did not prevent them from doing so. The efforts of the fathers in the Pueblo Indian area led to the founding of the Spanish colony of New Mexico in 1598 under Juan de Oñate as its first governor. This step increased the strategic importance of the Paso del Norte area for maintaining contact between Mexico and New Mexico. A monument later erected in the plaza of San Elizario tells how on 4 May 1598 Oñate claimed the locality for Spain.[2]

When Oñate in his turn despaired of finding significant wealth in New Mexico, it was again the friars who kept the core commitment to the colony, on whose fate hung that of the Paso del Norte area as well. It was also the friars who, in 1656, founded the first mission at the Pass, for the Manso Indians, complete with a little church. This first mission attempt collapsed after two years in the midst of a quarrel between the secular and church authorities in New Mexico, but the friars lost no time in picking up the pieces to start again, this time on a permanent basis.[3]

The ongoing presence of a Spanish-led settlement at Paso del Norte dates from 8 December 1659. On that day, humble Franciscan Fray García de San Francisco y Zúñiga founded a renewed mission for the Manso Indians, called Nuestra Señora de Guadalupe. Construction began on a church building, which took completed form in January 1668. The Guadalupe Mission, considered by one friar to be even more beautiful than the mission churches of New Mexico, still embellishes the spot. Thus the first enduring architectural statement of the border town ethos was an expression of faith. The downtown area of present Cd. Juárez now extends out around it.[4]

The Indians missionized were not without their own culture and history. The valley had known trade in the Classical Period of the first millenium A.D. Farming villages had existed there at that time, producing such crops as maize, beans, and squash, as well as utilizing the local lechugilla plant to make a distinctive jam. However, the local economy had suffered a setback in the tenth century due to the advent of the Apaches, migrating from the far north. By the time the Hispanic missionaries arrived, the Mansos, Sumas, and other local Indians had reverted to a hunting and gathering existence, living in grass huts and with the males going naked.[5]

In some very significant ways, the mission presence represented an improvement for the natives. However, the acculturation of the local Indians did not occur without the application of a good deal of harsh discipline by the fathers. The friars had a difficult task to perform considering the relative potential for violence from the Indians, despite their incipient level of organization. The Manso tribe was in no way named for the Spanish word for "mild," but rather for their explanation in their own language upon first meeting the Spaniards that they meant them no harm.[6] However, some of the friars fell into inhumane practices. Horror stories are told about the cruelty with which the mission Indians were treated, including body-scarring floggings, sale of Indian children into slavery, and arbitrary executions.[7]

Nonetheless, the fiercest of the Indians were the tribes that took to horseback and then began raiding into the settlement. While very formidable Indians were ever present at a close distance, the long line of border towns coincided with the zone of comparatively manipulable natives in what is now northern Mexico. Not only were these Indians poorly organized, but their enthusiasm for fighting must have been deflated by the defeat of related tribes a bit farther south in the Chichimeca Indian wars of the late sixteenth century. The ability to work with the local Indians, albeit under strain, encouraged the spread of the mission system and facilitated a mixture of native with European blood. The relative calm and cordiality of today's border town residents echoes the amenability of the earliest inhabitants.

From the start made by Fray García de San Francisco, two other missions were founded in the region in the first decade of settlement. The second mission was San Francisco, set up to the southeast for the Suma Indians in 1665. The third, also for the Sumas, was Santa Gertrudis. In Paso del Norte's second decade of the 1670s, still other groups of Indians, including Jumanos, Tanos, and even some Apaches, were attracted to live at the Guadalupe Mission. At the same time, the first Spanish-speaking settlers besides the friars also settled down around the Guadalupe Mission, where they provided the principal way station for travelers moving between points to the south in Mexico and Santa Fe. This original religious commitment was an essential element in the launching of border town history. It is hard to see how the experiment could have survived without its idealism. The rapid interbreeding and cooperation of Hispanic and Indian settlers, despite the segregationist caste policy of the Spanish Crown, bred a spirit of cooperation.[8]

The First Survival Crisis

The 1680s in Paso del Norte illustrate a protracted feature of border town life, namely isolation on a dangerous frontier. Although since World War II the border towns have finally begun to achieve economic and political integration into their respective countries, previously they were strongly affected by problems of isolation from the mainstream of their own countries and by separation from each other.[9] For the first generation of residents in Paso del Norte, this isolation brought vulnerability to constant harrowing Indian attacks. This simmering dilemma boiled over in the 1680s.

The crisis announced itself with the arrival in September 1680 of 1,946 bedragled refugees from the Spanish colony of New Mexico. The Pueblo Indians had exploded into rebellion, and the Spanish rule in New Mexico had collapsed. This development left Paso del Norte as the northernmost outpost of Nueva España, bearing the full pressure of maintaining the border. After a period of adjustment in makeshift camps, the refugees were settled into five new local towns, segregated by ethnic identity. In 1681 the New Mexican Indian refugees were placed in three new Franciscan missions, called (in order progressively downstream from the Guadalupe Mission) Ysleta, Senecú, and Socorro. Due to a shift of the Rio Grande to the south in 1846, Ysleta and Socorro now lie in Texas. The Hispanic refugees formed two new towns of their own — San Lorenzo and San Pedro de Alcántara. To these new settlements was added a local presidio, that of San José, at a distance from the Guadalupe Mission. This fortress served as a base for the later reconquest of New Mexico. Various Hispanics settled around the presidio, whose governor acted as their mayor (the first such official in the area).[10]

Thus the first stage of the New Mexican Pueblo uprising swelled the population of the Paso del Norte area. However, it also gave a model of successful Indian revolt for the discontented elements among the local natives. A shortage of food in the crisis fed the dissatisfaction. The result was a local facsimile of the New Mexican revolt, which in 1684 to 1685 put the local settlers to a hard test. Warned of an anti-Hispanic plot, Governor Domingo Jironza ordered eight of the Manso plotters to be garroted. In reaction, Tiguas brought down from New Mexico mingled with the local Sumas and other Indian groups (including some Mansos) in an attempt to exterminate or drive out the Hispanics. The Sumas permanently destroyed their missions of San Francisco and Santa Gertrudis, as well as the Hispanic settlement of San Pedro. Despite a later attempt to re-Christianize the Sumas through the new mission settlement of Santa María Magdalena, their reversion to heathen status back in their old mountain homes proved to be irreversible.[11]

Paso del Norte's Hispanic community was hard hit. It fought back by executing the captured rebel Indian chiefs. Crops and livestock were destroyed, and food fell into short supply. Clothing, too, was affected, attendance at church dropping off due to embarrassment over lack of decent garb. At one point, with the local population in agitation, the town council despaired of success and petitioned the Spanish authorities for permission to abandon the region. Yet in the end, they managed to hold on and provided the base from which New Mexico was reconquered in 1692 to 1695. The population of the Paso del Norte area was halved from about 2,000 to about 1,000, distributed among five remaining communities. The three New Mexican Indian missions of Senecú, Ysleta, and Socorro survived. Two Hispanic settlements remained: Paso del Norte itself and the smaller San Lorenzo.[12]

Yet out of the crisis Paso del Norte emerged as a real town for the first time as, for reasons of defense, Governor Jironza moved the presidio and its surrounding Hispanic population to a site next to the Guadalupe Mission. Jironza also managed to breathe a spirit of hope back into the residents. He used a 2,500-peso grant from the Spanish government to build dams and irrigation canals, which helped put the local farming and ranching back on its feet. Paso del Norte began to enjoy profits from exporting such grape products as raisins, vinegar, wine, and brandy both north to Santa Fe and south to Mexico proper. By 1750, there were over 3,000 people living in the Paso del Norte area. A local school for children of the elite was established, which by 1807 was training 316 pupils. San Elizario, Senecú,

Ysleta, and Socorro joined Paso del Norte in founding schools. In 1797 a bridge was built from Paso del Norte to the north bank.[13]

The new mercantalist emphasis did not at once eradicate the asperity of life, for the growing trade induced the Apaches to raid all the harder both by the lure of its products and by creating competition for watering holes along the Apache migratory routes. The expansion southwards of Comanches in the Great Plains also brought greater numbers of Apaches into the region. The residents of the area called for more help, and in 1726, Coronel Pedro de Rivera visited Paso del Norte to inspect the problem. To the chagrin of the Paseños, Rivera suggested that the benefits did not warrant the military effort, so that Spain should reduce, not increase, the number of its troops in the north. He did concede that the forty-nine soldiers then stationed at Paso del Norte should be retained, although on a reduced salary. After the scare caused by Rivera's report, the Paseños were relieved just to keep the number of soldiers that previously had seemed inadequate. A *modus vivendi* with the Apaches was established by a policy of conciliation implemented in 1772. Until the end of Spanish rule, the Apaches held their peace in exchange for presents and food.[14]

The survival of Paso del Norte demonstrated the feasibility of introducing still more towns along the Indian frontier. It also laid down the model by which they could be launched. In 1701 the Hispanic presence came to the site of a second future twin town of the border, Sonoita, Sonora, across from the present Lukeville, Arizona, with the founding of the Jesuit mission of San Marcelo de Sonoydag by Father Eusebio Kino. This mission gradually grew into a service center for the surrounding farms and mines, but remained small. It would be linked by paved road to the outside world in 1925.[15]

In 1759 a presidio was built on the Rio Grande in the Big Bend region to protect a mission established nearby in 1683. The town of Ojinaga, Chihuahua, developed around this presidio by the middle of the next century as a way station on the route between Cd. Chihuahua and San Antonio. The name would be changed from Presidio del Norte to Ojinaga in 1867, in honor of Governor Manuel Ojinaga of Chihuahua (who two years previous had lost his life in the Juarista struggle against the French). The original name would be perpetuated in Ojinaga's twin town of Presidio, Texas.[16] A more significant development of twin towns occurred on the Lower Rio Grande.

The First Towns on the Lower Rio Grande

Spain's settlement of the Lower Rio Grande was inspired by the bourgeois-based movement of Enlightened Despotism, with its interest in bolstering the economy of the Spanish Empire. Before this program was adopted in full force under Carlos III (1759–1788), a more expansive government was developing in Spain in the early eighteenth century. More attention was being paid to the needs for the extension of the empire in reaction to a new Anglo presence in Spanish America, dating from the 1714 Treaty of Utrecht and its grant to the British of trading rights in four Spanish American ports. Under a series of illustrious viceroys of Nueva España, greater attention to provincial needs brought such reforms as an improved dam for Paso del Norte in 1766 and royal postal service to that town from 1783.[17]

Most importantly, Paso del Norte was now joined by a whole series of new Hispanic towns tracing the general line of the present U.S.-Mexican border from the Gulf of Mexico to the Pacific. Worried over the vulnerability of Nueva España during the War of the Spanish Succession, the viceroy, the conde de Revillagigedo, in 1745 prepared for the settlement of coastal Tamaulipas. The project was assigned to Coronel José de Escandón, el conde de la Sierra Gorda. Escandón's love for his native Santander gave the new province its name of Nuevo Santander, endowed it with a sprinkling of Santanderino town names, and brought in Santanderinos as pioneers alongside the mainstream of settlers from northeastern Mexico.[18]

The mood of idealistic sacrifice already established by Paso del Norte was continued by these new settlements. The northernmost of Escandón's new towns were located on the banks of the Rio Grande, to provide border defense against the marauding Indians from the north.[19] A flying squadron set up by Escandón moved between these towns in a harried attempt to discourage such raids.[20] The wild Indian attacks, combined with a lack of even basic amenities, guaranteed concerned cooperation. Even the mission Indians, fighting with bows and arrows under their own Indian captains, joined in the common defense against the fierce Apaches and Comanches. There was little local food production and even less currency to buy imported goods. The simple thatched-roof cane and mud *jacales* contained almost no furniture. As was typical of a frontier, women were in short supply, and the Hispanic men fraternized with the Indian women to produce a rapid blending of the two blood groups. Also,

the custom of holding stock and land in common maintained a certain egalitarianism. Ranch hands were mainly the rapidly Christianized and Hispanicized local Tamaulipecan Indians, whose love of beef and need for security made them willing collaborators. Finally, the planting of Indian missions in most of these towns continued the commitment to Christ.[21]

The general tendency of sharing livestock and cattle was naturally broken where individuals held ranches in more remote areas exposed to Indian attack. This principle applied to the land north of the river across from towns on the south bank. Such was the case for Nicolás de los Santos Coy and his son-in-law, Blas María de la Garza Falcón, who were among the ranchers who received grants from Escandón on 10 March 1753 for sheep and cattle ranching across the river from Camargo in the area of the later Rio Grande City.[22] In the area of the future Brownsville, José Miguel Ramírez founded the Rancho Ramireño by 1765, while José de la Garza in 1772 built the Rancho Viejo (then called the Rancho de Santa Petronilla).[23] The pattern of individual ownership of herds also applies to José Vázquez Borrego's isolated *hacienda* of Dolores founded in 1750 on the south bank west of Revilla and later abandoned.[24]

The first of the down-*rio* towns to be founded was Camargo, named for the town of Camargo a bit southwest of Cd. Santander in Spain. The site was chosen with an eye to dominating future river traffic at a point where the higher Hill Country disgorges the Rio Grande to meander on from there through flat lands to the Gulf of Mexico. The 378 settlers arrived from Nuevo León on 5 March 1749, led by Capitán Blas María de la Garza. It was the Augustinians who founded the mission there, with 500 Indians. After relocation from the original site, a colorful church was built, which is arguably still the prettiest in the Lower Rio Grande territory.[25]

Close on the heels of the founding of Camargo on 14 March 1749 appeared the slightly smaller and even poorer settlement of Reynosa. This name, too, was borrowed from an older town in Santander, Spain, in this case chosen to honor Viceroy Guemes y Horcasitas, who was born there. The original location chosen is where the small town of Reynosa Díaz now stands, west of the present city of Reynosa. This spot allowed the settlers to cross the river to mine salt from the Sal del Rey close to the present-day town of Edinburg for sale back in Nuevo León. The salt was used mainly to nourish livestock and to aid in the patio process of extracting silver from its impurities. The town's 238 founders, hailing from Nuevo León, were led by Capitán Carlos Cantú. The San Joaquín Order set up a mission east of the town for 300 Indians.[26]

On 10 October 1750 a third river settlement was launched on the road to Monterrey upriver from Camargo. Its original name of Moros was changed in 1754 to Revilla in honor of Viceroy Revillagigedo. The town was still later renamed Guerrero, but the original townsite has been swallowed whole by the waters of Falcon Lake. The settlers were led by Capitán Vicente Guerra, and this town, too, was provided a mission.[27]

Competition in River Town Foundings

Competition rapidly opened up between these first three towns as each vied to spread its influence and jurisdiction up and down the lower stretch of the river. The initial race pitted Camargo against Revilla, as Reynosa was at first preoccupied with problems of constant flooding of its ill-chosen site. In 1752, as the result of a petition to Escandón from a group of Camargoistas, they were allowed to found, at their own expense, what might be thought of as a colony of Camargo on a high, rocky spot over the Río Álamo two and a half miles before it pours into the Rio Grande between Camargo and Revilla. This colony of a colony was dubbed Mier, a name which had already in earlier years adhered to the spot. In 1715, as it is believed, Nuevo León's Governor Francisco Mier y Torres had pitched camp there during an expedition, so that the location was remembered as the Estancia de Mier. Some ranches had actually existed on the site since 1734. To these early efforts were now added nineteen families from Camargo and thirty-eight from the Nuevo León town of Cerralvo. For the first time, no mission accompanied the founding. However, a Franciscan-style church was built in the 1780s and 1790s. Capitán Florencio de Chapa led the settlers.[28]

Camargo's founding of Mier spurred Revilla to spin off a far more significant colony of its own upriver, in this case on the north bank of the Rio Grande. On 15 May 1755 Escandón responded to a petition from a group of Revilla families by granting them permission to launch the settlement of Laredo. Again, a town in Santander, Spain, inspired the town's name. The project had been spearheaded by José Vázquez Borrego, and the new town was led by his later son-in-law Tomás Sánchez. The importance of the settlement was guaranteed by its location at the major crossing of the Rio Grande on the main route between Monterrey and San Antonio, Texas.[29] So many settlers poured in from Revilla that the population more than doubled in the first decade.[30] In 1767 about sixty huts had been built on both sides of the Rio Grande.[31] As had occurred in Camargo's founding of Mier, Laredo was not at first given a mission. Only in 1789 did the Augustinians found a 500-Indian mission there. However, the main town church of San Agustín was begun from the outset.[32]

If Revilla had outdone Camargo's creation of Mier with the founding of Laredo, a group of ten families, nine of them Camargoistas, in 1774 set about planning to found another town with a significant future — Matamoros. The founding families had already established ranching interests in the area since 1749, when Matías de los Santos Coy had started the first ranch there.[33] Officially launched in 1784, the new population was at first called San Juan de los Esteros Hermosos. Capitán Ignacio de Ayala led the settlers, under the nominal legal authority of Camargo.[34] Here again, no missionary effort accompanied the founding. It was not until 1793 that missionaries from Zacatecas arrived and built a little chapel.[35]

Situated on the south bank toward the mouth of the river, the location of Matamoros, as of Laredo, was well chosen for eventual mercantile development. Its short-term advantage was that it offered ample water for cattle in the local esteros or lakes, formed from flooding of the Rio Grande over its lower southern banks. It was also more protected, being located farther downriver from the Apache and Comanche raids. As in the case of Laredo, a stream of settlers soon began the pattern of immigration which was to reach such avalanche proportions in the twentieth century.[36]

The Start of San Diego

The last town of the present border to appear in the period of Enlightened Despotism was San Diego, now lying at that border's westernmost extension. The California coast had been claimed by Spain since 1542. In that year, Juan de Cabrillo, a Portuguese explorer sent north by Guatemalan Governor Pedro de Alvarado, had discovered San Diego Bay, an accomplishment honored by the Cabrillo National Monument in San Diego. However, on a return trip in 1543, Cabrillo had broken his arm in a fall on San Miguel Island in that same bay and died when gangrene set in. He had been buried on the island, and no Spanish settlement had resulted. Only in 1769 did Carlos III decide that the area needed to be populated with Hispanics before Anglos, French, or Russians could grab it. Accordingly, from April into July 1769, coordinated Spanish expeditions converged on San Diego Bay.[37]

The first governor of the new province of Alta California, Gaspar de Portolá, established a presidio with forty soldiers at the spot. This historic site is now known as the Plymouth Rock of the Pacific Coast. A Franciscan mission was established by fifty-six-year-old Fray Junípero Serra, ex-professor from his native Mallorca in Spain's Balearic Isles.[38] The heavy population of local Indians congregated by Padre Serra in his mission of San Diego had been living by hunting rabbit and deer and by fishing and gathering, which was typical of the border natives. They had been living in makeshift shelters, the men and boys going totally naked, while the women and girls covered themselves with animal skins.[39] Padre Serra insisted on bringing in Hispanic settlers in order to provide farmers, skilled labor, and Christian models for the natives.[40] As a result, a group of Hispanics arrived on 26 September 1774.[41] Even at this early date, San Diego was thought of as a border settlement, for on 19 August 1773, Fray Francisco Palóu placed a large cross on a hill south of where Tijuana now stands — at the natural limit of San Diego's valley — to mark the boundary between Baja California (assigned to the Dominicans) and Alta California (of the Franciscans).[42]

This settlement, too, experienced early difficulties which were overcome only by a spirit of dedication. Nineteen men died of an illness which gripped the settlers in their first days. The Hispanics were so sick that the Indians were able to take advantage of the absence of a stockade. The natives sacked the mission, killed one of the men, and even stripped the clothing from the ill. A wooden stockade was subsequently thrown together, to be replaced in 1778 with stone. The first crop planted was destroyed by an inundation. By the start of 1770, Governor Portola concluded that the settlement would have to be abandoned if a ship did not arrive with supplies by the morning of the Feast of San José on 19 March. However, balding Serra's short and corpulent body, filled with a zeal for saving the natives, did not shrink from their mortifying his flesh with stones, whips, and torches. Serra led the friars in prayers that the mission be saved. On the evening before the given day, a passing ship which had lost an anchor fortuitously decided to pull into the harbor, saving the settlement.[43] The harbor was good, the soil was responsive, and the beauty of the site inspiring, so that San Diego, like Matamoros and Laredo, was soon prospering. By 1790, it was producing all the grain it needed.[44]

With this settlement, a chain of Hispanic towns demarcated the whole line of the future U.S.-Mexican border. The settlements had a long way to grow, and many other towns would later spring up along the course they had traced, but the geographic outline of their distribution was complete.

CHAPTER THREE

Family Trouble:
Class Division and Corruption

It is sad to watch the original ideals of a young family break down. Such a devolution became marked in the family of border towns in the 1760s. It is tempting to speculate what might have been accomplished in the last two hundred years in the border towns had the initial aspirations not been lost. However, the changed goals opened their own new path of promise and loss.

Unequal Distribution of the Land

Already in the 1750s, the original system of shared lands came under attack from the new towns' leading families, who were eager to carve out great estates for themselves. Paso del Norte saw the first establishment of sizable *haciendas* in the 1750s. In Paso del Norte, notable beneficiaries included descendants of early settlers. Diego Tiburcios de Ortega, whose family had moved to the area in the late seventeenth century, in 1751 won a grant to the largest ranch in the region, stretching out on both sides of the river. The military officers also benefited. Francisco García, military commandant in the 1780s, set up what became the wealthiest of the local ranches, that of Sta Teresa, seven miles northwest of town on the south side of the river.[1]

At the same time, the leading families of the Lower Rio Grande towns began to call for the removal of Escandón, who was blocking land division. Escandón feared that great land holdings would discourage further settlers, but the opposition point of view maintained that the lack of individual holdings was a disincentive to making improvements. In response to the complaints against Escandón, in 1757 the viceroy sent José Tienda de Cuervo to hold an inspection or *visita*.[2] Escandón and his views weathered that first onslaught, but in 1766 continued complaints brought Viceroy Carlos de Croix to dismiss Escandón and place him on trial. Escandón's replacement as governor of Nuevo Santander, José Fernando Palacios, in 1767 held a second *visita*, which led to the coveted land grants. The beneficiaries were so delighted that they barely winced at the simultaneous reduction of their military garrisons and the ending of their local exemption from tribute.[3]

The early community spirit now faded into one of class contention and exploitation as the new land grants established a typical Spanish-American contrast between the few wealthy "haves" and the masses of the deprived "have-nots." Grants of both town lots and rural estates were made on the basis of seniority. Captains were given four *sitios* (17,712 acres) of ranch land and four *caballerías* (424 acres) of farm land. The original settlers received two *sitios* (8,856 acres) of ranch land and two *caballerías* (212 acres) of farm land. The sons of original settlers and others who had lived in the region for six years or more got two *sitios* of ranch land.[4] From this time on, border towns were dominated by a ranching elite which maintained a sharp class superiority over the poverty-ridden masses.[5] In the 1780s residents began to be listed by ethnic status either as (prestigious) Spaniards or as (unprestigious) mestizos, mulattos, or Indians. Given the fact that one's listing in the caste system could be purchased, the reference was really to social/financial status rather than to racial identity. Use of *don* and *doña* as marks of respect for one's betters came into common usage, and marriage between the ethnic groups was rare even after it became legal.[6]

The land distribution was not made without protest over its inequity. Spanish government inspectors questioned the justice of the land grants in Reynosa, where six intermarried families dominated most of the land and local offices.[7] Many of Laredo's residents fought against the overwhelming power of Tomás Sánchez. In 1768 these residents moved to a new location on the south side of the river, where they set up a town government under their control. Sánchez won the support of the governor of Nuevo Santander, a move which allowed him to return the seat of government to the old location and to personally assume the office of mayor. However, the two factions continued to quarrel. Sánchez incarcerated the town treasurer in 1771 on a charge of embezzlement and sold the man's property at a public auction to recoup the funds. The local priest sided with the opposition and refused to greet Sánchez at his church door for mass. When the obdurate curate died, Sánchez saw to it that a clergyman sympathetic to him took the position.[8]

The issue of land distribution might have led to more trouble at the outset had local residents not been distracted by an intensification of the threat posed by the wild Indians swooping down from the north. The increased Indian pressure brought a special inspection in 1766 to 1768 by the Marqués de Rubí. On Rubí's suggestion, in 1772 the Crown established a line of presidios (including at Laredo) exactly along the route of the later U.S.-Mexican border, with San Antonio, Santa Fe, and the California towns left as advanced outposts to the north. Local men between ages eighteen and sixty were formed into auxiliary military companies. In 1776 these local units were trained to employ added mobility as *compañías volantes*. The towns of the later border were that year grouped for the first time into a common administrative unit, along with regions to their north and south, with the establishment of the commanding general of the internal provinces. The seat of this unit was located initially in Arizpe, Sonora, and subsequently in Cd. Chihuahua. A plan of 1780 would have turned Paso del Norte, like Santa Fe, Albuquerque, and Taos, into a walled town. The Paseños rejected this suggestion, fearing what would happen to their scattered ranches if they developed a passive reliance on town walls. This refusal meant that Matamoros would be the unique example among the border towns to later draw a brick girdle around her girth. However, for added protection an additional presidio, that of San Elizario, was built downstream from Paso del Norte in 1789.[9]

Government Corruption

The new mood of exploitation was accelerated by the shift from the reformist Enlightened Despotic reign of Carlos III to the corrupt government of his son, Carlos IV. The new king was dominated by the foolish Queen María Luisa and her opportunistic lover, Manuel de Godoy. A tidal wave of unbridled money-making and power abuse now swept through the Spanish Empire and over the towns of the future border. The change can be glimpsed in Matamoros (to use the present name of San Juan de los Esteros, which was rechristened Refugio in 1796 and then Matamoros in 1826). The Zacatecas missionaries who had come to the town turned their attention to administering their extensive land donations, to lending money at usurious rates, and to enjoying the gracious life. Coming to identify with the local ranching elite, they lost their original missionary spirit and opened themselves up to charges of cupidity.[10] Visitors noted the hypocrisy, alcoholism, and lechery of the clergy, here as elsewhere along the border.[11] Their greed became legendary in the local folklore.[12]

The dominance of the early leading families in Matamoros/Refugio met with an organized opposition of the sort already exhibited in Laredo. The Ballís led a move of newer families, largely coming in from Reynosa, to take over town leadership from the original Camargoista clans which had founded Matamoros. Widowed Rosa Mᵃ Hinojosa de Ballí in 1790 received vast amounts of land north of the Rio Grande across from Matamoros. Beside the La Feria Grant, centered on the Rancho La Feria, Rosa inherited the Llano Grande Grant to the west. Her eldest son, Capitán Juan José, in 1798 moved to his own San Salvador del Tule Grant, northwest of the Llano Grande Grant. Rosa bought Rancho Las Casteñas to the east of her Rancho La Feria for her middle son, José Mᵃ (nicknamed Chico). The youngest son, Padre Nicolás, educated in Spain, traveled between the ranches, officiated in Matamoros' first chapel (built compliments of his mother), and founded a mission for the fierce Karankawa Indians on what became known as Padre Island.[13] He gained possession of the Rancho de San Juan de los Esteros outside of Matamoros/San Juan, as well as of the Rancho Santa Cruz, at the southern end of the offshore sand strip now named Padre Island in his honor.[14]

From this ranching base, the Ballís shaped a faction that for a brief time challenged the Camargoista political leadership in the town. After the town government had been established in 1796, complete with an adobe, palm-roofed town hall, it had initially been dominated by founding families from Camargo. The first mayor, from 1797 through 1799, had been Capitán Ignacio de Ayala.[15] He had turned the office over to his *consuegro*, José Cayetano Girón, who was followed in turn in 1801 by Capitán José Manuel de Goseascochea, a former Camargo judge married into the local de la Garza clan.[16] The next year, in 1802, the Ballí faction enjoyed success when Juan José Ballí, who had held the post of mayor of Reynosa in 1799, became mayor. The family's ascendency lasted through much of the decade, with the Ballís' relative Vicente López de Herrera, chief judge of Reynosa, as mayor in 1803, 1805, 1806, and 1807, and with Chico Ballí as mayor in 1804.[17]

The Camargoista faction fought back hard. In 1803 Juan José Ballí was arrested on the suspicion of insurrectionary plotting and the next year died in prison.[18] At the same time, Padre Nicolás Ballí's position as local clergyman was placed under the authority of Padre José Felipe de la Garza, appointed as his superior by the bishop of Nuevo León.[19] In 1805 Chico Ballí retired from active politics due to ill health.[20] By 1809, town politics lay securely back in the hands of the original Camargoista families.

Other border towns evidenced the same problem with corruption which fueled the conflicts in Matamoros. Reynosa's urgent need for a change of location to escape from the periodic flooding of the original site met with a lack of concern from the governors of Nuevo Santander.[21] Repeatedly during the reign of Carlos IV, floods destroyed buildings and bred epidemics. To compound the dilemma, the location was devoid of proper drinking water (the river water being unsuitable), lacking in a source of stone (so that the adobe buildings dissolved in each flood), and deprived of any church to minister to the residents.[22]

When in 1806 an especially devasting flood chased the townsfolk to higher ground, shortly after still another request for translation of the town site had been ignored by the latest governor, Capitán Antonio Ballí made a direct appeal to the viceroy. As a result, at long last, permission was granted that year. Reynosa relocated to its present site, next to where a local mission had been founded. Here they could build on high and dry terrain, with a good fresh water source from wells, local limestone for construction, and religious pastoring from the friars. Between 1810 and 1835, the church of Nuestra Señora de Guadalupe rose on the new plaza. Its bell tower, all that remains of the original structure, is now attached to a modern church. The "Old" Cemetery was laid out, where Capitán Ballí and the other town fathers lie in graves long devoid of headstones.[23]

In Laredo, the mood of the times found expression in an application of the old *obedezco pero no cumplo* syndrome of seeming to comply while not really getting the job done. The *alcalde* posted, but did not bother to enforce, such unpopular viceregal decrees as a prohibition of card games and a ban on the sale of tobacco and mescal.[24] In Paso del Norte, the prevailing corruption expressed itself, as in Matamoros, in the slack attitude of the clergy. The Guadalupe

Mission's goal of Christianizing the Indians of the settlement was fulfilled and its Indians were intermarried with the Hispanic residents of the town, so that the church was placed under a secular priest. The four remaining missions were poorly tended. The two friars who were supposed to care for them spoke no Indian tongue and allowed the churches to sink into a state of filth in which bird and bat droppings besmirched altars and other furnishings.[25] In San Diego, official neglect could be seen in the delapidated condition of the presidio.[26]

Start of Trade with Americans

The prevailing graft offered a tempting situation in which to start illegal trade with Americans.[27] After all, by this time many a merchant in central Mexico was happily smuggling with British partners, covering his trail with the ubiquitous *mordida* system. By defiantly establishing trading contact with Americans, the border towns began to play their own role in shaping the history of the continent. The Anglo-American presence they called to the area pointed the way to a very different future than their rulers in Madrid and Mexico City would have wished or envisaged. The *norteños* were frustrated by the refusal of Carlos III's government to allow legal trade with other nations. The Spanish mercantalist system directed all of Mexico's Atlantic trade via Veracruz, a prohibitively distant outlet for much of northern Mexico.[28] This ruling held back border town growth, for the Americans were the natural trading partner. The wealth from such a trade was badly needed to allow the border towns to grow and to gain strength for repulsing the wild Indians.

Not all of the border towns were properly located to form contraband contacts with American traders. It was the towns at the three crucial points for trade—Matamoros and San Diego, with their ports, and Paso del Norte, with its control of the major pass over the Rocky Mountains—which were best situated then as now to prosper from international trade. Such towns saw the early establishment of illegal commerce with its attitude of *"Cuando sabes no dirás, cuando ves no juzgarás, si quieres vivir en paz"* ("Your tattling will cease and judging others decrease if you want to have peace").

Matamoros' new contraband trade looked mainly to New Orleans, which since 1763 had been dominated increasingly by American and British merchants.[29] After 1804, the city was part of the United States. The de la Garza clan was notable in developing

Matamoros' trade on this early illegal basis. José de la Garza in 1775 established the first home in Port Isabel (then called Punta de Isabel or Frontón) at the southwestern end of the Laguna Madre inside the Brazos de Santiago. He subsequently brought in other settlers to join him there, and a contraband trade with Louisiana pirates was soon in operation.[30] Another settlement with a similar *raison d'être* was Boca del Rio (later called Bagdad) on the south bank, toward the river mouth. From 1777, a mixture of Hispanic and Italian families began moving in to that location.[31] Under the stimulus of the black market trade, Matamoros' population swelled from under one hundred families to over 2,000 people in the first decade of the nineteenth century.[32]

In Paso del Norte, Anglo-American traders first put in an appearance when in 1804 Napoleon handed the Louisiana Territory over to the United States, a transaction which made the Americans the Colorado neighbors of Hispanic New Mexico. While Lewis and Clark were exploring the northwestern part of the new territory, St. Louis merchants were attempting to lay out the Santa Fe Trail for trade with New Mexico. Probing farther south, an increasing number of these innovators, including James Purcell (Dimas Procell to the locals) and Lawrence Durocher (Lorenzo Duroret) made their way to Paso del Norte from 1806 on. Those Americans with government or dubious connections were less welcome. Ellis Bean, who had taken part in Philip Nolan's filibustering expedition into East Texas in 1800, and U.S. Army Capt. Zebulon Pike were both sent under arrest to Cd. Chihuahua for questioning. To keep strategic military information out of American hands, it was decided in 1808 that local Americans were not to participate in campaigns against the Indians.[33] This ruling must have made the area all the more attractive to Anglo merchants, who could concentrate all the more on business.

In San Diego the first foreign merchants were the French, whose ships pulled into the harbor in 1786. The British appeared on their heels, with the expedition of George Vancouver stopping at San Diego in 1793. The British and French presence increased through the 1790s. However, the Americans were the main foreign presence by the second half of the 1790s. This was the period in which the Yankee merchants were laying down a prosperous trade around the Pacific which would come to include hunting for whale oil, taking Yankee rum to Sydney to exchange for wool, picking up tea from China, and obtaining sea otter pelts, cattle hides, and tallow from California.[34]

A more casual official approach to halting the contraband trade was applied in Matamoros, in contrast to a somewhat more vigorous policy in Paso del Norte and a bit more serious effort in San Diego, reflecting perceived vulnerability to foreign takeover in each of the border towns. At the turn of the century, Spanish officials were ordered to halt all foreign ships trying to land or trade in San Diego. Yet such was the eagerness of the locals and foreigners alike to benefit from the commerce that Yankee ingenuity at once hit on a formula for circumventing the prohibition. In March 1800 the American ship *Lelia Byrd* was allowed to dock when its captain explained that the ship had run out of supplies. By international law, any port was obliged to aid a ship in distress. The local authorities soon discovered that the sad story was just a ruse, for the mariners were caught trading and were forced to fight their way back to their ship.[35]

However, this in no way discouraged the use of the pretext of being in distress, and one ship after another made use of it through the following years. In 1804 the local authorities made one further try to stop the practice by refusing help to foreign ships claiming distress. In 1806 they imprisoned four Americans caught smuggling. But when in July another American ship, the *Racer* tried unsuccessfully to scare the presidio into releasing the prisoners, the incident did persuade the authorities to back off their questionable refusal to help ships in trouble. Thus, the trade carried on under this ruse picked up as strong as ever. Even the *Racer*, once again experiencing problems, returned to trade in 1807.[36]

The waffling of official policy allowed increasing numbers of Anglo-Americans to settle in San Diego, as in Paso del Norte, in this period. The first four Americans took up residence in 1798. Claiming that their ship had sailed off without them, they managed to find employment working at the presidio. Some of the settlers were clearly interested in guiding the trade from the San Diego end. Yankee John Brown, who had been caught trying to smuggle out otter pelts in 1803, jumped ship and requested resident status in 1804. All in all, the illegal American trade helped San Diego to grow from a tiny village. At the turn of the century, private buildings began to be constructed outside the enclosure of the presidio. And in 1803, the mission added a new crop—olives.[37]

Padre Hidalgo's Revolt

The Spanish government was a hindrance to development but not an insuperable barrier. The very laxity of corrupt government allowed the border towns to work around the laws. This *modus vivendi* helps explain why, when Padre Hidalgo's revolt exploded through much of the rest of Mexico, the leading border towns did not participate. Another factor was their remoteness. When a liberal parliament in Cádiz was established under British protection in opposition to Napoleon's takeover of Spain and an initial call to send representatives was issued, the notice arrived too late for border representatives to arrive in Spain in time to participate.[38]

When Padre Hidalgo's independence revolt began on 16 September 1810, the only segment of the border to join in the revolt were those towns which were being left behind by the sweep of change in this period. Specifically, the towns of the Lower Rio Grande upriver from Matamoros (then called Refugio), realizing that their growth was coming to a halt, lashed out against being relegated to history's backwater. These towns, from Guerrero (then still called Revilla) down to Reynosa, found their insurrectionary leader in Bernardo Gutiérrez de Lara of Guerrero. A blacksmith and mechanic with a wife and children, he came from one of the town's founding families. His liberal ideas may have been picked up from his elder brother José Antonio, a priest educated in civil and ecclesiastical law in Monterrey at a time when liberal priests of the type of Padres Hidalgo and Morelos were proliferating through Nueva España. When Bernardo would later meet Padre Hidalgo, he would carry with him a letter of introduction from José Antonio.[39]

The people of Guerrero/Revilla had seen their hopes for joining Matamoros in trade with the United States stirred and then disappointed. In 1800, Philip Nolan, Irish-born horse trader and protégé of Gen. James Wilkinson, had made contacts in town. However, in March 1801, Nolan had been killed on a filibustering expedition in Texas, and the promise of continued growth through trade he had held out to Guerrero had disappeared with him. Nolan's local contacts may have included the Gutiérrez de Lara family, for when, eleven years later, Bernardo sought aid in Louisiana for his rebellion, he contacted three men once closely associated with Nolan.[40]

When news of Padre Hidalgo's revolt first reached Guerrero/Revilla, Bernardo Gutiérrez de Lara jumped to espouse the cause. From his hometown, his agents distributed propaganda leaflets to the downriver towns to the east and Laredo to the northwest, urging them to join Guerrero in revolt. His incendiary tracts popped up as far away as San Antonio to the north and Cd. Victoria (then called Aguayo) to the south. These propaganda efforts did much to revolutionize Nuevo Santander and Texas, whose governors were both toppled.[41] Along the Lower Rio Grande, Mier, Camargo, and Reynosa joined Guerrero in its agitation. An official Spanish report told how that section of the river was a "hotbed of rebellion."[42]

On 16 March 1811, Bernardo Gutiérrez de Lara met Padre Hidalgo and Ignacio Allende at the Hacienda of Sta M^a near Saltillo on their flight north after their defeat at the Puente de Calderón. Commissioned as a *teniente coronel*, Gutiérrez de Lara was sent back home with orders to complete his organization of the revolt there and then to move on to the United States to seek help from President James Madison. Hidalgo and Allende were captured a mere four days after Gutiérrez de Lara's departure, to be sentenced and shot, but Gutiérrez de Lara held to his instructions and escaped into Louisiana. In the spring of 1813 he led a troop of filibusters back into Texas and captured San Antonio on 1 April.[43]

Gutiérrez de Lara's plan was to use Texas as a base for the reconquest of the Rio Grande towns in his own Tamaulipas homeland. He accordingly lost no time in sending a force of men south under Felipe Garibay and José Mª García Salinas (nicknamed El Cantareño). This force progressed through the Rio Grande region, from where Gutiérrez de Lara's wife and children moved to rejoin him in San Antonio. It then continued on to the outskirts of Monterrey. Meeting with military defeat there, Garibay's troops fell back on Gutiérrez de Lara's *rio* towns in July. Gutiérrez de Lara was ousted from power in San Antonio and returned to the United States. Eleven days later, on 15 August, the rebel cause in Texas went down in defeat. The disaffected *rio* towns reverted to Spanish control and were subjected to a 9:00 P.M. curfew and strict control of all travel, especially to Texas.[44] Most of the property of the Gutiérrez de Lara family had already been confiscated since 1811, and Padre José Antonio kept a low profile as a priest in Monterrey.[45]

Laredo (like Matamoros) remained aloof from Gutiérrez de Lara's call to arms. The reason for Laredo's loyalty seems to have been its dependence, exposed as it was on the Indian frontier, on the local Spanish garrison to contain the raids of the Comanches and Apaches. Thus, Laredo's town government swore loyalty to the

Crown and set up six companies to help fight insurrection, while the commandant of the presidio took measures to control travel in the area and forbade public dances, the bearing of arms, and the sale of alcohol.[46] This attitude allowed the Spanish forces to use Laredo as a staging area for their counterattacks against Texas. In 1813 all Laredo men between ages fifteen and sixty were organized into auxiliary companies. The Laredo troops were repulsed in their first attempt to reconquer Texas, at Alazán Creek on 16 June 1813. However, another effort from Laredo met with success at the Battle of the Medina River on 15 August of that year.[47]

While containing dissident elements, the three towns already profiting from illegal trade under the Spanish Crown (Matamoros, Paso del Norte, and San Diego) held loyal, rather than rock the boat of contraband wares. It was in vain that a group of rebel sympathizers in Matamoros in 1811 penned a manifesto of discontent with the government. The de la Garza Camargoista faction, once more in control of the town government and benefiting from the new trade contacts, took measures to block any rebel takeover. José Domingo de la Garza was *justicia mayor* in the loyalist town government in that year.[48] The de la Garza clan was closely tied to the Morales family, which provided the mayor who first declared that Matamoros would remain loyal to Spain.[49] A son-in-law of the late José Salvador de la Garza, José de Goseascochea, gave his life fighting the revolt. A captain in the Spanish provincial forces, he fought under the royal governor of Texas, Manuel Salcedo, and shared his defeat and execution.[50]

Furthermore, the de la Garzas continued to be prominent in the town government in the following decade, when the supporters of Spain had emerged in a strong position. The mayors of the last ten years of Spanish rule included Blas Mª de la Garza VI in 1815 and José Domingo de la Garza in 1816. The desire to please Spain was stronger in Matamoros at this time due to the hopes placed in the town's application to the Spanish Crown for permission for a port. The fact that Spain later granted this request (in 1820) is a measure of Crown satisfaction with the town leaders' loyalty during the revolt.[51]

The opposition was also handicapped by the fact that its natural leaders, the Ballí clan, had been dealt a heavy blow in the years immediately before the revolt, as described above. Ex-mayor Juan José Ballí was dead and Chico was in failing health, so that of the three brothers only Padre Nicolás Ballí was still able to act. José Mª

Villarreal, of a family intermarried with the Ballís, joined Bernardo Gutiérrez de Lara's rebel forces, fighting in his filibuster invasion of Texas in 1812.[52] Padre Ballí himself, although clearly a conscientious and dedicated priest, left his religious duties, abandoned his Rancho de San Juan de los Esteros outside of Matamoros, and retired to his ranch on Padre Island. He apparently left the Rancho de San Juan in some haste, for when he later returned, after the political crisis had passed, he found the ranch dilapidated and important papers, including his deed to Padre Island, missing.[53] In the last years of viceregal government, the Ballí family and its allies were notably absent from municipal government positions, and reappeared only with the collapse of Spanish rule.[54]

Loyalty also won out in Paso del Norte. The military authorities were able to organize special patriotic companies, called *fernandinos*, to fight potential insurrection and to set up a committee of surveillance. Two men were arrested in 1811 on a charge of rebel sympathies. A Paseño merchant by the name of Luciano de Torres García was accused of selling goods to Coahuila rebels, and sympathetic letters of Felipe Montoya of Ysleta to leaders of the revolt were intercepted. However, both men were released after Padre Hidalgo's capture and execution.[55]

Timely concessions played an additional role in holding San Diego loyal to the Crown. In 1811 a treaty allowed at least the Russians to come legally to California in search of sea otter pelts. The first contact of San Diegans with Russians had occurred five years before. José Darío Arguello's daughter, Concepción, had accepted a proposal of marriage in 1806 from a Russian noble, Nikolai Petrovich Rezanov, during his visit to San Francisco from the Russian colony in Alaska. Rezanov died in Siberia before the planned wedding, and Concepción did not learn of his fate until 1842, through a chance remark from an English visitor. Nonetheless, she had remained true to him, finally becoming a nun rather than marry another man.[56] The Russian contact this story recalls was now legalized. It also must have helped to improve relations between the Crown and San Diegans when, in 1813, a dam was built in Mission Gorge, from which an aqueduct supplied the mission with enough water to allow an export of grain starting in 1817. There were a few rebellious rumblings in San Diego, as in Matamoros and Paso del Norte. Padre Panto was poisoned by his cook in June 1812, and in the same year a soldiers' plot was broken up by the arrest of three men, including Sergento

José Mª Pico, the father of Pío Pico and Andrés Pico of later fame. All the same, the tiny town held loyal.[57]

The Impact of Padre Hidalgo's Revolt

The result of the years of revolt for the border towns was that the loyal towns, which were already starting to prosper from the clandestine commerce, continued their growth through the rest of the 1810s. It was said that in this period Jean Lafitte himself, based since 1817 in Galveston, was making Port Isabel one of his ports of call. The shallow waters of the Laguna Madre offered a tempting shelter from the larger Spanish war ships that hunted pirates. A fifteen-foot well in nearby Laguna Vista is today marked with an explanation that Lafitte had it dug.[58] Both American and British merchant interest in the area continued to build. In 1817 they lent financial support to landing a revolutionary force under Padre Servando de Mier and Francisco Mina on the coast a ways south of Matamoros.[59] With its illicit commerce, Matamoros grew to the point that in 1814 a primary school for boys was founded.[60]

The simultaneous growth of Paso del Norte was acknowledged in July 1814 by the establishment of an elected town government under a mayor. Its political stability and economic well-being allowed the town to participate, as no other towns of the later border did, in elections to send representatives to the Spanish imperial parliament in 1814. Meeting in Paso del Norte's town hall on 11–14 March, twelve electors chose delegates to both provincial and national deputations. Francisco José de Jaúregui was to be sent to Spain, but never got a chance to set out because King Fernando VII crushed the experiment and returned to the old system of absolute monarchy. Again, when in 1820 Rafael Riego launched a liberal revolt in Spain and restored the parliament, delegates were chosen in Paso del Norte on 24 and 25 September. Pedro Pino was sent off to Spain, but his story was summed up in the sardonic phrase, *"Pino fue y Pino vino"* (Pino left and Pino returned). Pino got only as far as Veracruz, where he learned Mexico was breaking away from Spain, and so returned home.[61]

San Diego, too, continued to prosper using the contraband formula in the late 1810s. The Russians proved too weak a force to play effectively against the Americans, whose merchants continued to pour in on one ship "in distress" after the next. The British and the French followed suit. To complete the parallel with larger Matamoros, some of the French merchants, and most notably the unpredictable Capt. Hippolyte Bouchard, were dubbed pirates here as well.[62]

In contrast, the stagnating towns of the Lower Rio Grande upriver from Matamoros, most of which had joined the revolt out of desperation, suffered even more than before. The civil war had uprooted much of the society, causing some people to flee from the area, while refugees from other regions streamed in.[63] The disruption also heartened the wild Indians to accelerate their depredations. The Carrizo Indians were crushed in 1812 by a force from Reynosa, but the Apaches and Comanches were not so easily contained.[64] The countryside became so dangerous that both ranching and farming suffered from a lack of help, and both meat and vegetable production dropped off. People turned to imported food sources, but these were also in scarce supply since muleteers hesitated to transport goods along the Indian-ravaged roads. What goods did make it through were expensive, so that the local folk tended to fall into debt. Many of the poor sank into peonage to pay their obligations, turned to banditry, or simply ran off. In short, an economic depression settled in which lasted in Laredo for a decade, but from which Guerrero/ Revilla, Mier, and Camargo have hardly ever really recovered.[65]

As so often happens when troubles hit a family, some of the children are more marred than others, and usually these are the ones who were already suffering from problems. The border sisters had seemed much more similar in their innocent infancy. In their reactions to government corruption, some of the sister towns were strengthened, while others were left behind, stunted and scarred.

CHAPTER FOUR

A Change of Father:
Start of the American Presence

A change of father can be a traumatic event for the children in a family. It certainly proved to be so for the border towns of mother Mexico when, in place of the original Indian father, an alternate parent nation was introduced in the form of the United States. The new family arrangement would prove to be, in its own way, just as stormy as the old one, and just as fruitful.

The Legalization of Foreign Trade under Iturbide

A changed attitude of support for the border towns' American trading links was opened up with Mexican independence in 1821. Mexico's first native head of state, Agustín de Iturbide, first as president and then as emperor Agustín I, in the period from September 1821 to March 1823, lent his support to northern commercial aspirations. This brought a flood of newly legal trade but in no way ended the contraband, which was already so well entrenched that it has survived as a major facet of border commerce to this day. High customs duties and a long list of goods which could still not be imported (as a means to encourage domestic industry) guaranteed the survival of the old smuggling activities, with the accompanying *mordidas*, crime, and violence.[1]

Matamoros (which retained the name of Refugio under Iturbide) had good reason to celebrate the coming of independence with grand festivities, for it was now lifted to the rank of a municipality and experienced an economic boom with an influx of foreign business

and businessmen.[2] Many members of both the old Camargoista and Reynosista factions now let bygones be bygones and joined hands to share the benefits. Loyalist mayor Domingo de la Garza led the way in swearing fidelity to the new regime, while José M[a] Villarreal, the freedom fighter, became a town councilman in 1820 and 1821 and then mayor in 1826, 1830, and 1831. Francisco Ballí acted as a town councilman in 1823 and 1824.[3] Guerrero/Revilla's rebel leader Bernardo Gutiérrez de Lara himself returned from the United States to become the first constitutional governor of Tamaulipas.[4]

The anticipation in Matamoros was so great that the local officials did not wait for approval to be officially granted to start registering ships moving between its port of Boca del Rio and its main partner port of New Orleans. The meager selection of local trading wares — essentially cow hides, mules, and wool — was exploited for all it was worth to supplement metal currency in exchange for a wide variety of American and European manufactured goods.[5] Seeing the heartening results, in 1823 Rafael García submitted a request to found the town of Port Isabel at the favorable harbor location where a village already stood. This request would eventually be granted, in 1839.[6]

Although El Paso, disappointed by the failure of the Spanish parliamentary plans, at first showed a lack of enthusiasm for Iturbide's conservative government, it did take advantage of the opportunity to increase trade with the Americans.[7] So did San Diego. Already in 1821, a trading route was opened up from Santa Fe to California by William Beckness. Two years later, the first foreign trading house in California was opened in San Diego — the English-owned McCullough, Hartness and Company. A new optimism regarding the town's future led to the founding of grand town houses by some of the families who would dominate the little settlement through the Mexican period. The Carrillos seem to have been the first family to build a house below the presidio, perhaps in 1821. The sons of late Sergento José María Pico built their house in 1823. Santiago Arguello also became prominent as a commander at the presidio.[8] Laredo, too, now began to share in the upswing of fortunes by finding its own niche in the budding trade of the Norte. Namely, it turned to a major emphasis on sheep farming, so that wool became its chief export item.[9]

The Trading Bonanza under Guadalupe Victoria

The fall of the first Mexican empire and its replacement by the first Mexican republic brought a decision of lasting importance regarding territorial identity to two of the border communities. As the boundaries of the new Mexican states were determined, both Laredo and Paso del Norte were detached from what has often been argued to be their natural territorial identities. Laredo was included not in Nuevo León, as it reasonably requested, but in Tamaulipas. This decision made geographic sense only with the inclusion in Tamaulipas of the Wild Horse Desert, stretching between the Rio Grande and the Nueces. When that stretch of land would be lost to Texas in 1846, the new town of Nuevo Laredo would be left in a tiny, illogical Tamaulipecan panhandle.[10] Likewise, the decision to include Paso del Norte in the state of Chihuahua rather than in the territory of Nuevo México meant that after the Mexican-American War the new town of El Paso would be included in the state of Texas rather than in New Mexico, from which it had already been excluded.[11] However, the initiation of the Mexican republic brought no change of policy regarding trade and immigration for the towns of the later border. The first president, Guadalupe Victoria, headed the liberal Federalista Party, which found strong backing in the Norte and favored the *norteño* policy of Anglo immigration.

Matamoros, which in 1826 was given this name in honor of one of the leaders of the *independencia*, Mariano Matamoros, built a customhouse at Boca del Rio on the south bank of the river near its mouth. The town that sprang up there would soon be called Bagdad. The customhouse was established at such a remove from town because ships did not want to follow the excessively tortuous eighty-mile course of the meandering and shallow river on to Matamoros, which lay only twenty-five miles away by road.[12] However, ships soon showed a preference for entering the Brazos de Santiago Pass into the Laguna Madre a ways farther north to unload at the west side of Santiago Island. The entry here was eight feet deep, which was safer than the six-foot-deep clearance over the sandbar at the mouth of the Rio Grande required to dock at Boca del Rio.[13] Ox carts and flatboat ferries completed the transit of goods between Santiago Island and Matamoros.[14] Port Isabel, whose hopes for attracting ships were disappointed, pluckily turned to development as a beach resort for *norteño* families.[15]

Contraband goods were unloaded anywhere along the coast

beside the official ports. Martín de León, the de la Garza-related Cavazos family, and American merchant Sanforth Kidder were all charged with black market trading. De León made contact with a New Orleans pirate named Raimond La Fou and founded his own port at the southern end of Padre Island to foster such trade. Even the first American consul in Matamoros, Daniel Smith, was accused of favoring smugglers.[16] With the resulting economic stimulus, Matamoros grew from 2,320 residents in 1820 to 7,000 by 1829 and to 16,372 in 1837.[17] In 1824 the United States established its consular post in the town. In 1828 the town gained a weekly postal service, with its first newspaper, *Noticioso*, following in 1831.[18]

Paso del Norte's economy benefited, too, as trade in both mining and ranching products flowed along the Santa Fe-Chihuahua Trail. In 1826 Paso del Norte was granted the status of a *villa*, and the town's first public school opened its doors. The growing prosperity of the local ranchers was reflected in the success of Juan Mª Ponce de León, who in 1827 established a ranch north of the river across from Paso del Norte on land where downtown El Paso, Texas, now stands. He built a flour mill by the river dam and established a monopoly on the transport of goods to and from Paso del Norte. His property became the richest local ranch of the decade, bustling with one hundred ranch hands.[19]

San Diego geared itself more to a mercantile identity under the governor of California, who was sent out by President Guadalupe Victoria, Gen. José Mª Echeandía. Even though Monterey was designated as the official Californian capital, Echeandía ignored this fact and established his center of government from 1825 to 1830 in San Diego. He then carried out various changes aimed at supporting San Diego's economic growth. For one thing, the town's first school was established. Only eighteen students showed up initially, but after Echeandía stepped in to order parents to send their children, 339 pupils were enrolled in 1829. The Russian interest in local sea-otter pelts received further encouragement, in an ongoing but futile Spanish attempt to offset the American presence.[20] The military, which was viewed as supporting anti-middle class, conservative politics in Mexico at the time, was low on Echeandía's list of priorities. Behind in their pay and short on food and clothing, some of the soldiers in the San Diego garrison protested in October 1828, only to be reassigned to other locations. This weakening of the military was pushed to the point that it encouraged Indian uprisings.[21]

The church, another traditional support of the rival Centralista Party, was undermined along with the military. The secularization of mission land, which had begun with the fall of Iturbide, was promoted. Most of the mission Indians were declared "emancipated." Only some of the Indians were given a little land of their own, in violation of the original missionary plan to turn the missions into self-supporting Indian settlements, and even this little bit of land was in large part gambled away or neglected. The Indians subsequently drifted away from the region or found work on the new private ranches. Some of the land and Indians were left assigned to the San Diego Mission, since it provided support for the local garrison by supplying workers and money through pressed loans. However, the governor's demands for labor and money weighed heavily on the moribund mission. At one point, Echeandía went so far as to send soldiers to confiscate whatever grain they could find there.[22]

The mission land was granted in large estates, forming the basis for a new layout of great private local ranches. The first of these estates went in 1823 to Capitán Francisco Mª Ruiz, former presidio commander. Juan Bandini, from a prominent Italian family which had migrated via Spain to Peru, received the Rancho de Tecate, present site of the twin cities of Tecate, California, and Tecate, Baja California. Manuel Machado set up the Rancho El Rosario, where the town of Rosarito now stands. In 1829 San Diego Mayor Santiago Arguello, brother to Iturbide's former governor of California Luis Arguello, received the Rancho Tía Juana, south of San Diego.[23]

With this development, San Diego joined the general pattern of the future border towns in creating an economic and social elite of a handful of ranching families. The most prominent of them were the quartet of the Bandini, Pico, Arguello, and Estudillo clans. The importance of each family was announced by the construction of a new large home in town in addition to its great ranch house, some of which were served by over one hundred Indian ranch hands. In addition to the Pico and Carrillo homes, already constructed under Iturbide, Juan Bandini and Capitán José Antonio Estudillo, assigned to the presidio, built town houses in 1827. Francisco Alvarado put up his house at about the same time. The Bandini home became the town's main social center, while the Estudillo home, famed for its central tower and balcony used for watching bull and bear fights or for housing musicians, was chosen by novelist Helen Hunt Jackson as the setting for the wedding of her protagonist Ramona. These families consolidated their identity as a ruling caste of *gente de razón* by heavy intermarriage. For example, Santiago Arguello's son José Ramón married a Pico girl, while one of Santiago Arguello's daughters was wed to Juan Bandini and another became the wife of Governor Echeandía's secretary.[24]

The goods produced by these ranches emerged as the new main source of trade for San Diego, as ranching products already were for Matamoros, eclipsing the declining supply of sea-otter pelts. Hides and beef fat, used for candle tallow, were exported. The pejorative cognomen "greaser" was originally an innocuous term given by Anglo traders to the local scrapers of the fat or grease from the cattle hides in preparation for the sale of both. Beef formed the staple diet, and clothing, furniture, and even door hinges were shaped from cow hides. Adobe walls were topped by decorative and protective cattle horns. Rodeos, organized to separate and brand cattle, became central social and sporting occasions, as well as business events. San Diego's fame as a trading port in the Mexican period was spread by three books. One was a guide book about southern California written by Benjamin Morrell, who visited San Diego aboard the ship *The Tartar* in 1825. The second was also a travel account, by James Pattie, telling of his trading expedition from Santa Fe to San Diego by land route in 1829. The third was a novel entitled *Two Years Before the Mast*, written by one of the Yankees who visited the town in 1836 and again in 1861, Richard Henry Dana. By 1830, San Diego's population had reached 530, still behind Paso del Norte and Matamoros but healthily growing.[25]

The Influx of Anglo Settlers

The trickle of American merchants who had established a local town presence earlier now became a strong current. While the two ports of Matamoros and San Diego naturally drew in the highest numbers of Europeans, the dominant settlers and traders in all of these towns were Americans. As far as the Gulf trade went, the British preferred to concentrate on the more lucrative business to be found in Veracruz.[26]

In Matamoros, foreigners soon dominated such lines of work as medical practice, silversmithing, the jewelry trade, carriage making, millinery, carpentry, and mechanics. Besides Anglo-Americans (mainly Yankees) and Franco-Louisianans, there were Englishmen, Irishmen, Frenchmen, Germans, Castilians, and a sprinkling of Italians in evidence. Each ethnic group maintained its own coffee houses and billiard halls, as well as its distinct national style of home architecture.[27] Prominent figures among Matamoros' foreign community included such Americans as Connecticut Yankee Charles Stillman, a distance merchant who settled in Matamoros in 1828, and Stephen F. Austin's cousin Henry Austin, who in 1829 began to operate a ship called the *Ariel* on the river between Matamoros and Camargo. The most notable of the Castilians was José San Román, a business partner of Stillman.[28]

As to Paso del Norte, in April 1823 John Heath of Missouri, an empresario like his friend Stephen F. Austin, had won a grant from the Paso del Norte town council to buy the El Brazito Grant across the river thirty-three miles north of town and to settle a colony of 150 Catholic Missourians there. This grant failed with the untimely fall of the Iturbide government before the colony could get established. The colonists went back home, leaving Heath financially ruined. Nonetheless, other Americans with clearer grants were more successful. Americans soon dominated the town's business activity. Coming in by 1828, Hugh Stephenson from Kentucky via Missouri engaged in trade along the Chihuahua Trail, developed mining, and ran a local store.[29]

In San Diego, the Yankees further expanded their trade. In 1826 Bostonian William Gale formalized the hide trade between San Diego and his hometown, in the name of the Bryant and Sturgis Shipping Firm. Two years later, his company built a storehouse to hold the otter hides it purchased prior to shipping them out. James Pattie blazed a more direct trail between Santa Fe and San Diego in 1829, followed later the same year by an expedition along the same route led by Ewing Young, with the participation of Kit Carson.[30] The Americans joined in the local entertainments, including bull and bear contests, bull fights, cock fights, and horse racing, along with heavy betting and practical jokes. On one occasion, Señor Lugo placed an exploding cigar at the disposal of his guest, Alfred Robinson. The joke literally backfired, for Robinson never got around to picking up the cigar, and forgetting his subterfuge, Lugo himself smoked it in bed that night, to the detriment of both his mustache and his wife's nerves.[31]

Even in out-of-the-way towns Americans began to put in an appearance. Yankee peddlers appeared on the streets of Camargo in the 1820s, coming up the river by boat and then heading along the road to Monterrey. The first Americans in Laredo in this period, too, were in transit along the San Antonio-Monterrey road, although some stuck around long enough to get in trouble with the local authorities.[32] Some of the newcomers secured a local niche by marrying into the older Hispanic families. In Matamoros, both Adolphus Glaevecke and James Power married into the prominent de la Garza extended clan.[33] In Paso del Norte, Hugh Stephenson wed the sole daughter and heiress of the wealthy Ascárate family.[34] In San Diego, rancher Juan Bandini married four of his five daughters to Yankees: to merchant Abel Stearns (in 1841), to innkeeper Charles Johnson, to Dr. James Winston, and to Lt. Cave Johnson Couts. In the last case, the girl literally fell into her husband's arms when the railing on her roof gave way while she was watching a column of cavalrymen pass. Also in San Diego, English trader John Forster married a sister of Pío Pico; American trading post operator Jonathan ("Juan Largo") Warner married an Anglo foster daughter of the Picos; and Capt. Joseph Snook wed a daughter of Juan Bautista Alvarado.[35]

The most romantic marriage story of San Diego was that of Henry Fitch. An American who came to San Diego in 1826 and opened a successful mercantile store, Fitch rapidly acculturated, calling himself Enrique, joining the Catholic church, and taking Mexican citizenship. Richard Henry Dana, Jr., in his *Two Years Before the Mast*, disparaged Fitch as big and vulgar; Joaquín Carrillo's daughter Josefa either took a different view or admired these qualities. With her encouragement, the next year Fitch received permission from Joaquín to marry the girl. However, when a call was made at the wedding ceremony to voice any objections "or forever hold your peace," Domingo Carrillo spoke up against the match. The rumor was that he was motivated by Governor Echeandía, who wanted to marry Josefa himself. On the suggestion of Josefa, and with the help of her cousin Pío Pico, the couple eloped in 1829 on a ship bound for Valparaíso, Chile, and an uninterrupted wedding ceremony. Over a year later, they returned with a newborn son. Henry was arrested by Echeandía's order, but he would be freed by a judge on the conditions of performing penance and of donating a fifty-pound bell to the Los Angeles church. Fitch complied. The couple was then allowed to settle down in San Diego, where Josefa gave birth to ten more little Fitches.[36]

The Debate over Anglo Colonization

The number of Anglo-Americans in the towns under consideration remained slight compared to the great influx of Anglos into the largely unsettled lands to the north, especially eastern Texas and northern California. A very serious policy dispute opened up over the desirability of this Anglo colonization. Anglos offered the only ready supply of immigrants at that time due to underpopulation in Mexico. On the one side of the debate were those who felt that the advantages of having Anglo-American settlers rapidly populate these regions outweighed the risks. Placing Anglos on the outposts of the wild Indian territory offered a buffer for the hard-hit northern Mexican towns, promised a bonanza in real estate speculation, and brought the population build-up essential for accelerated economic growth.

In Matamoros, the prominent de la Garza family encouraged American immigrants. Domingo de la Garza acted as mayor of Matamoros/Refugio in 1822, when a policy of welcoming foreign immigrants was being encouraged. After a period of several official about-faces in immigration policy, Juan José de la Garza acted as sub-mayor of Matamoros in 1834, a year in which policy again swung back to encouraging American immigration.[37] Blas Mª de la Garza Falcón VII moved to what is now the Nueces or Kleburg County area and would later supply provisions to the Texas rebels.[38] Martín de León, husband of Patricia de la Garza and father-in-law of Rosalia de la Garza, founded an Anglo-American colony at Victoria, Texas.[39]

On the other side of the argument was the danger that the Anglo settlers would prove loyal to an expansive United States rather than to their new Mexican nationality. There is no question but that important elements in the United States were actively interested in the acquisition of the region by their country. In 1829, for example, the first American minister to Mexico, Joel Poinsett, offered $5 million for setting the border along the Rio Grande River, an offer repeated by his successor.[40] The Ballís seem to have represented the anti-immigration frame of thought in Matamoros. That they should have done so makes sense from the standpoint of the threat Americans posed to the vulnerable position of the Ballís' ranch on South Padre Island. Since 1817, the presence in the area of Lafitte, who had come to an understanding with the Americans in 1815, must have made the Ballís nervous. Lafitte had not respected Hispanic claims in his takeover of Galveston Island, and the purported semi-annual drinking orgies of the pirates was not designed to ease their worries. The Ballís might well have felt qualms over Martín de León's founding in 1823 of a pirate-linked port at the Brazos de Santiago. At that time, the Ballís were still six years away from reconfirmation by the Mexican government of their Spanish title to the island.[41] The Ballís had good reason to fear a hostile Anglo-Texan encroachment down the Laguna Madre, as developments in the late 1830s and early 1840s would prove. Thus, it is no surprise to find that the Ballís, in contrast to their rivals the de la Garzas, seem not to have been involved in schemes to plant American settlers on Mexican soil. When in 1842 the anti-immigration Gen. Adrián Woll made an official call for Mexican nationals to abandon their ranches north of the river, the Ballís were among those ranchers who cooperated, while Juan Antonio Ramírez de la Garza seems to have stayed on.[42]

Thus, under the leadership of Guadalupe Victoria, the border towns plunged head-first into their fateful interaction with Anglo-America. The Spanish Crown and the Mexican Centralistas were correct in warning of the problems which would ensue from this policy. Geographic determinism might have dictated this development to occur on one basis or another. Had Europeans never conquered into North America, the meeting of forest and desert peoples might have created Aztec-Iroquois twin settlements along the same line. However that may be, it was Guadalupe Victoria's policy that initiated the transformation of the future border towns from a Mexican-Indian to a Mexican-American identity.

Centralista Reaction under Anastasio Bustamante (1830-1832)

The disagreements between the Federalistas and Centralistas reached a point of armed conflict in 1828, when Centralista President Manuel Gómez Pedraza illegally removed many Federalista officeholders and was overthrown in a Federalista reaction. Vicente Guerrero, who replaced him, continued Federalista policies down into 1830. At that point, the Centralistas struck back and put in Anastasio Bustamante as president from 1830 to 1832.

The policy of encouraging American trade and Anglo settlement was now halted. On 6 April 1830, President Bustamante closed the Mexican frontier to American settlers. An army under General Mier y Terán was sent from Matamoros into Texas to enforce the new ruling.[43] Laredo, whose economy (the wool exports to the south) did not rely on foreign trade, endorsed Bustamante's coup d'état.

Laredo also hoped that an appreciative national government would send more help for repelling Indian attacks on its exposed position. At any rate, Laredo was upset that the previous Federalista state governments of Tamaulipas paid more attention to Matamoros, which with its flourishing sea trade had become a far richer source of government revenue.[44]

However, the three main towns carrying on trade with the Americans — Matamoros, Paso del Norte, and San Diego — were hard-hit. Matamoros suffered from a new Tamaulipas state tax of 1830, applied exclusively to American shipping. Worse, in February 1832 the National Congress closed Matamoros' port, forbidding all foreign trade there. The authorities tried to allay the outburst of local indignation by an abortive scheme that merely rubbed salt in the wounds. It was suggested that the Matamorense merchants compensate for the loss of their considerable maritime trade with New Orleans and New York by trading with the tiny Irish Catholic farming community of San Patricio by the Nueces River on the border of Tamaulipas and Texas. In support of this suggestion, a new road was laid out between Matamoros and San Patricio. A four-day party to initiate the proposed trade was held in June 1832, complete with bullfights, races, and games.[45] With a Centralista garrison occupying Matamoros, at times under the direction of a severe General Mier y Terán, there was little that Matamorense trading interests could do in way of protest.

Paso del Norte was hit in 1831 by a renewal of Apache attacks, as it became clear that the Spanish commitment to conciliation had been abandoned in favor of a get-tough policy. Francisco García lost his cattle and sheep to the raids, and his misery found no lack of local company.[46] San Diego now lost to Monterey its role as residence of the California governor by decision of the new governor, Col. Manuel Victoria.[47] José Mª Padrés led a group of ranchers including Pío Pico, Juan Bandini, and Juan Bautista Alvarado in trying to complete Echeandía's division of the mission lands before the new Centralista government would put a stop to the attack on the church. The local presidio was seized in November of 1831. However, Governor Victoria countered the move and banished Padrés from California.[48] No more secularization was allowed in Governor Victoria's year in office.[49]

Brief Return of the Federalistas (1832-1834)

In 1832 the Federalistas surged briefly back to power for a couple of years under the acting presidency of Valentín Gómez Farías, a doctor from Zacatecas who had led the north in revolt against Bustamante and had become Santa Anna's vice-president. Once again, Anglos were allowed to settle in Mexico, while the Centralista bastions of church and army were attacked. As a result, the Anglo-American influence continued to grow in the future border towns.

The return to Federalista rule was not smooth in Matamoros. A 300-man Federalista army under Col. José Antonio Mejía was landed at Brazos de Santiago on 29 June 1832 and fought its way across the river at Burrita to occupy Matamoros. While the Centralista forces under Col. José Mariano Guerra fled south, the local merchants gave the entering troops a warm welcome. The congratulations were premature. Colonel Guerra, strengthened by a contingent of troops under Col. Mariano Paredes, took the Federalista soldiers by surprise by wheeling around against Matamoros. Caught offguard, Colonel Mejía sailed off to Texas. However, it did not augur well for a long tenure of Centralista control of Matamoros that the Mexican government was Federalista and that Mejía went to Texas with funds from local business interests and accompanied by Texan Federalists Stephen F. Austin and Col. John Mason. Knowing Mejía would be back, the Centralistas hurriedly began a fort west of town on the river. Known as Fort Paredes, it would be the first step in what would later extend into fortifications around the whole town. However, Fort Paredes did not save Colonel Paredes. After the U.S. schooner *Grampus* boldly appeared in July 1832 off Brazos de Santiago, a mutiny of nervous Centralista soldiers returned Matamoros to Federalista control on 19 August 1832. A mood of restored goodwill between the local Anglos and Hispanics prevailed in Matamoros as profits returned.[50]

Paso del Norte also experienced a business upswing. As trade in textiles and dry goods flowed unimpeded down the Santa Fe and Chihuahua trails under the presidency of Gómez Farías, profits for those shipments that made it through averaged about fifty percent and rose as high as twice that percentage. One new Anglo businessman to appear on the scene in both Paso del Norte and Cd. Chihuahua in this period was an Irish-American from Kentucky named James Magoffin. True to the Irish stereotype, he was said to be possessed of wit, gregariousness, and a knack for storytelling. Magoffin launched into the Santa Fe-Chihuahua Trail trade in 1832, dealing in copper and other goods, including suspected contraband sales of weapons, ammunition, and alcohol to Apaches. Having been U.S. consul in Saltillo from 1825 to 1831, he came to Paso del Norte already equipped with an array of Spanish attributes, including a knowledge of the Spanish language, the Spanish name Santiago, and a Spanish wife (of the same Veramendi family into which Jim Bowie married). He also soon acquired Mexican citizenship.[51]

In San Diego, Gómez Farías' term of office saw a scramble to continue the secularization of the missions which had been halted under Bustamante. José Figueroa oversaw the process as the new governor of California. José Mª Padres, banished for having tried to hasten that development, now returned to California as its military chief. Helped by the national Secularization Act of 17 August 1833 (in the writing of which San Diego rancher Juan Bandini had a hand as a delegate to the National Congress), mission land again began to be handed out in vast parcels. The Pico family would come to hold 150,000 acres. Santiago Arguello, Jr., in 1833 received the Rancho Milijó, running from his father's Rancho Tijuana west to the beach. A mood of conspicuous consumption accompanied the despoiling. Josefa Carrillo de Fitch developed a taste for compulsive gambling. After she threw away $1,000 in a single card game, her husband Henry Fitch convinced the mayor to grant him a legal separation. Only when Josefa promised to reform her ways was marital harmony restored.[52]

The dissolution of the missions was again accompanied by the typical Federalista attack on the position of the army. The presidio of San Diego was reduced to twelve impoverished soldiers under their commandant. At the same time, American trade and immigration were encouraged by the new special director of colonization, José Mª Híjar. Capt. Henry Fitch led the emergence of an Anglo business community, dominating shipping and merchandising. San Diego emerged as the center of the hide trade of California. Fitch financed the fur trade hunters and prospered to the extent that he sent his sons to be educated all the way from Honolulu to Charleston. Among the new American settlers were William Heath Davis, who wrote a description of San Diego in his *Seventy-five Years in California*, and Thomas Wrightington, a Massachusetts shoemaker who came on a hide ship in 1833 and served as mayor of San Diego in 1844. Tom Wrightington ran a *pulquería* until one night he fell from his horse and, being too drunk to get to his feet, provided a feast for the coyotes.[53]

San Diego's growth was also fostered by the community being allowed to organize as a town with an elected mayor. Diegueño leaders had complained to Governor Figueroa of the capricious government they had suffered under the uncooperative military *comandante*, Santiago Arguello. Juan Mª Osuna was chosen as the first mayor over Pío Pico in December 1834, with Juan Bautista Alvarado as one of the two town councilors and Capt. Henry Fitch as town attorney. One result was growing tax revenues; in 1834 Governor Figueroa was able to introduce a new tax on foreign hide salting factories.[54]

On his deathbed in 1835, Figueroa appointed José Castro to be his successor as civil head of the Californian government. The Diegueños complained that the post belonged to Estudillo as senior *vocal* of the *Diputación*, despite the illness that had been keeping him from Monterey much of the time. Castro stepped out of the problem by handing over his post to the military *comandante*, Teniente Coronel Nicolás Gutiérrez in January 1836. Juan Bandini expressed the continuing Diegueño discontent with the government in Monterey, heading a memorial complaining about the decline of farming and commerce, among other issues.[55]

With such moves, many of the leading border town residents closed their ears to the Centralista Cassandra cries against the Trojan Horse represented by the Anglo presence. Which party was espousing the best plan for the future of their region is a moot point. Nonetheless, as soon as a new Centralista government came to power in Mexico City, the freedom of action of the local leaders was sharply reined in.

Santa Anna's Military Action Against the Anglos (1834–1836)

When Antonio López de Santa Anna assumed his active presidency and dismissed the National Congress in a Centralista coup in 1834, the Federalista program for development of the Norte was again reversed. Deposed President Gómez Farías symbolically headed for New Orleans, where he joined Texan Lorenzo de Zavala, who had set up a New York bank to promote Anglo investment in Texas. Parts of the Norte refused to accept Santa Anna's coup. Santa Anna first crushed a revolt in Zacatecas and then turned his attention to Texas. Sandwiched between these hot points to the south and to the north, the towns of the future border waited to learn the impact on their own fate.

Matamoros fumed with frustration. George Fisher's newspaper,

El Mercurio del Puerto de Matamoros, printed by John Southwell, fulminated against Santa Anna until the president brought the paper under control.[56] In November 1835, Martín de León's son Fernando and his brother-in-law José Mª Carvajal were caught red-handed supplying arms and supplies for the Texas rebels at Matagorda Bay. They were brought back to Matamoros under guard, but both managed to escape, doubtless with local help. Fernando escaped at Brazos de Santiago and Carvajal from Matamoros.[57] The Centralista officials treated U.S. Consul Daniel Smith with such disrespect that in April 1835 an American warship appeared at Brazos de Santiago and sent one of its officers to a Mexican military vessel to demand an explanation. Santa Anna's government was in no mood to back down, so that instead of winning an apology the move only brought a confused round of fire between the ships, the hasty withdrawal of the Americans, and the execution of the U.S. naval envoy.[58] By June, American trading ships were being denied the right to dock.[59] When, that September, another U.S. warship appeared at Brazos de Santiago, the Mexican navy proved equally combative.[60] The Texans grew bolder after Gen. Martín Perfecto de Cos was repulsed from San Antonio in December 1835. Texas ships harried Mexican shipping in the Laguna Madre, and a Texan raid for horses led by Dr. James Grant hit the ranches around Matamoros in January 1836. Centralista forces in Matamoros feverishly threw up the new Fort Guerrero on the river at the east end of town in a response of self-protection.[61]

In Paso del Norte, anti-Centralista sentiment moved into seditious planning as well. In 1836 Hugh Stephenson was charged with having smuggled gunpowder, and his partner Archibald Stephenson was fined on a similar accusation of illegal trading. The anti-Centralista mood was so strong in California that U.S. President Jackson in 1835 offered to buy San Francisco Bay from Mexico. Santa Anna sent Coronel Mariano Chico as the new Constitutionalista governor of Alta California. In May 1836, Chico forbade retail trading on foreign ships and declared Monterey the only port of entry for goods coming by ship into California. The San Diegans ignored the orders, causing Chico to complain that Americans were landing at will and continuing to sail away with hides and sea otter pelts. Juan Bandini, collector of customs, who grumbled against Governor Chico, was convicted for smuggling.[62]

While some of the bigger towns held their breath, little Reynosa put up its dukes and asserted itself against Centralista bullying. The

Centralista governor of Tamaulipas tried to take over Reynosa's traditional jurisdiction of the nearby salt lake with its lucrative salt trade, and when Reynosa mayor Manuel de la Fuente objected, the governor replaced him with his own appointee. However, the men of Reynosa, joined by sympathizers from Guerrero, formed a makeshift force which retook Reynosa and ran the governor's man out of town. With the fellow river towns, from Guerrero to Matamoros, expressing sympathy for his stand, de la Fuente determined to hold on to the position he had so courageously defended—at least until Santa Anna would show what he could or could not do in Texas.[63]

Once again, Laredo played the part of the odd town out among the towns of the border to be, by expressing support for Santa Anna's takeover. As had been the case previously at Bustamante's ascent to power, Laredo's stand was influenced by its own situation. Its economy was still not tied significantly to American trade, nor had large numbers of Anglos moved to the town, and the pro-Matamoros bias of past liberal Tamaulipas state governments stung Laredo's sense of justice. However, this Centralista stand did not help the town. During the military campaign in Texas, late in 1835, the Centralista army confiscated Laredoans' horses without due remuneration.[64]

By the time of Santa Anna's confrontation with the Texas rebels, the Centralistas had thus already alienated the most significant portion of the populations of the future border towns. Their refusal to accept Santa Anna's leadership or to heed his warning of the danger of losing land to the United States would lead to their being placed, so to speak, in a *palenque* between two clawing eagles—a ruffled Mexican and an aggressive American one. Yet, the resulting *pelea de gallos* was partly a response to the towns' own economic policies. Locked after 1848 into a border town identity, they would benefit from the conjunction of the two societies. This change, partly of their own making, would be their curse—and their blessing.

Border Violence under Bustamante (1836–1841)

On 21 April 1836, Santa Anna was defeated and captured at the Battle of San Jacinto. The Centralistas turned back to Anastasio Bustamante, who reassumed the presidency from 1836 to 1841. The aftershocks of the Texas Revolution rapidly swept over the towns of the future border. Texas had succeeded in breaking away from Mexico, and the next year New Mexico briefly did the same. There was a danger that other regions of Mexico's alienated Norte would be motivated by the Texan victory to defy the Centralista government in their turn. This threat led to tensions for the towns of the future border. Moreover, Laredo and other Rio Grande towns found themselves now located on an exposed war front, hit by crisscrossing raids between Texas and Mexico, Indian attacks, and economic disruption.

San Diego was also caught up in the impact of Texas' independence. In August 1836 a California revolt was launched in Monterey, driving Governor Chico on to a ship and out of the area. His place was briefly taken by Nicolás Gutiérrez, who in November was driven out, in turn, by a man with a San Diego background named Juan Bautista Alvarado. Alvarado declared Alta California a free and sovereign state. The San Diego *ayuntamiento*, with the active participation of Juan Bandini, Santiago Arguello, and Pío Pico, decided to hold loyal to Mexico, splitting southern from northern California. Juan Bandini, who was the most committed to action, led a force north, while Arguello suspected Pío Pico of secretly supporting Alvarado. With the Diegueño force headed his way, Alvarado agreed to a compromise in which California continued as a state of Mexico, but with Alvarado as its governor. San Diego received permission for a local customhouse.[65]

However, bad blood between San Diego and Monterey continued. In March 1838, Governor Alvarado's forces under José Castro defeated a group of Diegueños under José Antonio Pico at Rincón Pass, north of Los Angeles. Andrés Pico was one of the seventy Southerners captured. Then at midnight on Christmas of 1838, Castro's force in a surprise move occupied San Diego. The townsfolk were gathered dancing and watching a *pastorela* at Juan Bandini's house. Bandini and Estudillo managed to escape, but several men were taken prisoner. Headed north with his catch, Castro stopped for the night at San Luis Rey Mission, where he was received by the mission administrator, Pío Pico, two of whose brothers were among the prisoners. Pío sent out agents to gather a force under José Antonio Estudillo and stalled the bibulous Castro by plying him with food and wine. Estudillo hid a group of men in the trees outside the mission, but at the last minute he lost heart and led them back away again. So, wined and dined without knowing the reason for such abundant hospitality, Castro moved on, unhindered and unsuspecting. The prisoners were later released.[66]

Having won the upper hand, Governor Alvarado took a harsher stance toward San Diego. In June 1839 he appointed the English hide dealer William Hartnell to look into Indian complaints over misadministration of the secularized mission lands. In the ensuing investigation, the president of the Southern Missions suggested that Pío Pico should be thrashed from head to foot for his mishandling of the San Luis Rey Mission. The governor used force to remove Pico from his control of the mission and also ended the Arguello control of the San Juan Capistrano Mission and Bandini's management of the San Gabriel Mission.[67]

The disruption on the eastern border was not so easy to resolve. Matamoros was sandwiched between an angry and restrictive Centralista government to the south and a pugnacious and expansive Texan republic to the north. Mayor Juan Molano's request that defeated Gen. José Urrea's Centralista forces evacuate the town did not salve feelings. Instead, General Urrea subjected his twenty-three Texan prisoners to harsh treatment. Two Americans, William Howell and Captain Potter, were placed under house arrest at Matamoros' Proctor Hotel for criticizing the humiliation being meted out to the Texan prisoners. However, with the aid of hatter Robert Love, Howell and Potter escaped to Texas.[68] Urrea also harassed U.S. Consul Daniel Smith. Smith's house was searched, a mare and two mules were confiscated, and his stepson and another youth were briefly arrested for their purported plans to make a getaway to Texas.[69] George Fisher was fined $1,000 for the anti-Centralista views of his *El Mercurio del Puerto de Matamoros* and was exiled.[70]

Raids swept back and forth between Texas, which claimed the whole territory south to the Rio Grande, and Mexico, which refused to recognize Texas' independence. Texas' interest in the area rested in two considerations. For one, Texans and Mexicans competed for the privilege of rounding up the cattle and especially the horses of the Wild Horse Desert. The horses were brought for sale to the market in Laredo. Laredoans, who traded the animals on into the Mexican interior, were willing to buy from Mexican and Anglo alike due to the income. The other point of interest was in the more distant but richer trading routes that entered Mexico at the two ends of the Rio Grande: Paso del Norte's Santa Fe-Chihuahua Trail at the western end and (more in contention at this point) Matamoros' Gulf ports at the eastern end.[71]

In July 1836 both of Matamoros' main ports — Brazos de Santiago and Boca del Rio — were hit by a month-long Texan naval blockade. Business was hard hit even after the blockade was lifted.

The hands of the Mexican military were tied by understaffing. Nicolás Bravo, the distinguished *independencia* fighter and ex-vice president, was in January 1837 appointed to command the troops at Matamoros. However, even his capable leadership was hamstrung. Finding his position futile given the government's denial of his repeated requests for reinforcements, Bravo resigned his post in frustration.[72] The resulting Mexican military vulnerability invited continuing bold moves from enemies of the country. In April 1837 an American warship entered Brazos de Santiago in search of two American schooners impounded by the Mexican navy. With guns blazing, it freed them and escorted them back into the Gulf. Later that month, another ship was brought captive by the Mexican navy into the same harbor, and its passengers were imprisoned in Matamoros. One of the prisoners was a previous Texan minister to the United States named William Wharton. When Wharton's brother, Col. John Wharton, came to Matamoros to work for William's release, under a truce arrangement, he, too, was arrested. Nonetheless, both brothers managed to escape.[73] As if the hostility of the Texas and American navies were not enough, in April of the following year of 1838, the French navy launched its own temporary blockade of Matamoros' ports, as part of the Pastry War between France and Mexico.[74]

Laredo was the town which was placed most in jeopardy by the Texan claim, lying as it did on the north side of the Rio Grande. It was all the more vulnerable, given the inadequate size of the Mexican military force in the area. After meeting with no response from requests for additional troops, the mayor shaped local civilian volunteers into an informal fighting unit to help combat Indian attacks. A Texan force under Erasmus "Deaf" Smith tried to grab the town for Texas in March 1837, but was repulsed in the battle of the Arroyo de Chacón five miles outside of Laredo.[75]

The breakdown of Mexican control along the Rio Grande and the general collapse of Mexican military prestige with the defeat at San Jacinto encouraged some Indian tribes to escalate their depredations. Comanches and Apaches alternated in their raids on the towns and ranches of the region. Towns the whole length of the later border were affected. In April 1836 the new Indian boldness was announced by a Comanche war raid which penetrated all the way to the Matamoros area and drove off horses over the dead bodies of their owners. The marauders met with such little resistance that they started to return every full moon, driving off cattle and mules as well as horses. In August 1836 they even rode shooting right past the Matamoros army barracks, in an Indian equivalent of a modern Bronx cheer.[76] Paso del Norte's best defense against Apache raids was a band of Indian fighters called the War Society Against the Barbarians, formed in 1839. Its Irish leader, James Kirker, and his men turned the Apaches' love of scalp hunting back against them, proudly displaying their Indian scalps in public.[77] The scalp trade was so rewarding that Kirker began including black Mexican scalps along with those of the Apaches.[78]

San Diego shared the burden of the rising Indian threat. Juan Bandini's Rancho Tecate was one of the ranches sacked and destroyed in 1837. That April, an attempt to kidnap Josefa Carrillo de Fitch during her husband's absence on business was foiled when the plan was overheard and two of Fitch's friends were waiting for the Indians' arrival. The conspirators were arrested and shot, and when Captain Fitch returned, he rallied ten sailors from a hide ship in the harbor along with fifteen local men and drove the Indians up into the mountains. Yet San Diego, too, called in vain for more adequate military protection.[79]

Rather than finding solutions for the disruption of the local economies, the Mexican government only compounded the crisis by imposing a higher tariff in 1837. Designed to increase government revenues, the measure had the opposite effect of causing many of the American commercial firms to move away. In Matamoros, the economic disruption was compounded when many soldiers deserted and formed bands of up to a hundred thieves.[80] San Diego's population would decline to a meager 150 people by 1840. In 1838 it was deprived of its town government, which was being administered from Los Angeles. The town's humiliation was made complete when, in December 1841, its first bishop turned up his nose upon arrival and, despite being cordially housed at Juan Bandini's home, within four days he transferred his new see to Santa Bárbara.[81]

The First Republic of the Rio Grande

At the end of 1839, a group of businessmen in the Lower Rio Grande towns decided to fight back in an attempt to restore their pre-Santa Anna prosperity. They, too, now planned to form their own small country. Texas had shown the way, while both New Mexico and California had already briefly experimented with similar secessionist schemes. Ex-Mayor Juan Molano of Matamoros and Padre

Lira of Camargo endorsed the plan, and José Mᵃ Carvajal (an in-law of both the de León and the de la Garza families of Matamoros) participated in the scheme. Molano's in-law Coronel Antonio Canales formed a private army of 600 men, including a contingent of Texans, on the north side of the Rio Grande across from Mier.[82]

Crossing the Rio Grande, the revolutionary force established its initial headquarters at Carvajal's recently built castle across the Rio San Juan outside of Camargo. Coronel Francisco González Pavón led a 600-man force down from Guerrero, but Coronel Canales, marching upriver, defeated it at Alcantro Creek near Mier on 3 October. In one sense, however, Alcantro Creek was a Pyrrhic victory, for canny Carvajal had his arm shattered, leaving the expedition more one-sidedly under the indecisive and inconsistent Canales.[83]

Canales' first mistake was waiting for a month before leading his 1,000 men downriver to confront the 1,500-man army under Gen. Valentín Canalizo in Matamoros. Canales' procrastination allowed Canalizo to hurriedly have a trench or small moat dug entirely around the land sides of Matamoros. A town wall would later rise along this circuit, linking riverside Fort Paredes (to the west) to riverside Fort Guerrero (to the east). Seeing Canalizo's larger force waiting with eighteen cannons ready to protect this moat line, Canales lost heart and pulled out on the very day he had arrived. It would have been better at least to have tried at Matamoros, for without that port town, the attempt to form a separate nation on the Lower Rio Grande was doomed to failure. Instead, Canales decided, with little logic, that larger and more distant Monterrey would make an easier prey, and so he led his army off in that direction instead.[84] After a skirmish outside Monterrey discouraged him there as well, Canales marched his increasingly disoriented army north to Laredo. There, in January 1840, he proclaimed the new Republic of the Rio Grande, complete with a constitution, a two-room capitol, and a flag. The inauguration of Jesús Cárdenas as president was held that same month in Guerrero.[85]

In 1840 Canales thrashed out in still more directions. First, he tested the possibility of expanding up the Rio Grande into Coahuila, only to pull back after a military setback there. From March to June, a Centralista force occupied Laredo until Canales' band of mixed Federalistas and Texans retook the town. That summer Canales led his troops south against Cd. Victoria, which, perhaps to his own surprise, he actually succeeded in capturing. The best logic from there

would seem to have been a push against Matamoros, whose Centralista garrison was now cut off from outside aid. Canales turned instead to an attempt to capture Saltillo. The resistance at that town was so intense that his Texan soldiers accused Canales of leading them into a trap in order to exterminate them. With his troops quarreling among themselves, Canales found himself pushed back by Gen. Mariano Arista all the way to Camargo. On 8 November 1840, Canales surrendered in exchange for a pardon for himself and his men. The first Republic of the Rio Grande was at an end.[86]

Canales' fiasco left the situation worse than before. Foreign incursions into the Rio Grande region continued unabated. In January 1841, John Hays, one of Canales' Texan volunteers, led a group of Texas Rangers from San Antonio in an expedition to intimidate Laredoans from competing for the feral herds in Wild Horse Desert. Some of the local horses were rounded up but then returned, the Texans explaining that the exercize had been intended only as a warning to respect Texan claims. In the spring, Hays led the Rangers back again in search of a wagon train robber. In a battle east of town, Hays pushed his way into Laredo over the dead bodies of nine Mexicans, but did not find the suspect.[87]

No remedy for the economic decline was forthcoming. Even Matamoros, the healthiest economic center of the area, was described by an observer as simply "dwindling away."[88]

Santa Anna's Stronger Measures (1841–1844)

The Centralista Mexican government exhibited renewed energy in tackling the Texan and American challenge after Antonio López de Santa Anna returned to power in 1841. Santa Anna placed an equestrian statue of himself in the Zocalo in Mexico City showing his arm pointing north. Local wits claimed that the dictator was pointing toward the national mint, which he intended to plunder. However, Santa Anna was pointing the way to renewed military action in the Norte, and he set about turning the symbolism into reality.

Several steps were taken to try to discourage an American presence. The measures started small and then escalated. At first, a policy of levying forced contributions on foreign merchants was implemented. Next, only foreigners with a safe-conduct pass, issued sparingly and only in Mexico City for one year at a time, were allowed to do business in Mexico. In 1843 all land trade with the United States was prohibited, as frontier customhouses were closed. In 1844, it was decreed that only those foreigners who were naturalized citizens, married to Mexicans, or heads of families resident in Mexico could henceforth engage in retail trade. Many American merchants were obliged to sell their wares hurriedly at a great loss.[89]

The Mexican army simultaneously resumed the offensive. In September 1842, Gen. Adrián Woll recaptured San Antonio, although he was not strong enough to hold it for more than nine days. Dragging prisoners with him, he retreated to Matamoros.[90] There he established the Rio Grande as his line of strength, calling all Mexicans to retreat south of that river away from exposure to Indian and Texan attacks.[91] However, the Vanderbilt Steamship Company threatened to cease trade with the area if its ships had to hazard entering the shallow mouth of the Rio Grande to land at Boca del Rio, and this brought a renewal of the Mexican occupation of the Brazos de Santiago area. Port Isabel became more favored at this point, with William Neale's stagecoach line providing transportation from there to the Rio Grande ferry landing across from Matamoros.[92] The stronger anti-Texan stance found expression in the appearance of a new Matamoros newspaper in 1843, called *El Latigo de Texas (The Whip of Texas).*[93]

The Texan response to Woll's expedition to San Antonio came in December 1842, when Gen. Alexander Somerville led about 800 Texans in a looting spree of the Rio Grande towns from Laredo through Guerrero to Mier. When the main force headed back to San Antonio, some of the soldiers stayed behind for more pillaging under the leadership of Col. W. S. Fisher.[94] On Christmas Eve, these men camped at the Rancho de Casas Blancas outside of Mier. Any religious thoughts on that holy occasion were shattered when a 633-man Mexican army from Matamoros, under Gen. Pedro Ampudia, suddenly appeared and took up positions in Mier. In a battle fought through darkness and rain through the night of 25-26 December, Ampudia managed, despite heavy losses, to push the Texans back against the Rio Álamo at the edge of town. Then he sent Coronel Antonio Canales (pardoned for his part in the Rio Grande Republic rebellion) with the cavalry to surround them, and was able to force their surrender.[95]

Ampudia conducted his 242 Texan prisoners downstream to Matamoros, resisting Canales' call for their execution. The prisoners kept up a spirit of spunk, charging around on all fours and bellowing when herded into a cattle pen. In Matamoros, sympathy for the prisoners was expressed by Anglos and Mexicans alike. William Neale went to give money to each man from Kentucky, where he had once lived. When the Kentucky men were asked to step forward, they hesitated, thinking they were to be shot. Instead, non-Kentuckian Capt. Ewing Cameron and after him all the men came forward, to share the fate of their Kentucky companions. To their pleasure, they found that this brought each of them a share in Neale's distribution of money. Loreta Lojero pawned her jewelry and went from door to door to raise money for their legal defense, going along with them to Mexico City to stand by them during their trial. While the prisoners were being marched south to judgment, they attempted to escape, only to be rounded up and decimated. They were obliged to draw beans from a pot while blindfolded to decide who would (by drawing a black bean) or would not (thanks to a white bean) be shot. One of the men warned Cameron to dig deep, where there were white beans, thus saving the captain for the time being. Nevertheless, he was executed later on.[96]

Santa Anna's confrontational approach precipitated dramatic events in San Diego too. That town reacted negatively to Santa Anna's new governor of California, Manuel Micheltorena, who was committed to heading off the growing American influence. Micheltorena, a subordinate of Santa Anna in the Texas campaign, brought with him a tough army, including 500 released criminals. These ex-convicts arrived with nothing more to wear than some old blankets. In their hunger, they stole food and supplies from the residents. Micheltorena gave possession back to the friars of twelve of the twenty-one secularized missions, including those of San Diego, San Luis Rey, San Gabriel, and San Juan Capistrano. The Californios, determined to preserve the American trading position, turned back to the old ruse of allowing American ships to come into port "to make needed repairs."[97]

Doubtless encouraged by the failure of General Woll's invasion of Texas, in February 1844 the Californios rebelled again. Micheltorena was defeated at a "battle" at Cahuenga Pass over Los Angeles. No men were killed, but when the Anglo riflemen he had brought along refused to fight, Micheltorena gave up and returned to Mexico. Pío Pico was made governor of rebel California, Andrés Pico captain of the militia, and Juan Bandini secretary of state, with the seat of government in Los Angeles. The next year, Juan Alvarado detached northern California as a separate nation governed from

Monterey. San Diego became one of the *partidos* of southern California, under Santiago Arguello as its subprefect. The last of the mission land was now handed out by Governor Pico. He sold San Luis Rey Mission to his brother José Antonio Pico and the Cot family, and auctioned off San Juan Capistrano Mission to John Forster and James McKinley. The Guadalupe Mission south of Tecate was granted to Juan Bandini, and the remainder of the San Diego Mission land went to Santiago Arguello.[98]

Important elements in the border towns had by this time opted to break away from the Centralista regime at all costs and to pursue a policy of inviting in still more Anglo-American contacts for the sake of material advancement. What followed, in the Mexican-American War, was not the solution to their problems that most border residents had in mind. On the other hand, it cannot be maintained that the border towns have always been helpless victims of distant national policies. In this case, as in others, they played a role in determining their own future. The frontier identity which had shaped these towns from the start was about to be given a more permanent stamp, for the struggle against the Centralistas would lead into a war which would place them on one of the world's longest borders.

The Mexican-American War

Santa Anna was unexpectedly toppled by Gen. Mariano Paredes in 1844, when he decided to relieve Paredes of his command due to that general's losing battle with the bottle. The Mexican leader most active in heading off Anglo encroachment was thus removed at a time the fragmentation of the Norte was inviting American adventurism in the area. Liberal José Herrera, who followed Santa Anna as president, was in office only briefly. His successor, the same Mariano Paredes, while sharing Santa Anna's Centralista stance, lacked his alertness. Paredes' rigidity played right into the hands of U.S. President Polk and the expansionist schemes of important elements of his Dixie-based Jacksonian Democratic Party. Only a Mexican attack on soil perceived in the United States as being American could have persuaded U.S. Secretary of State James Buchanan and Secretary of the Navy George Bancroft to vote for a declaration of war. Polk ordered Gen. Zachary Taylor to lead an American army in the occupation of northern Tamaulipas at the start of March 1846, boldly claiming this area as part of recently annexed Texas. As a local saying put it, *"Mas vale llegar a tiempo que ser invitado"* ("It's more important to arrive on time than to be invited"). Taylor built Fort Polk at Port Isabel and Fort Texas (later called Fort Taylor and then Fort Brown) across the Rio Grande from Matamoros, in hopes of provoking a Mexican military response. President Paredes' determination to fight for the territory underlay Gen. Mariano Arista's decision to send some troops across the river. On 25 April these soldiers killed or wounded sixteen soldiers of an American scouting party. With cabinet solidarity achieved, Polk was enabled on 11 May to obtain a declaration of war from Congress.[99]

In preparation for the confrontation, Matamoros hurriedly completed the construction of Fort Casa Mata to shore up the town's defenses in the area of Fort Guerrero, across the river from where Fort Texas (Fort Brown) was being hastily constructed.[100] Then, on 2 May, General Arista laid siege to Fort Texas. Its commander, Maj. Jacob Brown, for whom the fort was subsequently named, became one of the fatalities.[101] When General Taylor tried to lead 2,000 reinforcements from Port Isabel to rescue Fort Texas, General Arista twice drew up his forces to bar the route. The battles of Palo Alto on 8 May and of Palma de la Resaca the following day resulted as Taylor's men each time blasted their way through the Mexican ranks.[102] These defeats convinced General Arista to pull his 4,000 surviving soldiers out of Matamoros on the night of 17–18 May. Taylor occupied Matamoros on the heels of his retreat.[103]

After the future Civil War general George McClellan had laid out the military highway up the north bank to supply his troops, General Taylor moved his army by boat upriver first to Reynosa in June 1846 and then to Camargo. In July 1846, Capt. Richard Gillespie rode into Laredo with a troop of Texas volunteers and took possession of the town without bloodshed.[104] From Camargo, Taylor led his men through Mier to reach Monterrey in September.[105]

Meanwhile, in San Diego, American marines had landed in July 1846 to take possession of the town. They built Fort Stockton, complete with a moat and drawbridge, on a hill over the town. That October, the American soldiers in San Diego found themselves suddenly besieged by a revolt of the Californios. The siege lasted until the end of the month, when reinforcement troops were landed and crushed the town rebellion. It took three more months to pacify the rest of California.[106] The last border town to see fighting was Paso del Norte. The town fell to Col. Alexander Doniphan in December 1846 as a

result of his victory over Capitán Antonio Ponce de León at the Battle of Brazito, twenty-eight miles northwest of town.[107] The war, along with the military occupation of the Mexican border towns, was brought to an end by the Treaty of Guadalupe Hidalgo on 2 February 1848.

Local Reaction to the American Conquest

The border town residents were divided in their reaction to the American takeover. Before the coming of the war, many of the local Anglos, Irishmen, and Germans seem to have been speculating on the possibility that the United States would make good its claim to the Rio Grande boundary. After having experienced the threat to their interests posed by Bustamante's government, some of the Anglos, with the renewed encouragement given to Americans under Gómez Farías, preferred to invest on the north bank of the Rio Grande. Following the bold appearance of the U.S. *Grampus* off Brazos de Santiago in 1832, momentum was apparently given to investment decisions based on the ability of the United States to protect American interests north of the river and on American determination to establish a Rio Grande boundary. Anglo investment in Matamoros began to concentrate on the north bank. In that same year of 1832, Frederick Banks built a beef-curing and soap-making factory on leased land at Port Isabel.[108] In 1834, John Stryker received a grant to the Banco de Sta Rita on the riverbank north across from town. This land was free to claim, thanks to the latest of the Rio Grande's relentless shifts to the south. Stryker formed a little settlement there which would swell with American refugees in times of Centralista crackdown in Matamoros, and it became the first permanent Anglophone village on the Lower Rio Grande.[109]

The pattern of Anglo, and also German, interest in the north bank across from Matamoros continued under the Centralista governments. English-born William Neale came to Matamoros in 1832 after mercenary military service with Mexican forces and a period of living in Kentucky. He had intended to settle down as a house painter, but finding that occupation unprofitable, he switched to running a stagecoach line between Boca del Rio and the Rio Grande opposite Matamoros.[110] Adolphus Glaevecke moved to Matamoros from Germany in January 1836, marrying into the de la Garza extended clan. Convinced, according to his own explanation, that the United States was going to make good on Texas' claim to all territory down to the Rio Grande River and cause the north bank to boom, he settled there on the Rancho San Pedro, about fifteen miles west of the later town of Brownsville.[111]

A ways up the Rio Grande, the same pattern prevailed. Henry Clay Davis had first come from Kentucky to Camargo in the 1830s to buy horses for the U.S. Army. Davis had joined the Mier Expedition in 1842, been taken prisoner by General Ampudia, and after his release returned to Camargo. There, on 24 March 1846, he married Hilaria de la Garza, a descendant of Capitán José Antonio de la Garza Falcón, on the understanding that he would settle down on her inheritance north of the river from Camargo. There he set up the Rancho Davis. He worked at founding a town on the site at what was called Davis' Landing, and after the war this plan would succeed in launching Rio Grande City.[112] Also in the 1840s, Charles Stillman of Matamoros bought parcels of land a few miles farther upriver across from Mier, on which the settlement called Roma began to take shape.[113]

In Paso del Norte, too, the local Anglos manifested an interest in the north bank of the river. Hugh Stephenson, who had been in the area since 1828, established his ranch and house "La Casa Grande el Alto" at Concordia on the north side of the Rio Grande. James Magoffin built a house on land owned by Alejandro Ramírez on the north side of the river. On 19 December 1836, the Texas Congress asserted a claim to the north bank of the Rio Grande all the way into New Mexico. In June 1841, Texas President Mirabeau B. Lamar sent an expedition of 270 men to conquer the claimed territory. The Texans were rapidly taken prisoner and sent south to be tried. However, the claim to the Rio Grande's left bank remained, as the Paso del Norte Anglos were well aware. The Magoffins and Stephensons led the local Anglos in hailing the expedition prisoners as heroes, showering them with clothing, food, champagne, and tobacco on their transit through Paso del Norte. Mexican historian Carlos Mª Bustamante even claimed the Anglo-Americans of the upper Rio Grande had been the instigators of Lamar's attempt. By the second half of the 1840s, various Anglos had settled north of the river in and around a small community first formed in 1827 and called Ponce de León Village for its founder, Juan Mª Ponce de León.[114]

When the war came, local Anglos, Irishmen, and Germans moved to help the American takeover. As soon as Taylor occupied Matamoros, many of the American residents of the town crossed

the river to group into a settlement on Stryker's property.[115] Back in
Matamoros, General Ampudia, suspicious of Adolphus Glaevecke,
ordered the German-born rancher to report to him each morning.
Nonetheless, Glaevecke managed to offer his services to General
Taylor and worked as a U.S. scout, a beef and wood supplier, and a
courier, all at considerable risk and without any significant pay for
his services.[116] Francophone residents of Matamoros also joined with
these other groups to act as a fifth column.[117]

Matamoros' foreign merchants rapidly reaped the fruits of the
occupation, raking in profits from sales not only to Taylor's army,
but also to the people of the expanding occupied zone. As imports
were not charged any customs duty by the Americans until the Walker
Tariff of 31 March 1847, sales mushroomed for a time, and new
American merchants moved in to share the bonanza.[118] For the ten
months in which this favorable mercantile situation prevailed,
Matamoros sprouted such indices of wartime prosperity as store-
front lighting and a multiplication of vaudeville theaters, saloons,
and dance halls.[119]

The same pattern can be detected among Paso del Norte Ameri-
can-born residents. When the war broke out, James Magoffin was in
Missouri on his Santa Fe Trail business. He accompanied Senator
Thomas Hart Benton to the American capital, where he was commissioned by President Polk to smooth the way for Gen. Stephen
Kearny's army as it moved down the upper Rio Grande River. In his
meeting with the governor of New Mexico, Magoffin negotiated
surrender without a fight by arguing that resistance would be futile.
He planned to try the same tactic in Paso del Norte, but was arrested
en route in the town of Doña Ana and sent to Paso del Norte as a
prisoner instead. However, the former leader of the scalp-hunters,
the Irishman James Kirker, went out to greet the American troops
under Alexander Doniphan as they headed into Paso del Norte.[120]

The reaction of the Hispanic Mexicans to the American invasion was divided between fierce hostility and resigned acceptance.
Antonio Canales, José Mª Carvajal, and young Juan Cortina of the
de la Garza extended clan, all of whom fought against the invasion,
provide prominent examples of Hispanic Mexicans who fought for
the integrity of Mexican soil.[121] However, other Hispanic residents
reacted less negatively to General Taylor's early Spanish-language
proclamation that the lives, property, and religious customs of all
residents would be respected. Leading local Hispanic Mexicans who

cooperated with the American military included Miguel Salinas, who rented land to General Taylor for the construction of Fort Texas/ Fort Brown, and Juan Antonio Ramírez, who lent Taylor a carriage for use while Fort Texas was being constructed.[122]

Once Taylor was in command of Matamoros, he sought a wider support from the local Hispanics by putting out an army-printed bilingual Spanish-English newspaper named *The Republic of the Rio Grande and the People's Friend*. As this clumsily propagandistic title indicates, Taylor hoped to repopularize Antonio Canales' old scheme to establish a separate republic to encompass Matamoros and the other south bank river towns. The effort failed so clearly that the paper was soon transformed into the purely English-language *The American Flag*.[123]

Laredo's overwhelming Hispanic population, long desperate to end the Indian threat and to boost its economy, received the Texan force under Captain Gillespie in friendly fashion. Laredo's mayor, Andrés Martines, led a town meeting which assured the Americans of local cooperation and expressed a hope that the Americans would provide the long-needed protection from the wild Indians. Content with this submissive attitude, Gillespie and his men left the town on its own until November, when Mirabeau B. Lamar launched Laredo's American administration.[124]

Hispanic leaders of Paso del Norte took part in the resistance to the American invasion. Rancher Antonio Ponce de León led the Mexican force that fought the U.S. troops north of town. Several Hispanics, including the town prefect and the local priest, Padre Ramón Ortiz, were subsequently arrested by Colonel Doniphan for anti-American activities. The American presence was not rendered more palatable by the rioting of some inebriated American soldiers or by the use made by other soldiers of documents from the town archives for lighting candles.[125]

The San Diego Hispanics proved to be the most energetic in resisting the U.S. takeover. However, here too the reaction was far from unanimous. Besides receiving the encouragement of such Anglo residents as the American settler Albert Smith, who joined the occupying forces, the new U.S. establishment was supported by such local Hispanic leaders as Santiago Arguello and Miguel Pedrorena, who accepted commissions in the American army. Such friendly families even invited the American soldiers to their social occasions. Juan Bandini played the part of munificent host to Commodore Stockton at his home. Yet other Diegueños were determined to fight. Andrés Pico formed a resistance band called *Los Galgos* (The Greyhounds), and José Antonio Carrillo formed another styled *Los Hilachos* (The Ragamuffins). The views of the American John Warner seemed sufficiently hostile to bring his arrest. Their determined hostility to the American occupation was rooted in the fact that in San Diego the American invaders were taking power away, not from a distant and hated Mexican conservative government but rather from a local liberal government in the hands of the San Diego elite themselves. Pío Pico was their governor down to his farewell proclamation and brief exit from occupied California, while his brother Andrés Pico was the military leader of the resistance to the American takeover.[126]

In October 1846 the small American garrison was warned that Andrés Pico was planning to descend on San Diego with his nearby force of rebels, and took refuge on a whaling ship in the harbor. The natives thereupon raised the Mexican flag over the abandoned presidio. Seeing this, the next morning Albert Smith left the ship and managed to slip unnoticed during lunch hour into the presidio, where he put the cannon out of commission. Bringing two of their own functional cannons ashore the next day, the Americans scattered the Mexicans and reoccupied the presidio. Smith shimmied up the flag pole and changed the flags once again. One of the town *señoritas*, María Antonia Machado, dared the soldiers' displeasure by grabbing the American flag, stuffing it into her blouse, and hurrying home with it. From a nearby ridge, the rebels kept the Americans on the defensive until Commodore Stockton brought in reinforcements. Meanwhile, Andrés Pico's troops kept a U.S. force under Gen. Stephen Kearny under pressure in two battles some thirty miles northeast of San Diego. Only when Kit Carson made it through the enemy lines to urge Commodore Stockton to rush in reinforcements was Kearny rescued and the rebellion brought to an end in January 1847.[127]

By their eagerness to bring in American settlers and investment and by their erosion of Mexican unity through opposition to the Centralista governments, the towns of the new border now about to be established had played their part in bringing on the Mexican-American War. Some residents had done so wittingly, others unwittingly. Indeed, the U.S. military occupation proved to be helpful in some ways to the interests both of those people who were speculating on an American victory and of those who merely wanted a government favorable to trade. The postbellum situation brought a rapid proliferation of border towns with a growing population and trade. It also at long last ended the danger to life and limb posed by Indian raids.[128] The border towns had shaped their own future in a dramatic new direction. That future would lie along the path of bicultural, bilingual diversity — a path lined with roses, full of thorns.

CHAPTER FIVE

Belated Twinning:
Start of the Twin Cities

In a gush of blood and pain from Mother Mexico out of the Mexican-American War, a younger set of baby towns came squalling into the world. The Rio Grande River, which delineated the eastern half of the new border, invited settlements on both banks. The preexistence of Mexican towns on the south side of the Rio Grande necessitated the establishment of U.S. forts on the north bank across from them, and these American forts provided the cores of new U.S. towns. Laredo's pattern was an exception, reversing this general process by spinning off a twin town on the Mexican side. The production of twin cities along the border's western half would follow later.

The new international border was drawn on 2 February 1848 by the Treaty of Guadalupe Hidalgo along natural river boundaries through most of its extent, being defined mainly by the Rio Grande and the Gila River. The only land boundaries were the relatively short distances between the Rio Grande and the headwaters of the Gila and again from the mouth of the Gila (where it runs into the Colorado River) straight west to the Pacific. The 1853 Gadsden Purchase, which would add to the United States a strip of land south of the Gila River, would replace a logical geographic border with an arbitrary and invisible line across the deserts from West Texas to the Pacific. In the pre-Civil War atmosphere of sectionalism, the American government sought the territory for a planned southern railroad route. Santa Anna, Mexican head of state for one last time, sold the territory to refurbish his treasury and preserve his power.

In the conditions of the Treaty of Guadalupe Hidalgo, the southern river towns, including Matamoros, Reynosa, Camargo, Mier, and Guerrero, all lost their community's lands on the north side of the river.[1] It was mainly on these previous *ejido* lands that American towns sprang up. These new settlements gained an early economic advantage when in 1852 the American government increased the number of approved trade routes for foreign bonded goods into Mexico and allowed two years, rather than just one, for such merchandise to be sent out from Texas ports. Reductions in Mexican tariff duties in 1849 were an inadequate stimulus for the Mexican towns, and many Mexicans moved north across the river.[2] Smuggling augmented the advantages of the American towns. Far lower prices — even as much as one-fourth lower — could be found in the towns on the American side. In an attempt to halt the contraband trade, the Mexican government on 20 November 1848 set up one customs post in Matamoros, with authority as far as Reynosa, Camargo, and Mier, and a second one covering the area from Guerrero to Nuevo Laredo.[3]

The twin towns found themselves placed in an international milieu. The potential cultural creativity inherent in this situation has been long in emerging, but the mere presence face to face of two great permanently planted cultures made border town life more colorful and varied. The establishment of new towns on the U.S. side of the border brought in a stronger Anglo presence there. New Anglo-Americans joined the earlier immigrants in such towns as Brownsville, Laredo, Eagle Pass, Del Rio, and El Paso. Many of them came to provide goods and services both to the local residents and to the U.S. army posts. The development of new businesses also attracted a considerable immigration of Hispanics from both interior and frontier Mexico. In most cases, the Anglos formed the ruling elite of the new towns.[4] The Treaty of Guadalupe Hidalgo confirmed the older Hispanic land titles on the north side of the border, and many Hispanic Mexicans chose to become American citizens.[5] However, Mexicans frequently were forced to sell part or all of their lands to pay legal fees or lost them through fraud.

The change also brought a fresh spiritual impetus. Along with the founding of churches came a dedication to winning souls for Christ in defiance of the frontier flavor. The Catholic church now demonstrated in the American settlements the spirit of zeal that had once marked it in the older Mexican towns. French clergymen were especially noteworthy among the Catholic spiritual leaders. The

Oblate Missionaries of Mary Immaculate made a major impact in the Lower Rio Grande area, starting with the arrival of Fathers Telmon and Soulerin in Brownsville in 1849. The missionaries suffered through a period of being lodged in a half-ruined shed and conducting services in an empty shop until better quarters could be obtained. By mid-1850, seventeen Oblate Fathers from the Archdiocese of Lyons in France were already at the work for which they would remain famous for the rest of the century — riding to bring spiritual succor to outlying ranches and rural chapels.[6]

In the 1850s and 1860s, Father Keralum, trained as an architect in Paris, built a series of French Gothic churches, including Brownsville's Church of the Immaculate Conception (the present cathedral), the Sáenz-Fernández Chapel at the Toluca Ranch near Progreso, Roma's Church of Our Lady of Refuge of Sinners, and the Church of San Agustín in Laredo.[7] Patrons included Mifflin Kenedy in Brownsville and the García family in Roma.[8] The Oblate Fathers were reinforced in their effort in Brownsville when at the very end of 1852 the first four of the French sisters from the Incarnate Word Convent in Lyons arrived. The next year, they launched the Villa María boarding school for girls.[9] In 1862 the Oblate Fathers opened a comparable school for boys — St. Joseph's.[10]

Of the first Protestant churches to be built in Brownsville — the Methodist, the Presbyterian, and the Episcopal — the Presbyterian seems to have been the most fervent in soul-winning. In 1852 Presbyterian missionary Melinda Rankin of New Hampshire opened a school for Mexican girls, and in 1854 a Presbyterian boys' mission school followed, the work of the first minister, Hiram Chamberlain. Reverend Chamberlain, whose daughter married Richard King, started his first services aboard his future son-in-law's steamship for lack of better facilities.[11] He energetically extended his mission work to the ranch areas around Brownsville, setting up Sunday school groups where there was poor access to his church in town. Melinda Rankin also busied herself with distributing Bibles and religious tracts. By founding fourteen missions in Mexico, she launched the history of the Presbyterian church in that land.[12]

Where Relations were Troubled

The twin cities, often said to be so similar that if you have seen one you have seen them all, were actually quite distinct from their inception. A relatively tranquil existence in this decade marked relations between the sets of towns where Hispanic leadership and culture prevailed in both twins. However, the more common type of twin town set to appear in the 1850s was characterized by the prevalence of a more Anglo flavor in the town on the American side. Signs of intertown strain were more common in such a case.

The Case of Brownsville/Matamoros

Brownsville, named for the major killed in the siege of Fort Texas/Fort Brown in the Mexican-American War, was the creation of land speculator and merchant Charles Stillman. One of the earliest and also most successful of the Anglo merchants to establish himself in Matamoros, this Connecticut Yankee had both the knowledge of the area and its people and the shrewdness and position of respect to act on that intelligence. Thanks to Stillman's decision to make the local U.S. Army quartermaster a junior partner of his scheme, he received advanced reports on the exact location of the new site chosen for a relocation of Fort Brown. Stillman then located his town next to it so that it would be protected by the army while attracting business from the soldiers. The site also stood on a ridge of land relatively free from floods.[13] He purchased this spot, which had been the location of Matamoros' northern *ejido* or village commons, from families who had leased plots there from the town.

Some legal difficulty was posed by the fact that Matamoros had originally bought the land from Francisca Cavazos but never paid her, but the conflicting claims were eventually worked out in court.[14] Challenges to Stillman and his town location arose from various rivals. John Stryker promoted Santa Rita, which was briefly the first county seat of Cameron County. Asa Wheeler tried to launch the town of Mansfield, and a group of squatters led by steamboat captain Patrick Shannon proposed a town to be called Shannondale. All challengers were vanquished.[15] A conflicting claim to the same site was made by another group of land developers, including William Neale and two men who were in the area as part of General Taylor's entourage, County Judge Israel Bigelow and lawyer Stephen Powers. The group had received permission to incorporate the site as a city and then, under Bigelow as Brownsville's first mayor, had claimed all the land in the corporate limits.[16] This threat, too, was overcome. However, the defeated set of men continued to oppose Stillman's control of the town by forming a Blue Party faction to counter Stillman's Red Party.[17]

Stillman named the central streets of the new town for members of his family — St. Charles Street for himself, St. Francis for his father, and Elizabeth Street for his wife.[18] He donated land for Washington Park for the benefit of the public.[19] To guarantee good access between Matamoros and Brownsville, he founded one of the ferry services between the towns.[20] Brownsville's greatest advantage was its connection to the Brazos de Santiago harbor — the only major port on the Gulf of Mexico between Corpus Christi and Veracruz.[21] Port Isabel was chosen as the landing site inside the Brazos de Santiago, and a U.S. customhouse was located there in May 1849.[22] Grasping the importance of Port Isabel to Brownsville, Stillman worked in collaboration with a New Orleans produce broker named Simon Mussina, who simultaneously had bought out the old town of Port Isabel and was developing a new American port town there. As the new owner of the main local newspaper, *The American Flag*, Mussina promoted the advantages of both Brownsville and Port Isabel.[23]

In its first century of existence, Brownsville was dominated mainly, but not exclusively, by its Anglo merchant families. At the head of those Anglo merchants already settled earlier in the area stood Charles Stillman himself. Operating his Brownsville to New York trade from the Brownsville end, he moved with his Connecticut bride into a new brick house at the corner of Washington and Thirteenth streets (which is today a museum). His wife would move to New York after delivering Charles' two eldest children in Brownsville, so that he henceforth saw her only on summer vacations.[24] William Neale, who had long run a stagecoach line on the north bank, continued to prosper by providing transportation between Port Isabel and Brownsville.[25] Prominent among the new Anglo families recently arrived in the area were Mifflin Kenedy from Pennsylvania and Richard King from New York. These two Irish-Americans had become friends working on Dixie riverboats together. When Kenedy was hired as a captain of one of General Taylor's Rio Grande boat transports, he had called in King to be his pilot. The two men now went into partnership with Stillman to monopolize steamboat traffic on the river.[26] The interest of Kenedy and King later shifted to the northern Wild Horse Desert, where they concentrated on building the Sta Gertrudis Ranch into the largest ranch in their country.[27]

Brownsville's position as a port town facing the Atlantic drew in many German and French-speaking immigrants. As late as forty

years after the town's founding, it was still considered advantageous
for the local postmaster to be able to speak not only English and
Spanish, but also French and German.[28] Jews and Italians were also
prominent settlers from the first.[29]

Seventy-five percent of Brownsville's 2,000 residents in 1858
were Mexican-Americans.[30] Hispanic families from both the old
ranching elite and the new mercantile class were also very prominent
from the first. For their part, many of the Anglo families were quite
Mexicanized in customs and bilingual English-Spanish in speech (as
was Brownsville in general) and were typically intermarried with the
Mexican elite.[31] The old Mexican ranching elite was represented by
such extended families as the de la Garzas and the de Leóns. That
famous in-law of both, José Mᵃ Carvajal, settled in Brownsville despite
having fought Taylor's invasion.[32] Estefana Goseascochea de la Garza
lost some of her land due to a challenge to her land titles in the
American takeover, but she managed to retain the bulk of her holdings.[33] The Ballís remained well represented in Brownsville, although
their status was reduced due to less success in defending their land
claims.[34] Leading Hispanic merchants included José San Román,
dealer in dry goods, who transferred his business from Matamoros
to Brownsville, and Miguel Fernández, who owned an import-export
store on Market Square and later the town's Merchants National
Bank.[35] Francisco Yturria gives a prominent example of a Hispanic
who fit into both land-holding and merchant categories. Son of a
decorated Mexican captain, Yturria had established a mercantile business in Matamoros. In 1848 he chose to settle in Brownsville, while
still maintaining a base in Matamoros. He later founded the Yturria
Bank. He also extended his land holdings to over 250,000 acres,
including the San Martín Grant, previously held by his wife's family,
and the Yturria Ranch north of the later Raymondville.[36]

Soon so much trade was moving between Port Isabel and
Brownsville that Brownsville, which now could import American
goods duty-free, took over Matamoros' old importance as the main
port town connecting Brazos de Santiago to northeastern Mexico. A
"Cart War" erupted between Anglo and Mexican-American
wagoneers for control of this lucrative business. So much of the trade
crossing the Rio Grande was contraband, to avoid Mexican duties,
that Boca del Rio blossomed into a sizable town as a smuggling empo-
rium and was renamed Bagdad for its sinful flavor. The passage
through Brownsville of myriad forty-niners, headed for San Francisco

via northern Mexico, also brought customers.[37] Brownsville thus took shape rapidly, with a two-story brick city market completed in 1852 and a public school operating in the new courthouse from 1854. Henry Miller, starting in 1849, operated the two-story frame Miller Hotel (at first called the Cameron House) in close proximity to the ferry crossing.[38] In Brownsville's initial boom, it looked as though there was not enough room for two important towns by the mouth of the Rio Grande and that Matamoros had lost out to Brownsville.

The Case of Hidalgo/Edinburg

McAllen, the principal town which would arise north of the river across from Reynosa, did not yet appear in the late nineteenth century. However, a tiny town called Edinburg was founded on the north bank immediately across from Reynosa. Today known as Hidalgo (while the name Edinburg has shifted to a newer neighbor), this town's identity seems destined to be swallowed up by rapidly growing Greater McAllen. Hidalgo was launched after the Mexican-American War out of a tiny settlement called La Habitación. The founder, John Young, consolidated his local holdings and position by marrying Salomé Ballí of the old Ballí land-holding clan. He profited from various sources of income, including ranching, salt sales from the Sal del Rey (the road to which was improved by Charles Stillman), operating a river ferry and a hide yard, and selling lots and running a general store in his new town. The burg was dubbed Edinburg after the capital of Young's homeland, and was made the seat of the new Hidalgo County in 1852.[39]

Reynosa's Troubles

Because Hidalgo/Edinburg failed to grow significantly, due to lack of population in the sparse ranching chaparral, it did not pose the sort of challenge to Reynosa that Brownsville did to Matamoros. Nonetheless, Reynosa found itself at a disadvantage in this period. Bypassed by the river trade between the Gulf and Mier (from where goods headed by land for Monterrey), Reynosa's location was not yet crucial for trade. It had lost some of its families and ranches on the north side, leaving it with a little over 4,000 inhabitants, and it no longer controlled the lucrative salt beds. The town and its ranches were also now plagued by continuing rustling raids staged by Anglo and Hispanic outlaws from such disparate north bank bases as Rio

Grande City and Brownsville. The Anglo-Americans of the north bank were feeling their oats from the American success in the Mexican-American War, and many of them were pressing their psychological advantage against the south bank. The Reynosa area was especially targeted because, lying as it did off the main mercantile routes, the goods of certain big business backers of the outlaws were not thereby placed in jeopardy. Mexican investigators claimed that Richard King and Adolphus Glaevecke were two of the beneficiaries of these illegal round-ups. Texas District Judge N. P. Norton was tried but acquitted for leading a raid that robbed 3,418 pesos from Antigua Reynosa. Frederick Matthews in 1852 successfully robbed and sold in Texas 400 head of cattle. Thaddeus Rhodes led other raids from his Rosario Ranch in Hidalgo County, and in 1856 boldly freed a captured gang member from a Mexican prison.[40]

The Case of Rio Grande City/Camargo

Henry Clay Davis, already locked in a struggle against the Stillman faction for control of slightly older Roma upriver, had been hoping to launch still another town directly across the Rio Grande from Camargo on his Rancho Davis. The founding of U.S. Fort Ringgold on the spot on 26 October 1848 provided the economic base to realize his dream. Capt. Forbes Britton helped Davis lay out the lots and left his name attached to the town plaza. Davis dubbed the new town Rio Grande City and gave an example to others by building its first brick house, which still stands.[41] An energetic entrepreneur, Davis encouraged trade by plowing a furrow (due to the lack of roads) to guide wagons along the route from Corpus Christi through Laredo to the new town. Rio Grande City also became the county seat of Starr County, with Davis acting as its first county clerk.[42]

The Case of Mier and Roma

In at least one case, namely Mier and Roma, a rough start of a twin city set had already grown up on the Lower Rio Grande before the war. Roma had emerged under the guiding hand of Charles Stillman of Matamoros, who in the 1820s had bought land from the richest ranching family of the area, the Garcías, and laid out the town on the site. After the Mexican-American War, Anglo and European entrepreneurs further developed the town. By 1853, Roma had 1,000 inhabitants. From the first it became known as a town built around illegal trade. Major Emory of the U.S. and Mexico Boundary Survey, who came through Roma in 1857, was amazed to find so many grand houses, like the two-story Cox house built in 1853, and large warehouses. The major noted that there was no conspicuous legitimate trade or significant population to explain their presence, and was subsequently informed that smuggling was the true economic base of the town.[43]

A struggle for control of Roma and its vigorous black-market trade opened up after the Mexican-American War. One group, which might be labeled the Mier-Brownsville faction, was headed by the Garcías of Mier, who had dominated Roma before the Mexican-American War, and their ally Charles Stillman. The Garcías, after working with Charles Stillman to launch the town, cooperated after 1848 with Stillman to make Roma the last stop upriver of the steamboats of Stillman, King, and Kenedy. Mifflin Kenedy especially promoted the town's growth. The other faction, which might be dubbed the Camargo faction, was headed by Henry Clay Davis, married earlier into the de la Garza family of Camargo. Davis was promoting the new town of Rio Grande City downriver and was eager to expand his interests to Roma as well.[44] Davis gained an advantage in controlling the first steamboat landing with its river dock facilities. Some of the local merchants, including Nestor Sáenz, located their establishments at Davis' landing. However, the Stillman, King, and Kenedy partnership fought back by building their own rival steamboat landing.[45]

Mier leaders again voiced their discontent with being left, after the loss to the United States of the Wild Horse Desert, in the illogical, long panhandle of Tamaulipas rather than joined more naturally to Nuevo León next door. Feeling that some concession needed to be made to local resentments, on 11 February 1853, the Mexican government briefly transferred the towns from Mier through Nuevo Laredo to Nuevo León. However, Tamaulipan protests brought a reversal of the decision a mere two months later. Blocked at every turn, Mier and Roma settled into the difficult business of illegal trade under heavy surveillance with the restricted opportunities of a backwater region.[46]

Competition between the Twin Towns of the Lower Rio Grande

One of history's ironies was played out in the Lower Rio Grande towns at this time. Earlier, the local Hispano-Mexican leaders had brought in Anglo-American businessmen to help develop the region, only to be disappointed at the way success in this goal was achieved. Now, Anglo-American businessmen tried to manipulate the interest in a lower tariff on the part of the Mexican leaders (who hoped thereby to develop the region), only to be disappointed at the way success in their goal was achieved.

The period of the 1850s on the Lower Rio Grande was shaped by the dynamic Anglo entrepreneur. His name changed from town to town; it was Charles Stillman in Brownsville and Henry Clay Davis in Rio Grande City. Yet his story was generally the same: He had come to the area earlier in the expectation that his business expertise would help the region blossom. The local Hispanic leaders were not wrong in believing that he could do this job, but they had miscalculated on the trauma that would result for their society.

Especially in those cases where a more American-flavored town developed across from an established Mexican town, potential existed for an impassioned competition to spring up between them. This tendency was most pronounced in areas of strong trading profits. Such competition between adjoining towns is best seen in the case of Brownsville and Matamoros, due to the early commercial development of the region. An initial rush to invest in Brownsville occurred, with the early business stimulus from the California Gold Rush traffic passing through it. However, various problems soon arose to plague town developers. Legal squabbles over property and charter rights in the city, an early dominance by a handful of business interests, a lack of concern for building such infrastructure as a hospital or school building, deaths from yellow fever and cholera epidemics, and insecurity from ongoing Indian raids all combined to frustrate many of the first settlers. Both Brownsville and Matamoros were hurt by high Mexican import tariffs. As a result, already by mid-April 1850 Brownsville saw an outmigration of early pioneers.[47]

Some of the Brownsville leaders hoped to resolve their problems by coercing the Mexicans to lower the tariff on goods moving into Matamoros. Knowing that the Matamoros merchants would also be enthusiastic for this proposal, and not foreseeing the negative impact that such a change could have on their own town, these men decided to coerce Mexican authorities into granting a local free-trade zone. Headed by Richard King and Mifflin Kenedy, with Charles Stillman possibly as a less visible third, this group decided to force the tariff change by supporting a second scheme to create a compliant Republic of the Rio Grande out of Mexican territory. It was hoped that this scheme would either succeed or scare the Mexican government into lowering the tariffs.[48] José María Carvajal, veteran of the first Republic of the Rio Grande, and José María Canales, son of the leader of that earlier attempt, were chosen to head the movement.[49] John S. "Rip" Ford was assigned the rank of colonel to head the Texan troops to be recruited.[50]

The program was made public outside the town of Guerrero on 3 September 1851 as the Plan of La Loba. Two weeks later, Carvajal led an army of combined Mexicans and Texans across the Rio Bravo from Rio Grande City and attacked Camargo. With Guerrero, Mier, and Camargo under his control, Carvajal then marched his thousand some troops downriver through Reynosa to besiege Matamoros. The scheme worked like a *curandero* charm. The commander of Matamoros' garrison, Gen. Francisco Ávalos, hastened to lower the tariff and to end the prohibitions on the import of certain items. This move converted Carvajal's army into a superfluous relic. In an ironic preparation for the Día de los Muertos, Carvajal devoted the ten days and nights preceding that festival to a bloody attempt to take Matamoros from General Ávalos. Carvajal's forces captured Fort Paredes and surged on to the Plaza Hidalgo at the heart of town, but could not hold what they had taken. In recognition of this tenacious defense, Matamoros was awarded the title of *"Invicta y Heróica"* (undefeated and heroic). Finding all of his efforts to be futile, Carvajal withdrew upriver. Gen. Antonio Canales, who had held aloof from this attempt despite his sons' involvement, led a pursuing army that pushed Carvajal back. On 21 February 1852, he defeated Carvajal on the banks of the Rio San Juan outside Camargo and cleared Mexican soil of their presence.[51]

Matamoros' Free Trade Zone (1858)

Brownsville soon learned that the political probing of its merchants had created a Frankenstein's monster which would come back to stalk it. While the Centralista Mexican government of Santa Anna subsequently reinstated the tariff, Ávalos' measure had received too much local support for it to be suppressed. The Centralistas had developed an impossible suspicion of the liberal Matamorenses.

However, in 1855 Centralista President Santa Anna was forced from power and Centralista Gen. Adrián Woll had found it advisable to use the cover of darkness to sneak out of town. The triumphant Federalistas turned a smiling countenance to Matamoros' pleas. The town's reward came (appropriately for Irish-Americans King and Kenedy) on St. Patrick's Day of 1858 in the form of the authorization of a free trade zone strip twelve miles wide along the south bank of the Rio Grande from its mouth through Nuevo Laredo.[52]

The result was a bonanza for Matamoros. The local big merchants rushed to reopen stores in that south-bank town, selling American and European goods at low prices.[53] Matamoros' population leaped from less than 12,000 people to 40,000 by the end of the 1850s. Its newly founded (1859) Instituto de San Juan provided a higher level of secondary education for the youth of both Matamoros and Brownsville.[54] Yet, as Matamoros waxed, Brownsville waned. To avoid paying American duties, European ships now preferred to debouch their goods at Bagdad (the old Boca del Rio) rather than at Brazos de Santiago, despite Bagdad's more shallow entry and less protected location.[55] Fort Brown was closed in March 1859, compounding the blow to Brownsville.[56] Richard King and Mifflin Kenedy started to shift their attention to their ranches farther north in the Wild Horse Desert.[57]

Matamoros' strengthened position vis-à-vis its twin town was also reflected in a renewed local Hispanic resistance to the American occupation. This opposition found expression partly in an outbreak of cattle rustling raids hitting now in the opposite direction, from south of the river into the ranches around Brownsville. The boldest of the resistance leaders-cum-cattle rustlers was a north bank rancher named Juan "Cheno" Cortina, himself resettled on the south side of the river. A member of the prominent old de la Garza clan, red-headed and explosive, Cortina cut his ties to Brownsville in a highly dramatic fashion. Outlawed for wounding a city marshal, whom he found roughly arresting an unruly former ranch hand, Cortina took revenge by shooting up the town. Adolphus Glaevecke and the city marshal were intended as his two main targets. As the sun rose on 28 September 1859, it silhouetted Cortina leading a band of about 200 armed men into town. Before the town could throw off its sleep to call on Matamoros for help and form a resistance, five men (including William Neale, Jr., two other Anglos and two Hispanics) were murdered, and all the prisoners had been freed from the town jail.[58]

Two days later, Cortina officially proclaimed himself champion of the local Mexicans against the Anglo-American oppressors. Another proclamation in November added a religious postscript, stating that God had called Cortina to this task. This clarification of his goals brought a steady swelling of Cortina's ranks which would gradually propel him from the status of *ranchero* Robin Hood through Mexican general to governor of Tamaulipas. With as many as 500 men at his command, Cortina laid siege to Brownsville and rounded up livestock belonging to Charles Stillman and other area ranchers. A town militia named the Brownsville Tigers was thrown together by Capt. Mifflin Kenedy and led by Capt. W. B. Thompson, with a Mexican-American company commanded by Francisco Yturria. The Tigers joined forces with a Matamoros unit under Lieutenant Colonel Laranca and Cortina's cousin Col. Miguel Tijerina. In October 1859 their combined units attacked Cortina's El Carmen Ranch, only to be driven in a humiliating route back to Brownsville.[59]

American troops were rushed back to Fort Brown. In December 1859, Maj. Sam Heintzelman led 150 regular soldiers plus 198 Texas Rangers commanded by Rip Ford in chasing Cortina's band up the north bank of the river. In a battle near Rio Grande City, Cortina's troops were scattered. Cortina swam his horse across the river and reestablished his camp on the south bank at La Bolsa Bend. This spot became Cortina's base for conducting cattle raids across the river and for attacking riverboats. Even though in February and March 1860, Rip Ford commanded counterraids against Cortina's camp, Cortina was able to maintain his harassment of the Brownsville region for several years to come.[60]

Reynosa was another of the various towns of the Lower Rio Grande delta to be affected by Juan Cortina's insurrectionary activities. In March 1860, his band was hanging out at the Rancho La Mesa on the outskirts of town. Two forces, one from Brownsville and the other from Matamoros, moved to try to catch him there. The crafty Cortina gave them the slip, leaving the American and the Mexican forces to blunder into each other in a mistaken exchange of fire at the ranch. Provided with the information that Cortina had moved on to Antigua Reynosa, Rip Ford attacked that town the following month. Finding Cortina again gone, the frustrated Texans headed for Reynosa itself. Angered by the repeated violation of their jurisdiction by Texan gunmen, the men of Reynosa hurriedly sent the women and children out of town and prepared to fight. Ford rode into their crossfire coming out of side streets and down from roof tops when he entered Reynosa's town plaza. He called out that he was just looking for Cortina, to which the Reynosans shouted back that this was not Cortina's Rancho La Bolsa and that Ford was on the wrong trail. The Texans were forced to backtrack across the river, sourly firing some shots back into the town as they disappeared on the far bank.[61]

Trouble between Eagle Pass and Piedras Negras

The double founding of Eagle Pass and Piedras Negras is the one notable case where, in the wake of the Mexican-American War, a set of twin border towns sprang up at a remove from any previous town settlement. The point where the old Saltillo-San Antonio highway had earlier crossed the Rio Grande at Paso del Águila would probably have seen town development long before, had it not been for raiding Indians. San Juan Bautista Mission and Presidio had been too weak to counteract this threat. With the vigorous Texan campaigns against the Indians after the Mexican-American War, and especially with U.S. Army plans to locate a fort on the north bank, the time seemed ripe for investment. However, the local smugglers had by this time shifted their river crossing some thirty miles upstream as a more convenient place to avoid border guards.[62]

In 1849 San Antonio merchant James Campbell set up a trading post on the spot of this latest ford of the river. Texas ex-commissary general William Cazneau agreed with Campbell's estimate and started a ranch there as well. Campbell's store flourished through sales to the soldiers of the new Fort Duncan, as well as to the forty-niners coming through on their way to California. Campbell did such a good business that one forty-niner named Henry Matson settled locally and with an investment in two kegs of liquor opened a saloon in a borrowed army tent set up by the river. This saloon prospered even more than the store. Here San Antonio banker John Twohig bought up land and sold it in lots as a new town in 1850. In this fashion, the whole town of Eagle Pass essentially grew up centered around a booze hole. Twohig saw to it that stagecoach contact to San Antonio was established in 1851. Eagle Pass also became the seat of the new Maverick County in 1856. However, growth was limited by the ranching monoculture of the area, by its remote location, by continuing Indian raids, and by the rough-and-tumble tone established by stranded gold rushers, adventurers, and outlaws.[63]

Here we have an example of twin towns being born in rapid succession. Piedras Negras appeared in the same year of 1850, impelled by a Mexican desire to hold the south side of the river from any possible American incursion out of Fort Duncan. A Mexican fort was accordingly built on the south side of the river alongside a new Mexican town populated from the surrounding river settlements. The local coal outcrops gave the town its name of Piedras Negras ("Black Rocks"). Relations were troubled between more Americanized Eagle Pass and Piedras Negras. Bad feelings flared up when in 1855 James Callaghan led an American force south of the river in pursuit of raiding Indians. Instead of finding them, Callaghan's men exchanged blows with a Mexican force on the Río Escondido. The Americans then grabbed Piedras Negras, looting and burning it before returning to Eagle Pass.[64]

The Case of El Paso/Paso del Norte

As in the case of Brownsville, there were also several candidates for the site of the new main American town across the Rio Grande from Paso del Norte. The pre-existing north bank towns of Ysleta, Socorro, and San Elizario were too far from Paso del Norte to compete seriously. The main contenders by the end of 1849 were Franklin, Magoffinsville, Concordia, Frontera, and El Molino. This list equates to the interests respectively of Franklin Coons, James Magoffin, Hugh Stephenson, T. Frank White, and Simeon Hart. The five contending sites for the new town thus reflect the Anglo leadership in the region. One factor in deciding which town would succeed was the choice of the seat for the new El Paso County. The decision here was postponed when in 1849 San Elizario, at a remove from the principal competition, was chosen for that honor. A more important question was which spot could attract the new population coming into the area. Here the town of Franklin, superimposed over the former Ponce de León Village, won an early advantage thanks to its location most directly across the river from Paso del Norte. When gold rushers began to pour through the area, they preferred to stop here. Their presence influenced the third main factor in the competition, namely the site of a U.S. Army post. To protect these transients, in September 1849 a fort was built on the site. With this move, Franklin's success was guaranteed.[65]

Not having the advantages of international influences like those enjoyed by the port towns of Brownsville and San Diego, land-locked

El Paso was more dominated from the start by its smaller Anglo-American component of merchants hailing mainly from the northern United States via the Santa Fe Trail from Missouri. The contrast between the Anglo population (numbering 144 in 1860) and the Mexican population (with 263 families in 1860) was made all the starker by the difference between the pious Mexican farmers for whom this was home and the rough new Anglo settlers for whom this was an escape.[66] Frequent transfers of land ownership to Anglos further exacerbated the polarity of cultures. While Benjamin Franklin Coons, a St. Louis merchant in the Santa Fe Trail trade, bought the property of Juan María Ponce de León, James Magoffin simply took over that of Alejandro Ramírez. Magoffin claimed the ranch property by right of having lived in a house there, while Ramírez had never actually lived in his log cabin on the land. Ramírez fought Magoffin's claim in the American courts down to 1872, but in vain.[67]

James Magoffin advertised the good fortune of this Anglo set by being a generous host, serving imported delicacies by the light of improvised chandeliers. Simeon Hart built up a collection of books at his ranch house (which is now El Paso's Hacienda Cafe). Intermarriage helped to depolarize the situation somewhat. Simeon Hart provides a reminder of the tendency of these Anglo leaders to marry into older Mexican families. Hart was a New Yorker who had grown up in St. Louis, Missouri. He had come into the area as an American soldier in the Mexican-American War. After being wounded in battle and nursed back to health by the Siqueiros family of Santa Cruz de Rosales, Hart at age thirty-four married one of the Siqueiros girls, age seventeen.[68]

Another of the new Anglo leaders was Ben Dowell, a settler from Kentucky who arrived as a penniless soldier in the Mexican-American War. Starting as a supervisor of Juan Ponce de León's vineyards, Dowell married Juana Márquez of Ysleta and soon was prospering as a farmer and businessman. His adobe business establishment acted as store, saloon, game room, post office, and general social center for the men of the town. His organization of horse racing on a dirt road outside of town, with accompanying betting, was a big success. As a farmer, he brought the cultivation of alfalfa and sweet potatoes to the area. As a town leader, he was active as the first mayor (in 1873), postmaster (from 1857 to 1860), justice of the peace (who eradicated one shady character with a blast of buckshot as he entered his saloon door), and organizer of the local Masons.[69]

Benjamin Franklin Coons worked so feverishly to expand his new town that he failed to reap the benefits. In a slightly premature effort to open a trade route from San Antonio, he lost his investment when his expedition fell apart in trying to cross the difficult and dangerous territory. While Coons failed in his attempt, others soon succeeded. Coons himself went from one blow to the next. He lost his rent from the army when the post was moved forty miles to the north to Fort Fillmore in September 1851. Even worse, the removal of army protection allowed the Apaches to hit the town with raiding parties. Coons drifted on to California, and Franklin returned to its old name of El Paso. Its ownership passed via Juan Ponce de León and then his widow in 1854 into the hands of Kentuckian William ("Uncle Billy") Smith. Smith joined with five other men to organize a townsite company and handed out plots in an unsystematic fashion that is still evidenced in the higgeldy-piggeldy street layout of El Paso's downtown section.[70]

When the army deigned to return to the area in January 1854, it settled at Magoffinsville, founding Fort Bliss. However, El Paso's position as the main town had already been established. Its prosperity was increased by a new trade in copper from mines brought into the United States as a result of the Gadsden Purchase (or the *Venta de la Mesilla*) in 1854. Regular stagecoach connections ran east to San Antonio and north to Santa Fe from 1853 and west to San Diego from 1857, solidifying El Paso's role as transportation hub of the region.[71]

El Paso and Paso del Norte, like Brownsville and Matamoros, started their coexistence with a mood of sibling rivalry. Mexican resentment over the loss of the north bank brought sympathy for rustling raids onto the ranches across the river. When El Paso rancher James Magee chased rustlers of his cattle south of the Rio Grande, he found himself arrested and jailed in Paso del Norte. An American posse which crossed the river to free him failed to do more than leave two of their men dead. Relations were embittered, not due to a free trade zone on the Mexican side (as in the case of Matamoros), but because of the exact opposite, a forty percent duty on American goods imported into Mexico. It was the wrong formula for revenge. Paso del Norte's north-south trade (all it had) was crippled, while El Paso was able to capitalize on routes from east, north, and west. Seeing the decline of the southern town, more than 5,000 Pasoans shifted by 1856 from Paso del Norte to El Paso, which emerged as the main commercial center for both banks of the river.[72]

Where Relations were Calm: The Case of the Laredos

In the one notable case where a new town sprang up on the south side of the border across from what had been a Mexican settlement, the tension between the twin towns was less pronounced. This was the situation with the two Laredos, where a former Mexican town fell on the U.S. side of the border and spun off a similar twin city on the Mexican side. Nuevo Laredo was formed in 1848 by some 500 of old Laredo's 1,173 residents. These people preferred to pull up stakes and resettle south of the river rather than become American citizens. If one can believe the story, even Laredo's population of dead folks dropped, as some residents dug up their deceased family members for reburial in Nuevo Laredo. In August 1848 the first town government was appointed and "elected." While waiting for the construction of their church, worshipers had to settle for a frame store with a leaky roof, which forced them at times to hold umbrellas during the service. However, the town rapidly began to take on a more respectable form. A military garrison was built in 1850, and in 1851 the Church of El Niño de Atocha began to take shape on the Plaza Principal.[73]

The anti-American mood of Nuevo Laredo was echoed back in old Laredo. The town leaders of Laredo in 1848 petitioned both the U.S. and Mexican governments for permission to remain in Mexico. This wish was strongly felt despite the advantages of being in the United States, including being protected from Indian raids (consolidated by the establishment of Fort McIntosh in 1849), becoming the seat of the new Webb County in January 1848, being granted greater political participation, having debt peonage abolished, and being granted a lighter tax obligation. Furthermore, although members of the tiny new Anglo merchant community won most of the posts in the first county election, the old elite Hispanic families retained their hold on most of the land and the town government. The Benavides family, headed by Bacilio Benavides, an ex-mayor of Mexican Laredo, remained especially powerful in town politics, as the first mayor, a county judge, and a state representative. Bacilio's brother, José del Refugio Benavides, and his nephew, José de los Santos Benavides, also served as mayors in the 1850s.[74]

The route to success for the new Anglo merchants lay through close cooperation with the Benavides family. Edmund J. Davis, a lawyer who moved from Florida in 1850, formed a close political alliance with the family that helped him in this decade to win the posts of alderman, customs collector, district attorney, and district judge. Hamilton Bee, from South Carolina, married the daughter of a local mayor and became a father-in-law later to a Benavides boy. Raymond Martin, who had come from southern France via New Orleans, was helped by his cooperation with the Benavides clan to develop and dominate the local sheep industry. Indeed, the few Anglos became more Hispanicized than the Hispanics became Americanized.[75]

Nuevo Laredo received its economic baptism from the Tamaulipas free trade zone. The stimulus this brought allowed the town by the end of 1859 to boast of almost a thousand residents, with an elementary school, a newly laid-out central plaza (now the Plaza Benito Juárez), and a rapidly rising church.[76]

The Towns with Missing Counterparts

In two major cases, there was no twin town to create a mood of rivalry. Yuma and San Diego saw no Mexican counterparts yet in this period. Yuma was a new American town which sprang up where no Mexican settlement had been located. San Diego was an older Hispanic town taken over by the United States.

The Case of Yuma

Town twinning came later along the younger western extension of the new international border. The absence of a properly navigable river boundary in this area, or of any river boundary after the Gadsden adjustment, together with the extreme aridity of the desert, meant that major development would have to wait for the introduction of large-scale irrigation. This left most of this part of the border for the time being without significant towns at all. The two notable exceptions were Yuma and San Diego.

Yuma, Arizona, grew up around an army post established under the command of Major Heintzelman to hold the juncture of the Gila River with the Colorado. Seeing the potential for a town to serve the soldiers, a consortium of San Francisco businessmen headed by John McLemore purchased the site and divided it into lots for sale. José Redondo, one of the leading local ranchers and farmers, moved to the new town, founded businesses, and became the mayor. He grew to be so rich that when he died in 1878, a group of townsfolk tore up his ranch in a vain search for buried stashes of money, despite the protests of the Redondo family.[77]

The usual border town denizens of this period were present in Yuma, from naked Indians bribed for their votes to (sometimes publically naked) bordello girls. One of the prostitutes just coming into town advertised her wares by taking off all her clothes while an Indian pulled her across the river on a log. Another young woman, as late as 1916, chose Main Street for her flirtatious self-exposure. The first local madam was Sarah Bourginnis, a six-foot-tall, red-headed "Sasquatch" from Tennessee who had followed Zachary Taylor's army through northern Mexico in the Mexican-American War. At the war's end, she had made her way via El Paso to Yuma, where she opened a bar and brothel. She carefully located her establishment across the Gila River in Mexico, where Major Heintzelman could not interfere with the two teenage girl "orphans she had taken in." The Gadsden Purchase placed her business on American soil, but her arrangement survived, thanks to Sarah's great popularity with the troops. She would be given a military escort, a gun salute, and burial in Fort Yuma's military cemetery at her death in 1866.[78]

The Case of San Diego

More Americans moved into San Diego in the 1850s, while still leaving its Mexican flavor intact. The bilingual residents continued to break confetti or perfume-filled *cascarones* over each other's heads, to wear *serapes* and *rebozos*, and to dance the *jota* and *jarave* while balancing water-filled glasses on their heads. Juan Bandini was elected the first county treasurer and José Antonio Estudillo the first county assessor. However, the old families lost standing due to the expense of trying to defend their land titles in court, given the carelessly written deeds and maps of the Hispanic period. Whaling, freshly legalized, brought in more Yankee businessmen. The Panama Steamship Line, specializing in the transport of gold prospectors to California, regurgitated on San Diego the lawless type which had already exerted an unsettling effect on Brownsville, Eagle Pass, and El Paso.[79] The filibusterer William Walker in the 21 January 1854 issue of the *San Diego Herald* published his plan to make Baja California and Sonora states of the United States.[80]

San Diego prospered under the new developments, growing back to 650 non-Indian inhabitants already in 1850. The more vigorous handling of the threat from wild Indians made the town all the more attractive to settlers. In 1850 it became the seat of newly created San Diego County. In the following decade, the town gained a hotel, a public school, a Masonic lodge, an Episcopal church, a new Catholic Church of the Immaculate Conception, a stagecoach line to Los Angeles, an English-language newspaper (*The San Diego Herald*), and a river dam. On the other hand, the town, isolated from the rest of the state by its mountain ranges, lost the political and economic leadership of southern California to Los Angeles.[81] Had this not occurred, San Diego might have brought a much earlier prominence to border culture. As it was, the town remained bounded by the general border provincialism and obscurity, although never as much as other border towns.

San Diego was incorporated as a U.S. town in 1849, with Joshua Bean as its first mayor. Yet it failed to produce a successful town father in this decade, as in other large border towns, due to the failure of the main candidate for this post, William Heath Davis. (The three Davises of this period in Rio Grande City, Laredo, and San Diego bore no family relationship to each other.) Davis, a ship owner who had first visited San Diego as a boy in 1831, was persuaded by U.S. border surveyor Andrew Gray that the future of San Diego lay along the bay rather than at the inland site of old San Diego. Davis accordingly rallied José Antonio Aguirre, Miguel de Pedrorena, A. B. Gray, W. C. Ferrell, and T. D. Johns to join him in buying 160 acres there and launching a new town. For a couple of years, the new site seemed to be catching on. Two hotels were built, and the *Herald* was set up as the town's newspaper. There were even hopes, stirred by the *Herald*, of making San Diego the capital of a separate state of Southern California.[82]

However, in 1851 the town was held back by the last major local Indian uprising. This revolt was led by Chief Antonio Garra, a former pupil at San Luis Rey Mission who was receiving advice from William Marshall, a sailor turned Indian. Lieutenant Patterson lured Garra into attacking his troops by disguising them as vulnerable emigrants and then slaughtered the Indians. Both Garra and Marshall were captured and executed, the former by firing squad and the latter by hanging. Adding to the disruption, a band of unruly volunteers from San Francisco, calling themselves the Hounds, tardily came to help fight the Indians and remained camped outside of town. There they caused trouble and refused to leave until the sheriff shot a leg off of one of their ringleaders and chased off the rest.[83]

With all the upset, the new town of San Diego failed to take off, and by April 1853 a general exodus back to the less propitious site of the old town had set in. The abandoned site was dubbed Davis' Folly, and in the Civil War even Davis' expensive wharf would be hacked down for firewood by the Union soldiers. A separate state of Southern California was approved by a referendum in 1859, but the legality of the move was thrown into question at a time when the pro-Southern sympathies of the area made the move look like a plot to add another pro-slave state. As a result, California remained intact, and San Diego failed to emerge as capital of a new state. Nor did a filibustering expedition into Baja California under William Walker in 1853 and 1854 succeed in adding that area to the United States and San Diego's hinterland. San Diego had awakened out of all of its big dreams into the harsh reality of stagnation.[84]

While San Diego was not paired with a twin town yet in this period, there were foreshadowings of such a development. The eventual founding of a twin town south of San Diego in 1889 was heralded by the establishment of the boundary line by the Treaty of Guadalupe Hidalgo on 2 February 1848. The Mexican government maintained that it needed a part of Alta California so that the peninsula of Baja California would not be cut off from the rest of Mexico. The U.S. negotiators accepted this reasoning. They accordingly chose a border line drawn straight from the middle of the Gila River at the spot where it joins the Colorado River to the Pacific Coast at a point one league (ca. three miles) south of the southern edge of San Diego. This decision placed the site of the future Tijuana just south of the border. While the border line had been a natural one geographically along the Rio Grande, it became (after the Gadsden Purchase) less logical to the west. South of San Diego it became unnatural, cutting into two parts the intermittent Tijuana River Valley, which had been the southernmost region of Mexican Alta California. Not only was the upper river valley, by being placed in Mexico, divorced from its mouth in the United States, but the mountain configurations which cut San Diego off from the north also cut off Tijuana from any easy outlet to the outside world except across the border to San Diego.[85]

Since the founding of Tijuana would not come until 1889, the ranching population of the area where the town would later be established was sparse in contrast to that of San Diego. The potential for friction was nonetheless present, for the main ranchers of the Tijuana area, Santiago Arguello (who became a naturalized American citizen) of the Rancho Tijuana, his sons of the Rancho Milijó and the Rancho El Rosario, and José Bandini with his ranch property, store, and restaurant, were men in the process of being displaced from their prominent position in San Diego.[86] It is true that Juan Bandini became San Diego's first justice of the peace under the American system and that his son-in-law, Abel Stearns, prospered, driving around in a carriage imported from Boston. However, many of the old landholders were brought to financial ruin by the expense of trying to prove their land titles in court. The land deeds of the pre-American period had been too vaguely defined to allow for security of title of their Hispanic owners in an age of bad faith. One deed defined one property line as running "thence northward to the point whereat a buzzard roosts upon a yucca stump."[87]

In this fashion, during the first decade of the present U.S.-Mexican border, the twin city phenomenon was born in trauma, culture shock, and occasional exultant economic development. The twin sisters, after years of slow and uneven birth, had appeared in a sudden gush of nativity from the irregular union of their two vigorous but dissimilar parent nations. Products of violence, they would long be treated with the neglect that is the frequent lot of bastard children. Yet it is also true that illegitimate progeny tend to grow up to haunt their parents, and the case of these rapidly growing twin cities would be no exception.

CHAPTER SIX

Soldiers Court the Sisters: The Civil Wars and Reconstructions

As the twin sister towns of the border grew into young maturity, rival beaux began to knock at their door. In this courtship, Matamoros and Brownsville were the belles of the ball. The thrill of the courting years can serve to patch over sibling rivalries and draw together pubescent sisters sharing dating secrets. This proved to be the case for the twin sisters of the eastern border. While the civil wars spelled loss for towns along the western end of the border, they brought great economic gain to the Lower Rio Grande border towns. Here the civil wars demonstrated that the American and Mexican towns were linked by some common interests and could benefit by working together. The mutual benefits and the crisscrossing of factional alliances between towns helped draw twin sets closer together, healing some of the divisiveness of the 1850s.

Towns that Suffered from the Civil Wars

Too remote from the core areas of both countries, the western border towns found themselves thrown more on their own resources during the disruption of the two national economies. The histories of San Diego and Rancho Tijuana offer examples of this situation.

The Case of San Diego and Rancho Tijuana

San Diego, lying as it did at the Pacific terminus of a trading route out of Dixie, was generally sympathetic with the South throughout the Civil War. However, the Yankee sea captains had played a major role in the early Anglo community, and opinion was sharply divided. Some of the local secessionists were arrested. The town's economy hurtled into a crisis in the civil wars due to the collapse of trade with both Mexico and the eastern United States and to the halting of immigration into California. Since there seemed to be no better use of the town's wharves, they were burned as winter fuel by the army in 1862.[1] Unemployment spawned cattle rustling on both sides of the border. In 1861 bandits caused the Arguello and Bandini families to flee from their ranches into San Diego. As the problem persisted, in September 1864 the Arguellos set up on their Rancho Tijuana an early fiction of a town government with a court and a police force under José María Bandini.[2]

The Case of El Paso and Paso del Norte

El Paso and Paso del Norte likewise suffered economic dislocation and population stagnation. This misfortune was partly due to El Paso's leaders backing the wrong side. The Mexican population was generally indifferent to the issues in the U.S. Civil War, but the Anglo-Americans were almost unanimous in support of the Confederacy. This was not because they were from Dixie, for most were not, nor because most owned slaves, for this was impractical in a non-plantation zone beside a national border that offered easy escape into Mexico. Their Southern sympathies were economically motivated by hopes that Jefferson Davis, the president of the Confederate States, would make good his promise to build a transcontinental railroad through El Paso. James Magoffin and Simeon Hart were especially active in rallying the town's support for Texas secession from the Union. Hart intimidated the only two men who opposed secession (two brothers from Indiana — the town surveyor Anson Mills and younger William) and was accused of bringing in hundreds of residents from Paso del Norte to further cinch the vote for leaving the Union. James Magoffin put up a Confederate flag over the town as the Union army pulled out of Fort Bliss. Anson Mills headed for Washington, D.C. to seek a commission, but his brother William stayed in the area.[3]

Lt. Col. John Baylor and a Texan force occupied Fort Bliss in July 1861 and used it as a base for an anti-Union campaign in New Mexico. Troops headed out that same month to launch the struggle for that territory. El Paso's leaders also worked to win Confederate access to Mexican mining products and a Mexican Pacific outlet for

Dixie cotton. When the U.S. consul in Paso del Norte carelessly crossed over to El Paso on business, he was held for questioning. However, the war in New Mexico went badly, and in May 1862 the Confederates retreated back to the El Paso area. By August, their situation even there seemed so exposed that the Confederate troops abandoned El Paso, returning to Central Texas. With the occupation of Fort Bliss by Union troops that same month, many town leaders made themselves scarce by either following the Confederate forces east or (like James Magoffin) transferring their residence to Paso del Norte. They were wise to do so, for other Confederate sympathizers who stayed behind were indicted for treason. Property of Confederate sympathizers was confiscated and sold at rock-bottom prices. Simeon Hart's possessions were purchased by William Mills.[4] El Paso naturally suffered from the loss of civic leaders, the confiscation of wealth, and the hostile military occupation.

The border towns were also caught up in civil war in Mexico at the same time. The traditional role of the border towns as bastions of support for the liberal cause in that country was underlined when from August 1865 to March 1866 Benito Juárez established his liberal opposition government in Paso del Norte. The presence of a friendly Union government across the Rio Grande gave an added attraction to this choice. The Union officers cooperated with the U.S. government-sanctioned sale of arms and ammunition to Juárez and included Juárez's son and his cabinet members in their social functions. Gen. James Carleton even placed Simeon Hart's abandoned Rancho El Molino at Juárez's disposal, although he found it preferable to remain on Mexican soil.[5]

Towns that Benefited from the War

The towns of the Lower Rio Grande held a primacy of importance among the border settlements in this period. Located closer to the hearts of both the United States and Mexico, these towns were stimulated rather than stunned by the effects of the civil conflicts, at least in their early stages. Local leaders cleverly reached out to turn the civil wars to their own benefit, attracting unprecedented wealth to themselves and their towns. This is not to say that the towns did not experience turmoil from factional feuding and destruction from military clashes.

Factions in the Texas Border Towns

By the end of the 1850s, border town residents had begun to choose sides between the factions that would tear at their two countries in the coming half decade of civil wars. In the towns on the American side, residents argued the polarized positions of the Democratic and Republican parties. The main Texas border town leaders were generally pro-Confederate in their leanings. This preference was no more for reasons of origin than it had been in El Paso, for similar reasons. Here, too, there were few Southerners among them, nor was it because they held slaves, as the aridity of the region and the proximity to the border as an escape hatch discouraged the holding of significant numbers of slaves. More importantly, the political affiliation of the main leaders here was determined by the opportunity to prosper from their links to the Democratic Party and the Confederacy. These factors were especially important in Brownsville, which had a predominance of Yankees, Louisiana French, and Europeans in the non-Hispanic segment of its leadership. The proximate Union blockade of Confederate ports promised to divert Southern trade through Brownsville and Matamoros. Furthermore, the Southern Democratic Party was granting government contracts to the steamship company of Stillman, Kenedy, and King, the leaders of Brownsville's pro-Confederate Red Party. Even at that, a strong Union sympathy existed, organized in the local Blue Party.[6]

In contrast to El Paso, Brownsville's Mexican-American community was not so neutral on this issue. A faction headed by the controversial Juan Cortina, from his base south of the river, expressed a vigorous opposition to Dixie and its commitment to expansion at the expense of Latin America. In March and April 1861, Cortina led his band in an anti-Confederate move briefly back across the river into Zapata County. There, at Redmond's Ranch, he clashed unsuccessfully with a force of Texas Rangers sent out against him from Laredo. While some Mexican soldiers did sign up to fight in the local Confederate forces, they mutinied in 1863, killing and wounding several Brownsvillites.[7]

In Laredo, Santos Benavides and his clan, which still dominated the town, provide an example of Mexican-Americans who took a strong pro-Confederate stand. Their main concern was to nourish the cotton trade between Dixie and Mexico via Laredo by their political allegiances. They thus maintained close support for the Texas Confederates as well as contacts with Governor Santiago Vidaurri of Nuevo León.[8]

Factions in the Mexican Border Towns

A similar political dichotomy emerged in the Mexican border towns as residents reacted pro or con to Benito Juárez's new Reforma program in 1857 to 1859. While mainstream border opinion supported Juárez, a significant opposition existed as well.[9] The French invaded Mexico in 1862, followed by Maximilian, the new foreign emperor of Mexico imported in an attempt to shore up the cause of the Centralistas against the Federalistas under Benito Juárez. As Federalistas became Juaristas and Centralistas took on the designation of Imperialistas, the border towns divided into factions supportive of one or the other. The cotton prosperity, connected as it was to the Imperialist-sponsored trade with Britain and France, encouraged an Imperialista party in all of the towns, but the underlying liberalism of *norteño* society sustained a strong Juarista opposition as well. Juárez's Laws of the Reforma, with their attack on Catholic church privileges, had brought some of the border Catholics to rally behind the Centralista cause. The economic stimulus brought by the French and British ships (coming to trade via the towns with the Confederacy) also inclined some of the local business interests to support the French-backed Centralistas. Yet, both factions took advantage of the trading boom.

In Matamoros, a group of ambitious Juaristas including Juan Cortina, Bernardo Yturria, Servando Canales, and José María Carvajal formed the Rojo or Red faction in hopes of grabbing power from the group of families which had been dominating the town government. The latter group, including members of the Longoria, Tijerina, and Cavazos families, rallied to defend their interests by forming the Centralista Crinolino Party under a yellow banner, a local variation on the usual green.[10] Confusingly, the red banner thus stood for political conservatism in Brownsville, but liberalism in Matamoros.

At the outset of the struggle, in 1861, Reynosa joined Matamoros in backing the anti-Reforma Crinolinos. When Jesús de la Serna, head of the Tamaulipas Rojos, was elected governor of Tamaulipas in that year, the Crinolino leader, Cipriano Guerrero, challenged the decision, initiating fighting between the two factions. Following Matamoros' lead, Reynosa declared for Guerrero and his Crinolinos. De la Serna thereupon sent a Rojo army to subdue these border towns. As the two armies seemed ready to fight for Reynosa on 21 October, news arrived of the imminent invasion of Mexico by the French. Called away to the struggle against the invaders and weakened by their arrival, the Rojo commander at once retreated.[11] Reynosa was thus enabled to continue under Centralista leadership.

As in Matamoros and Reynosa, Nuevo Laredo's society was polarized at first between factions. Here the red flag was waved by Juarista Chinacos in the face of green (rather than yellow) banner-bearing Imperialista Mochos. Juarista *señoritas* danced in red shoes and dangled ax-shaped pendants around their necks (for chopping down tradition), while their conservative counterparts wore green footwear and displayed the Christian cross. When the French invaded Mexico in 1862, Governor Santiago Vidaurri of Nuevo León made plans to absorb Nuevo Laredo into his state. However, the defeat of the French on "Cinco de Mayo" (5 May) of 1862 at the Battle of Puebla caused Vidaurri to back off. The Juarista liberals gained and held the upper hand, for which Benito Juárez later rewarded the town by raising it to the status of a *villa* under a mayor and town council.[12]

In towns on both sides of the river, the spiritual revival that had marked the 1850s was now undermined as the clergy allowed itself to be swept into the partisan acrimony. Both Catholic and Protestant clergy identified generally with the conservative parties in the two countries, polarizing the churches. Brownsville's pro-Confederate congregations forced such Union sympathizers as Episcopal minister Daniel Shaver and Presbyterian missionary Melinda Rankin to leave town.[13]

The First Conservative Ascendancy (1861-1863)

Difficulties were also created by the clash of hostile military forces, although the cooperation between friendly factions on both sides of the Rio Grande drew the twin towns closer together. In March 1861 the Union forces at Fort Brown were replaced by troops loyal to the Confederacy.[14] Many of the local Unionists either made their way to the Northern states or relocated to Matamoros, while some of their property was confiscated.[15] Santos Benavides of Laredo formed and took command of a company of Texas Rangers, eventually obtaining the rank of colonel. He led these Rangers in May 1861 to confront an anti-Confederate movement inspired by Juan Cortina in Carrizo Springs. On the twenty-first of that month, Benavides' Rangers pounced on Cortina's men in the process of pillaging Carrizo Springs and defeated them, killing seven and capturing eleven of the enemy.[16] In December of 1862, Benavides followed a guerrilla band under Octaviano Zapata south of the river and dealt it a knock-out blow near Camargo.[17] The Union blockade of Confederate ports rapidly materialized, in July 1861 extending to Brazos de Santiago. This move launched the great diversion of Dixie cotton exports and other trade in and out of the Confederacy via the ports of Bagdad, Matamoros, and Brownsville. The passage of these goods over the Rio Grande could not legally be prevented since that river had been declared an international waterway by the Treaty of Guadalupe Hidalgo.[18]

Confederate power on the U.S. side of the Rio Grande spilled over to cause fighting on the Mexican side as well. In the fall of 1861, fierce fighting erupted for control of Matamoros. As army clashed against army in this period, the town would complete a brick wall around its land sides by 1865, making it the only walled city on the border. Unfortunately for tourism, the wall did not survive past the early twentieth century.[19] In a struggle originating in a disputed election for governor of Tamaulipas, a conservative Crinolinos army grabbed control of Matamoros for their yellow banner on 9 September, causing the upstart Rojos leaders to flee across the river. Regrouping in Brownsville, the displaced Rojos followed José María Carvajal from 21 October to 31 December 1861 in a bid to recapture Matamoros. The fighting was fierce, with buildings going up in flame block by block as Carvajal's troops pushed their way toward the Plaza Hidalgo. However, in the end, the Rojos were repulsed north of the river. A mere three days later, an army arrived sent by Nuevo León's Governor Vidaurri, who was ambitious to extend his own sphere of influence. This force imposed a tense truce between Matamoros' two parties. The attempt was strained; Yellows and Reds refused to merge into a neutral Orange.[20]

The First Liberal Ascendancy (1863-1864)

After landing with a force of 6,000 Union soldiers at Brazos de Santiago on 2 November 1863, U.S. Maj. Gen. Nathaniel Banks occupied Brownsville four days later. The Confederate forces evacuated the town without a fight, but after having set fire to Fort Brown and to hundreds of bales of cotton. The fire spread out of control and burned part of the town as well, while citizens rushed in a panic to cross by ferry to Matamoros. The cotton trade was obliged to shift upriver, crossing mainly at Laredo. In late 1863, at a time when the Confederate command had disappeared for the time being from the rest of the Rio Grande, Colonel Benavides' Laredo alone maintained

Dixie's commerce with Mexico. When a Union force advancing from Brownsville menaced the town, Benavides got up from a sick-bed to engage it at Zacate Creek to the east. Despite difficulty in staying on his horse due to his illness, he persevered through a three-hour battle, so that the Union forces decided to withdraw that night under the cover of darkness.[21]

The Juaristas soon managed to work their way back to control of Matamoros, which was placed under the control of Gen. Manuel Ruiz. On 6 November 1863, the same day the Union army was occupying Brownsville, a force under Juan Cortina captured Matamoros in the name of the Centralistas. However, this did not represent more than a fleeting change of party control. The unpredictable and opportunistic Cortina, previously a Juarista, almost immediately reverted to his original loyalty, only to switch sides twice again.[22] When the Imperialistas seemed to be winning and Juan Cortina, at that time Tamaulipas governor and military commandant, championed their cause, Reynosa also decided to support them. Cortina made Reynosa his base of action for a time, before returning to Matamoros and a Juarista identity.[23]

The Second Conservative Ascendancy (1864–1865)

One last period of Confederate trade returned to Brownsville when in July 1864 the Union troops retreated to Brazos de Santiago.[24] Momentarily switching back to the Imperialista camp, Juan Cortina on 9 July 1864 raided upriver from Matamoros and captured Nuevo Laredo. Mayor Pioquinto Treviño was pulled from his house and required to hold a town meeting at which allegiance was sworn to Maximiliano. Before leaving Nuevo Laredo, Cortina installed a new government. The new town heads included a member of his Cortina clan, who was married to a woman of the prominent local Benavides family.[25]

Cortina soon decided to switch sides again, a move that put him in the eye of a new military storm blowing in from the Gulf. In September 1864, Imperialista troops under Gen. Tomás Mejía landed at Bagdad and prepared to attack Matamoros. To support Cortina's hold on Matamoros, on 6 September 1864, Col. H. M. Day led about 900 Union soldiers in an attack on a Confederate outpost at Palmito Ranch, halfway between Brownsville and Brazos de Santiago. The resulting First Battle of Palmito Ranch is perhaps unique in military history as being a four-way battle between four separate armies.

Cortina advanced to bombard the Confederates from across the river, only to be countered by Mejía's Imperialista troops moving west from Bagdad. Mejía then took Matamoros from a temporarily cowed Cortina. By 11 September, Rip Ford's Confederates and Mejía's Imperialistas had carried the day.[26] Matamoros was declared the capital of a new imperial territorial division.[27]

The Second Liberal Ascendancy (1865–1866)

With Juan Cortina having switched his allegiance once again to the Juaristas, in March 1865 Nuevo Laredo dared also to return to a pro-Juarista town government. Nonetheless, people feared a violent return of Cortina when his local relative was accidentally trampled by a spirited stallion. However, the man's young widow, María Benavides, traveled to San Fernando to calm Cortina, who accepted the news with equanimity.[28] The Juarista cause won a further triumph when in April 1865 a force under Gen. Miguel Negrete took control of Reynosa for the remainder of the war, using it as a base to hit at Matamoros.[29] In the next month, May 1865, another Union attempt to retake Brownsville was halted, at the Second Battle of Palmito Ranch. Only with the arrival of the news of the end of the American Civil War did Brownsville surrender to Union occupation at the end of that month.[30]

Through the rest of 1865, one Juarista attack after another beat against Mejía's Imperialista defense of Matamoros.[31] Mejía's hold on the town was also strained by a destructive six-day riot perpetrated on 5-11 January 1866 in Bagdad by black Union troops visiting from across the river.[32] Bandits played their role by harrying the trade route between Bagdad and Matamoros, while Juaristas rendered trade on to Monterrey unsafe.[33] Then in June 1866, a Juarista force under Generals Servando Canales and Mariano Escobedo attacked a great merchant convoy escorted by an 1,800-man guard while it was passing through Camargo from Matamoros to Monterrey. In the battle of Las Lomas de Santa Gertrudis outside Camargo, the guard was driven off, and 200 wagons with a rich cargo were captured.[34] In that month, Mejía surrendered Matamoros to the Juarista Generals Jose María Carvajal and Juan José de la Garza.[35]

Still Matamoros' situation remained unstable, for Juan Cortina expelled Juárez's General Tapia from the town in September 1866. A subsequent siege of Matamoros by Tapia only led to a cholera epidemic that raged through his trooops and took his life. General

Escobedo was appointed by Juárez to replace Tapia. In November, Escobedo unleashed what was to be one of the bloodiest of the many battles in Matamoros' history. The moat dug earlier around the town was a formidable barrier swept by crossfire, and getting past it proved highly costly to the attackers. However, Escobedo's men swam past their comrades' shot and drowned bodies to carry the day and occupy the town. Cortina, who had lost on the military front, succeeded for the time being in the diplomatic arena, reconciling himself with Juárez.[36]

Through all of this kaleidoscoping of occupying armies, many residents had played a shell game of shifting locations between Matamoros and Brownsville.[37] The period had been emotionally unsettling, but financially rewarding. Its effect was to tie residents of both sides closer together, wedding American to Mexican border town mercantile and political interests. The exacerbation of intertown relations in the 1850s had seemed to be establishing an irreversible mutual hostility between the twin towns. The civil wars, for all their disruption, brought the first basis for amicable relations between them as refugees from each side found succor on the other bank of the river. Future periods would witness a constant see-sawing from one mood to the other, but the poison of unmitigated enmity had been met with a timely antidote.

Economic Benefits

Property confiscations marked most of the wartime changes in town control along the Rio Grande.[38] Those who escaped the slings of outrageous fortune in one town by moving to its twin often found themselves later subjected to its arrows on that side due to the continuing shifts of party fortunes. However, such were the business opportunities that the overall financial balance rested in the black. The principal impact of the Civil War in this region was to boost prosperity and draw twin towns into closer cooperation to best benefit from it.

No towns profited more from the civil wars than Matamoros and Brownsville. For the duration of the hostilities, these two towns briefly moved ahead of Paso del Norte and El Paso as the leading border towns in size and wealth on their respective sides of the border. Matamoros' population swelled to 60,000, while its port of Bagdad attained a population of 15,000 people, with up to 300 ships loading or unloading at a time.[39] The most lasting cultural fruit of this prosperity is Matamoros' principal town theater, now called the Teatro de la Reforma.[40] Charles Stillman, Mifflin Kenedy, Richard King, Francisco Yturria and other Brownsville merchants relocated there for its greater business opportunities and protection from Unionist attack.[41] From the standpoint of the cotton trade, it hardly mattered which faction such a chameleon as Cortina claimed to join. Local business profits knew no partisan consistency.[42]

Brownsville's prosperity grew as well, as many merchants kept a subsidiary store in that town for handling the American side of their business. The town's population increased from 2,500 in 1860 to 25,000 in 1865.[43] A new ethnic element of Jewish merchants, notably from New York City, was attracted by the prosperity to settle locally. Their names included A. J. Bloomberg, G. M. Raphael, and Louis Cowen (Cohen) in Matamoros, and Solomon Ashiem in Brownsville.[44]

The other towns of the Lower Rio Grande also profited to an extent from the cotton trade. Reynosa benefited both from that commerce and from the occupation of the town by the Juaristas. When, in April 1865, Juarista general Miguel Negrete occupied Reynosa with 2,000 soldiers, he proved to be a great benefactor to that town. While he used Reynosa as a base for attacks against Imperialista general Tomás Mejía in Matamoros, Negrete in 1865 and 1866 rebuilt public buildings, opened elementary schools, and sponsored other constructive projects.[45]

Camargo and Mier in this period acted as transfer stops for European manufactures headed via Bagdad to Monterrey and for Dixie cotton from Roma moving via Bagdad to Europe. The trade, second in importance only to that of Matamoros, was significant enough to attract the stationing of a Confederate military camp at Roma.[46]

Laredo and Nuevo Laredo also enjoyed the good times that came with the cotton trade, which crossed the Rio Grande in great quantities at this point as well. The resulting prosperity allowed Laredo merchants like Raymond Martin to profit from sales of imported items to local customers. Laredo squeezed this advantage down to the last shipment to cross the border. Santos Benavides' determination allowed Laredo to continue to enjoy its trade boom down to June 1865. Only at that late date did he finally accept the inevitable and dismiss his troops.[47]

Even a set of twin towns as far upstream as Piedras Negras and

Eagle Pass, watched by a Confederate force posted in the latter town, felt the positive impact of the cotton trade. The towns were lucky in escaping action during the wars, with the exception of skirmishes against outlaws and Indians. The line between these two latter categories was blurred by white outlaws who disguised themselves as Indians to conceal their identity. Law and order was difficult to maintain due to the understaffing of the local garrison as a result of war needs elsewhere.[48]

The Postwar Adjustments

The decade following the end of the civil wars brought a return to the antebellum divisiveness between the twin towns of the border. The tensions of the 1850s reemerged as the area shrunk back from the exceptional wartime trade. Once again, the free trade zone of the Tamaulipan border placed the towns of the south side of the Rio Grande in a distinctly stronger position. Their twins on the north side were already disadvantaged by the weight of Reconstruction. Economic woes further added to the political problems. The Texas border towns faced a postwar depression, heightened by the continuation of U.S. tariffs at their high wartime rates.[49] Only San Diego escaped this pattern, lacking as yet a Mexican counterpart and benefiting from the return of immigration and trade with the ending of the American War Between the States.

Reconstruction

Under the rule of Radical Republicans, committed to harsh treatment of ex-Confederates, Brownsville lost its short-lived prominence. Radical Republicans ran the Brownsville government from 1868 to 1872, while Radical Republican Edmund J. Davis, a former resident of Brownsville, seved as governor of Texas from 1870 to 1874. German-Texans, who along with Mexican-Texans had been the strongest ethnic block opposed to the Confederacy, were notably well represented on Brownsville's town council in this period. The heated partisan sentiments boiled over in the billiards room of the Miller Hotel into a fight between Republican Sheriff Rudolph Krause and the ex-Confederate officer Rip Ford. Krause's throat and ears were none the better for the scuffle, while Ford's hand received a gunshot wound.[50]

Brownsville could not compete with Matamoros' business vigor in this period. Its population and commerce both declined.[51] Charles Stillman gave up on the area, retiring to New York City in 1866. As the steamboat business of his old partners, King and Kenedy, declined, Richard King also relocated—to his Santa Gertrudis or King Ranch far to the north.[52] Cattle rustlers including Juan Cortina and the Canales family crossing from Mexico plagued the ranches around Brownsville with massive losses of livestock.[53] The hemorrhage of livestock was so serious that a detachment of Texas Rangers was sent to patrol the area. The result was a series of violent showdowns, but no respite from the rustling.[54] The construction of a Rio Grande Railroad track from Brazos de Santiago to Brownsville in 1871 helped somewhat, but not enough to reverse the decline.[55]

Laredo also came under a Radical Republican yoke. In 1868, Texas Governor Andrew J. Hamilton appointed Samuel Jarvis from New York to be the Republican mayor of Laredo, among other appointments. Jarvis had as a youth left his well-heeled family to join a filibustering adventure in Nicaragua. After his release from prison there, he had made his way to northern Mexico as a soldier in Zachary Taylor's army. Settling in Lampazos, Coahuila, he had taken a Mexican wife and raised a family. Newly come to Laredo at the end of the Civil War, Jarvis organized the Republican Party there in defiance of the old Benavides control. Jarvis left his imprint on the town by repulsing raids from Kickapoo Indians, opening a new cemetery, and taking a cue from Charles Stillman in Brownsville (where Jarvis had briefly stayed before coming to Laredo) by naming some of the streets after members of his own family.[56]

Jarvis' leadership shattered the former monolithic control of Laredo by the Benavides family. At the beginning of Reconstruction, Santos Benavides, as a former Confederate officer, was for the time being barred from holding public office and saw his home seized, being forced to move to his Charco Largo Ranch outside of town. In 1872, a group of Mexican soldiers were arrested at that ranch for weapons smuggling. A polemical war opened up between the anti-Jarvis *Fronterizo* of Matamoros and the anti-Benavides *Nueces Valley*, with scurrilous attacks flying right and left. Laredo might have been more seriously affected by Reconstruction had it not been for close cooperation after 1870 between the new Texas Reconstruction Governor Edmund J. Davis, who had lived in that town as well for a time, and Laredo's dominant pro-Confederacy Benavides clan. Davis' close political alliance with the Benavides family survived Davis' move out

of Laredo and his Civil War service as a brigadier general in the Union Army. Even while governor, Davis returned repeatedly to Laredo, visited with the Benavideses, and represented them in court. Jarvis stepped down in the autumn of 1872, but left behind him a two-party system, with an ongoing challenge to the Benavides family.[57]

In this period, Eagle Pass was controlled by a gang of desper-adoes under John King Fisher. King Fisher had grown up in Goliad, where as a youth he had been incarcerated for a robbery attempt. After the Civil War, many families had moved from Goliad to Eagle Pass. They found their new home infested with bands of thieves of all sorts — Anglos, Mexicans, and Apaches. One of the new settlers remembered the ornery King Fisher and called him in as a cattle guard. King Fisher caused such a reign of terror that at times the county judge slept away from his home for fear of being murdered. So efficient did Fisher prove to be that the rustling problem was soon contained. By claiming the unbranded cattle among the herds he retrieved, he was able to establish his own large ranch, complete with a sign at the entrance reading "This is King Fisher's road; take the other one."[58]

In El Paso, the local pro-Confederate leaders had to fight to regain their confiscated properties after the Civil War. Joseph Magoffin received the ranch of his late father James only in 1869, while it took until 1873 for Simeon Hart to obtain his property from William Mills. Bob Dowell, who had remained on friendly terms with William Mills, was able to return to town and his property on favor-able terms. Besides, Mills had an interest in resuming the old racetrack gambling with the help of Dowell's speedy horse. In the meantime, under Texas Governors Hamilton, Throckmorton, and Pease, Wil-liam Mills headed a Radical Republican domination of the town gov-ernment through his "Customhouse Ring" (a reference to Mills' post as collector of customs from 1863 to 1869). Various ex-Union sol-diers remained in El Paso to collaborate with Mills' administration. Typical of the early Anglo settlers, they took local Mexican wives and became bilingual. Local Mexican-American leaders also became allies, and were granted lesser political offices. Mills' machine was tainted with fraud, bribery, ballot stuffing, intimidation, and vote purchasing from the largely illiterate Mexican-Americans.[59]

The election of Edmund J. Davis as Texas governor spelled the downfall of Mills as it had of Jarvis in Laredo. Even though a Radical Republican himself, Davis swung his support behind Albert Fountain, a previous follower of Mills. Fountain was able to assume control of El Paso's Republican machine, while Mills lost his post of customs collector. The shuffling of offices from Mills' supporters to backers of Fountain brought hard feelings, culminating in a shoot-out at Ben Dowell's Saloon. Two men were left dead, and Fountain was wounded. Fountain's administration was no more honest than Mills' had been. Yet Fountain held on until, amidst charges of fraud and oppression, his regime gave way to El Paso's first mayor over an incorporated city in May 1873.[60]

El Paso also suffered economic woes in the Reconstruction period. Mail and stage contacts with San Antonio were disrupted by Apache and Comanche attacks in the Pecos region. The problems reached a crescendo in 1877, when Fort Bliss was shut down. Law and order departed with the last soldier. That October, the so-called Salt War erupted when Judge Charles Howard tried to buy out the salt beds east of town and to charge a fee for removal of salt, which had hitherto been a free and common commodity. In a showdown at Solomon Schutz's store, Howard gunned down the representative of the local Mexican-Texans. Subsequently, Howard and two of his followers were taken prisoner by a mob of Mexican-Texans and shot. An unruly posse from Silver City, New Mexico, which ostensibly came to help restore order, only added to the destruction.[61]

The Continuation of the Tamaulipas Free Trade Zone

A Juarista attack on Mexico's Catholic clergy, with its conservative sympathies, constituted a counterpart to the partisan revenge occurring under Reconstruction in the Texas border towns. In Matamoros, the two priests in charge of the town church were thrown into prison. The building was placed under the control of one of Gen. José María Carvajal's officers. A test of wills followed as Father Olivier refused to hand over the keys to the church and his jailers refused to let him or his fellow priests eat or drink until he gave in. The result was that a key was handed over and the fathers were released—too soon, it turned out—for this was not the correct key, and the priests had escaped to Brownsville before the deception was realized.[62]

However, the mood of contention in the Mexican border towns fostered by the attack on the church was counteracted by the economic uplift provided by the continuing free trade zone. This arrangement allowed these towns to experience economic prosperity after the ending of the Civil War trade.[63] As a result, the Mexican border towns included in the free trade zone enjoyed populations three times the size of their Texas counterparts. This situation exasperated the Texan border leaders, who made repeated efforts to scotch the free trade zone. Brownsville's Mayor Edward Downey lobbied against the zone in Washington, D.C., in 1870. However, the victorious Juarista governments refused to comply.[64]

The free trade zone helped to ease but not to halt Matamoros' decline from its fabulous wartime boom. From a high of 60,000 in 1866, the population fell to 13,700 by 1873, but without the free trade zone it would certainly have fallen lower still.[65] Progress was still detectable in this period. In 1867 the town's first telegraph was put up — to Bagdad, four years before the telegraph came to Brownsville.[66] Juan Cortina was placed, a wolf to guard the sheep, in charge of local troops assigned to suppress banditry. Cortina continued his depredations north of the river, but did help to improve commercial safety on the Mexican bank.[67] A settlement sprang up at Santa Cruz, on the peninsula extending north of Matamoros at the site of the river crossing to Brownsville, and a mule-pulled streetcar line from the Brownsville ferry into the center of Matamoros went into operation in 1873.[68]

The *zona libre de comercio* gave a boost to the upriver towns as well. Mier was enabled to add a clock tower to its church in 1872. A girls' school was founded, and the first newspaper was published.[69] Roma across the river continued its ongoing and irrepressible contraband activity. This illegal business financed Roma's notable Euro-Spanish style buildings which the German-born architect Heinrich Portscheller designed in this period. Roma also saw the arrival of the (military) telegraph in 1876.[70]

Nuevo Laredo likewise prospered and grew at this time. A town hall was built, the Plaza Principal was improved, a public school was founded, street lights were put up, and an extensive residential zone was added.[71]

In 1869 the Federal Congress of Mexico extended the border free trade zone west through Coahuila and Chihuahua.[72] The possibilities offered by the free trade zone underlay the founding of a new Mexican town in this period — Cd. Acuña. The idea to found a town on this spot was born in 1866 in the brain of a Capitán Leal, who was looking for a spot to settle himself and his sixty soldiers now that the civil wars were at an end. Leal's request for official status for his settlement was granted in 1877. After various changes, the town received its present name in 1912 in honor of Saltillo poet Manuel Acuña, who had committed suicide in 1873 at age twenty-four. This recognition of a poet, rare enough in the annals of town history, is no surprise from a Mexican border town, where verse is cultivated and prized. Victor Hugo once suggested that Paris be renamed for him; he should have lived on the Mexican border. True to the forces governing border development, a twin town, Del Rio, appeared simultaneously in 1868 on the American side of the river.[73]

As a result of the extension of the free trade zone to its area, Paso del Norte prospered and grew to 10,000 people. El Paso's 3,700 inhabitants across the river found their main social outlet in Paso del Norte. The most notable regional leaders of the day were residents of the Mexican town. Ramón Ortiz, come from Santa Fe, New Mexico, to act as the curate of Nuestra Señora de Guadalupe, was touted as the main town host. Dr. Mariano Samaniego was a local boy trained in medicine by Louis Pasteur at the University of Paris. His brother-in-law, Ynocente Ochoa, rancher, merchant, and partner of Luis Terrazas of Cd. Chihuahua in the founding of the Banco Mineiro de Chihuahua, was the richest man in town.[74]

The Postwar Boom in San Diego

San Diego, which was not affected by Reconstruction, enjoyed a smoother development in this period. The postwar resumption of east-west trade and western immigration in the United States brought a new upswing for California.[75] The real estate promoter who virtually single-handedly plugged San Diego into these currents was Alonzo Horton. Horton had learned ingenuity and hard work when as a boy in upstate New York he had to help his blind father feed their family by making baskets. He had gone on to work in a wide variety of occupations. Falling ill of consumption when only twenty-three years of age, he had headed to the drier western clime of Green Bay, Wisconsin. In his five years there, he had jumped into his first experiment with town development by founding the town of Hortonville. He did such a solid job that the town still exists today.[76]

Caught up in the California Gold Rush fever, Horton struck his own vein of gold by opening a store to serve the other gold rushers. He experienced a major setback when he was attacked and robbed of all his wealth by a mob of Panamanians while he was crossing the Isthmus on a trip home. Bad luck may have caused Horton many problems, but he always bounced back thanks to his ingenuity and Puritan-based hard work. He fetched a bride from Wisconsin and built up a new business, selling furniture and househould goods in San Francisco.[77]

Horton's involvement with San Diego began when he attended a lecture depicting the great potential of the site, with its excellent harbor, its healthful climate, and natural beauty. Without having made a personal evaluation, Horton broke through the shocked protests of his wife and impetuously sold all of the stock of his San Francisco store within three days. When in early 1867 Horton first set eyes on the town on which he had blindly staked everything, he felt reassured over his decision. It certainly seemed the best spot for his health. His lifelong tubercular hacking permanently disappeared before two weeks were out, and he would grow downright robust on the dry San Diegan air.[78]

Before investing his money, Horton staked out the townsite and concluded that it needed to be moved down to the edge of the bay, a spot then occupied only by Santiago Arguello. After handing ten dollars to the county clerk to persuade him to place lands along the bay for sale at an auction, Horton laid the groundwork for making a successful bid. While not a church-going Christian, he made social contact with the local priest, attracting his attention by placing five dollars in silver in the collection plate. In exchange, the priest proved helpful in rallying the men Horton wanted to act as his trustees.[79]

At the auction, Horton found no serious rivals for the property, and was amazed that it was valued at only seven to ten cents an acre. He had started the auction with a bid of one hundred dollars for a tract of two hundred acres, or a rate of fifty cents an acre, a bid met with guffaws from the spectators. Horton's high esteem for the land raised his taking price for the whole purchase to twenty-seven cents an acre, a rate still considered a bargain by Horton, though foolhardy to the local residents. One cynic remarked, "That land has lain there for a million years and nobody has built a city on it yet." Horton had a retort ready: "Yes, and it would lay there a million years longer without any city being built on it if it depended on you to build it."[80]

Horton's dream was helped by the timely Gold Rush that hit his incipient settlement in the third year of its building, at the very start of 1870. For five years, prospectors engaged in a feverish competition for stakes in the mountains some sixty miles south of the border. Gems discovered in 1872 on the American side of the border added to the boom. Mail service was introduced to connect the rest of California to the mining developments. Horton, in a trip to San Francisco, stirred competition between steamer lines, thereby reducing the cost of transport to his town. He also convinced Western Union to bring telegraph contact to San Diego in 1870 by personally paying one-quarter of the needed subscriptions to interest the company, in return for half the telegraph earnings for the first three years. Diversification of the local ranching and whaling economy was also helped by a major development of bee farming, which made San Diego the world's largest producer of honey by 1880. Under this impact, the present city of San Diego rapidly took shape on the location of its present downtown section. Horton even painted free the two sides of all unpainted houses facing the bay, to give a more pleasing impression for potential settlers.[81]

Horton logically concentrated first on building a new wharf. A well providing potable water was dug. A fire department, a gas works, and a chamber of commerce were formed. The future Balboa Park land was set aside for that purpose. Buildings proliferated, including by 1871 a courthouse, the Horton House Hotel, the Bank of San Diego, a public school house, a private secular school, and an Episcopal school. By 1883, a public library, a telephone company, a YMCA, and an opera house had been added. The ethnic complexion of the new town shifted as the remaining Indians were removed in 1876 to a nearby Indian reservation and non-Catholic English-speakers poured into town. A Jewish synagogue was founded, as well as a Unitarian Society center, and Episcopal, Presbyterian, Baptist, and Methodist churches — the last named on land donated by Alonzo Horton. The destruction of the bay by the San Diego River was halted by the diversion of that waterway into False Bay in 1877. The new town was served by two newspapers, *The San Diego Union* and *The San Diego Weekly Bulletin*. When fire gutted much of the old town in 1872, the will to rebuild it faltered. Just as the town took root, Horton was hit by a legal suit challenging his right to the land as having been won illegally. It was too late; San Diego was another Hortonville in fact, though not in name.[82]

The civil wars thus acted as an object lesson in the mutual interests that could be shared by towns on both sides of the border in an atmosphere of cooperation. It was a lesson poorly absorbed, but salubrious nonetheless. The civil wars also taught the importance of the border during periods in which Mexican-American relations assumed special significance. The decade following the civil wars saw a return to the previous divisive rivalry between most sets of twin border towns. The additional quarreling between postbellum factions within the towns further heightened the ill will. Being caught up in international politics was proving to be a risky business for the line of twin sisters.

CHAPTER SEVEN

The First Job:
The Gilded Age

The Gilded Age represented a major turning point in border town history. Mexican President Lerdo de Tejada had blocked plans to build a railroad connection between the United States and Mexico, warning that grave problems would arise if the two countries were linked by a common transportation network. "Let there be a desert between strength and weakness," he said. He was right in foreseeing the coming problems. He was wrong in feeling that the solution was to resist the forces of change. *"Camerón que se duerme, se lo lleva la corriente"* ("The sleeping shrimp is carried along by the current").

Opposition leader Porfirio Díaz championed the forces which were eager to make this transportation link. Yet he did so without adequate preparations for the resulting problems of rapid population growth. As a result, the border towns have been hurtled ever since down a path of overpopulation, underemployment, and increasingly complex problems in American-Mexican relations. Various attempted remedies have been tried; none have yet solved the ills. There is still hope today that the next experiment will offer the solution.

Porfirio Díaz's Revolt (1871-1876)

When General Díaz launched his movement to grab control of the government, important elements in the Mexican and American border towns rallied behind him. American backers were especially interested in Díaz's promise to encourage American investment in Mexico. When Díaz announced his Plan of la Noria on 8 November 1871, it was met with enthusiasm by elements in towns all the way from Nuevo Laredo to Matamoros. Brownsville merchants provided arms and supplies. Brownsville's Francisco Yturria was one of those who befriended Díaz. Yturria later benefited from the good relations by winning permission to build a telephone line from the Yturria Building in Matamoros to the Yturria Bank in Brownsville. The information gleaned by listening to the conversations being relayed yielded inside information which Yturria used to business advantage. John King Fisher of Eagle Pass also became such a good friend that Díaz gave him a handsome pistol and provided him with a bodyguard to escort him to his social functions. It took five years for Díaz's plans to meet with success, years in which support for him in the border towns continued to grow. Porfirista sentiment was running so high by 1875 that the town government of Nuevo Laredo imposed a curfew of 11:00 P.M., with only the *serenos*, who called the hour and weather, permitted to be on the streets for the rest of the night.[1]

Díaz accordingly in December 1875 moved his center of operations for a time to Brownsville. Mayor Manuel González of Matamoros (a later president of Mexico), Gen. Lauro Villar, Juan Cortina's half-brother Sabas Cortina, and William Neale's grandson William A. Neale were among those who rallied around his cause. Neale even set up a fake cannon made of stovepipe and old cart wheels, with pumpkin cannon balls, pointing in derision at the real cannons of the Matamoros garrison across the river. Díaz's Matamoros supporters would be rewarded with high posts in Díaz's government.[2] In 1881, Díaz would personally come to Matamoros in a gesture of appreciation.[3]

Action picked up when, on 2 March 1876, a force of Porfiristas took Reynosa by surprise.[4] The uprising spread next to Nuevo Laredo. During the night of 13 March 1876, Porfiristas and Lerdistas clashed in the main plaza in a donnybrook which left many dead and injured. When morning came, Díaz's followers held the site. This success emboldened Díaz himself to cross the Rio Grande in April and to organize a force at the Rancho de Palo Blanco outside Matamoros.[5] He and his general, Manuel González, then led 500 men in an attack on Gen. Jesús Toledo's troops holding Matamoros. Toledo's own soldiers were unenthusiastic for the government cause. Hearing them sarcastically singing the lines "*Voy a partir a lejanos regiones, de donde nunca jamás volveré*" ("I'm leaving for distant regions from which I'll never more return"), Toledo got the drift of their message and deserted for the "distant region" of Monterrey. Matamoros fell, an eager apple, into Díaz's outstretched hands.[6] However, Díaz's forces suffered a defeat outside of Monterrey, after which Matamoros was occupied in a surprise move by a government force under Gen. Mariano Escobedo. Díaz consequently transferred his base of operations to his native Oaxaca.[7] That proved to be a wise move, for by December 1876 Díaz had taken control of the national government.[8]

Porfirio Díaz's Impact on the Border

Díaz's policies propelled border town development in a major new direction. The Porfiriato did away with the old Mexican border free trade zone, which had benefited the Mexican towns but at the cost of placing local Mexicans and Americans at cross purposes. In its place, the new government brought an even greater economic stimulus by patronizing the building of railroad links, which now for a second time drew twin city sets closer together in their interests.

At first, Díaz felt obliged to hold and even extend the free trade zone, to thank the border towns which had played such a leading role in bringing him to power. Thus, by 1885, Díaz had extended free trade along the entire border.[9] However, the industrialists of interior Mexico complained that the zone allowed foreign goods to compete unfairly with Mexican manufactures. Furthermore, Porfirio Díaz's links to the United States and his encouragement of U.S. investment in Mexico opened Díaz to U.S. pressure to end the border free trade zone. As American border merchants continued to complain, in 1878 Mexico was informed of a joint resolution in the U.S. Senate and House of Representatives to again call for the abolition of the zone. In 1884 the protest was repeated, and in 1889 the national platform of the Democratic Party called for the zone's abolition. That same year, the chambers of commerce in El Paso, Eagle Pass, Laredo, and Brownsville linked up to lobby the Texas state government for help in bringing an end to the zone.[10]

As a result, the free trade zone was dismantled bit by bit. The first step was taken when, in 1891, all goods manufactured in the free trade zone and sent into interior Mexico were subjected to ninety percent of the normal duties. As the United States, with its cheaper and better goods, was uninterested in their products, this left the Mexican border manufacturers with only the feeble local market. In contrast, the Federal District and Monterrey benefited from American investment bringing increased industrialization in this period. Monterrey emerged as an important industrial center, and other northern cities were helped by advances in small industry, commerce, and mining. In 1905 the free trade zone itself was abolished, to allow Mexican-made products an advantage in the border markets. The change greatly increased the cost of living in the Mexican border towns. The fall in world prices for silver, Mexico's currency base, further aggravated the rise in living costs. Many residents responded by moving across the border.[11]

Linking Up of the U.S. and Mexican Railroad Systems

In 1881 the Southern Pacific Railroad reached El Paso, and the two Laredos were joined to both the U.S. and Mexican rail networks. The next year, the Santa Fe Railroad linked San Diego to Arizona and points farther east, while Nogales was joined to the U.S. rail system. In 1888 the Mexican national railroad also reached Nogales. The railroad was completed to Brownsville only in 1904 and to Reynosa and Matamoros only in 1905.[12] Business increased as the trains shipped out cargo. The middle border towns shipped out large amounts of mining products, while the eastern and western ends of the border saw the introduction of irrigation and large-scale farming. The American towns took the initiative in launching farms. An urgent need for quantities of farm workers was met by workers from the Mexican side of the border.

The interdependence of the twin cities was thus everywhere reinforced. The resulting build-up of population added significant new towns to the family of twin sister cities and gave a major growth impetus to those already in existence. The rush to obtain farm work on the north side of the border initially depopulated some of the towns on the Mexican side, but the depopulation soon turned into a problem of overpopulation. Far more workers than could be absorbed migrated to the Mexican border towns from interior Mexico and then found themselves barred from entering the United States.[13] The end result for the border towns was an infusion of energy so tremendous that everything that went before seems like a prologue. The border towns not only mushroomed in activity and population, but also proliferated in number, completing the full string of twin towns as we have known them since. Yet lack of planned preparation for the massive immigration that was set loose into these towns launched a problem with runaway poverty which has yet to be resolved.

The border towns blossomed one after another as the magic wand of the railroads touched them. These towns will be considered in the chronological order of the arrival of their rail links.

The Boost to El Paso

The coming of the railroad transformed the two towns of the Pass first. District Judge James Hague, owner of El Paso's first piano, led the push to bring trains to that town. Hague donated a large urban strip of land for use by the railroads, spurring a race between competing railroad companies for the privilege of arriving first. The Southern Pacific completed a track from Los Angeles in May 1881. In the next two years, the Texas Pacific from Fort Worth and the Atchison, Topeka, and Santa Fe from Santa Fe added rail ties to the east and north. Paso del Norte, renamed Cd. Juárez in 1888, received its rail link south to Mexico City in 1884.[14]

The railroad allowed El Paso to become the most important smelting center of the U.S. Southwest. The first local smelter was built in 1885, using the products of the mines of Chihuahua, Texas, New Mexico, and Arizona.[15] The Guggenheims' American Smelting and Refining Company was especially prominent. El Paso's agriculture did not respond strongly to the presence of the railroad in this period because the area's shortage of water made large-scale irrigation unfeasible.[16]

The town converted from a sleepy outpost of 800 residents into a city of 39,279 in 1910.[17] A Chinatown with its typical Chinese restaurants and laundries (a hallmark of many western border towns in this generation) was formed by ex-railroad workers. Streets were paved, electric lights were introduced, a water system was installed, a fire department was formed, and a telephone service begun. Streetcars (mule-drawn to 1902 and electric thereafter) crisscrossed the town, connecting El Paso with Cd. Juárez by a bridge across the river. The downtown section emerged with a post office, a First National Bank, theaters, and the largest hotel in Texas, the Grand Central. Country clubs also appeared. In the first decade of the twentieth century, before it was decided that rest is more vital than climate in recovering from pulmonary tuberculosis, El Paso won a reputation as a health center, with various sanitoriums. The first public school for Anglos was established in 1883, for blacks in 1885, and for Hispanics in 1887. The first high school was constructed in 1902.[18]

El Paso's early reputation as a border Babylon had long attracted a worldly element of Anglo settler, and only in the 1880s were the first town churches built. The Catholic (St. Mary's), Episcopalian, Presbyterian, Methodist, and Baptist churches all appeared, followed in 1899 by a synagogue (Temple Mount Sinai) for El Paso's German Jewish community.[19]

The foundation for El Paso's cultural establishments was laid down. The Myar Opera House was built and the El Paso Symphony Orchestra was founded in 1893, a public library was established in 1895, and a chamber of commerce was created in 1899. El Paso's concern with architecture began to emerge at the start of the twentieth century. The main influence here was Henry Trost, an architect of the Louis Sullivan and Frank Lloyd Wright schools. Trost combined these Chicago schools' ideas with Spanish mission style and New Mexican pueblo style to produce a new type of U.S. Southwest architecture. Imitations spread along the border west to San Diego and east to Weslaco, Texas, with its 1928 city hall, library, and museum.[20]

Anglo business leaders now more than ever monopolized the running of the town, especially after El Paso in 1884 became the new county seat in place of Hispanic Ysleta. Anglo-Americans, pouring in with the railroad boom, briefly formed a majority in El Paso, although the Anglos once again lost this position by 1900 due to massive immigration from Mexico. Taking menial jobs for the most part, the Mexican newcomers concentrated in two slum communities — Chihuahuita near the international bridge and La Mesa, on a plateau north of the downtown section. The old integration between Anglos and Hispanics gave way when in the 1880s separate schools were built for Anglos and Mexican-Americans (as well as for blacks).[21]

Cd. Juárez did not initially share the advantages from the railroad enjoyed by El Paso, since the hub of the railroad lines was located in the northern twin town. In order not to lose its traditional superiority over booming El Paso, Cd. Juárez asked the Mexican government to be included in Tamaulipas' free trade zone. The request was granted. The brief period from 1885 to 1891 in which the free trade zone was stretched to Juárez brought the town's biggest growth to that time. By 1887, factories had arisen, notably those bottling wine and brandy, and grand department stores had been built. In addition, three new town newspapers appeared.

Cd. Juárez took on the earlier cosmopolitan flavor of Matamoros and Brownsville as Anglo-Americans, Englishmen, Frenchmen, Germans, and Spaniards were drawn in by the business opportunities. However, with the slow demise of the free trade zone beginning in 1891, many of these businessmen, along with their employees, shifted their base of operation to El Paso. A shortage of water, due to rising use of the Rio Grande in Colorado and New Mexico, caused a sharp cutback in agricultural production at the same time. As a result, Cd. Juárez's population fell from 29,000 in 1890 to 8,780 in 1900.[22]

The Boost to Laredo and Nuevo Laredo

Laredo had long protested having to take second place to Matamoros and Brownsville. Finally, it got its chance to surge forward by getting a head start on the new rail linkage being made from the major Texas cities through Monterrey to Mexico City. In 1881, two railroads reached Laredo. The first was Uriah Lott's line from Corpus Christi; the second was Jay Gould's line from San Antonio. By mid-1882, the Mexican National Railroad line between Nuevo Laredo and Monterrey was almost complete. A low-water railroad bridge carried the first passenger train, with Gen. William Sherman aboard, from one town to the other on 8 March 1882. The first vehicle bridge followed in 1889. In 1910 a proper high railroad bridge would be put in place over the Rio Grande. The two Laredos were quite right to greet the coming of the railroads with a huge fiesta lasting from Christmas Eve of 1881 through the following New Year's Day. Great amounts of freight with the accompanying jobs were diverted from the Brownsville route to Laredo.[23]

Laredo experienced a major transformation under the impress of the railroad. Rail transport gave a major push to wool and coal exports north. Refugio Benavides, of the dominant old ranching clan, joined forces with Charles Callaghan to launch the mining of surface deposits of coal north of town. The Benavides family, Callaghan, and Raymond Martin (a Frenchman married into the local García family) dominated the sheep ranching between them. Laredo's population grew, and its first bank, a larger city hall, a city market, six public schools, two private schools, an opera house, Methodist, Baptist, Presbyterian, and Episcopal churches, and numerous saloons, gambling places, dance halls, and houses of prostitution appeared. Population in Nuevo Laredo also began a rapid growth, and a new *mercado* arose in 1881.[24]

The Boost to San Diego and Tijuana

San Diego was the next border town to receive a major impetus toward faster growth with the arrival of the railroad. The Santa Fe Railroad began service to the city in 1882. Farms proliferated with the incentive for agricultural expansion that the railroad brought. In 1888 the completion of a new dam on the Sweetwater River brought both electricity and irrigation to the region. The San Diego Irrigation Company was accordingly founded to bring water to the city and surrounding farms.[25]

In the resulting prosperity, new residential communities sprang up: La Jolla, Pacific Beach, Coronado, Escondido, La Mesa, and Ocean Beach. San Diego's sewage system, mule-pulled streetcar, and high school were launched. New denominations appeared with the founding of the Congregational and Christian churches in 1886 and of the Lutherans and Seventh Day Adventists in 1888. San Diego now assumed a position as a cultural leader among the border towns. A literary magazine, *The Golden Era*, went into publication in 1887, the same year in which the Louis Opera House opened. The Fisher Opera House followed in 1892. In 1889 the Torrey Pine Forest Preserve, containing rare species of trees, was set aside by the town council.[26]

The intellectual emergence joined with other factors to give San Diego a reputation for radical eccentricity and extremism. California attracted large numbers of people looking for adventure and a better life into a relatively rootless society. John Steinbeck in his short story "The Red Pony" addressed the frustration of Californians who found themselves halted by the Pacific Ocean at the end of the frontier. Such frustrated pioneer energies may have found partial outlet in exploring the frontiers of thought.

Free-thinkers and political radicals became part of the local scene. In 1893, Katherine Tingley's Center for the Universal Brotherhood and Theosophical Society, gathering Gnostic-influenced Rosicrucians of the Swedenborg and Blakian variety, opened its doors on Point Loma. Five years later, the same woman founded the School for the Revival of the Lost Mysteries of Antiquity. In keeping with this local penchant for the unusual, in December 1915 the town council would hire a rainmaker named Paul Hatfield. If his hocus-pocus was able to bring enough rain to fill the reservoir, which had been drastically lowered by drought, Hatfield was to receive $10,000. The results were more than the town could handle. It rained so much that already the next month the San Diego River was smashing through dams and spilling its waters over the area, killing people and causing over $3 million of damage. The flabbergasted town councilors refused to pay Hatfield, accusing him of willfully exceeding orders. A Pied Piper whose revenge had already been wrought in his initial work, Hatfield moved on to other successful contracts, including a stint in Central America.[27]

San Diego suffered a local recession in the 1890s. A panic hit the national bank, two hotels burned in suspected insurance scam arson, and Alonzo Horton lost most of his fortune. However, the town's economy bounced back in the first decade of the twentieth century. The turning point came in 1905, when the U.S. government opened San Diego's port to competing mercantile shipping lines, ending the previous monopoly of the Pacific Mail Steamship Company. The port boomed, and it did so all the more with the opening of the Panama Canal in 1907. It also helped that in 1890 tourmaline and in 1903 topaz were discovered near town. The mining of these gems provided San Diego with another major industry. From a population of 17,700 residents in 1900, San Diego jumped to 39,578 people in 1910.[28]

The burst of growth in San Diego, stirred by the coming of the railroad, spilled across the border to stimulate the founding of Tijuana on 11 June 1889. There are various theories regarding the name of Tijuana, which was taken from the Arguellos' ranch on the site. One claims that a *Tía Juana* (Aunt Jean) once lived on this ranch, giving it her name. Other explanations have it that Tijuana is a corruption of an old Indian word or that the ranch was named for the preexisting Rancho de San Andrés de Tiguana close to Loreto, Baja California. A customhouse had stood on the site since 1874, and a tiny settlement with a grade school had sprung up around it.[29]

It was the Arguello family which gave the push for founding a real town, carved out of their own ranchland. They accordingly laid out a rectangular street plan around the typical central plaza and began selling lots. The new town was officially accepted by the Mexican government on 11 July 1889. It grew slowly at first, due to San Diego's recession in the 1890s, and entered the twentieth century with still only 242 inhabitants. However, the recovery of San Diego at the start of the century gave a source of tourist dollars for Tijuana, which thus oriented itself to entertaining Californians from the very first of its existence. In 1903 gas street lighting was installed, along with the construction of a bullring by L. Loperena and a greyhound racetrack by John Russell. By 1910, Tijuana's population had tripled in one decade to 733 people.[30]

The Boost to Eagle Pass and Piedras Negras

Eagle Pass and Piedras Negras also made progress in this period thanks to the coming of the Southern Pacific Railroad in 1882 and the Mexican National Railroad from Mexico City in 1892. The railroad at once gave a boost to local cattle ranching, which was aided also by the introduction of barbed wire in 1883. Rail transport also stimulated the development of coal mining. In the 1880s, F. H. Hartz started the mining outside Eagle Pass, transporting the coal to San Antonio. In the 1890s, Louis Dolch came to dominate the industry from his mining settlement at Dolchburg outside of Eagle Pass. At the end of the century, the Southern Pacific Railroad leased the mines from Dolch. As the trains allowed Eagle Pass to form a solid economic base, the Maverick Hotel was built in 1880, St. Joseph's Academy for girls and the Simpson Bank in 1883, and a Victorian Neo-Gothic courthouse in 1885. Piedras Negras was helped by the brief extension of the Mexican border free trade zone to Coahuila in 1888. For two years, business thrived and public buildings were erected. However, the dismantling of the free trade arrangements brought a decline in population again, from a height of 15,000 down to 10,000 by 1906.[31]

King Fisher's "protective" gang by this time had been removed from Piedras Negras, after the Texas government had sent some Texas Rangers commanded by Captain McNelly to arrest him in 1876. King Fisher surrendered without a fight, and emerged from the consequent court trials a changed man. Moving with his wife and daughter to Uvalde, he became an active churchgoer. He was shot to death by gunslinger Ben Thompson when he made a futile attempt to reestablish peace in San Antonio's Vaudeville Theater.[32]

The residents might have been too precipitous in dismissing King Fisher, for the rapid expansion of the north bank cattle industry attracted a bevy of rustlers based across the river in Mexico. American troops were at times brought into action to chase the bandits. The situation was complicated by the fact that Indians were involved in the conflict on both sides of the fighting. Kickapoo Indians, Algonkians who in the mid-nineteenth century had moved from the Great Lakes to Kansas and Oklahoma, had fled on farther south to escape being herded onto a reservation. They had taken refuge in Coahuila and been granted land there by the Mexican government. Their hatred of the Americans for stealing their homeland gave an added incentive for their rustling of cattle from the ranches around Eagle Pass. To chase them down, the U.S. Army employed black Seminole Indian scouts. These half-breeds were a mixture of Seminoles with escaped black slaves who in the antebellum period had made it to Florida. Sent from Florida to an Oklahoma reservation in the late 1840s and early 1850s, many of these Indians, too, had escaped to settle in Coahuila. They, like the Kickapoos, had come to combine Spanish speech with Indian dress (including an occasional buffalo horn headdress). It was perhaps the fact that they had picked up Southern Baptist worship that made them less anti-American. Instead of raiding the north shore, they signed up as scouts with the American forces, earning a reputation for dependability and bravery.[33]

The U.S. Army's employment of the black Seminoles was viewed with suspicion in Mexico, and in April 1877 two of these scouts were accused of treason and imprisoned in Piedras Negras. Lt. Col. William Shafter led three U.S. cavalry and two infantry companies in a raid from across the river in an attempt to rescue them. He seized the town jail, only to find that the two Seminoles had already been transferred to Saltillo. However, one escaped and the other was later released. Angered by Shafter's occupation of Piedras Negras, the Mexican government stationed Gen. Gerónimo Treviño in Piedras Negras with the command to prevent further such incursions. However, in a meeting in Piedras Negras between Treviño and his American counterpart Gen. E. O. C. Ord in June 1877, a private agreement was made. The U.S. cavalry could continue to pursue *bandidos* south of the river as far as 150 miles into Mexico, provided that there were no Mexican troops in the area and Treviño was given advanced notice. Eventually, the Kickapoos were allowed to hold dual U.S. and Mexican citizenship and to travel back and forth between the two countries.[34]

The discovery of oil and gas fields in Texas accelerated a general shift away from coal as a fuel. The need for local coal especially fell off when in 1902 the Southern Pacific Railroad converted most of their locomotives from coal to oil-burners. Louis Dolch was unsuccessful in finding other good customers for the coal, but he compensated for this loss by turning to irrigated farming. In 1904 he began to grow onions and figs on 400 acres of land he cleared and irrigated. His success caused other farmers to imitate him. By 1909, eight irrigated farms were thriving in the region.[35]

The Boost to Yuma and Los Algodones

Although Yuma lost its army post of Fort Yuma in the 1880s, this blow was more than compensated by the coming of the railroad. In 1883 the Atchison, Topeka, and Santa Fe Railroad connected to Yuma. The sight of the trains brought in crowds of gaping naked Indian men. The residents of Yuma were used to the sight, but it unnerved passengers staring from the train windows, so that all pantless Indians were officially barred from entering the train station.

The trains had a rich cargo of mining products to pick up at Yuma, from recent strikes of silver, gold, and lead. The location of a state prison in Yuma from 1875 gave an additional boost to the town's financial health. With the construction of Laguna and Imperial dams, rapid growth set in, and Yuma's population increased from 2,500 in 1900 to close to 5,000 in 1914.[36] Yuma's growth as a railroad stop encouraged the Mexican side of the border to sprout a town as well, at a spot cater-cornered downriver from Yuma. In 1887, Los Algodones was founded as a cotton-growing region using water from the Colorado River for irrigation.[37]

The railroads eventually gave rise to large-scale irrigated farms. The potential was slow to be realized because of lack of funds for irrigation dams until the 1902 National Reclamation Act gave federal assistance for this effort.

The Boost to the Two Nogaleses

The two Nogaleses sprang up from scratch in response to the arrival of the rail link and to the last brief phase of the Mexican border free trade zone. The site was a natural one for a railroad stop, being located at a natural north-south pass through the high desert region called the Pimería Alta for its native Pima Indians. These Pimas had long lived in river valley farming villages, surrounded by the more primitive hunting-and-gathering Pápago Indians. The Jesuit missionary Francisco Eusebio Kino had begun the Christianization of these Indians in 1678. With the secularization of the local Jesuit mission upon the expulsion of the Jesuits in 1767, the Elías family had emerged as the principal landholders. When the Treaty of Guadalupe Hidalgo left part of the Nogales Ranch in the United States, the Elías family had lost the part of its ranch north of the new border, despite a legal battle to retain it. It was nonetheless the Elías family's Rancho de Los Nogales (Walnut Ranch) which gave the name to the two new twin towns.[38]

When it became clear that a railroad was being built to the spot, Nogales, Arizona, was hurriedly founded in 1880, complete with an anticipatory customhouse. The founding of Nogales, Sonora, followed in 1884. The Santa Fe Railroad arrived in the region that same year, to pick up local mining products, most especially copper from the mines at Cananea. Local ranch products also found a new outlet.[39] In 1888 the Mexican National Railroad formed a connection with the Mexican interior as well.[40]

The Arizona town enjoyed a faster takeoff than its Sonoran counterpart. From having had only one frame and one adobe house plus a dozen tents in 1882, Nogales, Arizona, three years later boasted a school, a church, and a few businesses. Nogales, Sonora, received a telegraph link to the rest of Mexico in 1887, and two years later had become Sonora's second most important town for imports and exports after Guaymas. The short period in which the border free trade zone was extended to this area gave an early boost to Nogales, Sonora. Mexicans from farther south regularly traveled to Nogales to shop while the arrangement lasted, bringing additional income for development. Thanks to this business and to a tendency of the local ranchers to establish town houses there, by 1891 it had grown to 2,500 inhabitants. Its first primary public school was built at the start of the new century.[41]

As in some of the other border towns by this period, the ethnic flavor was cosmopolitan. In Nogales, Sonora, Anglos and Frenchmen were much in evidence as merchants, while most of the small shops in and outside the *mercado* were owned by Chinese brought in with the railroad construction. Already in their first decade of existence, the two Nogaleses were given an object lesson in the difficulties of inter-municipal cooperation along a touchy border. In March 1887 the mistress of Mexican Col. Francisco Arvizu, who was stationed at Nogales, Sonora, left him and took refuge in Nogales, Arizona. The colonel sent a Señor Rincón to convince her to return, but she asked U.S. law officers to escort Rincón back across the border. As Rincón was being brought to the Mexican guard station, confusion arose. Objections by the Mexican patrol to the rough handling of Rincón led to a shootout in which a Mexican guard was killed. Tension rose, and a detachment of U.S. cavalry was rushed to police the Arizona community until the situation calmed down. Tempers might have flared up more violently had not the two towns been so tightly interlaced by social, family, and business ties.[42]

The black market commerce typical between twin towns was all the more difficult to control here due to the fact that some of the buildings of Nogales, Arizona, were snuggled right against the border line. International Street, between the two towns, lay entirely on Mexican soil. Advantage was taken of this proximity most notably by John Brickwood, who had made his way from Illinois and married a local Mexican woman. Brickwood built a one-story frame saloon and gambling house in 1884, complete with a painting of a winking woman over the bar. Since one wall was smack along the border line, this allowed sales to be made on his porch of tobacco free of American taxes and of liquor free of Mexican taxes. Only in 1897 was the problem alleviated when all buildings in Nogales, Arizona, were required to be removed to a distance of sixty feet from the border.[43] A fence was placed along the dividing line, crossed by a land bridge built in the early twentieth century.[44]

In 1899, with the coming of the Ferrocarril de Nacozari, Agua Prieta, Sonora, appeared at the Guadalupe Pass over the Sierra Madre Occidental as a transit town for picking up mining products. Its twin town of Douglas, Arizona, was launched in 1900, with an emphasis on copper smelting. Naco, Sonora, and Naco, Arizona, to the west of Douglas and Agua Prieta, followed in 1901 as another, smaller border gateway. Named for the barrel cactus fruit, the two Nacos served the surrounding copper mines.[45]

The Boost to Calexico and Mexicali

In 1901 the Southern Pacific Railroad stimulated the founding of another brand new set of border towns, Calexico and Mexicali. In May of that year, the California Development Company, a subsidiary of E. H. Harriman's Southern Pacific Railroad, opened the Imperial Canal. This canal brought water into the Imperial Valley from the Colorado River via the Mexicali Valley in Baja California. Only in 1936 would the construction of Boulder Dam allow a water-distribution canal entirely on American soil to supply water to the region.[46] Irrigation allowed the formation of rich farms on both sides of the border, attracting large numbers of farm workers.[47] In 1904 the first train arrived in Mexicali. Two years later, a railroad line was commenced from Mexicali through Los Algodones to Yuma.[48]

The two new twin cities of Calexico, California, and Mexicali, Baja California del Norte, emerged out of an area recently inhabited by the Cochimies Indians. Like the native Indians along most of the border line, these folk were simple hunters and gatherers whose males went nude, and who had no more permanent shelter than covered saplings bent together. Mexicali was developed by Guillermo Andrade, a banker from Hermosillo, Sonora. In 1874 Andrade set up the Compañía Mexicana, Industrial y Colonizadora de Terrenos del Río Colorado. Andrade was backed by wealthy and archconservative Gen. Harrison Gray Otis and his son-law, Harry Chandler (co-owner of the *Los Angeles Times*). These two Los Angeles moguls operated through their Colorado River Land Company. Winning a large grant in the region from Díaz's government on the pretext of planning to settle Cucupás Indians on it, Andrade used the money to lay out farms instead.[49]

In 1904 Andrade sold all his rights in the area to Otis and Chandler. Since the Mexicali Valley farmland was now entirely owned by Otis and Chandler through their Colorado River Land Company, using two Tijuana residents as legal fronts, the new inhabitants settled only in Mexicali itself, making that the sole town in the Mexicali Valley. The resulting giant *latifundia* was devoted to raising cotton, becoming the largest cotton farm in the world. Flooding was a worry for the residents in the early years until the building of Boulder/Hoover Dam in 1931-1935 brought better control.[50]

Chinese workers smuggled in from California provided the mass of the farm workers here. Mexicali itself was majority Chinese, an outpost of distant Peking set down amongst the taco eaters and tequila drinkers. Even Japanese and East Indians were more numerous than native Mexicans. There was concern that such a non-Mexican English and Chinese-speaking population might nourish Harry Chandler's purported hopes of turning Baja California into a new state of the United States. Arizona Senator Henry Ashurst five times tried to push Congress to acquire a port on the Gulf of California. In 1915 the U.S. government filed a charge against Chandler for violating the neutrality laws.[51]

The Boost to Brownsville

"A cada santo se le llega su día" ("Every saint has his day"), but for some it arrives later than others. The railroad came quite late in the Porfiriato to Brownsville and Matamoros, and they suffered from the delay. Through the last two decades of the nineteenth century, their economies were hard hit by a loss of trade to the two Laredos. Local business leaders on both sides of the river frantically threw up one scheme after another to link their towns with the national railroad systems of the United States and Mexico. In 1882, 1884, 1888, and 1892 plans were made, only to fall through in turn. Potential investors outside the area simply found the Laredo route too satisfactory to bother with Brownsville.[52] Economic stagnation and lack of change resulted. The establishment of the first public school building in 1889 was one of the few signs of improvement in this period, and only one-fourth of the town's school-age children attended at that.[53]

The tearing down of most of the walls that had come to circle Matamoros' land side provided a poignant symbol for this period's dismantling of previous gains. Business languished as Matamoros became a ghost of its former self, with whole blocks of buildings standing empty.[54] In 1882 Tamaulipas state government offices transferred to Cd. Victoria. Bad hurricanes in 1880 and 1889 played their part in bringing the demise of Puerto Bagdad.[55] In 1891 an anti-Díaz revolt on the south bank of a group of Matamorenses and Brownsville Mexican-Americans led by Catarino Garza, a resident of both towns, only brought more loss.[56] Garza's expedition was organized on the north bank and then crossed the Rio Grande close to Mier. Rallying local followers, Garza pushed downriver, only to be defeated and forced to recross the river.[57] A lonely exception in Matamoros' stagnation was its ongoing commitment to education, culminating in the founding of a Tamaulipas state teacher's college in the town in 1898.[58]

Brownsville was tied into the American railway network on 7 June 1904 with the arrival of the first train from San Antonio and Corpus Christi.[59] The tracks were built by the St. Louis, Brownsville, and Mexico Railroad, which was later absorbed into the Missouri Pacific.[60] On 5 May of the next year, the connection was completed on from Matamoros to Monterrey.[61] A railroad and passenger bridge between Brownsville and Matamoros was erected in 1910.[62] A proposal to lay down a direct line from Matamoros through Cd. Victoria to San Luis Potosí was abandoned as too costly.[63]

The start of large-scale farming on the north bank of the Rio Grande accompanied the arrival of the railroads and their transportation of the farm products to northern markets. Land speculators from the northern Midwest (at first former soldiers from Fort Brown and railroad magnates, and then land development companies) bought the land cheap, cleared the brush and irrigated the fields, and then resold the land to Anglo-American farmers from the same region. The new owners then turned to using Mexican workers from south of the river.[64] These workers came in large numbers. Henceforth more Mexicans entered Texas each year than had come during all the period under the Viceroyalty of Nueva España.[65] One major new crop was citrus fruit. In 1904 an ex-Texas Ranger by the name of H. G. Stillwell launched the first commercial orange and grapefruit orchards outside of Brownsville.[66] Experiments with growing cotton on irrigated farms were launched. Farm towns sprang up at regular points along the railroad route between Brownsville and Mission.[67]

Brownsville woke up again. The telephone arrived in that same year of 1904, along with a bottling works, a steam laundry, and the founding of the Cameron County Medical Society.[68] An electric power and light plant, a sewerage plant, and a waterworks were built in 1908.[69] The Brownsville Business Men's Club for urban improvement was formed in 1909, the same year that the new high school began its football competitions.[70] In 1910 the Brownsville Country Club was born. Brownsville in 1912 would add an electric streetcar line plus a telephone system, and in 1913 its first sidewalks.[71] From 6,305 residents in 1900, Brownsville's population rose in 1910 to 10,511.[72] Matamoros showed new energy in this period as well. A bullring was opened in 1905,[73] and in 1907 telephone service was initiated.[74]

The restored prosperity on the north bank led to a new problem as the population in Matamoros built up faster than employment could be provided. The unemployment encouraged another outburst of cattle rustling based on the south bank and aimed against the north bank ranches. Texas Rangers like the aggressive A. Y. Baker were called in to fight such outlaws as Jacinto Treviño.[75] In trying to contain the *bandidos*, the Texas Rangers entered into their most desperate and hence most violent period, leaving a legacy of hatred of the "Rinches" among the local Mexicans and Mexican-Americans.[76]

The Boost to McAllen

On 20 August 1904, with the tracks having being laid west of the new town of Pharr, Capt. John McAllen and his son James moved to start their own town on the route ahead. McAllen was a Scot who had started his life in the Rio Grande Valley as a clerk in his compatriot John Young's store in Hidalgo/Edinburg. After Young's death, he had married the widow Salomé Ballí, which brought him into control of 80,000 acres of ranch land. McAllen and his son now organized the McAllen Townsite Company and built a depot at a spot he hoped would sprout an important new town. This site, now called West McAllen, lost out, however, to a location two miles east, where the present city of McAllen was born.[77]

McAllen proper, at first called East McAllen, was launched by Briggs and Swift of Louisiana. They gained the advantage by paying for their own railroad depot, hurrying into irrigated farming, and effectively promoting their town.[78] McAllen benefited from lying roughly at the nexus of various farm towns surrounding it in all directions. Hidalgo (the old Edinburg) lay to the south. Pharr and San Juan, founded in 1906, were located to the east, the latter on John Closner's San Juan Plantation. Edinburg, founded in 1908 and at first named Chapin until in 1911 it was given the county seat and the name of old Edinburg, lay to the north. Mission, named for an Oblate mission on the site, was founded to the west in 1908.[79]

Wisconsin-born Sheriff John Closner was one of the leading developers of irrigation in this region of Hidalgo County, with his Rio Grande Valley Reservoir and Irrigation Company, formed in 1908. Lloyd Bentsen was also a notable developer of this area. Cotton, oranges, and grapefruit received the main emphasis. Under this impetus, McAllen rapidly took shape as a new town. John Closner's Hidalgo Telephone Company provided it with telephone service from the outset. In 1909 the main town newspaper, *The McAllen Monitor*, was founded.[80] The initial impact of McAllen's railroad on the twin town of Reynosa was negative. At first, so many south-bank residents rushed to receive the higher farm wages across the river that by 1909 Reynosa was temporarily turned into something close to a ghost town.[81]

Tecate, California, likewise received its initial impetus from the railroad. John Spreckels, a California sugar magnate, spurred the town's founding in 1907 by bringing the San Diego-Arizona Railroad through the region.[82] Its twin town of Tecate, Baja California, was launched in 1918. By 1990, Tecate, Baja California, had grown into a clean, quiet town of 52,000.[83]

Relative Decline of Small Towns

The towns lying off the main railroad crossings fell into relative obscurity, even where side lines brought them a limited growth. Ojinaga's trade was lost to the new railroad route from Cd. Chihuahua via El Paso to San Antonio. The Kansas City, Mexico, and Orient Railroad through Ojinaga to Chihuahua would be completed only in 1930, and the bridge over the Rio Grande linking Ojinaga to Presidio only in 1950. By this time, it was too late to regain control of the trade. In 1990, Ojinaga still had only 24,000 residents.[84] Cd. Acuña also finally linked up to the railroad system in the 1930s, but was too far off the main route to benefit greatly.[85]

Even in the surge of Porfirian development, some of the more out-of-the-way towns remained mired in the old mood of hostility between the twin towns. This was the case for Rio Grande City and Camargo, where a low point in their innertown relations was reached in the summer of 1877. Two Mexican *bandidos* attacked the Rio Grande City jail to release fellow gang members, leaving the jailer shot, his wife slashed, and another man wounded. Despite calls for extradition, only one of the culprits was ever handed over.[86] Seven years later, bad feelings boiled over between Mier and Roma. In 1884 a quarrel between the towns over possession of a tiny island in the Rio Grande led to an unsuccessful assault on Mier by thirty Americans.[87] The same mood of rivalry prevailed between Ojinaga, Chihuahua, and Presidio, Texas. In an argument over the kidnapping of an American, U.S. forces from Presidio bombarded Ojinaga in December 1876. The American managed to cross to Presidio two days later.[88]

Tensions between Residents and Black Troops

One perplexing development of the first decade of the twentieth century was the repeated explosion of tension between residents of the American border towns and black troops assigned to local forts. Since this phenomenon occurred at various points along the border as early as the Civil War period, reaching its apogee in the early twentieth century, there is a suggestion of some general problem prevailing along the border. Black troops may have been stationed there on the misassumption that racial difficulties could be avoided given the relatively good racial relations between Anglos and Mexicans. As early as the Civil War, however, the stationing of blacks by the Union army had proven explosive in Brownsville and Bagdad. In 1875, Gen. Edward Ord transferred black soldiers from the Rio Grande Valley to the high plains, replacing them with white soldiers, because, he said, "when the colored troops went out, the Mexicans avoided them and, in some instances, attacked them." While he alluded three times to the poor relations between blacks and Mexicans, he hazarded no explanation of their cause.[89] One author suggests that the strain resulted in part from the behavior of the black soldiers as uneducated ex-slaves recently liberated from bondage and boiling over with righteous indignation due to years of mistreatment.[90] Incidents were not restricted to the border towns, erupting in 1917 in Houston, as well as elsewhere.[91]

The mood in El Paso grew tense when, in 1899, a company of black infantrymen was posted to Fort Bliss. Despite the presence of a small black community in El Paso, which had its own school dating from 1883, along with a black Baptist and a black Methodist church, complaints proliferated. There were more than the usual percentage of arrests for the drunken and disorderly conduct often associated with a military base, and insults were showered on the black soldiers in the streets.[92]

The Anglo and Mexican communities in this period were establishing a *modus vivendi*. The health of the new twin towns depended on striking a good tone of cordiality between the two ethnic groups in the face of the legitimate resentments of Mexicans over the loss of their national territory and the superciliousness of some of the Anglos over their successful grab of the region. Such a mood of goodwill was, bit by bit and in the face of repeated major setbacks, being achieved. The strain of this effort may have made it difficult to accommodate the raw sensitivities of the badly buffeted blacks as well. To the black soldiers themselves, who must initially have looked forward to being assigned to a region noted for its relative interracial harmony, this must have seemed one disappointment too many to bear. It would have been only human had the black troopers responded to the scowls with defiant comportment of their own. A flow of blood resulted in two tragic cases.

The first explosion came on 13 August 1906 in the notorious Brownsville Raid. As midnight approached, up to 200 shots were fired into homes and businesses by a group of men rushing along streets next to Fort Brown. One man was killed and another wounded; the fatalities could have been higher. While the identity of the attackers was never definitely established, the black troops were blamed and given dishonorable discharges, changed sixty-seven years later to honorable discharges. The circumstances are still confused. A black, Pvt. James Newton, had been pistol-whipped for jostling a white woman in passing on the street. Later, the same Private Newton was kicked by Texas Ranger A. Y. Baker for arguing loudly against the cost of the ferry to Matamoros. Another black private was shoved into the water in the same incident. The claim that still another black soldier had thrown a white woman to the ground had caused the troops to be confined to the fort in the evening by an 8:00 P.M. curfew, two nights before the "shoot-em-up."[93] Wherever the guilt lay, it is clear that the setting for an explosion of ethnic resentment existed.

In 1916 a fracas occurred in Del Rio when white prostitutes refused black patronage.[94] Another incident followed in Nogales two years later. At 2:00 in the morning of 27 August 1918, an exchange of fire between border guards occurred. When a Mexican tried to rush across the border, refusing to stop on command, a U.S. border guard fired past him. Seeing this, a guard on the Mexican side shot and killed his American counterpart. To quell the general exchange of fire that ensued, black American troops stationed at Nogales, Arizona's Fort Huachuca pushed their way into the Mexican town. Soon the black troops were running out of control, shooting at women and blocking aid to the wounded. Before they were convinced to pull back north of the border after a full day of fighting, thirteen people had been killed and fifteen wounded.[95] A local *corrido* or ballad was written about the incident, including the following lines:

> *Una caballería de negros*
> *Que venía entrando voraz*
> *Ahí quedaron tirados*
> *El resto corrió pá tras.*
>
> *Hirieron a dos mujeres*
> *Las balas americanas*
> *Y dijeron "No hay cuidado"*
> *"Somos puras mexicanas."*
>
> *El que muere por su patria*
> *Muere con todo honor*
> *Al sepulcro lo acompaña*
> *El pabellón tricolor.*[96]

That is, in rough translation:

> A force of blacks coming on horseback
> who crossed the border eagerly
> found themselves either pushed back
> or pinned down firing desperately.
>
> The bullets from American guns
> injured two out of our women,
> who said, "Never mind our wounds,
> we're red-blooded Mexicans."
>
> Whoever dies for his homeland
> will lie with honor in his grave.
> To the tomb will go with him
> The three-colored flag of the brave.

The black explosions remind us that while the Porfiriato brought new population growth and increased wealth, it did not bring economic or social justice. The twin sisters were reaching maturity with many of their juvenile problems dangerously unresolved.

Border Cities Politics and Government during the Porfiriato

Political conditions in the border towns during the Porfiriato and the corresponding Gilded Age in the United States were similar to those found throughout the two nations and not unlike those of their cross-border counterparts. The phenomenon of the urban boss was widespread in the United States and provided quasi-authoritarian local government based on the votes of immigrants. The authoritarian *caciques* who had controlled local governments in Mexico were gradually replaced as Porfirio Díaz implemented his *pan o palo* policy of eliminating independent power centers.

Politics in the American Border Towns

Gilded Age urban bosses in the United States gained power by creating a skillfully organized operation for winning elections and controlling local governments. The political "machine," as such an operation is known, provided basic services or favors to individuals as well as disparate groups or interests. The votes obtained from Mexicans and Mexican-Americans as a result of services provided for them or their employers enabled borderland bosses to hold power.

"Lacking any tradition of participation in electoral politics, [Mexican-Americans] did not view themselves as independent voters or as an aggrieved interest group with the potential power to organize and force their demands on public officials."[97]

Manipulation of the ethnic Mexican vote became an enduring characteristic of American border towns. Often this procedure involved support from Anglo leaders by means of public jobs and patronage for Mexican-American politicos or *jefes* who could organize and deliver Mexican votes. During the Gilded Age, Mexican-Americans were enticed to an evening *pachanga* from which they could depart in the morning only after being marched to the polls. Frequently, Mexicans were imported from across the border and paid to vote illegally.[98]

Undoubtedly, the most powerful of the borderland bosses was James B. Wells, Jr., of Brownsville, who became known as the political boss of South Texas and whose influence reached all the way to Washington, D.C. Wells began his rise to power through association with an earlier political leader, Stephen Powers. Although increasingly powerful in Cameron County politics, Powers was not able to consolidate control prior to his death in 1882. During his last years, however, he was in a position to groom a successor. Impressed by Wells' performance in a land suit, Powers invited the young lawyer to form a partnership in 1878. Wells married into Powers' family and soon joined the inner circle of the Blue Club, the dominant local political party affiliated with the Democrats. Under Wells, the Blue Club became the vehicle for gaining public office for his allies, who usually followed Wells' orders.[99]

Jim Wells maintained the support of area ranchers and Brownsville merchants by using his influence to promote favorable state legislation and railroad development, to hold down property taxes, and to secure deployment of Texas Rangers and army troops to keep order along the border. The third component of Wells' constituency, and ultimately the source of his power through their votes, was the population majority of lower-class Mexican Americans. Wells relied on his merchant and rancher allies to turn out the vote of those dependent on them, but he also established a personal relationship with those potential voters. Under attack at the end of his career for his manipulation of Mexican-American votes, Wells defended his relationship:

So far as I being a boss, if I exercise any influence among those people because in the 41 years I have lived among them I have tried to so conduct myself as to show them that I was their friend and they could trust me, I take no advantage of them or their ignorance. I buried many a one of them with my money and married many a one of them. It wasn't two or three days before the election, but through the years around, and they have always been true to me.[100]

Jim Wells obviously engaged in the same kind of paternalistic activity that characterized the operations of big-city machines by providing his own informal welfare system. Wells used the power of the ballot to benefit himself and his allies financially and to enable him to wield state and even national influence.

The first decade of the twentieth century saw both the peak of Jim Wells' power and influence and the beginning of his downfall. By 1900, Wells had created a system of allied local bosses throughout South Texas and was serving as chairman of the state Democratic committee. Jim Wells' counterpart in the "upper valley" was Sheriff John Closner. Wells played a crucial role in Closner's rise to power in Hidalgo County when he supported Closner's election as sheriff in 1890 in order to end the feuding among Democratic leaders. Wells and Closner remained allies, but Wells was clearly the senior partner. Closner was a tough law-and-order man, and not averse to violence; he sought to please his constituents with an attempt to eradicate cattle rustling. Closner's primary interest, however, was economic development. He installed the first modern irrigation system in the region, promoted railroad construction, and engaged in land speculation.[101]

One of Sheriff Closner's land development schemes played a major role in the establishment of what would become the primary American border town in that area. As the railroad moved west through Hidalgo County, Capt. John McAllen, a major landowner, organized a townsite carrying his name. When McAllen's company failed to develop the site promptly, a rival townsite was established under the leadership of Closner. The completion of an irrigation canal to the new townsite assured the triumph of Closner's East McAllen, which attained a population of 1,000 by 1911. McAllen was incorporated in that same year, and Frank G. Crow was unanimously elected mayor.[102]

Another of Sheriff Closner's land development schemes initially met with little success, resulting in political manipulation. Closner entered into partnership with County Judge D. B. Chapin to develop a townsite six miles north of McAllen. When the project failed to prosper, Closner and Chapin came up with a scheme to move the county seat from the border town of Hidalgo to their vacant townsite, named Chapin. Opponents of the plan surfaced and local newspapers asserted that "excitement is at fever heat. Some of the more nervous ones fearing trouble requested the governor to send rangers."[103] Closner and Chapin obtained a favorable vote from county citizens on 10 October 1908 and the following day transported the county records to the new location.[104] A falling out between Closner and Chapin, together with aspersions concerning Chapin's character and a murder charge, led to a decision in 1911 to change the name of the new county seat to Edinburg.[105]

In contrast to the new frontier developments in government and politics in Hidalgo County, Laredo had already a century of governmental and political experience. The dominant figure in Laredo politics in the late nineteenth century was Raymond Martin, a French immigrant and merchant who had become the wealthiest man in Webb County by 1860. Martin invested in sheep-raising and is believed to have amassed over 90,000 head by the early 1880s.[106]

Competition for political leadership of the growing town heated up. Raymond Martin, becoming fluent in Spanish and marrying into the García family, had recently built a coalition in 1875 to challenge the old Benavides ranching family and their Democratic Party. Competition between their rival ferry services added a business dimension to the political struggle.[107] Martin's faction had succeeded in grabbing control of the town offices starting in 1876. Martin's brothers-in-law Rosendo and Julián García had served as mayor for the next three years.[108] The new money in town gave Santos Benavides a chance to try to grab back power. Allying with Daniel Milmo of the new Milmo National Bank in September 1884, Santos and his son Juan Benavides started the Reform Club. James Penn supported the effort with his *Laredo Times*, attacking Martin as "Old Barnacle," leeching off the town government. A Penn poem announced:

> Soon will be known the people's choice,
> against the Barnacles they shout;
> and all Laredo will rejoice
> to turn the Mugwumps out.

The Reform Club adopted a *guarache* (sandal) as its symbol, in token of the lower class supposedly suppressed and exploited by Martin. Martin's faction by an extension of the same symbolism was labeled the *Botas* (boots). The fact that both groups were a mixture of rich and poor, as of Hispanic and Anglo, did not deter the use of such emotional symbolism.[109] Yet these tactics, coupled with parades and free-beer rallies, failed to restore Benavides' faction to office in the elections of 1884 or 1886. After the loss in the second election, Botas rubbed in the Guarache failure by announcing a plan to bury a sandal with funeral rites in token of the demise of the defeated party. As the Botas marched to the mock funeral, a group of angry Guaraches manning a cannon blocked their way in the Saint Augustine Plaza. The result was a shootout in which up to 250 men took part, leaving sixty people killed and many more wounded. Federal troops, the state militia, and the Texas Rangers were all sent in to restore order.[110] The Guaraches, with the exception of a brief period in 1895 to 1900, never did enjoy much success. By 1910, the Botas-based Independent Club had beaten out all serious opposition. The town government remained firmly under the Old Barnacle's *botas*.[111]

Although the Botas retained political control of Laredo after the elections of the mid-1880s, politics remained tense and confrontational. As an expedient in their efforts to challenge the long-dominant Democrats, Laredo Republicans founded the Independent Club in 1894. In 1897 Louis J. Christen, who had begun his career as a Guarache, was elected mayor on the Independent Club ticket. A smallpox epidemic in 1899 resulted in violence and the election of Democrat A. E. Vidaurri as mayor in the biggest political upset in Laredo history. Independent Club power returned, however, with the election of Amador Sanchez, who held the office of mayor until 1910.[112]

Democrat Bota control of Webb County government remained relatively undisturbed despite the turmoil in the city. José María Rodríguez, a native of San Antonio, married into the influential Benavides family and held the post of county judge for thirty-five years beginning in 1878. Similarly, Antonio M. Bruni, an Italian immigrant who became a merchant and livestock raiser, held office as Webb County treasurer for thirty-five years beginning in 1896. A Democrat, Bruni became head of the Independent Club as Republican influence declined.[113]

El Paso was incorporated as a city at the beginning of this era, in 1873; voters chose Ben Dowell as their first mayor. In 1876 land

developer Joseph Magoffin was elected county judge and four Mexican-Americans were elected to the county commission. The tran-
quility of the El Paso area was shattered by the outbreak of a bloody
civil disorder known as the Salt War in 1877. A shifting contingent
of primarily Anglo entrepreneurs attempted to assert a claim to the
lands near El Paso which had traditionally provided salt for local
inhabitants. A falling out among the salt "ring" politicos led to
shootings and conflict between Anglos and Mexican-Americans.[114]

El Paso's growth accelerated rapidly with the arrival of the railroad in 1881. The new administration of Mayor Joseph Magoffin
(former county judge) made substantial progress in providing civic
services. The growth of El Paso provided sufficient population to
warrant an attempt to relocate the county seat from Ysleta to El
Paso. Fraudulent votes in the ensuing election brought victory for
El Paso, and with it an end to Mexican-American political power.
The Anglo business and professional establishment in El Paso had
taken control.[115]

During the 1880s a Democratic "boss" emerged in the person
of Charles R. Morehead, who reluctantly agreed to run for mayor in
1889. For once the Republicans were able to mount a formidable
challenge and their candidate, Adolf Krakauer, won an election filled
with mudslinging and vote fraud. It was discovered, however, that
Krakauer had not taken out his final citizenship papers, and another
Democrat, Richard Caples, was chosen in the special election that
followed. The defeat of the Republicans marked the beginning of an
extended period of domination by a political machine known as the
Ring.[116]

As El Paso changed from an individualistic, wide-open frontier
town to a family-oriented, respectable western community, demands
for reform and the elimination of the vices of saloon, dance hall, and
gambling casino steadily increased. Democratic Ring nominee C. R.
Morehead defeated a reform ticket in 1903, but the losers organized
the Citizens' Reform League to keep the pressure on the city authorities. In 1904 Mayor Morehead gave in and ordered the closing of
the saloons, dance halls, and brothels. The gamblers and girls
promptly moved to Ciudad Juárez. Real reform government would
come later.[117]

The El Paso experience of transferring the seat of government
was repeated in San Diego during the frontier years of the Gilded
Age. Only four years after the founding of "modern" San Diego by

Alonzo Horton in 1867, the board of supervisors loaded the governmental records into wagons and moved them from Old Town to the new San Diego. The following year a new city charter went into effect and the newly completed courthouse became the county seat. In 1889 another new city charter provided for the election of a mayor, the first being Douglas Gunn.[118]

Clearly, the single most important influence on the San Diego of that era was John D. Spreckels, who "discovered" the city during a summer cruise on his yacht in 1887. With the enthusiastic support of the city fathers, the wealthy Spreckels poured money into a great variety of development projects. Economic power soon translated into political power. The dominant California Republican Party exerted its influence in San Diego through Spreckels and his local political "boss," Charles S. Hardy. Already the debate over the direction of development was beginning to take shape: railroads and smokestacks versus beautification, climate, and tourism. Although John D. was nicknamed "Smokestack" Spreckels because of his industrial enterprises, he also owned the famous Hotel del Coronado and insisted that the city council include a landscape architect.[119]

Politics in the Mexican Border Towns

When Porfirio Díaz succeeded in taking power in Mexico in 1876, he depended for support on the political *caciques* who controlled states, districts, towns or military and police units through a system of personal loyalty or economic dependence. Díaz sought to preserve his position, however, by consolidating power at the national level. He rewarded loyalty and severely punished opponents who refused his largess; even presumably loyal public officials, especially military officers, were frequently transferred to keep personal loyalties from developing. Local officials continued to be elected in the towns and cities, but the real power was in the hands of district officials known as *jefes políticos*, of whom there were 300 throughout the nation.[120]

Utilized extensively by Porfirio Díaz, the *jefes políticos* operated with considerable autonomy and were responsible only to the president of the Republic. They exercised virtually complete control over the districts under their jurisdiction. Consequently, local government operated during the Porfiriato with whatever degree of authority was permitted by the *jefe político*. The local governmental entity was the *municipio*, which consisted of a city or town of some consequence and the surrounding villages and rural area. (The American county is a roughly comparable entity.) The government of a *municipio* consisted of a council of six elected *regidores*, who usually selected the mayor from among themselves. Since each *regidor* was responsible for a particular area of local administration, the local system was similar to the commission system in the United States.[121]

The Rio Grande Valley provided a classic example of the elimination of a potential power rival to the dictator. Juan N. Cortina, scourge of Brownsville and Valley ranchers, general, governor, and mayor of Matamoros in 1874 and 1875, had been jailed in Mexico City for cattle rustling. When he heard that Díaz had captured Matamoros, Cortina escaped, declared for Díaz, and returned to Matamoros. A political rival attempted to eliminate Cortina, but Díaz found it expedient to hold his fractious supporter under house arrest in Mexico City for the rest of his life.[122]

The *paz porfiriana* settled in on the political scene in Matamoros. The long-time system of electing multiple mayors came to an end in 1873, but elections still occurred annually. Several men held the office more than once, and Rafael Solis served ten years as mayor. Despite the support provided by Matamorenses for his revolution, Díaz did little to reward the city. Economic devolution led to political decline as Tamaulipas state offices were transferred to Ciudad Victoria.[123]

Like Matamoros, Reynosa provided support for the Díaz revolution from the start, when Díaz passed through the town with his forces. The inauguration of a new municipal government building in 1899 seemed to set the stage for a livelier political scene in Reynosa during the last decade of the Porfiriato as competitive political clubs, the Círculo Rojo and the Círculo Verde (also known as the Club Político Union), appeared. They would play an active role on the local political scene for the next two decades.[124]

The Porfiriato was inaugurated in violence and bloodshed in Nuevo Laredo, as local forces supporting Díaz fought against Lerdista troops in the public plaza. The first few years of local government under the new regime were marked by chaos and corruption as members of the city council engaged in intrigue and sued each other. The most bizarre developments occurred beginning in 1883, when the mayor was accused of serious crimes and was forced to step down. His replacement, Pablo Quintana, promptly organized a gang which derailed and robbed the train from Monterrey of 8,000 pesos' worth of silver bars. Quintana and his gang were captured, but amazingly

Quintana was selected to serve in 1884 as mayor, a position he was unable to fill due to his incarceration. The town councilors were no better; some of these also were brought to trial for various crimes. The town treasury was plundered until it amounted to only fifty-seven pesos to pay thousands of pesos of debts. One local joke told about an American who came to city hall asking for "El Señor Quiroga." Misunderstanding him to be asking for *"el señor que roba"* (the man who robs), the official replied, *"Aquí todos roban"* ("Here everybody steals").[125]

Reform was brought to Nuevo Laredo's town government only in 1885, when Santiago Belden was elected mayor. The vigor he showed alternately as mayor and as head of public works is memorable even a century later. First, as a *sine qua non*, he put the town's finances back in order. Not waiting for full solvency to jump into town improvements, he borrowed money. When asked how he could build a water plant with no funds, he referred to how Moses had drawn water from a dry rock with his staff and said he would repeat the miracle by use of IOUs to the Banco de Monterrey. The improvements he brought to the town between 1885 and 1892 included its first telephone service, an electric streetcar line, electric street lighting, a fire department, a drinking water system, street paving, a rural school, and the Casino de Nuevo Laredo. As the town blossomed, a large theater hall was built and weekly band concerts in the Plaza Juárez commenced. When Belden died, symbolically on Mexico's main national holiday of 16 September 1892, there was a massive turnout for his funeral, with three days of official mourning throughout Tamaulipas. A statue of Belden was erected on the Plaza Juárez. After the death of Belden the Díaz dictatorship, through the state government, imposed its choices for local authorities, choosing prominent and competent men to continue Belden's progressive works.[126]

On the western end of the border, what had been a Baja California pueblo made up of a handful of *ranchos* began to emerge as an authentic border town around the turn of the century. The official founding of Tijuana occurred on 11 July 1889, when judicial authorities authorized an urban development plan. A Mexican customs port had been established at Tijuana in 1874 to collect tariffs on goods headed to Ensenada, but the proximate cause of the 1889 development was a brief Gold Rush in Baja California. The *jefe político* of the northern district of Baja California, Luis E. Torres, approved the political establishment of Tijuana as a "municipal section." Population in 1900 amounted to only 242.[127]

Much of the growth of Tijuana during this epoch was a reflection of development in San Diego. In 1900, Tijuana became the first subprefecture of the *municipio* of the northern district of Baja California. The local government provided public lighting, using oil lamps, in 1903. The opening of the port of San Diego to all commerce in 1905 resulted in the installation of tourist attractions including a greyhound track and a bullring.[128]

The transformation of the border towns under Porfirio Díaz's pro-American policy had thus been dramatic. Many sleepy little communities had become vibrant cities overnight. However, these benefits had come without planning for the attendant ills. When vastly more workers than could be accommodated surged from interior Mexico to the border, growing numbers of them found themselves trapped in Mexican border towns which had no means of employing them. Slum housing, with its accompanying disease and illiteracy, proliferated. A new situation of explosive desperation grew up along the sensitive border, where it could not be ignored forever with impunity. In 1907 Díaz's government addressed the problem by arranging for 200 unemployed men in Cd. Juárez to receive low-paying jobs with the Chihuahua railroads. The compensation was so low, however, that the offer was ignored. Next, the government advertised in interior Mexico that employment was unavailable in either Cd. Juárez or El Paso. This measure, too, had no effect.[129] Yet the dangerous situation that existed demanded remedies. The subsequent history of the border towns is largely the story of the various efforts employed — so far ineffectively — for trying to resolve the dilemma.

By the end of the nineteenth century, Mexico and the United States had thus agreed to end their common-law family feud, though no formal union was as yet proclaimed. Their new relationship promised an improved status for their neglected offspring, the twin border towns. These communities began to benefit from the rapprochement of their parent nations, but only partially. So long as no legal agreement was sealed, they would be as children under a shadow.

CHAPTER EIGHT

Fire in the Family Store:
The Mexican Revolution

The impact of the Porfiriato on the twin sister towns of the border can hardly be underestimated. From struggling apprentices, they had emerged as blossoming young businesswomen. Yet the first promise of a rapid entry into economic maturity was thwarted in most of the towns by the political unrest of the subsequent Mexican Revolution. For a decade, business development was stymied for those of the sister towns which were most directly caught in the crossfire. The international significance of these cities was again underlined as the First World War in Europe affected relations between the United States and Mexico. As previously, local interests in these towns conspired to manipulate outside forces to their own ends. However, in contrast to the civil wars of the 1860s, this time the two sides of the border shared less of the wartime prosperity and more of the wartime misery.

The border towns played a significant part in the Mexican Revolution, again demonstrating their traditional role as a leading liberal influence within Mexico. The supply to the rebels of weapons and provisions through the border towns and the use of these towns as a refuge for insurrectionaries were fundamental to keeping the revolutionary fires stoked. The Mexican border towns provided the Revolution with some of its leaders, and it was in their area that the Revolution was launched and many of the crucial battles fought. The American border towns sheltered new conspiracies and, when the problems created spilled over the border, helped to incur American intervention through their protests.

The Period of Fighting Concentration along the Western Border

The first stages of the Mexican Revolution, consisting of the revolts against Porfirio Díaz and Francisco Madero, inspired greater action along the western end of the border. The more theoretical nature of the earlier period appealed to the intellectual and experimental bent of the California coast, lying as it did farther from the control of central government. The latter part of the Revolution, involving the revolts versus Huerta and Carranza with their intensified power struggle, brought more fighting to the eastern end of the border. As the struggle for control of Mexico City escalated, possession of Matamoros, strategic and closer to the capital than other border towns, became more critical. The growing participation of the United States also highlighted Matamoros' key location between the two nations.

Cd. Juárez and El Paso remained politically involved throughout the decade, from the meeting between U.S. President William Howard Taft and Porfirio Díaz in 1909 to Pancho Villa's unsuccessful move to grab Cd. Juárez in 1919. The two towns' control of the rail nexus and their possession of the largest border population of that time guaranteed that they would remain in the thick of the agitation.

The Revolt against Díaz (1910-1911)

At the end of the first decade of the twentieth century, border towns participated in Francisco Madero's movement to vote Porfirio Díaz out of office and sponsor a real electoral choice. Liberal Mexican border elements had grown frustrated by Díaz's one-sided control of the government and his lack of reform. American border business interests were upset that Díaz had recently ended his long-time favor of American investments, in reaction against increasingly heavy-handed American political interventions in Meso-America. In 1908 Nuevo Laredo formed a local branch of the Anti-reelectionist Party.[1] A pro-Madero faction also formed in Reynosa.[2] On 26 June 1908 Benjamín Canales gave his life for this movement in an abortive resort to arms in Cd. Acuña (or Las Vacas, as it was then called).[3]

When in November 1910 disappointment over Díaz's manipulation of the elections led to outbreaks of revolt, the border towns were in the forefront of this challenge.[4] In Nogales, Sonora, a local revolutionary regime took shape under José María Maytorena, working with two other Hispanic and three Anglo rebel leaders. Maytorena maintained his hold on the town through two battles, those of Sahuaripa on 27 January and of Molino de San Rafael on 23 March 1911. The subsequent revolutionary movement in all of Sonora would grow from this base.[5] Piedras Negras (then called Cd. Porfirio Díaz) was attacked by Madero himself from Eagle Pass across the river, although without success.[6] In December 1910, rebel forces placed Ojinaga, Chihuahua, under a siege which would drag on for months. Presidio, Texas, across the river, swelled with refugees fleeing from Ojinaga and with one hundred U.S. cavalrymen sent to guard the town.[7]

At the western terminus of the border, the revolt was led by the controversial Ricardo Flores Magón. A native of Oaxaca who had become a member of the Partido Liberal, Flores Magón had fallen afoul of Díaz's regime by his editorial attacks printed in his *Regeneración* magazine. He had escaped incarceration to take refuge in the United States, where his brother Enrique had joined him. From that country, Ricardo had stirred strikes in Mexico, using his leadership in the internationally based IWW (standing not for "I won't work," as its critics claimed, but for "Industrial Workers of the World"). The "Wobblies" (as members of the IWW were dubbed) hoped to use international organization, especially between the United States, Mexico, and Canada, to compensate for structural weakness caused by their lack of crucial skilled workers, who were clustered in the American Federation of Labor. Both Eugene Debs' Socialist Party and Emma Goldman's Anarchists supported Flores Magón's activities. After the Mexican strikes had culminated in the Mexican worker revolts of Cananea, Sonora, and Rio Blanco, Veracruz, in 1906 and 1907, Ricardo was condemned to thirty-six months in an American prison for violation of the neutrality laws. However, neither his prison sentences nor Díaz's assassination squads and $20,000 reward on his head deterred Flores Magón from seditious opposition to the Porfiriato.[8]

From his base in Los Angeles, Flores Magón now called for the establishment of an independent Socialist government of Baja California, under a platform of maximum working hours, minimum wages, workmen's compensation, a six-day working week, and land redistribution.[9] Action followed words when, on 29 January 1911, José María Leyva crossed the border from Calexico with a private Magonista force of Mexicans and Americans, including for a short time Socialist novelist Jack London. Mexicali offered no resistance, most of its 462 residents fleeing in the opposite direction to Calexico and the protection of American troops hurriedly posted there. As the rebels took control of Mexicali, three local officials were arrested, one of whom was executed for refusing to cooperate. In February, a Federal force coming in from Ensenada was defeated in a small engagement outside Mexicali with ten government soldiers and six Magonistas killed. This victory emboldened the Magonistas to send a side force under U.S. Army deserter and Wobbly Stanley Williams to Los Algodones, where it burned the customhouse.[10]

The Magonistas knew they needed to take Tijuana if they were to succeed. Thus, a second insurrectionary band, under Luis Rodríguez, occupied Tecate, Baja California, on the route from Mexicali to Tijuana, on 1 March 1911. When a government force under Col. Miguel Mayol retook Tecate that St. Patrick's Day, with Rodríguez himself killed in the fighting, Leyva hastened from Mexicali to reclaim control. Defeated in turn by Mayol, Leyva handed over his command to Francisco Vásquez Salinas. Vásquez continued the pressure on Tecate. After a detachment composed mainly of Americans had torn up the outskirts of Tecate through April, on 9 May the force was thrown against Tijuana itself. Led by a Welshman named Carl Rhys Pryce, its 220 men sustained a battle for sixteen hours, while tourists came from San Diego to watch the display from across the border. As soon as the American detachment had taken the town, the tourists rapaciously poured in to sack it. Cognizant of the urgent need for financing if the Magonista cause were to prevail, Pryce charged the tourists fifty cents a person for the privilege of taking their booty back across the border. He also permitted gambling in Tijuana, skimming off a twenty-five percent tax. The money gained was sent to Flores Magón back in Los Angeles to purchase more weapons.[11]

Nonetheless, Flores Magón failed to build a proper base for his movement. He placed ideological purity and a determination to make Baja California independent of both Mexico and the United States ahead of making the sort of compromises that would have brought success. Thus, the big capitalist interests of southern California which had long encouraged filibustering expeditions to gain Baja California for the United States were scared into opposing rather than aiding him. He also alienated his American Socialist Party supporters by refusing to subordinate his movement to that of Madero. Seeing

Flores Magón's impracticality, even John Turner, author of the anti-Porfirista novel *Barbarous Mexico* and husband of an employee for Flores Magón's *Regeneración*, separated himself from the movement. On Turner's advice, Pryce decided to do the same, leaving command of the American detachment to Jack Mosby. The whole movement collapsed after Ricardo and Enrique Flores Magón, together with Pryce, were arrested in Los Angeles on 15 June 1911. With a group of Maderista railroad workers challenging them, the Magonista forces pulled out of Mexicali back to Calexico. There, after a farewell meal in one of the Chinese restaurants of the town, they disbanded. This left only Tijuana in Magonista control, and on 22 June 1911, Coronel Vega captured that town, too, from Jack Mosby's American detachment. The surviving American troops fled across the border into the waiting handcuffs of American authorities. Ricardo Flores Magón was imprisoned for violating the neutrality laws and later died at Leavenworth under suspicious circumstances.[12]

Where Tijuana had merely played at changing history, Cd. Juárez helped to make it. This town witnessed the first effective major military action of the Revolution — the battle of Juárez. The Maderista attack on the town was planned from El Paso, where Maderista Gen. Abraham González set up headquarters in the Caples Building. Acting within the limits allowed by the U.S. State Department, González recruited some American mercenaries to join his Mexican troops and purchased the needed arms and ammunition through El Paso's Shelton Payne Arms Company. In February 1911, Madero arrived in El Paso and crossed to take command of rebel troops which had taken up a position outside of Cd. Juárez. Repulsed from Casas Grandes, Madero returned to El Paso. He took up quarters in the Sheldon Hotel there, but kept his soldiers encamped at the Mexican side of a foot bridge, for easy access between the two countries.[13]

From the eighth through the eleventh of May, the Maderista troops attacked Cd. Juárez. Madero was haunted by the worry that American fatalities from stray bullets crossing deep into El Paso might cause an intervention by U.S. troops. At one point, with victory within his grasp, Madero's fear brought him to call for a retreat. However, his own general, Pascual Orozco, ignored the order, and after fierce house-to-house fighting, forced Porfirista Gen. Juan Navarro to surrender. Navarro's soldiers were stripped to their underwear and paraded through town in a modern equivalent of the ancient Roman triumphal parade. Indeed, the battle itself had been watched as a sort of neo-Roman gladiator show by civilians from both sides, many to their undoing from stray bullets. After the battle, these onlookers surged through the town to loot. The news of Madero's capture of Cd. Juárez helped convince Porfirio Díaz to step down and leave for Europe.[14]

The Revolt against Madero (1912-1913)

When word came that Díaz had renounced power, El Paso honored Madero with celebrations at his Sheldon Hotel and with a banquet at the Toltec Club.[15] A similar victorious mood prevailed in other border towns. The new Maderista mayor of Nuevo Laredo, Pedro González, met the call for reform by starting the custom of paying salaries to the mayor and town councilors in an effort to make them less vulnerable to bribes.[16] Nonetheless, Madero soon proved to be a bitter disappointment to both Mexican reformers and American businessmen. The Madero family introduced a nepotistic rule which placed personal power ahead of change, while its clash in mining interests with the Guggenheims soured American business on Madero's government. An early indication of border discontent came when Laredo's ex-mayor and present Webb County sheriff was indicted for plotting a revolt against Madero.[17] Soon the border was boiling again with revolutionary plots.

First of all, IWW agitation resurfaced in San Diego on 11 December 1911. The union's activities seemed to threaten the city's hopes for continued development. San Diego was rapidly emerging as an aviation center. Glen Curtiss had opened a flying school at North Island in the bay in 1910. With the successful hoisting of a plane from the waters of the bay to a cruiser, Curtiss proved in 1911 that the navy could realistically develop aircraft carriers. In 1912 the U.S. Navy and the U.S. Signal Corps founded the Rockwell Field Aviation Base on North Island. The next year, a naval coaling station went into operation at Point Loma, while a naval radio station began broadcasts from the city. Furthermore, plans were being made to hold the Panama-California Exposition in 1915 in celebration of the opening of the Panama Canal.[18]

Fearing that the IWW would scare off investment, the city council prohibited street speaking in downtown San Diego. A guard was assigned to patrol the county line with orders to hold out all Wobblies. On 10 March 1912, after forty-one men were arrested for street oratory, a free-speech demonstration staged by 5,000 protesters in front of city hall was broken up by spraying the crowd with water from fire hoses. Some residents decided that the official response to the IWW was insufficiently vigorous and formed a vigilante committee to run Wobblies out of town. In the tense atmosphere, a riot was set off on 8 May when the police shot one of the radicals. Nervousness climaxed with the arrival on 14 May of Emma Goldman, the head of the American violent Anarchists. Her career as an agitator had begun at the time of Chicago's Haymarket Riots in 1888 and had progressed through inspiring the assassination of President William McKinley with her inflammatory language. Her radical reputation brought her a reception at San Diego's train station by a hostile crowd of hecklers. After arriving with difficulty at the Grant Hotel, Goldman learned that her manager, Dr. Ben Reitman, had been kidnapped from his hotel room. While Dr. Reitman was stripped, tarred, and feathered, a mob outside the hotel shouted, "Emma, oh Emma, you put me in such a dilemma." In these circumstances, Goldman agreed to allow the police to rush her back to the station and place her on a train out of town.[19]

In February 1912 there was also renewed action in El Paso, where supporters of Emilio Vázquez Gómez plotted their own revolt. Vázquez Gómez had turned against Madero out of disappointment over being passed over for vice-president. At the same time across the river, champions of land redistribution were starting a campaign of burning and looting around Cd. Juárez. These men were called the Red Flaggers for their chosen leftist symbol.[20] Thus armed, the Red Flaggers attacked Cd. Juárez. Once again fearing that deaths caused by bullets straying into El Paso could cause an American intervention, President Madero ordered the town to surrender without a fight. This was done on 27 February.

In early March 1912 another ex-Maderista, Pascual Orozco, angry over Madero's backing of Abraham González as governor of Chihuahua, took command of the rebel troops in Cd. Juárez. El Paso's hardware firm of Krakauer, Zork, and Moye sold guns and ammunition to Orozco to distribute to his followers.[21] Orozco was undermined by the pro-Madera stance taken by the United States government. Additional American troops were rushed into El Paso's Fort Bliss, while in March 1912, President Taft declared an arms embargo. At the same time, Maderista government troops under Gen. Victoriano Huerta closed in on the town. Caught between two hostile fronts, Orozco went down in defeat.[22]

Whatever effects such border agitation might have had on undermining Madero's regime became a moot point in February 1913, when, in Mexico City, Madero was toppled, shot, and replaced by Gen. Victoriano Huerta.[23]

The Period of Fighting Concentration along the Eastern Border

The next two Mexican presidents, Victoriano Huerta and Venustiano Carranza, both perpetuated the old problems with their cynical lack of attention to reform and with their own hostility to American influence in Mexico. In the campaigns to topple first Huerta and later Carranza from national power, the eastern border towns came into a more prominent position in the fighting.

The Revolt against Huerta (1913-1914)

As in the previous revolts, the movement to overthrow Huerta took shape first in the border towns. On 13 March 1913 a rebel force grabbed control of Nogales, Sonora, from Mexican government troops.[24] The U.S. government once again permitted the purchase by rebel forces of arms and ammunition through American border towns, a decision that rapidly affected the Lower Rio Grande towns.[25] In May 1913 Gen. Lucio Blanco, leading a rebel force loyal to Carranza out of Coahuila, laid siege to Reynosa. After cutting the town's rail links, Blanco took the garrison by assault on the tenth of the month. The mayor was executed. Using Reynosa as his new base, Blanco occupied the towns upriver as far as Guerrero. Then, at the start of June, he moved against Matamoros.[26] Matamoros' walls had been largely dismantled during the security of the Porfiriato, and Maj. Estéban Ramos, responsible for the town's defense, had less than 300 men and zero cannons at his disposal. Spunky Ramos refused to surrender, telling Blanco to "Come on." He said, "This is my last chance and I am going to fight." The reaction of the average man was not so cocky; Blanco's appearance caused a general exodus of Matamorenses across the river to Brownsville.[27] There they joined Brownsvillites on the roofs to monitor the fate of their homes as Blanco attacked on 3 June.

In the first day of heavy fighting, Blanco's forces managed to secure control of the electric plant, located on the spot where Fort Paredes had earlier stood. On the morning of the second day, cannonading destroyed not only the army barracks but also the bull ring, the spires of the cathedral, and a dozen homes. Major Ramos, wounded and running low on ammunition, gave up the fight in the afternoon. He crossed the railroad bridge to Brownsville with about eighty of his men, and Blanco's men occupied the south end of the bridge as soon as they had crossed.[28] Still some of the defenders of Matamoros fought on through that night in a town lit by burning buildings. The next morning the last thirteen resisters, in their early teens, were captured and shot, even though prisoners taken earlier had been pardoned. The *corrido* "La Toma de Matamoros" records the shock of this execution of the juveniles:

> *Agarraron prisioneros*
> *a unos niños que pelearon,*
> *y otro día en el Parián*
> *a las seis los fusilaron.*
>
> *Pues los niños que pelearon*
> *con bastante decisión*
> *al enemigo causaron*
> *bastante admiración.*

That is:

> They made prisoners of some
> of the boys who'd also fought them,
> and the next day they took them out
> at six in the morning and shot them.
>
> For the boys that fought
> with such a dogged determination
> caused the enemy to feel
> a good deal of admiration.[29]

In all, the victory cost Blanco about 400 men, compared to 68 defenders killed. However, it brought him the rank of brigadier general, and it allowed Matamoros to become the main point of import of U.S. war munitions for the anti-Huerta revolt.[30]

While Blanco remained in Matamoros, from June to November 1913, he ran the town pretty much as he pleased. Casimiro Sada García, the elected mayor who had been imprisoned and replaced by Major Ramos, was restored to office. Like Ramos before him, Blanco pressed residents for loans to pay for his troops. He confiscated property of alien residents on phony charges and divided up local land

San Diego street scene — Fifth looking across Broadway intersection, ca. 1918.
— Courtesy San Diego Historical Society

John D. Spreckels, San Diego entrepreneur and power-broker, ca. 1911–1915.
— Courtesy San Diego Historical Society

U.S.-Mexico boundary, San Ysidro entrance to Tijuana, 1920.
— Courtesy San Diego Historical Society

Tijuana street scene, 1924.
— Courtesy San Diego Historical Society

Very early Mexicali street scene, ca. 1904.
— Courtesy San Diego Historical Society

Baja California Governor Abelardo Rodríguez, future president of Mexico, 1926.
— Courtesy Carlos Larralde, Long Beach, California

Juan Nepomuceno Cortina, controversial politico-military leader, as governor of Tamaulipas, 1864.
— Courtesy Carlos Larralde, Long Beach, California

Los Ebanos Ferry, last ferry crossing on the border, soon to be replaced.
— William Landry, Brownsville

James B. Wells, Jr., political boss of Brownsville from 1880s to 1910.
— Courtesy Brownsville Historical Association

Gen. Lucio Blanco (fourth from left) after the capture of Matamoros by Constitutionalist rebels in 1913.

— Courtesy Brownsville Historical Association

Capt. John McAllen, founder of the McAllen Townsite Company in 1904, for whom the city of McAllen was named.

— Courtesy Brownsville Historical Association

The Santa Cruz mule-drawn streetcar, which operated from the ferry-crossing to Brownsville to the main plaza in Matamoros.
— Courtesy Brownsville Historical Association

William Neale, English immigrant and Brownsville business and political figure in the mid-to-late nineteenth century.
— Courtesy Brownsville Historical Association

Federal Appeals Court Judge Reynaldo Garza and Brownsville City Commissioner Bernice Brown, daughter of Mayor Benjamin Kowalski, ca. 1980.
— Courtesy Brownsville Historical Association

Charles Stillman, major Matamoros merchant and founder of Brownsville at the close of the Mexican-American War.
— Courtesy Brownsville Historical Association

Mexican-American Mutualista Sociedad Benito Juarez of Brownsville, 1928.
— Courtesy Brownsville Historical Association

*President-elect Warren G. Harding (left) and Brownsville Republican leader
Renfro B. Creager during Harding's visit to Brownsville, 1920.*
— Courtesy Brownsville Historical Association

Governor Pete Wilson of California, formerly mayor of San Diego (in the 1970s).
— Courtesy Sirlin Photographers, Sacramento, California

Main Street, McAllen, ca. 1910–1915.
— Courtesy Hidalgo County Historical Museum

A group of Villistas celebrating the capture of Reynosa, 1915. In center, with white shirt and no tie, is A. Y. Baker, Hidalgo County Sheriff. Gen. José Rodrigues, commander of Villa's forces, stands at immediate right to Baker. Third to left of Baker is Gen. Absaul Navarro.

— Courtesy Hidalgo County Historical Museum and David Mycue

Early Hidalgo County power structure, from left: Deputy Sheriff A. Y. Baker, Walter Doughty, Sheriff John Closner, County Judge D. B. Chapin. Visiting site of new county courthouse, 1910.

— Courtesy Hidalgo County Historical Museum

Main Street, McAllen, ca. 1940.
— Courtesy Hidalgo County Historical Museum

McAllen Mayor Othal E. Brand
— Photo by PLG, Ltd.

James Wiley Magoffin, Chihuahua trader who arranged the peaceful surrender of Santa Fe to U.S. forces in 1846. He established Magoffinsville in what would become El Paso.
— Courtesy The Southwest Collection, El Paso Public Library (AS994)

Simeon Hart (bearded) founded an early Mexican-American family in Paso del Norte. Son Juan Hart (second from left) founded the El Paso Times.
— Courtesy The Southwest Collection, El Paso Public Library (3301)

Paso del Norte (Ciudad Juárez) in the 1870s.
— Courtesy The Southwest Collection, El Paso Public Library

El Paso in 1885, showing the Southern Pacific depot and the Pierson Hotel in center.
— Courtesy The Southwest Collection, El Paso Public Library (9167)

Guiseppe Garibaldi (left), Italian volunteer with the Mexican revolutionary forces, and Francisco Madero (right), soon-to-be Mexican president, during the Battle of Juárez, May 1911.
— Courtesy The Southwest Collection, El Paso Public Library (1452)

Iturbide Street, Laredo, ca. 1875.
— Courtesy The Institute of Texan Cultures, San Antonio

Santos Benavides, leader of an influential Laredo family, served as colonel commanding Confederate forces on the Rio Grande.
— Courtesy The Institute of Texan Cultures, San Antonio

Laredo City Hall and Market House, ca. 1890.
— Courtesy The Institute of Texan Cultures, San Antonio

owned by Huertistas to poor farmers to form the first *ejidos* of the Mexican Revolution. The Rancho Los Borregos, owned by Félix Díaz, son of ex-President Porfirio Díaz, was the first to be distributed.[31]

That fall, the anti-Huerta forces surged in Cd. Juárez as well. As the sun prepared to rise on 15 November 1913, Pancho Villa slipped his troops into Cd. Juárez by rail. Villa had captured a train to the south, stuffed his men and horses into its boxcars, and forced it to carry them into the border town. The surprise was so complete that Villa's conquest of Cd. Juárez proceeded with very little bloodshed. This success allowed Villa to use Cd. Juárez as his base for obtaining U.S. arms and ammunition and for subsequent conquests to the south, starting with Cd. Chihuahua that December.[32]

El Paso swelled with refugees from Villa's capture of Cd. Chihuahua, most of them taking the long desert highway to Ojinaga, from where they crossed to safety in the United States at Presidio. Gen. Luis Terrazas, with members of his wealthy ranching family, and Mariano Azuela, author of the revolutionary novel *Los de Abajo*, were among the émigrés. The refugees were at first tended at Fort Bliss, but the majority soon settled in the notorious slum called Chihuahuita.[33] Meanwhile, the Carrancista forces moved south along three routes from the border, from the northeast, the north central, and the northwest, until Huerta was forced to flee abroad.

The Revolt against Carranza (1914-1920)

The border also helped launch the last major round of the Revolution—the revolt against Carranza. The first agitation occurred in Tijuana; the first action with impact on the mainstream of national politics took place in Cd. Juárez; and the final confrontation of border conflict wrapped up in Matamoros. At the end of 1914, Tijuana was again occupied by revolutionaries, but only briefly.[34] Cd. Juárez saw a more serious insurrectionary plot develop under Pancho Villa. Villa was active in El Paso trying to bring the U.S. government to his side. He met in Cd. Juárez in January 1915 with the U.S. chief of staff, Gen. Hugh Scott, and was prevailed upon to cancel a planned attack on Naco, Sonora, due to fears the fighting might also affect the American side of the border.[35]

Instead, Villista troops moved east, grabbing Monterrey and then marching on Matamoros in March 1915. The attacking forces were under the command of Gen. José Rodríguez and Absaùl Navarro; Gen. Emiliano Nafarrate commanded the far less numerous government forces defending the town. In preparation for the siege, resourceful Nafarrate had hurriedly reconstructed the walls around Matamoros, complete with machine-gun nests, barbed wire, and a moat. He also flooded part of the low-lying land outside the walls, to cause the famous Villista cavalry charges to bog down. Nafarrate employed ruse, disguising a machine gun as a weak point in the walls. On 27 March 1915, the Villistas fell for the trick and charged through the weak point in the wall, only to find themselves in a long, narrow alleyway swept by machine-gun fire.[36]

With a loss of 250 men, the Villistas decided to retreat and try a surprise descent on the town from the north side of the river. They were counting on Nafarrate's outspoken anti-Americanism to have antagonized the Americans to the point where they would cooperate. However, Nafarrate threatened to fire on Brownsville if the Villistas were accepted, and the request was denied. The Villistas next tried making a surprise night attack during a lightning storm, but Nafarrate's strong defenses still held, despite heavy losses on both sides. After the arrival of a 400-man reinforcement on 10 April 1915 boosted Nafarrate's numerical inferiority to a less daunting one against four, that intrepid general took the offensive. A dawn raid through rain and mud outside the walls on 13 April caught the besiegers so unprepared that they were rapidly driven back. Losing heart, they called off the siege.[37]

World War I Complicates the Picture

Meanwhile, the outbreak of World War I in Europe had opened in the minds of some Mexicans and Mexican-Americans the possibility of playing Germany off against the United States. The most sensational application of this hope along the border was the Plan of San Diego, Texas. The conspirators had plotted an uprising of the Mexican-Americans of South Texas to commence on 20 February 1915 under the leadership of Basilio Ramos, Jr., of Nuevo Laredo. General Nafarrate from Matamoros, then busy strengthening the town walls in preparation for the coming Villista onslaught, had encouraged the plotters. Ramos had been angered over the prejudice against Mexicans which he encountered while working in a brewery in San Diego, Texas. He was determined to kill all Anglo men in Texas, New Mexico, Arizona, California, and Colorado, and either form another Spanish-speaking republic or rejoin the region to Mexico. Anarchist ideas similar to those espoused by Flores Magón inspired the inclusion of references to brotherly love and the communal ownership of ranches.[38]

Basilio Ramos had been arrested by the U.S. authorities in McAllen on the charge of conspiracy. This had occurred in January 1915, two months before the Villista attack on Matamoros. Freed on bail in consideration of the fantastic and improbable nature of his plot, Ramos had fled to a warm welcome in Nafarrate's Matamoros. However, after the repulsion of the Villista attack on Matamoros, the subversive plans were picked up that summer by two Brownsvillites, grocer Luis de la Rosa and Aniceto Pizaña. In their hands, the plan was expanded to include a black buffer state in East Texas and Oklahoma. De la Rosa had received a ring from Pablo Burchard, German consul in Monterrey. This fact, together with the discovery of secret meetings being held with German agents in El Paso by ex-Mexican President Huerta and revolutionary Pablo Orozco, stirred American suspicions of German involvement. More importantly, Carranza wanted to put pressure on the United States to bring it to recognize his government.[39] After launching several raids around the Brownsville area from the south bank, on 18 October 1915 sixty followers of de la Rosa, perhaps under his personal direction, derailed a train between Olmito and Brownsville. They then boarded and shot the surviving Anglos, robbing all of the passengers in the process. Two men escaped with their lives by claiming that they were Germans.[40] In the resulting panic, thousands of people with rural property moved out of the area. More than 200 residents of Brownsville at a town meeting sent an appeal to both the state and national governments for more military protection. The response was fast, as more than 20,000 soldiers were placed along the border by mid-November. De la Rosa went on to receive a commission in the Mexican army.[41] In the meantime the attacks from Mexico ceased, as a result of the American recognition of Carranza's government on 19 October 1915 — one day too late for the Anglos murdered on the train at Olmito.[42]

While these events were proceeding in South Texas, Pancho Villa was turning his wrath against the western border. In mid-October of 1915, Villa headed with 12,000 men to capture the little border town of Agua Prieta, Sonora, from Gen. Elías Calles and his 3,000-man army. Villa's plans were thwarted when Woodrow Wilson allowed another 3,000 Mexican troops out of Piedras Negras to be sent by rail through the United States from Eagle Pass to Douglas, Arizona, to reinforce Calles across the border in Agua Prieta. Despite a day-light assault on the town on 1 November 1915 and another that night, Villa was unable to take Agua Prieta and, after a couple of days, moved on to Nogales, Sonora. Yet he could not establish a base in that town either.

Feeling betrayed by the U.S. government, Villa's troops in January 1916 killed fifteen American mining engineers in Santa Ysabel, Chihuahua. When the men's corpses arrived in El Paso, a thousand Anglos headed for revenge to the city's Mexican district. Police tried to hold them at bay, declaring a curfew. Nonetheless, the first race riots in that city's history erupted, leaving both Mexicans and Anglos injured. Had the police not worked so hard to contain the confrontations, angry residents of Cd. Juárez might have crossed the bridge to join in the fray. One harsh measure taken to control the racial tensions was to raze the worst Mexican slum, forcing its residents to move across the river to Cd. Juárez.[43]

The Villista fury fell also on the little border town of Columbus, New Mexico. On 9 March 1916 a Villista force crossed the border from Las Palomas, Chihuahua, in a night raid that left many residents dead and buildings burned. Revenge against a local merchant who had cheated Villa, an attempt to grab arms and supplies from the local U.S. army camp, and a scheme to make Carranza seem like a U.S. puppet by having American troops pursue them have all been suggested as additional incentives to the raid. A pursuit by a thirty-three-man posse hastily thrown together by the town mayor left nearly a hundred of the remaining 200 Villista soldiers dead.[44]

Las Palomas was turned into a ghost town by these events. There were almost no people still living there when, on 15 March 1916, Gen. John Pershing with a 4,000-man army was ordered across the border in a futile eleven-month chase of Villa into the interior. Meanwhile, the Villista example encouraged a new spate of border rustling and other theft from bands crossing from the south side of the border.[45] In March 1916 anger boiled over in Cd. Juárez when the rumor spread that a fire in the El Paso jail, which had injured or killed twelve Mexicans and twenty-four non-Mexicans, had been deliberately set to murder the Mexican prisoners. In the resulting rioting, an Anglo streetcar operator was shot. In June of 1916 General Pershing's take-over of the most important of the border bridges caused talk of war between the U.S. and Mexico. Apprehension brought a mass exodus of Hispanics from El Paso into Cd. Juárez.[46] The departed Mexicans were replaced by other Mexicans fleeing the depredations of Pancho Villa in the Mexican interior. In that same month of June, 2,000 Mexicans were camped in a disease-ridden and flood-threatened slum constructed in the Rio Grande River bed while waiting for admission to El Paso.[47] So many wanted to cross north that the U.S. imposed a requirement of a literacy test and an eight-dollar fee. Many, impatient with the wait, made illegal entries.[48]

In an attempt to pressure the American government to withdraw Pershing's troops from Mexico, Carranza returned to the earlier policy of sponsoring incursions on to American soil. The policy was launched when two separate groups raided north across the Rio Grande on 14–15 June 1916. On the first day, some twenty-five Mexicans exchanged fire with an armed patrol near Brownsville, while on the next day a larger group of about a hundred men attacked U.S. cavalrymen thirty-eight miles outside of Laredo. With many Mexican-Americans and Mexican residents on the north bank sympathizing with Mexico, and the Texas Rangers taking ever more brutal steps to contain the situation, racial tensions mounted in southernmost Texas.[49]

American concern over German-Mexican collusion was heightened in March 1917, when the contents of the Zimmermann telegram were disclosed. Sent to Carranza's government from the German secretary of state, this dispatch proposed that Mexico declare war on the United States to reclaim the territory lost half a century before.[50] American fury over the proposal helped bring the American declaration of war against Germany. As American military attention shifted away from Mexico, bringing the withdrawal of Pershing's troops from Mexico, the border problems began to subside. President Obregón's reforms of the 1920s would further defuse the situation. Pancho Villa made one last attack on Cd. Juárez on 15 June 1919, only to be repulsed within the day by local forces aided by U.S. troops sent across from Fort Bliss.[51]

The Revolution's Impact on the Border Towns

For all its talk of social justice, the Revolution disrupted the lives of many border residents, especially on the Mexican side. The Mexican towns suffered wholesale depopulation due to destruction of property in the fighting and to the resulting crop shortages, hunger, and disease.[52] The American towns, with numerous Mexican refugees and economies tied to their twin communities, fared only slightly better. The advent of the First World War created more waves of migration sloshing back and forth across the border, further destabilizing the local population. At first, fear of the U.S. military draft caused a mass flight of Mexican-American farm labor back across the river into Mexico.[53] Yet by 1918, the resulting labor shortage and consequent easier immigration regulations were drawing in a new wave of Mexican workers to the American side. An influenza epidemic spread with deadly impact through the workers accumulated in Cd. Juárez in hopes of crossing the border.[54] Mexico's neutrality in the war also led to closings of border crossings for Mexican shoppers headed north and for U.S. tourists without a passport headed south, further hampering the border economy.[55]

The Negative Impact on the Eastern Towns

Since the hardest fighting of the Revolution occurred in the eastern section of the border, it is not surprising that the Revolution's impact was mainly negative there. Within that eastern zone, the Revolution naturally hit the Mexican towns much harder than their American counterparts. The Revolution's destructive effect on Matamoros can be glimpsed in the fate of local institutions. The two main high schools of the town, the Instituto Hussey and the Instituto Juan José de la Garza, both closed their doors. Troops converted the latter school into a barracks, throwing the library books into the mud for use as stepping stones.[56] The Scottish Rite Masons ceased meeting from 1911 to 1923.[57] Matamoros' population fell from 18,444 in 1900 to only 13,000 in 1920.[58]

The Mexican towns upriver were also adversely affected. Much of their population ended up as refugees in their twin towns on the Texan side.[59] Reynosa was almost completely depopulated by a series of sackings and robberies.[60] Similarly, hundreds of Mexicans fled from Piedras Negras to Eagle Pass to escape the war bands and the famine left in their wake.[61] Hundreds of families also left Nuevo Laredo, resettling with their businesses in Laredo. In 1914 Nuevo Laredo was badly burned by Huertista troops before yielding the town to Carranzistas forces.[62] Cd. Juárez was also hard-hit. Its public library, post office, bull ring, cock pit, and jockey clubs were among the buildings lost or damaged. Here, too, refugees poured across the river to El Paso.[63] The drowning of the revolutionary ideals in violence seemed well symbolized by the discovery in 1922 in the Rio Grande of the corpse of murdered revolutionary Gen. Lucio Blanco.[64]

The American towns fared less poorly, thanks both to their remove from the fighting and to the business brought in by U.S. soldiers posted to the border. However, they were stunted in their agricultural development for the course of the decade.[65] Brownsville suffered from bands of outlaws who ravaged the countryside on both sides of the river, rustling and murdering.[66] Brownsville's population squeaked ahead a bit from 10,517 in 1910 to 11,791 in 1920, a fraction of what it should have experienced after the start of irrigation.[67]

The onset of the First World War in Europe brought more problems for the north bank Lower Rio Grande towns in the form of tensions resulting from the German-linked border plots. It is true that in the period before the United States joined the war, some of the towns benefited from additional military garrisons. Fort Brown, which had been shut down as a military post in 1906 after the Brownsville Raid, was reopened in 1913.[68] The number of soldiers posted to Brownsville was boosted in 1916 to 30,000, a move warmly greeted by local merchants.[69] However, the revenue gained by the presence of the fort was a poor economic substitute for the lost farm prosperity. Eagle Pass' Fort Duncan, which had been in the process of being phased out, was beefed up again in 1916 to 16,000 soldiers for one last brief period.[70] However, after the U.S. declared war on Germany on 6 April 1917, the number of troops posted there was greatly reduced again.[71]

The More Positive Impact on the Western Towns

In contrast, some of the western border towns saw improvement in this decade. El Paso compensated for its loss of trade with Mexico by various means: by the stationing of tens of thousands of U.S. troops at Fort Bliss, by the arrival of well-to-do refugees from Chihuahua, and by the boost given to irrigated farming through the completion in 1916 of Elephant Butte Dam.[72] From 39,279 residents in 1910, El Paso grew into a modern-looking city of 77,560 by 1920.[73] The present University of Texas at El Paso grew out of the Texas School of Mines and Metallurgy founded there in 1914.[74]

Some of the revolutionary leaders in the West made responsible changes benefiting Mexican border towns. Álvaro Obregón and Plutarco Elías Calles both invested in the development of Nogales, Sonora, in the 1910s. Obregón opened a customs agency and fostered real estate development and mining. He also stood behind the founding in 1917 of the local chamber of commerce. However, Calles took some of the shine off his patronage by playing a role in the formation of a local anti-Chinese society.[75]

Likewise, Col. Esteban Cantú from Linares, Nuevo León, governor of the region and commander of the local military, gave notable patronage to Mexicali.[76] He made that town the capital of the state of Baja California del Norte — the only border town to enjoy such a status.[77] While Cantú commercialized vice and licensed gambling, he channeled the tax profits earned from them to urban improvement.[78] He made Mexicali a fitting seat for the state government by bringing in electric lights, then a fire department in 1918, a chamber of commerce that same year, a public library, a town hall, several primary schools, a commercial school, and a combined prep and normal school. Cantú's energy attracted the attention of Henry Chandler of Los Angeles. When the Colorado River Land Company failed to convince Cantú to lead a movement to break Baja California off from Mexico, Chandler armed a band of filibusterers to do the job. However, U.S. authorities arrested them before they could cross from California.[79]

San Diego experienced a brief setback in 1915 when the rains supposedly caused by rain-maker Paul Hatfield washed out the railroad tracks which had connected the city with Arizona. Instead of replacing them, the Santa Fe Railroad made San Diego a mere spur line out of Los Angeles, momentarily decreasing San Diego's importance as a railroad center. The same year, the Klondike Gold Rush also drew away some of San Diego's population. However, World War I represented the start of a period of real growth, thanks to the rise of local military installations. From 1919, San Diego became a major naval base for the U.S. Pacific fleet, turning it into a navy town. This new importance attracted the building of the San Diego and Arizona Railroad in the same year, counteracting the loss of the Santa Fe Railroad.[80]

The Last Flare-up

The border towns would see one last tardy flare-up of revolutionary fighting in March 1929, when Gen. José Gonzalo Escobar announced the Plan of Hermosillo, Sonora, in opposition to the imposition by President Plutarco Elías Calles of Pascual Ortiz as his successor. The revolt would affect three Mexican border towns: Nogales, Naco, and Cd. Juárez. Nogales, Sonora, and Cd. Juárez would both briefly be captured by rebel supporters.[81] American mercenaries hired by the rebels would be instructed to bomb Naco, Sonora, but would drop their bombs on its twin town of Naco, Arizona, by mistake.[82] This late flare-up would be an exception, however, as the border towns had long returned to the more complex attempt to solve their problems by peaceful means.

Politics and Government of Border Cities during the Revolution

Despite the turmoil brought by the Mexican Revolution, or perhaps in some instances because of it, most American border towns underwent substantial political and governmental changes during the second decade of the twentieth century. This was the era of the Progressive reform movement, which on the local level meant a revolt against bossism and a restructuring of municipal government. In the Mexican border towns local government was in the hands of whatever faction was exercising military control over that area. In some cases that meant frequent and volatile changes in local administrations and often a total breakdown in services. Indeed, Mexican border towns served as launching pads for several revolutionary thrusts into the interior.

Politics in the American Border Towns

Development resulting from the coming of the railroads and frequently the introduction of large-scale irrigation was a major factor in disrupting the political status quo of the United States border communities. In the case of Brownsville, "Boss" Jim Wells may have been the agent of his own political demise. After backing earlier unsuccessful attempts to build a railroad to the Rio Grande Valley, Wells served on the board of directors and as general counsel for the St. Louis, Brownsville, and Mexico Railway, handling the acquisition of land titles. The new railroad brought to the Valley thousands of land-purchasing midwestern Anglos who were not inclined to tolerate the manipulation of Mexican voters and the ensuing corrupt government.[83]

Probably Boss Wells allowed his business interests and his state and national political involvements to distract him from local conditions. This allowed Rentfro Creager to organize a new Brownsville political party composed of Republicans and disgruntled Democrats. The Independent Party platform condemned the Democrats for indulging in "machine methods, bossism, corruption, and graft" and promised "honest, efficient, economic, and wise business methods" in administering local government.[84] The Independents were already utilizing the rhetoric, if not the spirit, of the Progressives. Despite the new style, the Independents relied on many of the same electoral tactics used by Jim Wells, including the corralling of Mexican voters.

The initial challenge by the Independents in 1908 was turned back by a narrow margin, but in 1910 the new party succeeded in electing Benjamin Kowalski as mayor. The Independents also made a run at the Wells-controlled Cameron County government with only mixed results, but Wells was determined to regain control. The Wells machine accused the Independent city administration of excessive taxation and various abuses, but the Independents had compiled an impressive record in providing public services and utilities, as well as the construction of a new city hall and market. The Independents retained control in the election of 1912, but the results were disputed in the courts and—violently—in the streets. One perceptive local observer concluded that the "overriding concern of the Independent and Democratic leaders alike was the acquisition of political power, and both sides were willing to stoop to any tactic in their pursuit of that goal."[85]

Faced with the frustration and outrage of the Brownsville business community over the election scandals and violence, the Independents called for a compromise ticket for the next election and persuaded some leading Democrats to join them. The Independents also returned to their original reform strategy by proposing a new city charter based on the progressive commission plan of government with nonpartisan elections. Former Wells ally Augustus A. Browne was elected mayor along with the rest of the Independent slate in 1914, and he promptly delivered on the party's promise of a new charter, which actually established a city manager form of government.[86]

Jim Wells maintained his control over the Cameron County government until 1920, when he lost the county Democratic chairmanship. Wells himself described the results of his defeat: "Cameron County has ceased to be the 'Banner' Democratic stronghold . . . and it is now 'Anybody's and Everybody's County,' . . . which is due . . . to the fact that the 'Snow-diggers' are in the majority and fast increasing."[87] For all practical purposes competitive politics had come to an end in both the city and the county, and with it the importance of the Mexican vote. Mexican-American officeholders, who had been used to recruit the ethnic vote, nearly disappeared during this period.[88]

The Cameron County boss' Hidalgo ally, Sheriff John Closner, faced a similar problem at this time. The challenge to the Democratic machine in Hidalgo was delayed until 1914 due to the lack of any established base of opposition. When the Good Government League was finally established, it was due to the influx of Anglos, who exclusively comprised the membership. In consequence the league's campaign rhetoric added anti-Hispanic overtones to the usual condemnations of corruption. The league initially supported County Judge James Edwards, a former Closner ally who had been dropped from the Democratic ticket for promising to combat graft. Edwards proved to be an undependable candidate, and the league's campaign collapsed.[89]

The Good Government League achieved greater success in its attack on Closner by filing legal suits to force disclosure of county financial records. The large-scale graft in county government, and evidence of Closner's personal involvement that resulted from the lawsuits, brought Closner's political career to an end. The Closner machine, however, would live on for another dozen years.[90]

A prominent Laredo politico was ensnared by the Mexican Revolution in 1911. Amador Sanchez, mayor for the first decade of the century, had been elected sheriff of Webb County. Sanchez, a university graduate who had extensive ranching and mining interests in northern Mexico, became involved in the plans of Porfirian Gen. Bernardo Reyes to organize a revolution against the government of President Francisco Madero. Federal authorities indicted both Reyes and Sanchez for violating American neutrality laws, and Sanchez pled guilty in a Brownsville federal court. He was fined $1,200 and placed on probation.[91]

Any Laredo penchant for challenging the system must have been exhausted by the Bota/Guarache clash of the mid-1880s. The Republican-founded Independent Club remained dominant during the Revolution as it gained Democratic Bota adherents.[92]

Despite its preoccupation with the events and consequences of the Mexican Revolution, El Paso still found time to undergo its own municipal political revolt. The establishment Democratic machine known as the "Ring" had controlled El Paso government since 1889 under the leadership of Joseph U. Sweeney and C. E. Kelly. The Ring utilized all of the borderland political techniques for manipulating the Mexican vote, including paying voters, paying poll taxes, and "corralling" voters overnight in order to ensure their votes on election day. The Ring also took advantage of the fact that "the more acculturated and politicized Mexican-Americans could play a key role as mediators and ward bosses in Chihuahuita and the other Mexican settlements of El Paso."[93] These Mexican-Americans made the most of the situation by organizing to secure endorsements and favors from the Ring.

Both Republicans and reform Democrats sought to undermine the Ring's hold on the Mexican vote, but met with only limited success. Of greater importance in bringing down the Ring were the charges of corruption against Mayor C. E. Kelly, leader of the Ring during the early years of the Mexican Revolution. Kelly frequently demanded strong action by the federal government to protect El Paso, including military intervention. "I do not propose to maintain order in the City of Juarez," Kelly wrote, "but I do intend to protect life and property in the corporate limits of El Paso, Texas."[94]

Mayor Kelly's machine was attacked and weakened in 1913, when reformer Tom Lea won the Democratic county chairmanship. An increase in Anglo voters helped to minimize the Ring's domination of the Mexican vote, and in 1915 Tom Lea defeated Kelly in the race for mayor under the slogan "More Business and Less Politics."[95] The Ring was destroyed as a political force in El Paso.

Further reforms in El Paso became necessary with the coming of World War I. Newton D. Baker, President Woodrow Wilson's moralistic secretary of war, announced on 2 June 1917 that "El Paso must clean up. I am in receipt of daily reports showing social conditions to which our soldiers are subjected which can no longer be tolerated." Fear of losing the military prompted city officials to begin a crackdown on vice, especially prostitution and sale of alcohol to soldiers.[96]

At the western border extremity of San Diego, the Progressive reform challenge to boss rule began a few years prior to the onset of the Mexican Revolution. The attack on the political and economic dominance of the city by John D. Spreckels and his minions resulted in the adoption of a new city charter in 1905. The new charter reduced the size of the city council dramatically and implemented the Progressive reforms of initiative, referendum, and recall for the first time in California. In the mayoral election the same year, Capt. John L. Sehon was nominated by Progressive Independents on a platform that proposed a water development plan conflicting with the Spreckels' interests. Supporting Sehon was the *San Diego Sun*, owned by Eastern newspaper magnate E. W. Scripps, who had moved to a nearby ranch. The *San Diego Union*, Spreckels' newspaper, sprang to the defense of the existing city administration. Sehon won the election, but found it necessary to break into city hall at night to take possession of his office.[97]

John D. Spreckels had another card to play. On 14 December 1906, the Spreckels' interests announced plans to construct a railroad from San Diego to Yuma, thereby creating a direct link with the East. Mayor Sehon offered his congratulations, money poured into San Diego from investors, and even E. W. Scripps was induced to join the railroad construction project. Prosperity and the promise of a railroad enabled the Spreckels Republicans to regain control of city hall in 1907.[98]

The momentum for reform continued to build despite the temporary setback caused by Spreckels' railroad plan, and the charter amendments installed a modified "commission" form of government, which required elected commissioners to assume direct responsibility for particular city operations. Republican Progressives brought about the defeat of the Spreckels-supported mayor in 1909. Plans for an international exposition and the IWW fracas apparently disrupted the normal political currents; by 1913 the focus had shifted to a struggle between the advocates of "smokestacks" and the supporters of "geraniums." George W. Marston, a supporter of the Nolen Plan for civic beautification, was defeated in the race for mayor by Charles F. O'Neall, a real estate agent endorsed by those who favored more industry and commerce. Spreckels was not involved on either side.[99]

George Marston ran again for mayor in 1917 with the backing of most civic leaders, but his opponent, Louis J. Wilde, accused Marston of holding out "a beautiful figment of the imagination for the tourist and the pensioner." Wilde promised a real opportunity for prosperity for the working man and pensioner. Although Marston received strong support from both the Spreckels and Scripps newspapers, he was defeated by a wide margin in this early context of jobs versus environment. Wilde was reelected handily in 1919.[100]

Politics in the Mexican Border Towns

The Revolution completely destroyed the well-organized but authoritarian system of local government so carefully developed during the Porfiriato. In Matamoros the transition to the Madero regime provided little difficulty, but the overthrow of Madero raised questions of legality and loyalty. Shortly after the removal of Madero, the commander of the Matamoros garrison, Maj. Estéban Ramos, announced his allegiance to the counterrevolutionary movement and seized control of the city. Mayor Casimiro Sada García, who had taken office only the previous December, protested and was promptly jailed. His opponent in the recent election, Dr. Miguel Barragán, a former mayor, was given Sada's post.[101]

Major Ramos' control over Matamoros came to an end with the arrival of Gen. Lucio Blanco's Constitutionalist forces. Ramos escaped to Brownsville by the bridge at the end of the battle, but Mayor Barragan was forced to swim the Rio Bravo. General Blanco restored Mayor Sada Garcia to office, but Blanco ran Matamoros himself as he saw fit. On 1 July 1914 the Carranzista governor of Tamaulipas, Gen. Luis Caballero, appointed Amado Chapa Gómez as mayor and named a new city council. The military commanders actually controlled Matamoros through 1917. On 28 November 1915 Constitutionalist leader Venustiano Carranza arrived in Matamoros to a reception prepared by Maj. Alejandro López. Carranza took note of the belief that the first border town captured by the Constitutionalists had been Matamoros.[102]

In actuality, Reynosa had been "liberated" by General Blanco's Constitutionalist forces prior to their arrival in Matamoros. Reynosa previously had a strong pro-Madero political movement in the Club Politico La Union. When General Blanco seized Reynosa on 10 May 1913, one of his first actions was the execution by firing squad of the former mayor, Exiquio de la Garza. Constitutionalist *jefe* Carranza visited Reynosa on the same day that he arrived in Matamoros in 1915.[103]

As in Reynosa, Nuevo Laredo produced a pro-Madero movement even before the Revolution against Díaz. Lic. Pedro Gonzales was the principal founder of the Club Antirreleccionista, and when Díaz was deposed the government of Nuevo Laredo was turned over to Gonzales on 8 June 1911. The overthrow of Madero inaugurated a period of "anguish and terror" for the inhabitants of Nuevo Laredo, as federal and rebel forces fought for control of the city, and the inhabitants fled to the other side of the Rio Bravo. When Huertista forces were finally ousted from the city, they set fire to the municipal offices and destroyed many public properties.[104]

In view of the chaos in Nuevo Laredo, state authorities suspended elections and appointed Ezequiel Reyes to take charge of the local government. Reyes was a man of action who immediately began the work of cleaning up and restoring public services. Since there were no funds in the treasury and no business activity to produce taxes, Reyes spent his own money for the reconstruction. Succeeding administrations continued the work of restoring public services and began to receive some funds from the state government. Elections for the municipal government were restored in 1918, but after six months Gen. Reynaldo Garza, commander of the local garrison, ousted the new administration of Telesforo Macias for political reasons on orders from the state government. Politics continued to produce frequent changes in administration. In 1920 Telesforo Macias became mayor for the second time, but he was again ousted when the Obregón rebellion overthrew President Carranza.[105]

Ciudad Juárez was pivotal to the Revolution. Consequently, political and governmental power was often wielded by military authorities or their representatives. The El Paso/Ciudad Juárez area had been a magnet for anti-Díaz conspirators since 1893; when Madero announced his Plan de San Luis Potosí and guerrilla bands became active, the Juárez chief of police recruited hundreds of special officers to provide protection. When the rebels took the city, J. J. Flores, the city treasurer, was compelled to open the safe and turn over the city's cash to Pancho Villa. During times of stress in the succeeding years, the Flores family would relocate to El Paso. Flores himself became mayor briefly in 1913.[106]

During the Madero presidency, Chihuahua Governor Abraham Gonzales attempted to reform municipal taxation policies and remit taxes owed by the poor and the middle class. Despite his intentions not to intervene directly in municipal affairs, Gonzales ordered the *jefes politicos* not to allow gambling in their districts and specifically directed Gen. José de la Luz Blanco, the military prefect of Juárez, to close the casinos that the general had allowed to open. When General Blanco failed to act, Gonzales assigned local authority to Mayor Juan N. Medina, who also took no action because of the heavy dependency of the city on gambling for revenue. An exasperated Gonzales ordered Gen. Pascual Orozco and a contingent of troops to the border, where they raided the casinos and arrested the mayor. Gonzales also secured an amendment to the state constitution abolishing the position of *jefe politico*.[107]

With each change of military control came a change in municipal administration. When Pancho Villa seized Ciudad Juárez and

Chihuahua in 1913, his administration began a transformation of municipal authorities in accordance with revolutionary ideology. In 1916 municipal elections were authorized for the first time since Huerta seized power in Mexico City. By 1918, municipal officials were able to attempt to deal with the problems of migrants and the poor by establishing a Public Welfare Committee and providing public baths. The city council also asked the federal government to renegotiate a water allotment treaty with the United States. It was Ciudad Juárez tourist attractions — "watering holes, gambling tables, race track, bullring, cockfights, dance halls, brothels, honky-tonks, lewd shops, dope parlors, and the like" — that provided the taxes to support the municipal government and *mordidas* to support local officials.[108]

The impact of revolutionary violence on Tijuana and Mexicali was over by the time the Revolution began to affect the rest of Mexico. The Magonista/IWW takeover of the Baja California border towns provided authorities too preoccupied with revolutionary concerns to worry much about local municipal administration. When the radicals were ousted, the border towns were beset by the vices expelled by the reformers in San Diego. Julio Dunn Legaspy, commandant of the Tijuana garrison in 1911, noted with distaste the growth of vices dedicated to foreigners.[109]

Mexicali, which had come into existence only at the turn of the century, began governmental life as a municipal section under the *jefe politico*. The dominant figure during the Revolution in both Mexicali and Tijuana was Col. Esteban Cantú, who first came to Baja California as a federal army major assigned to quell the Magonista revolutionary threat. Cantú assumed command of the garrison in Mexicali in 1911, and managed to survive the power changes in Mexico City during the next three years. The shrewd Cantú subordinated the *jefes politicos* and military commanders in Baja California to his authority. Cantú was recognized as *jefe politico* by Pancho Villa's government in 1914, and was responsible for the creation of the *municipio* of Mexicali that same year.[110]

Isolated from the revolutionary turmoil in the remainder of the Republic, and incidentally any external authority, local government in Mexicali and Tijuana depended entirely on the goodwill and effective control of the *jefe politico*. Mexicali gained in prestige from Colonel Cantú's decision to continue to use the town as his base of operations, although without official sanction. Cantú's regime was very popular in the region, probably because it contributed significantly to the economic development. Dependent on local resources for public funds, Cantú imposed a variety of taxes and licensing fees (often on vice-oriented enterprises owned by Americans) to raise money to construct government buildings and schools.[111]

The best thing that can be said about the Mexican Revolution's impact on the border towns as a whole is that after a decade it was over, and the twin sisters could return to their activities as they had left them in 1910.

CHAPTER NINE

New Ups and Downs:
The 1920s and 1930s

In the sweet years of youth, when time seems to be standing still, valuable time is often lost for lack of a set plan. So it was in the years of youthful maturity of the twin cities of the border. The post-revolutionary period saw the border towns drifting along with no clear program for channeling the population growth which had been initiated during the Porfiriato. Economic development was disordered and uneven. When business was doing well, as was the case in the 1920s, the towns benefited. When the economy took a downturn, as it did in the 1930s, the border towns suffered.

The Farm Expansion of the 1920s

Both sides of the border found a source of prosperity in the 1920s — the northern side by completing the founding of the farms and the southern side by selling liquor and fun during the Prohibition era in America. However, the money earned was inadequately taxed for local improvements and poorly distributed to the bulk of underprivileged residents.

The last stage of the founding of farms north of the border, in the 1920s, was accompanied by major promotional campaigns aimed both at attracting agricultural workers from Mexico and at bringing in farm buyers from the northern Midwest of the United States.[1] In 1924, to facilitate the import of Mexican labor, the U.S. Immigration Service created a distinction between the shopper (allowed to cross from Mexico for up to seventy-four hours at a time) and the commuter (living in Mexico but working in the United States).[2] In the pitch made to sell farm plots to prospective midwestern investors, their gullibility was sometimes exploited. Some real estate speculators would purportedly bring a batch of people from up north into the Rio Grande Valley and show them a newly planted field. At the end of the week, the visitors would be taken past the same field, now ripe with full-grown heads of lettuce. The guests were told that such rapid growth resulted from the incredible soil of the "magic" Rio Grande Valley. The lettuce, of course, had actually been transplanted.[3] Charges of land fraud brought the U.S. Congress to launch an investigation in which Brownsville Mayor A. B. Cole was called to testify.[4] Even more advantage was taken of the poor Mexican farm workers. After being charged stiff fees for help in obtaining employment, they were radically underpaid by American standards. The flow of immigrants across the border became chaotic, with workers laid off during the off-season adding to the growing numbers of homeless aliens.[5] The U.S. Border Patrol, set up in 1926 to help handle the rush of immigrants, channeled but failed to contain the problem.[6]

El Paso benefited from growth in its natural resources industries (including new refineries of oil and copper), metal working, cotton farming, and commercial sales. The city's population reached 100,000 in 1930, still at that time the largest population for any city on either side of the border.[7] El Paso's resulting urban improvements included a civic center, a river front, a municipal airport, and new parks (notably Washington Park and Zoo, Memorial Park and Flower Gardens, and Dudley Field for baseball). Hotels and theaters sprang up, and the first radio station began business in 1929.[8] Laredo, thanks to its trade connections, became the second largest American border city in 1930 with 30,000 residents.[9] Brownsville benefited mainly from the success of the cotton, cabbage, tomato, potato, orange and grapefruit farms of the Lower Rio Grande Valley.[10] The construction of a highway system in the region contributed to its boom.[11] Brownsville burgeoned from 11,791 residents in 1920 to 22,021 ten years later. The first paved streets, an urban bus system, an international airport, a second international bridge, and the first large community hospital (now the Brownsville Medical Center) were important additions.[12] In 1926 a junior college was opened, later called Texas Southmost College, which would in 1991 grow into the University of Texas at Brownsville.[13]

Towns on the south side of the border also underwent an agricultural upswing. The new *ejidos* established in the 1910s played a noticeable role in such towns as Matamoros, Cd. Acuña, and Cd. Juárez.[14] Matamoros and Reynosa, stimulated by the presence of railroad transport, international bridges, and irrigation, turned to a major new emphasis on cotton farming. Reynosa's new bridge to the north bank was opened in 1926 as the only suspension bridge on the Rio Grande.[15] The new cotton farms around Matamoros, at first operating without the benefit of irrigation, catered mainly to markets in Germany.[16] Irrigation also brought an upswing of crop yields around Cd. Juárez, thanks to a new water-sharing arrangement with the American side. Yet cotton did not become the monoculture in Juárez that it was in the Matamoros and Reynosa regions, thanks to an equal emphasis on fruits like plums, peaches, apples, melons, pears, watermelons, and grapes, along with oats and such vegetables as sweet potatoes, chile, and beans.[17]

New communities appeared in the farming areas. In 1917, San Luis Río Colorado, Sonora, down the Colorado River from Yuma and Los Algodones, was launched as a military garrison, railroad town, and cotton- and sorghum-farming center on the new Yuma Valley Railroad line. Its twin town of San Luis, Arizona, appeared at the same time. Las Palomas, Chihuahua, across from Columbus, New Mexico, was founded in 1921 as a gateway town from land formerly held by the American Palomas Land and Cattle Company. (A name change in 1977 to Gen. Rodrigo Queveda has not caught on.) Also in 1921, San Pedro, Tamaulipas (the later Cd. Miguel Alemán), was founded as an agricultural colony across from Roma, Texas. It grew especially after 1953, when construction of Falcon Dam and Reservoir cut off the older town of Mier from easy access to a crossing to Texas.[18]

The farm expansion might have had a more beneficent effect on Mexican border town growth had it not been for three factors: a U.S. ban on the export of basic necessities (resulting from restrictions imposed in World War I), a Mexican government prohibition of the import to the border of cereals from southern Mexico, and the preference shown by merchants for selling commodities in the interior of Mexico rather than in the border towns. A narrowness of the local tax base, which brought bankruptcy to the town government of Cd. Juárez at the end of the 1910s, left Mexican border towns receptive to the development of sin industries in this period.[19]

The Nightlife Industry of the 1920s

In order to solve their financial problems, many Mexican border towns turned to the development of nightlife entertainment industry to attract Americans barred by Prohibition from drinking alcohol. The manufacture and sale of liquor were prohibited in Texas in 1918. The Eighteenth Amendment, declaring Prohibition, became U.S. law at the start of 1919, and the federal Volstead Act, which enforced it, took effect in 1920. As expected, the nightlife created new revenue and jobs. The resulting taxes were hotly contested between municipal and state governments, but in some of the towns they were used for town improvement projects.[20]

Everywhere, tourist restaurants, tourist bars, gambling houses, cabarets, racetracks, *palenques* (for cock fights), bull rings, brothels, lewd shops, dope parlors, breweries, and liquor distilleries appeared.[21] Cd. Juárez entrepreneurs took advantage of Cordova Island, a tiny bit of Mexico left by a shift in the Rio Grande on the north side of the river, to set up a bar, dance hall, and gambling casino in convenient reach of El Pasoans. However, Cd. Juárez's main nightlife centered on the south bank, with the Tivoli Gambling Casino, the Green Lantern and Irma's Houses of Prostitution on the Calle del Diablo, the Central Cafe, the Mint Bar, and other bars nearly every twenty feet for six blocks of the main street. The city had built its bull ring and racetrack previously in 1903 and 1905 respectively, and in 1926 added the Juárez Coliseum. The traffic crossing into Juárez was so heavy that two new international bridges replaced the older ones, and a trolley service commenced between El Paso and Juárez.[22]

Matamoros benefited from such restaurants as the U.S. Bar and the Texas Bar on its main plaza, with dance halls scattered in the vicinity. Some of its clientele was drawn off to the bars and dance houses which sprang up on the main plaza of the neighboring city of Reynosa, and to the like-named U.S. Bar and Texas Bar restaurants off Reynosa's plaza. The Reynosa bull ring was added in 1926.[23] The smaller Mexican border towns imitated the larger ones. Nogales, Sonora, saw the founding in 1923 of a brewery to provide beer for American tourists coming to visit.[24]

The most impressive growth was experienced by the towns of Baja California, thanks to the popularity of excursions across the border.[25] Among Tijuana's establishments was La Ballena, which advertized the longest bar in the world with a length of 510 feet. Baja California del Norte's governor, Abelardo Rodríguez, bought part of what remained of the old Rancho Tía Juana from the Arguello family in 1926, and with Baron Long and other American partners built the famous Agua Caliente luxury hotel on the land. Opened in 1928, the Agua Caliente's mixed Byzantine, Mudéjar, Renaissance, Baroque, and Mission-style buildings boasted hot spring baths, swimming pool, golf course, gambling casino, both horse and greyhound racetracks, and a private airstrip for direct flights connecting to San Diego and Los Angeles. Its Patio de las Palmas resounded with the sounds of parakeets, parrots, cockatoos, and crows.[26] Even tiny Los Algodones benefited, as a Yuma businessman opened a large bar there and ran a five-cent bus line from across the border for whoever would buy a five-dollar coupon book for the purchase of liquor at his saloon.[27]

In many cases, especially along the western half of the border, the business investors were Anglo-Americans shifting their interests from comparable establishments being shut down on the American side of the border. This was the case with Cd. Juárez, whose tourist restaurants, tourist bars (including Harry Mitchell's Mint Bar), gambling dens, breweries, liquor distilleries, and racetrack were principally owned by Americans relocating from an El Paso in the grip of reform. Louis Morris, a naturalized Mexican, founded B&M Distilleries; Wayne Russell of Denver set up the Mexican Distilling Company with a plant moved from Kentucky; and D & W Distillery also relocated from that state.[28]

Tijuana and Mexicali saw their own inrush of American investors from California, where *cantinas* and horse betting had been prohibited since 1911. The owners and their American customers were the same as before; only the locale shifted to south of the border. Tijuana's entertainment industry was dominated by fourteen American operators, who hobnobbed after 1924 at Tijuana's new Foreign Club. Tijuana's Tivoli Bar and Mexicali's El Tecolote Bar were owned by three cabaret owners forced out of Bakersfield: Marvin Allen, Frank Byer, and Carl Withington. Organized as the ABW Corporation, along with Baron Long of Los Angeles and Mafia-linked "Sunny Jim" Coffroth (Jack Dempsey's San Francisco boxing promoter), these men gained possession of the local gambling license and launched the Tijuana racetrack. Spanish-speaking Carl Withington, who was married to a Mexican woman, also founded the Mexicali Brewery in 1923. Other Americans, including a Johnson, a Jaffe, and a Baker, opened factories producing wine, which was distributed by bootleggers into California.[29]

Performing celebrities spread the fame of the Mexican border town attractions. In a boxing match held to inaugurate the Juárez Coliseum in 1926, Jack Dempsey knocked out four opponents.[30] He also boxed in Mexicali. Rita Hayworth, Laurel and Hardy, Jimmy Durante, and Buster Keaton performed at the Agua Caliente Hotel's Patio Andaluz in Tijuana.[31] Bette Davis acted in Mexicali, and Rudolph Valentino was married in its Teatro México, with the town mayor, Otto Moller, acting as his witness. The hit song "Mexicali Rose" was played by its composer, Jack Tenney, at the town's Climax Cafe, and two hits of the Mexican film industry, "Baja California" and "Roza de Bronce," were filmed in Mexicali in the 1920s.[32] The tourists themselves were sometimes big names. Charlie Chaplin frequented Tijuana's Casino Monte Carlo, as Will Rogers and Gloria Swanson did Tijuana's Sunset Inn ballroom. The guest list of Tijuana's Agua Caliente Hotel included Clark Gable, Bing Crosby, the Marx Brothers, and Douglas Fairbanks.[33] Babe Ruth, F. Scott Fitzgerald, and Al Capone also frolicked in Tijuana.[34] Visitors to Cd. Juárez included historian Will Durant, editorialist H. L. Mencken, and pilots Eddie Rickenbacker and Amelia Earhart.[35]

The upswing of prosperity brought various benefits to the Mexican border. Ciudad Juárez grew from 10,621 people in 1910 to 40,000 in 1930. This growth allowed it to maintain its status as the largest Mexican border town—a position challenged down to that time only by Matamoros during the civil war years. Tijuana's population mushroomed from 1,028 in 1921 to 8,384 at the end of the decade. Tijuana prospered from the programs of Governor Abelardo Rodríguez. Through his efforts, the city was given a chamber of commerce in 1926, a drinking water system, paving of the main streets, new schools, a dam (the Presa Rodríguez), and an airplane factory. The growth might have been still greater had the overwhelming majority of the town's employees not chosen to live on the U.S. side of the border to avoid the high cost of the American imports sold in Tijuana's stores.[36]

Mexicali also saw many urban improvements under the influence of Governor Rodríguez, especially since Mexicali served as the state capital. In 1924 Governor Rodríguez built Mexicali's municipal market. In 1925 the town's first fire station was constructed, and its library was rebuilt. Many new schools were opened, including an industrial school in 1926. The hospital and the government Banco Agrícola Peninsular (which issued farm loans) were founded in 1927.

Under Governor Rodríguez's direction, the town also began to take on a strong Mexican tone in place of the heavy Oriental flavor of its founding days (with five Chinese to each Japanese). This transformation was achieved by Rodríguez's order in 1924 that all employers, including Harry Chandler's still predominant Colorado River Land Company, must hire Mexicans for at least fifty percent of their workers.[37]

Ciudad Juárez modernized and cleaned itself up, laid down paved streets with street lighting, started a proper garbage disposal, and improved its water and sewage systems. It added trees, playgrounds, and parks, including the reopening of its Tivoli Gardens in 1928. A paved highway was opened from Juárez to Cd. Chihuahua.[38]

Reynosa's growth won it the rank of a *ciudad* in 1926.[39] Matamoros saw the founding of its first labor union, made up of restaurant, *cantina*, and hotel workers, in 1925. New social clubs were also founded, with the Rotary Club of Matamoros starting in 1927.[40] A badly needed canal to drain off flood waters was excavated there in 1923, and a public drinking water system was launched in Matamoros in 1926.[41] A full telephone system arrived in 1929.[42]

Despite the revenues produced, the nightlife industry brought problems of alcoholism, drugs, robbery, and murder.[43] The violence traditionally attracted to the border by the endemic smuggling received a new boost from bootlegging. Gun battles became a regular occurrence in such twin cities as Cd. Juárez and El Paso.[44] The decline was manifested in Tijuana by the contrast between the plethora of flashy *cantinas*, liquor stores, and night spots on the one hand and the one small church on the other. Everywhere, upstanding residents called for action to be taken to protect the moral fiber of their towns. A crackdown on the centers of vice of Tijuana in 1921 proved to be short-lived.[45] In 1923 a crowd formed in Piedras Negras, angry at the dependency of their town on the baser needs of American consumers. Calling for a restoration of the old Mexican border free trade zone, their threats against the director of the customhouse caused him to be transferred for his own safety.[46] A campaign to improve morality in Matamoros brought the dismissal in 1924 of corrupt judges and other officials. A new city ordinance forbade the sale of alcoholic drinks and closed all *cantinas* in the proximity of churches, schools, hospitals, work centers, and the train station.[47]

The crusade against the nightlife industry was weakened by the attack on the clergy by the Fascist-influenced Mexican government of President Calles in the late 1920s. At the height of the anti-clerical campaign, roughly half of the Mexican states closed most churches, barring approximately ninety-five percent of priests from conducting mass. Some states forbade all worship and expelled their clergy, large numbers of whom were banished from the country as well. Many residents of Cd. Juárez and other border towns were able to continue to participate in church services only by crossing to the American twin town.[48] It especially weakened the moral crusade that the churches were closed in the border cities most noted for their sin industries—Tijuana and Mexicali. A group of state-trained teachers desecrated Mexicali's only church, the Iglesia de Guadalupe.[49] Furthermore, not all of the reform talk that survived was actually ethically motivated. Pressure from Cd. Juárez's chamber of commerce to close the gambling casinos was partly backed by liquor interests which viewed the casinos as competition. Likewise, union objections to the gambling casinos enunciated by the *Confederación Regional de Obreros Mexicanos* were motivated by competition between the casinos on the one hand and the restaurants and bars with their unionized bartenders on the other hand.[50] Despite all the fuss, little permanent dent was made in the thriving nightlife industry, which brought in too much revenue to be easily suppressed.

Additional Sources of Prosperity of the 1920s

Other border towns were helped by such factors as new bridges, highways, and military installations. A bridge built south from Roma caused the little village of San Pedro de Roma to grow into a town which was later named Cd. Miguel Alemán. The growth of this new center drew importance away from older Mier, which would lose its customhouse in 1934.[51] A new highway inaugurated in 1928 between San Antonio and Mexico City made Nuevo Laredo Mexico's prime border port for volume of customs income, imports, and tourist crossings into Mexico.[52] Nuevo Laredo, with about 20,000 residents, briefly became the second-largest Mexican border town, after Cd. Juárez (which, however, was twice its size).[53]

San Diego's maritime emphasis was augmented in the 1920s by a revitilization of the local tuna industry, sending large fishing fleets to tap newly discovered banks off the coast of Ecuador. As the city grew, new highways linked it to the outside — in 1923 the Lee Highway to Washington, D.C., and in 1926 a highway link to Savannah, Georgia. The city airport was inaugurated in 1928.[54]

During the 1920s a lot of money was thrown around in the twin towns, but very little was spent to give the towns a strong middle-class foundation or to prepare the residents for more difficult times ahead. Those more difficult times were just around the corner, in the 1930s.

The Great Depression

Despite the bromide that border town poverty was already so extensive that residents could hardly tell any difference between the 1920s and the 1930s, the Great Depression did indeed hit the border towns hard. The two pillars of the local economies of the previous decade, farming and nightlife entertainment, were both adversely affected. As unemployment grew in the United States, large numbers of Hispanic farm workers, some of them legal residents, were expelled to Mexico under President Herbert Hoover's administration. The deportations caused El Paso's population to fall from 102,421 in 1930 to 96,804 ten years later. Tourism plummeted due to many factors: lack of money for leisure; the ending of Prohibition in the United States in 1933; the appearance of hordes of beggars in the Mexican border town streets; and the rising cost of goods in the Mexican border towns as a result of a thirty-eight percent devaluation of the peso vis-à-vis the dollar. President Lázaro Cárdenas' closing of Mexican casinos and brothels and prohibition of gambling in 1935 provided a further disincentive to the recent sort of tourism, while relieving many border towns of their seamier sides.[55]

The More Fortunate Towns

The port towns at the two ends of the border — San Diego, with Tijuana, and Brownsville — weathered the Depression better than their sisters. One helpful factor was the profit from their ports. San Diego continued to benefit from the major use of its harbor by the U.S. Navy and from the presence of army installations. Federal work projects were also liberally showered on the city. These projects allowed the building of a county fairgrounds, a racetrack, and a civic center. The opening of the Consolidated Aircraft plant in 1933 spearheaded a growing industrial emphasis. The success of the city's California Pacific International Exposition in 1934 and 1936, attended by President Franklin Delano Roosevelt himself, was an extra bonus. In the midst of these positive changes, the Communist-led riot in May 1933 proved to be little more than a curiosity.[56]

Tijuana managed to float through the first half of the Depression thanks to its prime location across from San Diego and close to Los Angeles. Its nightlife industry continued strong until 1935, the year in which Cárdenas' government prohibited gambling and related sin industries. At that time, Abelardo Rodríguez's Agua Caliente Hotel and other casinos ceased operation. The Agua Caliente found a new use housing Tijuana's Instituto Tecnológico. Hoping to squeeze a last bit of gain out of their investments through fire insurance, the American owners of some twenty establishments saw them go up in flames in 1935. A protest movement took shape, complete with a hanged worker hero named Juan Castillo Morales. Dubbed Juan Soldado, he was venerated as a miracle-working proletariat martyr. The fact that the man had been hanged on the sordid charge of raping and strangling a little girl failed to tarnish the shine of the worker saint.[57]

Tijuana's protest movement never came to a head, however, for two other developments took the place of the nightlife industry to shore up the town economy in the second half of the 1930s. First, many families were settled on new government *ejidos*, growing mainly wheat and corn. More effective was the creation in 1933 of a local border free trade zone around Tijuana. Ex-Governor Abelardo Rodríguez's influence with the federal government brought this concession. By 1939, the zone had been extended east along the whole border of Baja California del Norte. Boomtime returned to Tijuana. Stores and movie houses proliferated; a new hospital and three sanitoriums were built. A group of refugees from the Spanish Civil War chose Tijuana (and Mexicali) for their new home in 1939, bringing in new technical and educational expertise. The free trade zone was sufficiently successful to raise protests once again from the U.S. side of the border, including renewed proposals to buy Baja California from Mexico.[58]

Brownsville suffered less than many border towns thanks to the continuing expansion of its farm acreage, which doubled again in the 1930s. The agricultural expansion created a demand for labor that kept the wholesale deportation of Hispanic laborers to Mexico from being still worse. As it was, a labor shortage was created by excessive zeal in these deportations. Whole neighborhoods of people were sent packing across the river, to the tune of 450 Brownsvillites in one month of 1931 alone. The town's population held its own in this decade, but just barely, rising from 22,021 to 22,083 residents.[59]

Brownsville's economy also received a boost from the founding of the Port of Brownsville in 1936, rapidly emerging as one of the main cotton ports on the Gulf of Mexico.[60] It also helped that Highway 77 between Brownsville and Corpus Christi was completed in the second half of the decade, followed by the building of a network of hard-surfaced roads.[61] The founding of Brownsville's springtime Charro Days celebration in 1937 also served to draw in more of the scarce tourist dollars.[62]

Brownsville's better fortunes did not extend to its twin city of Matamoros. However, a short ways up the Rio Grande Valley from Brownsville and across the river, Reynosa also managed to experience an upswing in the 1930s. This growth was due to the tapping of irrigation water from two new dams, one near Reynosa and one near Camargo. The water was applied to a major expansion of Reynosa's cotton farming. The local cotton boom would last until the early 1960s, when under competition from the cotton of the Imperial Valley, the area would turn to growing sorghum and corn.[63]

The Harder-hit Towns

Most of the border towns experienced major setbacks in the 1930s. With the deportations from the United States and the continuing push of desperate job-seekers from inner Mexico, Matamoros' population bulged from 24,995 at the start of the decade to an out-of-control poverty and disease-ridden mass of 54,136 at the decade's end.[64] The city seethed with worker unrest.[65] The economic decline of the two Laredos was compounded by a disastrous flood of the Rio Grande in September 1932. Half of the international railroad bridge was destroyed. Many watching from the remaining side were swept away by an avalanche of water, joining the many victims of drowning, and buildings were churned away wholesale.[66]

In El Paso, factories cut back production, and stores shut down right and left. Crime proliferated, especially that connected with drug smuggling. As in other parts of the United States in this generation, the criminal identity was romanticized. The local equivalent of Al Capone and Lucky Luciano was La Nachás (Ignacia) Jasso de González, queen of the dope scene. La Nachás became head of her gang following the police shooting in La Popular restaurant of her husband El Pablote (Big Paul) González, wanted for 113 charges of murder. Big Paul's juvenile emulators formed themselves into street gangs and styled themselves "*pachucos*." They designed the zoot suit

as their distinctive dress, with the famous combination of wide-shoul-
dered and oversized suit coat, rolled up pants cuffs, tie, wide-brimmed
hat, long watch chain, and hair combed back into a ducktail. This
Paseño invention would spread all along the border and help precipi-
tate the Zoot Suit Riots in Los Angeles during World War II.[67]

Many of the workers laid off from jobs in El Paso lived in Cd.
Juárez, which choked on the build-up of unemployed poor families.
The relief offered by the Mexican government proved to be inadequate. It granted the town two percent of local customs duties and
offered free train rides to what few jobs were available with work
projects in the interior. Even this slim hope caused masses of desperate people to respond. One mother who showed up with six children
fainted from hunger at the train station. Farming *ejidos* were also
established all along the border to provide agricultural employment,
but many of these failed due to lack of equipment and poor soil.[68]

Nowhere along the border did the Depression have a more dev-
astating impact than on Nogales, Sonora. After the Banco de Sonora
went bankrupt, the Hispanic residents of Nogales turned their fury
against the local Chinese, who had dominated the town since its
founding. An Anti-Chinese League carried out attacks on this ethnic
group, which organized into its own Fraternal Union. The state government of Sonora showed no sympathy for the Chinese, perhaps
viewing them as a national security weakness on the border. The
Chinese first found themselves required to pay higher taxes and to
close their stores early, at 7:00 P.M. Then in 1931 they were sum-
marily ordered to leave the state. This expulsion turned Nogales into
virtually a ghost town for the rest of the decade.[69] The Chinese of
Mexicali were more fortunate; Mexicali still provides the border's
largest Chinatown.[70]

In the mass unemployment in Mexicali, men expelled from California farm work competed with locals who had not yet found jobs.
A popular demand rapidly took shape for expropriation and distribution of the lands of Harry Chandler's Colorado River Land Company. The state government's initial reaction was to arrest the
ringleaders of the movement and send them to imprisonment on the
Islas Marías in the Pacific. The movement only continued to gather
force, however, and won a sympathetic ear when Lázaro Cárdenas
became president of Mexico. After a mass protest rally of over 5,000
peasants, in 1937 Chandler was obliged to sell his land. He made a
hurried sale of the land to William Jenkins, an American who as a

Mexican resident could hope to get a better price for it. The Mexican government was thus obliged to buy it from Jenkins. The land was then divided among the local farm workers in a move Mexicali commemorates in its *Día del Ejido* every 27 January. The building between 1937 and 1947 of a rail connection between Mexicali and interior Mexico guaranteed the new *ejidos* the markets they needed to survive. The opening in 1937 of the local Banco Nacional de Crédito Ejidal allowed the distribution of farm loans to begin.[71] Mexicali rapidly took on a more Mexican look as Spanish-language signs replaced English ones, parks and plazas were rechristened with Spanish names, and the peso replaced the dollar as the main local currency.[72]

Some of the hard-hit towns worked innovatively to find a means of recovery. In 1938 Eagle Pass made the best of having lost its army base by establishing Fort Duncan Park, complete with museum, country club, golf course, and boy scout hall. Recreational facilities were also set up at nearby Maverick County Lake.[73] Like Brownsville in this decade, with its new Charro Days fiesta, El Paso established its famous Sun Bowl Carnival and games in 1935 in an attempt to draw money to the city. Three years later, it completed the twenty-seven-foot-high monument of Cristo Rey, with the fourteen stations of the cross on a mountaintop three miles from the center of town, at the meeting point between Texas, Chihuahua, and New Mexico.[74] Nevertheless, there was no easy answer for most of the border towns.

Politics and Government during the 1920s and 1930s

The keynote for political development on both sides of the Mexican-American border during the 1920s and 1930s was the establishment of partisan dominance. On the Mexican side, revolutionary chaos gave way to authoritarian stability as victors and presidents Álvaro Obregón and Plutarco Elias Calles fashioned a national political machine, the National Revolutionary Party, as their vehicle for political control. The national party exercised this control by determining the party's candidates for state and local offices and by replacing uncooperative officials.[75]

Politics in the American Border Towns

In Texas, state and county politics were dominated by the conservative wing of the Democratic Party in the tradition of the post-Reconstruction South. Although most municipalities operated under home rule charters, which gave them considerable independence of action, the power of the Democratic Party machine penetrated down to the local level: "Nowhere has this been more true than in the Rio Grande Border counties, where landowning and city elites have long effectively controlled both the economy and the political process, even throughout a dual-ethnic society."[76]

In Brownsville and Cameron County, political stability accompanied the prosperity of the 1920s. The Independent Party of the reform era established political dominance and gradually faded away from lack of opposition. Supported by Brownsville's socioeconomic elite, Mayor A. B. Cole held office throughout the 1920s. Similarly, Oscar Dancy was elected county judge in late 1920 and would hold that post, with one interruption, for fifty years. Judge Dancy's main focus during the decade was on the construction of concrete roads.[77]

The interregnum of Judge Dancy's long career occurred as a result of the election of 1932, and the economic impact of the Depression was clearly a factor in the anti-incumbency mood of the voters. Dancy could claim foresight for building the concrete highways, which required few repairs, in an era of funding shortages, and he was returned to office in the next election, after it became apparent that there were no simple political solutions to the Depression.[78]

At the time of his defeat, Judge Dancy said it appeared "as if everybody who was connected with taxes is beaten."[79] The tax burden, necessitated by bonded indebtedness, was also a problem in Brownsville, where a serious challenge to the political establishment was first mounted in 1935. Fausto Yturria, wealthy descendant of a pioneer family, headed the People's Party ticket in an unsuccessful race against Mayor R. B. Rentfro. One of the losing commission candidates was Robert Runyon, a photographer and botanist, who would constitute the major threat to Brownsville's elite establishment for the next twenty years.[80]

Runyon and other opponents of the Brownsville city administration organized a Greater Brownsville Party in 1937 to challenge the incumbents on the basis that the incumbents were Republicans who had meddled in Democratic Party elections and who had been in office too long. Runyon lost his race against Mayor Rentfro by a scant thirty-three votes, but the rest of his ticket was elected and Runyon was hired to run the city as city manager.[81]

Principled but temperamental, Robert Runyon became embroiled in a lawsuit against the *Brownsville Herald* and political disputes with his erstwhile allies on the city commission. When the city commission fired Runyon, he promptly filed for election as mayor. Running on a program of improvements for city parks, Runyon and his entire slate won by sizable margins in the 1941 elections. By mid-1942 the new mayor was in court, accused of ballot fraud. A hostile *Brownsville Herald* called for "the eventual permanent elimination of the Runyon political ring from our community."[82] The continuing controversies led to a thorough defeat for Runyon and his allies in 1943.[83]

Despite the bitterness of the political struggles in Brownsville in the early 1940s, the issues were the traditional issues of local government: taxes, debt, public services, and patronage. Robert Runyon's challenge to the elite establishment was not a proletarian revolution but an attempt by bourgeois entrepreneurs and businessmen to wrest power from an entrenched establishment. The early 1940s highlighted the bi-ethnic composition of Brownsville politics: for three terms the city commission had a Mexican-American majority composed of young business and professional men, including Reynaldo Garza, who would later become the first Mexican-American appointed to the federal bench.

In nearby Hidalgo County, the boss rule of Treasurer John Closner was supplanted by the boss rule of Sheriff A. Y. Baker. A former Texas Ranger, Baker had been Closner's deputy; when Closner was forced out, Baker moved in smoothly to take his place. A local newspaper editor accused the Baker Democratic machine of achieving "an all time high here for graft and corruption. Baker and his collaborators practically looted Hidalgo County of everything movable."[84] By manipulating the Mexican vote and fraud, Baker was able to continue machine control and the accompanying graft throughout the decade despite challenges from the Anglo settlers.[85]

A major break for the Hidalgo County reformers came in 1929 with the publication of an exposé of Hidalgo corruption in nationally circulated *Collier's* magazine. Particularly revealing was the account of the "Nickel Plated Highway to Hell," which cost the wildly excessive sum of $100,000 per mile and led only to facilities owned by county politicians.[86] Publication of the exposé facilitated the efforts of Ed Couch, Gordon Griffin, and Mayor Frank Freeland of McAllen, who formed a Good Government League, to attack Sheriff Baker and his clique. It took several elections before the reformers were able to overcome the endemic fraud; their efforts were aided by Sheriff

Baker's death in 1929. In 1930 Ed Couch was elected county judge, and he hired an external auditor to expose the corruption of the previous regime. Couch was reelected in 1932.[87]

There was no equivalent of the Democratic machine in the city of McAllen, but politics were tightly controlled nevertheless. A McAllen city commissioner explained the system: "Candidates are usually nominated on a ticket which is made up by a private group that invites the candidate to run. Anyone can run if he submits his name to the election commission, but independent candidates seldom have a chance. Last year there were ten candidates for the two vacant commissioner's posts, but the independents did not even show."[88] Because local government was in the hands of the Anglo socioeconomic elite, the general consensus was that politics was fair and clean. Since the McAllen leadership consisted of immigrants primarily from the Midwest, it was believed, at least by themselves, that they had not been infected by the border virus of corruption. O. P. Archer, who established a variety of enterprises including an ice cream parlor and the first automobile agency, held office from the beginning of the city and served as mayor from 1913 to 1923. Having operated under the general laws of the State of Texas since incorporation, the city adopted its first charter in 1925 to expand its size and function. Frank B. Freeland, a farmer and a Good Government League organizer, served as mayor during the charter adoption process until the end of the 1920s. An examination of city commissioners during the 1920s and 1930s reveals a consistency of membership and promotion to mayor from within the commission.[89]

One Mexican-American family, the Guerras, are considered to be among the founders of McAllen since they arrived from nearby Starr County in 1908, held economic status and social position comparable to the Anglos, and wielded great political power in the Mexican-American community. Anglo political leaders sought the support of these Mexican-American *jefes* because it was believed, with some truth, that they could deliver the Mexican vote. For many years members of this family were the only Mexicans on the McAllen city commission.[90]

If Brownsville and McAllen had local governments dominated by a "system," Laredo and Webb County were ruled by a machine, the all-powerful Independent Club. L. Villegas, mayor during the early 1920s, was succeeded in 1926 by Albert Martin, son of Raymond Martin, the nineteenth-century political boss of Laredo. The only serious challenge to Mayor Martin came in the election of 1932, but Martin survived this bitter campaign by a majority vote and continued to serve until 1940.[91]

One phenomenon of the 1920s that stirred emotions and raised tensions in Texas was the rise of the Ku Klux Klan. In 1922, Laredo and Webb County officials received letters informing them of the intentions of the Klan to "parade in the City of Laredo on the 19th of March." The Klan announcement was widely publicized by officials and the *Laredo Times* and was greeted with overwhelming hostility. On the day set for the march, armed police, deputies, and veterans turned out to give the Klan a rude welcome, but none of the white-robed bigots appeared.[92]

In contrast to Laredo, the Ku Klux Klan achieved considerable though transient success in El Paso. There the Klan exploited postwar economic conditions and the disorder accompanying prohibition to recruit reform-oriented local citizens. By September 1921, a local Klan chapter could boast of a membership of greater than 300 and was ready to launch a campaign against prostitution, automobile thefts, burglaries of homes, and other violations. Even reform Mayor Tom Lea joined the Klan, but later withdrew and opposed it.[93]

The reaction against the Klan was focused by the *El Paso Times* and included the sheriff and the chief of police, who threatened to jail any hooded paraders. Klan promises to reform and improve the schools, however, enabled Klansmen to take control of the school board in the election of 1922 and remove Catholics from administrative positions. Klan members found their way into other government offices, including the grand jury and the county. Finally, a legal maneuver by a Catholic opponent of the Klan publicized the names of influential prominent Klan members, prompting many members to resign rather than face public exposure. A Klan slate in the Democratic primary for the city election of 1923 was soundly defeated by a ticket headed by State Senator Richard M. Dudley. Other defeats followed, and by the summer of 1924 the Klan had ceased to be a political or social force in El Paso.[94]

The Klan's appeal in El Paso was due to its program emphasizing American moral values and reform, which had a respectable tradition in El Paso politics. Its failure occurred because a large proportion of the population was Catholic and Mexican. One historian concluded, "In a city that was socially and economically dependent on peaceful coexistence, moderation and common sense prevailed."[95] El

Paso was, however, a segregated city in which the Texas "white" primary election system was challenged in court by a local black doctor. Blacks constituted a tiny fraction of the El Paso population, but the Mexican majority, especially those living in the Chihuahuita slum, had little influence on public policy.[96]

The Anglo power structure produced solid, competent administrators during this era in El Paso. R. E. Thomason was mayor for most of the 1920s, went to Congress in 1931, and eventually became a federal judge. Thomason managed the city's finances well despite inheriting a million-dollar deficit when he took office in 1924. Ray Sherman, next elected mayor, faced the economic constraints of the Depression with a progressive administration that was still able to reduce municipal debt substantially.[97]

Depression-era El Paso faced a dual problem of local unemployment coupled with the reverse migration of Mexicans being forced out of jobs coveted by Americans. Mayor Sherman appointed a commission to deal with the program, but no simple solution appeared. County Commissioner W. T. Griffith offered a plan to have the county assume responsibility for all agencies dealing with unemployment and hunger. Griffith wanted to establish a public works program to be funded by bonds; the program was approved despite organized opposition from a Taxpayers' League.[98]

When Mayor Sherman decided against reelection in 1937, a three-way race opened the door for an "outsider," disabled veteran Marvin A. Harlan. Harlan promised to restore salary cuts suffered by teachers and to derive more money from utilities serving the city. Harlan was elected in a runoff, but found it difficult to keep his promises; his attempts to attack vice led to a scandal involving the police department, and he was accused of wasteful spending. Harlan's attempt to link his program with that of President Franklin D. Roosevelt proved unsuccessful in the next election.[99]

Political issues and scandals involving the police department and facilities became a major source of conflict in San Diego during the 1930s, but as the 1920s began, the major issue was John D. Spreckels and his dominance of public affairs. A major economic boom was under way in San Diego, and Spreckels began to reap the benefits from his investment of millions of dollars of the family fortune in city enterprises. During lean times Spreckels had offered to lease the Spreckels Building to the city for use as a city hall; the planning commission rejected this offer from the perspective that Spreckels was already too powerful without actually owning city hall. The mayor fired the planning commission.[100]

When a Spreckels company requested a trolley streetcar franchise, the city was split into two camps, each circulating petitions favoring the franchise or demanding a vote. The city council broke with Spreckels and ordered an election which narrowly approved the franchise. At a dinner he gave for San Diego business leaders in 1923, as his active life was drawing to a close, Spreckels expressed his feelings:

> Some years ago, when some of our peanut politicians were warning San Diego not to fall for the crafty schemes of the foxy "Spreckels interests," a certain well-known wit and sage said that my name must be John Demented Spreckels because if I were not crazy I would not subject myself to this constant yelping of village curs, but would sell out my holdings, put all my money in government bonds, sail away on my yacht, and let San Diego go to hell—or look to the bunch of anti-Spreckels knockers to save the city, under the highminded leadership of the *San Diego Sun*.
>
> Gentlemen, he did not know me, or he would never have suggested a surrender on my part. Whatever else I may or may not be, I am not a quitter.[101]

In 1926 both Spreckels and his long-time opponent, E. W. Scripps, owner of the *Sun*, died.[102] Spreckels' last fight concerned the construction of El Capitan Dam to provide a dependable water supply. An alternate location was proposed by a group of business leaders organized by George W. Marston and Ed Fletcher. After two elections and charges of bribery, voters approved bonds for the project by a three-to-one margin. But it would be a decade before the project's completion.[103]

By the late 1920s a major campaign undertook to modernize local government and institute civic reforms. Complaints of lax law enforcement and of corruption prompted a Progressive-style charter amendment providing for a city manager system. Although the citizens approved the new charter in 1931, city councilmen were reluctant to relinquish their prerogatives. For the next few years there was a constant turnover of city managers and police chiefs. Divided government created gridlock in San Diego in the mid-1930s over such issues as the location of a new police station and the regulation of vice. Ultimately, the reform element triumphed when Mayor Percy Benbough obtained a council majority. Thus ended the "open town" concept, and the professionalization of the police began.[104]

Politics in the Mexican Border Towns

As part of his program to reestablish national authority during his presidency, Álvaro Obregón purged Matamoros' elected officials on 9 December 1923 and installed Luis Rendón to run the city. When the state government appointed a new police commander for Matamoros, Mayor Rendón and the entire council resigned, claiming that their civilian authority had been undermined. When the Tamaulipas governor (and future president) Emilio Portes Gil began a campaign of moral reform in 1924, new Mayor Prudecio Roiz launched a local version, removing corrupt officials and cracking down on the vice-oriented establishments resulting from U.S. Prohibition.[105]

A doubling of the population of the Matamoros *municipio* during the 1930s, due to repatriations from the United States and the migration of the unemployed from the interior, produced tensions affecting the local government. A massive protest demonstration by farmers forced the resignation of Mayor Rafael Munguía Cavazos in 1935. Succeeding administrations made some improvements in public services, but a new governmental crisis occurred in 1941, when the departing mayor turned over the government to Tomás de Saro instead of Antonio de León, who had won the election. Although the de Saro faction attempted to hold city hall, hunger finally forced them out, and de León took office on 4 January.[106]

An agricultural and tourism development similar to that in Matamoros stimulated the growth of Reynosa to such an extent that in 1926 the Tamaulipas government authorized the official designation of "city." Territorial expansion of the city in 1928 was presided over by a council headed by Lauro Herrero Olivares.[107] The political stability and establishment domination of Reynosa was evident in the election of four mayors from the Tarrega family between 1917 and 1963.

The still turbulent conditions in Mexico during the early 1920s were clearly reflected in the governmental instability of Nuevo Laredo. In 1920 the garrison commander loyal to the successful revolt of General Obregón named Felipe Zepeda as mayor. Zepeda served nearly a year, but during 1921 four different men occupied the mayor's chair. Zepeda returned as mayor in 1923, but on 9 September he was ousted by Col. Enrique Torres and a group of citizens supporting the national rebellion of Adolfo de la Huerta. Even when local government was restored under legitimate authority, the Nuevo Laredo officials were confronted by a federal agency, the Junta Federal de Mejoras Materiales, headed by the customs administrator and equipped with tariff revenues to be used for public works. Gen. Esteban Baca Calderon, the customs chief, is fondly remembered in Nuevo Laredo for the modern water and electric plans and other projects he funded. The city council remained fiscally impotent.[108]

As the Depression settled in, the financial condition of the Nuevo Laredo government became more precarious. Mayor Amado Gonzáles Palacios, who had held that office for a term during the 1920s, struggled desperately during the early 1930s to restore a bankrupt municipal treasury. A catastrophic flood on 3 September 1932 placed additional financial burdens on the council, which had to provide emergency means of housing and feeding refugees. Political problems surfaced in 1935, when rival groups claimed to be the city council; the Tamaulipas governor intervened, disowned both "councils," and named a civil administration *junta* to take charge. In 1941 the city inaugurated the new Municipal and Federal Palace.[109]

The impact of American tourism on Ciudad Juárez, inspired by Prohibition, filled the coffers of local, state, and national governments with taxes in the form of fees, licenses, and concessions. The income allowed the government to transform the city through beautification and public works projects. Additional expenses involved the usual political propaganda and campaigns as well as *mordidas*. Intermittent closure of the gambling establishments resulted in unanticipated shortages of funds and telegrams to President Obregón complaining of the Chihuahua state government's failure to return a fair share of the revenues to the city.[110]

The notoriety of the presumably immoral atmosphere on the border prompted federal officials to impose early closing times in casinos and bars. Ulises Irigoyen, a community spokesman, accused federal officials of applying a double standard:

> While in Mexico City high public officials and ordinary residents go to bed at 3 a.m., in Juarez we are ordered to be asleep by 9 p.m., as though we were school children. In the nation's capital married and single women of the aristocracy carry on intimately with prominent bureaucrats, while at the border every couple is expected to have a marriage certificate; and while the clinks of champagne glasses emanating from the elegant metropolis casinos are heard all the way to the border, people in the interior are alarmed when someone drinks a glass of wine or beer in Juarez.[111]

The Depression, repatriation, and the end of Prohibition both diminished tax revenue and provided additional demands for city services. Difficulties were so great that Ciudad Juarez mayors often held office only a few months. When President Lázaro Cárdenas abolished gambling in Mexico, city officials could barely maintain normal services, and the mayor called for a boycott of American goods and services in a spate of resentment and frustration. The situation became so critical that the city could not maintain the water supply. The council petitioned for a greater share of customs duties and sent a delegation to Chihuahua City to explain the crisis. The Chihuahua government did agree to provide some funds to the city council, and the federal government funded a new waterworks and an improved irrigation system.[112]

The beginning of World War II saw not only the end of the Depression but the influx of soldiers to border forts like El Paso's Fort Bliss. Prohibition in Texas inspired renewed tourist activity that tripled revenues between 1941 and 1942, enabling the Ciudad Juárez council to undertake new civic improvement projects which transformed the city into a modern metropolis.[113]

The relative isolation of the Baja California border towns from the rest of the Republic continued to manifest itself in certain unique political developments. The removal of Col. Esteban Cantú as *jefe politico* in 1917 created a power vacuum from which Mexicali never recovered. During the 1920s the Mexicali council engaged in quarrels which included the exchange of gunfire and accomplished little. In 1925 District Governor Abelardo Rodríguez (later president of Mexico) dissolved the existing council in hopes of restoring stability. The election of a new council produced no improvement and added charges of electoral fraud. Destitute of funds and operating under a legal cloud, the 1927 council resigned en masse. A *junta* appointed by Governor Rodríguez instituted unpopular economizing reforms, but by the time its tenure ended the federal government had abolished local governmental entities in all territories.[114]

In Tijuana the 1920s began with growing concern over vice-oriented entertainment for tourists controlled by foreigners. Mayor Luis G. Beltrán appointed Julio Dunn Legaspy as police chief, with orders to close the centers of vice. When the new chief actually carried out his instructions, the foreigners succeeded in having him removed, and the establishments reopened. During this era, Tijuana's local government was a delegation dependent on the *municipio* council in Ensenada; the district governor and the council did provide some public works, including concrete paving of the main streets and expansion of the safe water system.[115]

District Governor Abelardo Rodríguez purchased the springs of Agua Caliente in 1926 and entered into a deal with Americans to build a new hotel, casino, and dog track. Agua Caliente became a luxury attraction bringing income and revenue to Tijuana, but its termination under President Cárdenas' orders added to the Depression-era problems of the city. Representatives of the Tijuana Chamber of Commerce traveled to Mexicali in 1930 to meet with District Governor José María Tapia, who then accompanied them to Mexico City to apply for a free trade zone. Federal officials were sympathetic, but a free trade zone for Tijuana was not implemented until 30 August 1933. The zone was extended to include Mexicali in 1935.[116]

To this point there had been no consistency in the relations between twin towns in each set. In the nineteenth century, the towns had mainly been caught up in a tug-of-war over which side of the border would gain the upper hand economically. In the early twentieth century, the towns had see-sawed over the issue of what to do with the burgeoning population of poor proletariat residents, who were hustled from one side of the border to the other as the fortunes of the towns alternated by decades. However, this pattern was about to change with the advent of the 1940s. The problem of the unemployed masses was going to grow so critical that only federal attention from the two parent nations could expect to cope with it.

CHAPTER TEN

Family Growth:
Postwar Prospects and Problems

World War II kicked off a major new stage in the history of the border towns. The immense need for labor in the United States created by the war, alongside the continued development of farmlands on the Mexican side of the border, caused a logjam of desperate, unemployed people looking for work. The two national governments were forced at long last to address the problems of the border towns. A series of measures followed, none of them fully successful, from the *bracero* program through PRONAF and the *maquiladora* movement to the proposal for a free trade zone of North America.

The *Bracero* Program

World War II transformed the relationship between border towns once again. There was a notable upswing in goodwill and cooperation between twin town sets, comparable to but less muddied than what occurred in the period of the civil wars. This improved rapport resulted from Mexico joining the United States in declaring war against the Axis powers.[1] Matamoros and Brownsville were concerned over German submarines in the Gulf, where in 1942 several ships were sunk off the Texas and Mexican coasts.[2] Tijuana and San Diego experienced nervousness over a possible Japanese attack, reacting with camouflaged buildings and precautionary dim-outs to make their cities more difficult to locate at night.[3] The many soldiers stationed in American border towns boosted the local economies. The ration-

ing of goods on the American side provided an incentive for taking advantage of the unrestricted shopping possible in the Mexican border towns.[4]

The increased demand for Mexican raw materials and manufactured products for the American war economy increased trade and spurred industrial and agricultural development in Monterrey and elsewhere in the north of Mexico. Cotton farming was now mechanized on the Mexican side of the border. The demand for cotton brought the greatest increase of population in this period in towns which emphasized this crop, namely Mexicali, Cd. Juárez, Reynosa, and Matamoros.[5] The drafting of large numbers of young American men into the U.S. military created a major demand for Mexican labor in the United States. The result was an acceleration in migration of Mexican workers to towns on both sides of the border. This trend has never flagged since that time.[6]

Perhaps as much as two-thirds of the deportees of the 1930s returned in the 1940s to the United States.[7] A strengthening of the Mexican and working-class elements of the American border towns resulted, most markedly in Brownsville at the eastern end, closest to the Mexican heartland. In 1993 the U.S. border counties in which minorities constituted more than seventy-five percent of the population were concentrated along the Lower Rio Grande. The U.S. counties along the western end of the border mainly still had a majority of Anglos.[8] San Diego in 1989 was still predominantly white and middle-class, with only about seventeen percent Hispanics, nine percent Asians, and five percent blacks.[9] As more migrants crowded into the Mexican border towns than the United States could or would accept, the Mexican towns began rapidly to outpace their American twins in population.[10] A critical situation was created in towns on both sides of the border, but especially on the Mexican side. Unemployed or underemployed families huddled into slums without basic services of proper housing, street paving, electricity, water, sewage, telephones, health services, education, or law enforcement.

In an attempt to control the monster migration, from 1942 to 1964 the two countries experimented with the *bracero* program. This program issued identification cards to those Mexican workers who were permitted to cross to work for American factories, farms, and railroads. By 1960, four million workers, including men, women, and children, had participated. The *bracero* program also stimulated an increase in naturalization of Mexicans as American citizens, as a segment of employers preferred this route for their workers to the uncertainties of *bracero* and illegal labor.[11]

The Postwar Prosperity

After the war, devaluations of the peso in 1948 and 1954 caused a phenomenal increase in border crossings. Americans enjoying the prosperity that came with victory in the war visited the Mexican border towns for shopping and entertainment. In the 1940s and 1950s, Cd. Juárez's trade increased by 240 percent, that of Nogales, Sonora by 279 percent, Nuevo Laredo's by 311 percent, Matamoros' by 682 percent, Mexicali's by 878 percent, and Reynosa's by a whopping 35,533 percent.[12] This change in its fortunes boosted Reynosa for the first time into the rank of one of the major cities of the border. Previously, it had been a small town, counting only 4,830 inhabitants still in 1930. By 1980, it would boast almost 200,000. This late takeoff has given Reynosa, like McAllen, a very modern flavor. In contrast to neighboring Matamoros and Brownsville, Reynosa and McAllen lack a historical dimension. Even the old cathedral of Reynosa has been torn down and rebuilt in contemporary style, with nothing more than its old bell tower remaining from an earlier period.[13]

Concern arose in Mexico over the continuing minimal wages and unheathful working standards of the *braceros* on American farms. Most laborers were worked through all the daylight hours without proper sanitary facilities and then herded to sleep under the open sky or in tents and shacks. Furthermore, it was difficult to protect the workers since so many of them were illegals outside the *bracero* system. To try to correct this dilemma, the two countries in 1947 cooperated in calling all illegals to come to border check points. From there they would be briefly crossed back into Mexico and then readmitted into the United States as legal *braceros*. Yet this remedy, too, only spawned new problems, as word of the "drying out" or legalizing of the laborers caused a new rush of migration to the border from central Mexico.[14]

A wage dispute erupted in the El Paso area in October 1948, which caused the Mexican authorities to withhold *bracero* crossing permits locally pending a resolution. International relations became strained when U.S. Immigration ignored the Mexican ruling and unilaterally let 7,000 workers into the country in the space of a week. When Mexico retaliated by temporarily suspending the *bracero* agreement, illegal workers made it across the border anyway as either *mojados* ("wetbacks," the river crossers) or *alambristas* ("fence jumpers"). This turn of events merely brought the situation back to the lack of regulation that had prevailed before the *bracero* program.[15] A new version of the *bracero* program was accordingly worked out in 1949, prohibiting the recruiting of Mexican workers in border towns, adding points of worker protection, and limiting work contracts to six months.[16] In 1951 the Migrant Labor Agreement granted Mexican laborers stays of up to eighteen months on American soil, provided that they not be granted jobs desired by American workers. The Mexicans participating in the program were to receive minimum wages plus transportation from Mexico and back. Reception centers were set up on the U.S. side of the border.[17]

Even then, illegal workers accounted for the majority of the farm hands. A massive effort by the Eisenhower administration from May 1953 to July 1954 to round up the illegals, a move dubbed "Operation Wetback," incurred the displeasure of the Mexican government as many thousands of people a week were forced back into Mexican towns all along the border. New instant slums were created in the Mexican border towns, sometimes on the unused but risky riverbanks. One makeshift camp in Tijuana crammed 15,000 deportees onto the dry but flood-exposed bed of the Tijuana River.[18] This year of woes for the victims of governmental abuse was climaxed in the Lower Rio Grande area by the great flood of late June 1954, which swept in a roar of destruction through the shanty towns of Cd. Acuña and Nuevo Laredo downstream.[19]

Agricultural Towns

The upswing felt by all of the principal border towns in the post-World War II period resulted in most cases from the sale of farm products. Competition in cotton production pitted border towns of the Lower Rio Grande against those of Baja California del Norte, with the latter enjoying the advantage. Agriculture in Brownsville and McAllen continued to expand. Brownsville's economy depended all the more on its farming in this period since Fort Brown was closed down in 1944 and business at the Port of Brownsville was adversely affected by the war. The distance of the port from supply points ruled out its use by the military, while U.S. government control of the merchant marine caused its civilian use to drop off as well.[20] Once the war was over, the port served mainly to ship out agricultural produce, mainly cotton, fruits, and vegetables from farms on both sides of the river, along with oil and gas.[21] These products were augmented in the postwar period by fishing, with a special emphasis on shrimping.[22] The Water Treaty signed by the U.S. and Mexican governments in 1944 allowed the building of the Falcon and Amistad dams, which freed farmlands from much of the previous periodic flooding.[23] The postwar period also saw the start of a significant trend of tourism to Brownsville, with Americans coming south to enjoy the warm weather and bicultural flavor of the city "on the border by the sea."[24] These developments sufficed to keep Brownsville's population growing, from 18,000 in 1940 to 48,000 in 1960.[25]

In the postwar period, Matamoros reached the height of its cotton production. Its exports to Western Europe, Japan, Canada, and India competed well with the higher-priced U.S. cotton. Matamoros also processed this commodity, businessmen from both sides of the river building cotton gins, compressing plants, and cottonseed oil mills. A modern highway was completed between Matamoros and Cd. Victoria in 1945. Matamoros grew in this period to be Mexico's second most important port for exports and eighth for imports.[26] As 60,000 workers surged into Matamoros from farther south in Mexico, the town's population increased by forty-one percent in the 1950s, reaching 92,952 residents.[27]

Matamoros' biggest rival as a border cotton town was Mexicali, whose agro-industry allowed it to become the largest business center on the border, slightly ahead of Cd. Juárez.[28] The town also enjoyed a political importance as the state capital of Baja California del Norte.[29] Along with Tijuana and Tecate, Mexicali was also made the center of its own new *municipio*. Gaining a sense of local pride, the town held its first local history congress in 1954.[30] Its first high school was built in 1963.[31] Calexico, across the border, also provided employment for the people of Mexicali as it shared in the farm boom. Eighty-five percent of the workers in its Imperial Valley commuted from Mexicali.[32]

The danger that salty irrigation water could cake and ruin the soil led in 1961 to a quarrel between Mexicali and Calexico over the distribution of the fresher waters from the Colorado River. Having first pick, the Americans were using the fresher water and passing water with a higher salt content on south. The Mexican practice of spreading water thinly over fields compounded their problem. By the end of 1962, angry demonstrations were being staged in Mexicali. Mexican cartoonist RIUS sarcastically suggested that the Mexicali Valley's name would have to be changed to Salinas or "Salty." The tension was relaxed when, in January 1965, an agreement on the salt content of water released from Calexico to Mexicali was reached between the two countries. Yet, with the near exhaustion of the ground water sources along the watershed of the Colorado River, the problem was merely postponed rather than resolved.[33]

Towns Emphasizing Industry, the Military, and Trade

The largest American border towns, San Diego and El Paso — both along the western stretch — had a combination of industrial growth and military investment to thank for their size. World War II brought San Diego a spate of aircraft construction and other government industrial contracts, as well as naval, air force, and marine base development. Where Brownsville's distance from the European and Pacific fields of war deprived it of what government patronage it had been receiving, San Diego's strategic location as a good port facing Japan turned it even more than before into a military town. New residents poured in to fill jobs in the defense industry. Nor did the trend stop with victory in World War II, for on the heels of that confrontation came the Cold War, with the conflicts in Korea and Vietnam. Added to this stimulus, after World War II San Diego gave a major push to establish itself as a tourist center. The end of the war saw the development of Mission Bay as a resort area, while two years later the city's mud flats were reshaped into a recreational zone. Fancy hotels arose, including the El Cortez with its trendy exterior elevator in 1956. A highway tunnel was pierced through the mountains north of town for better access from Los Angeles. The San Diego Philharmonic Orchestra was launched in 1950. Institutions of higher education proliferated with the founding of the University of San Diego for Women in 1949, of California Western University in 1952, and of the University of San Diego in 1954. There was also continued growth at San Diego State College, which would become the University of California at San Diego in 1971.[34]

Its heavy dependence on government spending and American tourism made San Diego unique among the border cities in that its development rested on factors that basically had nothing to do with being a twin city. While Tijuana looked very much to San Diego, San Diego virtually ignored Tijuana. One result was the lack of a sense of economic and cultural interconnection between the two, in stark contrast to the rest of the sets of twin sister towns.[35]

El Paso experienced an expansion of its industrial base with the addition of such new industries as textile manufacturing, food processing, petroleum refining, and construction. Older industries such as copper smelting and natural gas also grew. The military presence in the city increased to where the U.S. government was the single largest employer in 1950.[36] Artillery and rocket and missile development were local specializations at Fort Bliss from 1946, the same year that Biggs Air Force Base opened.[37] Tourism increased. Agricultural growth continued as well, with thousands of legal and illegal Mexican farm hands working the cotton fields.[38] As a result, the population of El Paso mushroomed from 96,810 in 1940 to 276,687 in 1960.[39]

Subsoil minerals provided a basis for industrial growth in some of the smaller border towns as well. Oil and gas production emerged as a major industry for Reynosa, starting with the drilling of the first gas well in the area by PEMEX in 1944. The oil and gas was refined in Reynosa, and some of the petroleum was turned into polyethelene products at the town's petrochemical plants. The natural gas went first to Texas, and then, by the time production reached its height in 1958, to the industries of Monterrey and other northern Mexican cities.[40]

Eagle Pass also benefited in this period from oil production, with many oil wells being dug especially in the mid and late 1950s. Industries processing local raw materials included the Reynolds Fluorspar Plant, the Tejas Barite Plant, Maverick Beef Producers, and the Big River Catfish Farm. The resulting employment pulled enough workers from south of the river to give Eagle Pass a Mexican-American majority to its population by 1970.[41]

The increased mining of local tungsten and molybdenum to serve the war economy allowed Nogales, Sonora, to begin recovering from the expulsion of its Chinese residents in 1931. The recovery was further helped by American tourism. The town's Fiesta de Mayo was launched as a promotional project. Liquor stores, a bull ring, and restaurants appeared. One of the restaurants, El Jardín de la Caverna, built up the appetites of its sanguinary customers by staging boxing matches while they ate.[42]

Yuma grew in this period as an army town. A U.S. air force training base and a military equipment test station were built in its rain-free environs during World War II. From 6,000 residents in 1940, Yuma quadrupled to 24,000 in 1960.[43]

Nuevo Laredo's main advantage continued to be the trade through it on both trains and trucks. The town acted as Mexico's top port for exports in this period.[44] A new highway, opened from Cd. Guerrero in 1947, gave further impetus to the town's expanding commercial activity. By 1955, a public library, two daily newspapers, five radio stations, several literary groups, a Seminary of Mexican Culture, and an Institute of Fine Arts had sprung up.[45]

Towns Emphasizing Entertainment

The Mexican towns across from the new big industrial American cities were in a position to return to an emphasis on nightlife entertainment. These towns drew in American tourists, who were referred to as *gringos* (purportedly from the once popular song "Green Grow the Rushes, Oh" sung in the Mexican War), *güeros* ("blondes"), *bolillos* ("white rolls"), or *gabachos* (from the English word "garbage"). Tijuana attracted an especially lively business from San Diego, as did Cd. Juárez from El Paso. Matamoros, due to its lack of tourist facilities, failed to draw as much of the tourist trade from Brownsville as it might have done.[46]

Tijuana's American tourists were drawn at first from the swarms of soldiers stationed in San Diego and then after the war from civilians enjoying the postwar prosperity. Both sin industries and arts and crafts shops proliferated. However, the jobs opened up by tourism could meet the needs of only a small percentage of the thousands of job-seekers who pushed in from interior Mexico. Most of these immigrants were hoping for employment in California, but found themselves trapped in Tijuana by the difficulty of crossing the border.[47] As a result of these developments, Tijuana became and has remained the border's fastest-growing city.[48] From 16,486 inhabitants in 1940 it came to have 59,962 in 1950. This population increase warranted the granting of Tijuana's own *municipio* in 1954, governed by a seven-member municipal council. Tijuana's first daily newspaper, *El Heraldo*, started publication in 1941. A jai alai center was opened in 1947, a bull ring was built in 1960, and a new highway was cut through the coastal mountains to the beach. However, around the inner core of positive developments emerged a vast *Cartolandia* ("Cardboardland") of makeshift barrios, as replete with crime and promiscuity as they were void of water and other basic services.[49]

Cd. Juárez's restored nightlife entertainments placed an emphasis on serving GIs from El Paso.⁵⁰ The continuing prohibition in Texas on the sale of liquor by the drink gave an added incentive for crossing the river. Civilian fun-seekers followed in the tracks of the soldiers. Juárez also specialized in offering Americans quickie divorces, bringing in via El Paso "freedom rider special" flights from New York City. Charlie Chaplin, Ingrid Bergman, Tony Curtis, and Jane Mansfield were among those who availed themselves of the service. Draft dodgers from El Paso's Fort Bliss helped build up Cd. Juárez's American alien resident population to 30,000 by 1955. In all, Juárez's population shot up from 48,881 in 1940 to 252,119 in 1960, making it Mexico's fifth largest city.⁵¹

For local reformers, a return to the bad habits that had been overcome in the 1930s was disheartening. A local *dicho* reminds us that *"La primera vez es muchachada, la segunda es sinverguenzada"* ("The first time a woman loses her maidenhood; the second time she loses her sense of shame"). As in the 1920s, ineffectual protest reform movements sprang up in the Mexican towns affected. Such a campaign was led in Cd. Juárez in the early 1940s by Mayor Antonio Bermúdez. One of the town residents put the mood of indignation into verse:

> *¡No es la Sodoma! ¡Es Atenas!*
> *Del Norte brillante estrella,*
> *del Bravo hermosa sultana.*
> *Es Ciudad Juárez, la bella*
> *india gallarda y lozana*
> *que de su destino ufana*
> *se yergue altiva y descuella*
> *en la tierra mexicana.*⁵²

This might be roughly translated as:

> It's not Sodom! It is Athens!
> brilliant star out of the North,
> fair sultan of the Rio Grande.
> It's Ciudad Juárez, of Indian birth,
> gallant, exuberant, and grand,
> which with destiny-guided hand
> displays its proud and upright worth
> through the Mexican fatherland.

Politics and Government during the Post-World War II Era

If anything, the economic recovery occasioned by World War II and the consequent end of the Depression reinforced the political stability of the border towns. In Mexico, the government political party changed its name from "national revolutionary" to "institutional revolutionary," reflecting the bureaucratized stability of the political system. This systematized political stability percolated down to the municipal level. On the American side, the Democratic Party was so dominant that politics took place within the context of that party (through primary elections) or in the nonpartisan setting that existed in several towns.

Politics in the American Border Towns

In Brownsville, the challenge to the political establishment mounted by Robert Runyon had been crushed in the early 1940s. The traditional business elite supported the regime of Mayor Herbert L. Stokely, who held that office for a decade beginning in 1945. Stokely was the immediate past president of the chamber of commerce, so it was not surprising that his administration would focus on such projects as a new civic center. Favoritism toward the elite in a transfer of park land was the issue which sparked the rise of a new challenge to the establishment. Margal M. Vicars, a laundry operator, was encouraged to run against Stokely in 1955 by other civic-minded young businessmen and Robert Runyon, who became Vicars' political mentor and close friend.[53]

Given little chance of success by the *Brownsville Herald*, Vicars waged a Populist-style campaign charging the Stokely administration with excessive tax and utility rates, reflecting Runyon's original attack on the establishment in 1937. When Vicars appeared to have achieved a razor-thin victory, the *Herald* noted "a sort of numb shock" among supporters of Stokely, who feared "that an enormous tragedy had overtaken Brownsville, the sort of political calamity one would assert, if, say, Liberace had been elected President."[54] Vicars' triumph, however, was diminished by the defeat of most of his allies, including commission candidate Robert Runyon. Even Vicars' narrow victory was in dispute, and his election was overturned seventeen months later in a lawsuit that reached the Texas Supreme Court.[55]

Vicars sought and achieved vindication in the next election; not only was he narrowly elected, but the other members of his ticket won a commission majority. Vicars' team won by carrying the heavily Mexican working-class precincts while losing the well-to-do Anglo neighborhoods in an election which brought out seventy-five percent of the registered voters. In the process, Vicars had made promises to fund new projects while reducing taxes and public utility rates. In trying to fulfill these promises, the inexperienced commission majority ran up a large deficit, causing the city's auditors to recommend reductions in spending and "drastic steps to cut personnel costs." Vicars saw his commission majority crumble and then suffered a stunning rejection at the polls when he sought reelection. The 1950s ended with the elite establishment again in firm control of Brownsville's city government.[56]

If Brownsville experienced a moderate political earthquake, McAllen and Laredo felt scarcely a tremor. During this era, the political leaders of McAllen continued to be businessmen with relatively extensive commercial and farming interests, although a few lawyers served as candidates and officeholders. Mayors during this period usually had served on the city council. C. W. Davis served as mayor during parts of three administrations, and Phillip Boeye held the position through most of the 1950s.[57] A member of the Guerra family held a council seat throughout the period as part of the political "system." A threat to the controlled Mexican vote appeared after the end of World War II as returning veterans, with a greater awareness of their rights, joined a new generation of American educated white collar workers in expressing independence from the Guerra political operation. One group of veterans founded a Spanish-language weekly newspaper which attacked the local organization of Mexican businessmen dominated by the Guerras and their associates.[58]

As McAllen grew, its government became more sophisticated. The first city manager was appointed in 1943, and William L. Schupp held the position for many years beginning in 1946. A new and extensive city hall was constructed in 1950. The low turnover of city administrators, such as the city manager and the chief of police, was further evidence of limited political competition in the city.[59]

Returning Mexican-American veterans of World War II also participated in the politics of Laredo, but were apparently willing to do so within the confines of the long-dominant Independent Club machine. A clearly paternalistic and sometimes tyrannical operation, the Independent Club was respected by both state and national politicians for its ability to deliver votes for the Democratic Party. The club elected Hugh Cluck to the mayor's office in 1940, and he held that post for fourteen years. Cluck was succeeded by J. C. "Pepe" Martin, Jr., grandson of the nineteenth-century political boss, Raymond Martin. On the few occasions when opponents appeared to challenge club-supported mayors, they were defeated by margins of two-to-one or more.[60]

Unlike the nonpartisan process in the other border towns, political decision-making in El Paso occurred within the Democratic Party. The Democrats were not tightly structured, however, and competitive factions scored electoral successes in the late 1940s. The *El Paso Herald*, claiming to speak for the "little people," supported Dan Duke, a railroad locomotive engineer, in unseating the incumbent, a wealthy industrialist in 1950. The rival *El Paso Times* supported a committee of some 200 of the business and professional leaders seeking outstanding candidates for public office. The *Times* and the committee backed fellow committee member Fred Hervey for mayor in 1952 and ousted Duke, the incumbent. Mayor Hervey served two very successful terms, and was succeeded by another committee-selected candidate.[61]

The 1950s was a period of physical as well as economic expansion. During his two terms, Mayor Fred Hervey brought in a new water supply, enabling new residential development, and annexed areas near the Rio Grande. The addition of perhaps 40,000 overwhelmingly Mexican-American citizens ironically served to undermine the Anglo political dominance of El Paso. As was the case in other border towns, second- and third-generation Mexican-Americans were entering clerical and service occupations, obtaining more education, and becoming more aware of their rights as Americans. Here as elsewhere, the catalyst for political involvement was the activist attitude of World War II veterans. In 1958 young, charismatic County Clerk Raymond Telles announced his candidacy for mayor. Telles' candidacy inspired record numbers of Mexican-Americans to pay the poll tax and register to vote.[62]

Telles' candidacy was strongly opposed by the influential business community and their committee, but he did have the support of the *Herald-Post* and had assembled his own team of reputable Anglo council candidates. In an election which received national attention, Telles and his team won a substantial victory. Some in the business community claimed embarrassment that their city had elected a

Mexican mayor, but many proved willing to adapt to the new situation. Mayor Telles acted with caution, sensitivity, and competence. By the time of the next election, Telles had so convincingly reassured the business and political influentials of his commitment to traditional political paths that he was able to run unopposed with tacit business support. It was generally believed that "distrust among Anglo-Americans resulted from their failure to recognize that ethnic Americans have been absorbing the beliefs, sentiments and values of the dominant culture for years."[63]

The issue of ethnicity had also proven important in San Diego at the beginning of the era. In this case, however, the issue did not concern Mexican-Americans, who constituted less than five percent of the population even after a fifty percent increase during World War II. At the start of the war, it was the Japanese and Japanese-American population that raised concerns. The San Diego city council did not wish to confront the issue directly, electing instead to forward to the Federal Bureau of Investigation a report suggesting their removal from the area.[64]

Strategically located, San Diego underwent a tremendous population growth during World War II. At the close of the war, city leaders were determined to hold on to the economic gains the war had provided. As stated in a chamber of commerce report, "We have these industries and payrolls. Our business and economic life has been geared to them." The report concluded that "we have no alternative than to bring about a retention of those payrolls and plan for the orderly development of a City and County to accommodate them."[65] In 1943 San Diego gained a leader for its development strategy in Mayor Harley E. Knox, a dairy owner. Mayor Knox and other leaders knew that water was the key to San Diego's future, and that water was across the mountains in the Colorado River. San Diego joined a county water authority and sought federal support, but it was not until late 1947 that a seventy-one-mile aqueduct was placed in service, barely in time to avert rationing.[66]

Mayor Knox and the planning director, Glenn C. Rick, anticipating the loss of industrial payrolls, turned to the development of recreation facilities to attract tourists. The administration secured voter approval for a bond issue to develop an aquatic playground at Mission Bay and pushed ahead with dredging plans. A reluctant Mayor Knox joined the effort to establish a mall of government buildings in order to get a convention hall, which he regarded as essential, but the mall project was defeated by the voters on several occasions by substantial margins. Knox also led the fight to create public parking lots in the downtown area.[67]

Years earlier, political and police corruption had caused the voters to adopt a city charter limiting the power of elected officials. Mayors and councils chafed under these restrictions, but the voters resisted changes, often defeating pay raises for elected officials. Eventually, some pay raises were approved, but the city manager system remained unchanged despite the rapid growth of the city and its government.[68]

Politics in the Mexican Border Towns

The nearly complete absence of autonomy in the local governments of Mexico was readily apparent during this era. The politically absolutist national system usually functioned under the guise of constitutional legitimacy, but the leadership of the ruling party frequently resorted to violence and thuggery to intimidate opponents. This was especially true in Matamoros after World War II. In 1947 the Tamaulipas governor, Hugo Pedro González, accused of ordering the assassination of a Tampico newspaper publisher, was replaced by Gen. Raúl Gárate. The new governor, in turn, forced Matamoros Mayor Ramiro Hernández to step down, and replaced him with Leonides Guerra. In 1948 the locally chosen PRI candidate, Cruz Villarreal, was opposed by Governor Gárate's hand-picked candidate, Ernesto Elizondo. Villarreal was verified as the winner of the election, and President Miguel Alemán came to Matamoros for his inauguration, but Elizondo hired gunmen and seized control of city hall in December of 1949. Supported by the governor, Elizondo unleashed a reign of terror on the local populace and Mayor Villarreal was jailed. Villarreal was released when he agreed to retire from politics, leaving Elizondo as mayor.[69]

Operating without hindrance, Mayor Elizondo razed some buildings and constructed others, including schools, and established a water and sanitation department. But when he shut down Boys Town, the lucrative prostitution center, Elizondo may have gone too far. Three weeks later, the mayor and his bodyguard were gunned down; suspicion of guilty knowledge fell on the police department, but no action was taken. Elizondo's friend and successor, Juan B. García, was the victim of a reform movement prompted at the national level by President Adolfo Ruiz Cortines. Both García and his patron, the Tamaulipas governor, came under attack by an anti-corruption campaign named Acción Cívica. Demonstrations launched by Acción Cívica in Matamoros led to a mob siege of city hall and culminated in Mayor García's resignation. In 1957 a new city hall rose on the site of the 1831 version under the next elected mayor, Augusto Cárdenas Montemayor, as the turmoil began to subside.[70]

The power relationship between state and local officeholders, so evident in Matamoros, manifested itself in Nuevo Laredo at the beginning of this era. Mayor Pedro Gonzáles, who took office at the beginning of 1945, had the satisfaction of seeing his son, Hugo Pedro Gonzáles, become governor of Tamaulipas. The tremendous growth of the city resulting from World War II produced many public improvements for Nuevo Laredo, but not under the auspices of the municipal government. The closing of Mexican gulf ports during the war had caused many customs brokers to transfer their operation to Nuevo Laredo, and the surge of trade across the border provided ample revenues for the Junta Federal de Mejoras Materiales. Col. Rafael M. Pedrajo, chief of customs, began a program of improving the water and electricity plans and paving streets, but his work was interrupted when he was shot by a subordinate at the customs office.[71]

Governor Hugo Pedro Gonzáles, suspected of complicity in the murder of a newspaper publisher, was removed from office at the orders of President Miguel Alemán owing to the national scandal. As in Matamoros, the new governor, Gen. Raúl Gárate, ousted the elected municipal officials and substituted an appointed civil administration. By the time of the next election, the term of office had been extended to three years. The new mayor in 1949 was Juan de Dios Hinojosa, local chief of the national labor union (CTM), which formed a part of the dominant political party, Partido Revolucionario Institucional (PRI). Hinojosa and his successors continued development projects, especially school construction, aided by public works emanating from the Junta de Mejoras Materiales, now separated from the customs administration. The effectiveness of the *junta* was limited, however, by the frequent turnover of administrators, amounting to twelve in a period of six years.[72]

The resources of Nuevo Laredo and its government were sorely tested by a great flood which occurred on 30 June 1954, despite the completion of Falcon Dam the previous year. President Ruiz Cortines rushed to the stricken city to focus attention on the magnitude of the disaster and to mobilize national relief aid. The municipal government and the local *junta* did what they could, but were over-whelmed; a Junta de Socorros was established to coordinate relief efforts.[73]

The growth of entertainment-oriented tourism before and during World War II brought development and prosperity to Ciudad Juárez, but at a price. City leaders were disturbed by the growing reputation of their city as a den of iniquity. In the early 1940s, Mayor Antonio J. Bermúdez launched a reform campaign, supported by the governor and President Manuel Ávila Camacho, aimed at eradicating the drug and prostitution vices. Bermúdez achieved some success, but conditions returned to "normal" under his successors. The growth posed additional problems for the city in the form of water shortages in the late 1940s, resulting in lack of water and sewer services for three-fourths of the city. City officials provided new wells, pipes, and greater water pressure, but the influx of migrants continued to strain even these improvements.[74]

During the 1950s, conscientious efforts on the part of the local administrations "fostered the proliferation of social, cultural, and economic institutions, giving Juárez a new look."[75] The tawdry image of the city began to abate somewhat: the Mexico City periodical *Punto*, and others, praised the administration of Mayor Pedro N. García for public works and social reforms. Despite the improvements, García's successor, Mayor René Mascareñas Miranda, reported at the close of the decade that "municipal revenues fail to increase at rate of the demand for public services because the income level of the great majority of . . . families barely allows for the satisfaction of basic needs, and they are unable to contribute toward public expenditures."[76]

The inability of the city administrations to overcome the multitude of urban problems facilitated the growth of political opposition among the business and professional community. Mexican business influentials condemned the widespread bossism and corruption in government, and resented government controls. Juárez chamber of commerce leaders and other businessmen formed a civic association and successfully managed a campaign to remove the Chihuahua governor in 1955. Civic association leader René Mascareñas Miranda was selected as the PRI candidate for mayor in 1956, but other association members supported Mascareñas' business partner, who was nominated by PAN (Partido Acción Nacional), a conservative, business-oriented party. A hard-fought campaign produced an exceedingly

close election won by the PRI candidate. By 1959, politics had
returned to normal with a traditional PRI candidate winning a big
victory over a PAN nominee. The government party had responded
effectively to local discontent, but in the process real partisan competition had begun in Ciudad Juárez.[77]

There was no partisan competition in the Baja California cities
at the beginning of this era for the simple reason that there was no
local self-government prior to 1953, because local political divisions
had dissolved in the 1920s. By the late 1940s, however, the territory
had grown so rapidly that representatives of Mexicali and Tijuana
joined those from the other cities in a formal petition for statehood.
President Miguel Alemán fulfilled a campaign promise by endorsing
the petition, and the Mexican constitution was amended to provide
for the creation of the new state. The new government of Baja California established the Organic Municipal Law, which provided legal
status for municipal governments in Mexicali and Tijuana.[78]

The first city councils of the new era of municipal government
took office in March of 1954. Most of the changes in city government dealt with procedural questions involving elections and holding office. Political power was completely in the hands of the PRI,
and municipal offices were political rewards for PRI activists or members of unions or *ejidos* which sponsored the local PRI. In the Mexicali
council, positions could function as rewards because the council had
no real decision-making authority. Mayors (council presidents) came
from the business elite of Mexicali, and were of a different social
level from the council members. The major goal of the council was
the promotion of economic growth, but much time and effort was
expended in providing traditional services. There was little interest
in regulation of business, and the council routinely deferred to the
business community.[79]

The political system in Tijuana bore a marked similarity to that
in Mexicali. The Tijuana municipal government had to face the problems of extremely rapid growth without the funding provided by the
national government during the territorial period. The major challenge was providing public services for the population explosion, and
local tax resources were inadequate. The major power sources were
found outside the local government, either in the state capital,
Mexicali, or Mexico City, or in the business community. The chamber of commerce was the most powerful local influence on government, having many overlapping memberships with both the PRI and
the council and even providing quasi-governmental functions.[80]

Failure of the *Bracero* Program

By 1964, the *bracero* movement, which had failed to either control the flow of Mexican workers into the United States or to alleviate the flood of unemployed residents into the border towns, was brought to an end. By this time, the great expansion of the farming economy had finished. Salt accumulation in the soil and excessive competition from too many areas of production caused the cotton boom to come to an abrupt halt in 1962. Mechanization of farming had also progressed to the point where the farms no longer needed the large numbers of workers required in the past.[81] The border towns were faced with a pressing need to find other outlets for employment and new plans for winning elusive prosperity.[82] The *bracero* program had failed to provide a lasting solution; new programs were about to appear.

CHAPTER ELEVEN

Parental Rapprochement: The *Maquiladora* Era

The twin sisters had grown up in a dysfunctional family, torn between quarreling parent nations. The dream of parental harmony dies hard, often lingering on into the adulthood of the affected children. Just as the troubled relations between those parent nations threatened to explode into a new row, a common project unexpectedly began to draw them together.

In the 1960s, the growing numbers of Hispanics in the American Southwest combined with the American civil rights movement to rally some of the border town residents behind a demand for more justice to Mexican-Americans. El Paso's city council in this decade insisted on equal access to rental and purchase housing.[1] Some Mexican-Americans joined the Chicano movement's call for an independent Spanish-speaking homeland for the Mexican-Americans carved out of the territory conquered by the United States in the Mexican-American War.[2]

For its advocates, such a Chicano nation would be a reclamation of the Mexican-Americans' original homeland, termed Aztlán. The historical basis for this claim rested on the fact that the Mexican-Americans were principally Mexicans sharing a partial blood inheritance from the Uto-Aztecan Toltec and Aztec tribes. The Uto-Aztecans had originally conquered their way into Mexico in the ninth century, coming out of their original homeland of Aztlán. This area from which they had been expelled by invading Athabascan Apaches and Navajos pushing south from Canada was that region later known as the U.S. Southwest. Thus, Mexican immigrants into the American border region were merely returning to their ancestral homeland.

In 1965 Chicano leaders at the University of Texas at El Paso demanded Mexican-American faculty members, administrators, and regents. Courses in Chicano studies with supporting library materials were also requested. One of the campus political science professors called on Mexican-Americans to vote for Chicano goals. As the movement gained steam, a student protest demonstration held in 1971 tried to occupy the Administration Building. Although thirty students were arrested, the demonstration attained its goal of bringing a change in administration, with a new policy of hiring Mexican-Americans. A dozen years later, Hispanics represented the largest ethnic group among UTEP's students. In 1972 the local schools launched a bilingual education program, and in 1977 the city elected its second Mexican-American mayor.[3]

The notion of claiming cultural lineage from the Uto-Aztecans of the region, who included a component of the colorful and civilized Pueblo Indians, helped inspire a notable creative outburst of Chicano art and writing. On the other hand, the idea of an independent Mexican-American nation (a recurring one with a certain parallel to the Québec Libre Movement in Canada) could have created rising tensions between Hispanics and Anglos, with repercussions for international relations along the border. Instead, attention was soon drawn away by the major new opportunities opened up with the start of the *maquiladora* program.

The settlement of the Chamizal dispute in 1967 heralded the transformation of the intercultural mood from conflict to cooperation. The Chamizal, a 400-acre tract of *chamiza* ("desert brush") land, had been transferred from the south bank to El Paso by a shift of the river in 1864. Mexico had continued to claim the strip, and an international arbitration commission in 1911 had approved Mexico's claim, but the United States had been reluctant to agree. President John Kennedy, eager for Mexican support in the deteriorating relations between the United States and Castro's Cuba, had signed a treaty in 1963 dividing the disputed territory between the two nations.[4] Mexico received 630 of the disputed acres, the United States 193 acres. Kennedy's successor, President Lyndon Johnson, who had supported the treaty, on 28 October 1967 in El Paso officially transferred the Mexican part of the Chamizal to Mexican President Gustavo Díaz

Ordaz. The two nations left a memorial of the new international amity in the developments they constructed on their respective parts of the Chamizal. The Mexican side sprouted a spacious park with a monument and waterfalls, a modern customhouse, and some buildings of the University of Juárez. The American side gave rise to a museum, theater, and landscaped grounds.[5]

The Crisis at the End of the *Bracero* Program

The Chicano movement's potential for disruption was increased by the crisis that followed the ending of the *bracero* program. In 1961, as the program began to unwind, the layoff of many thousands of Mexican workers left hordes of these displaced persons wandering the streets of the Mexican border towns. Cd. Juárez alone contained 20,000 unemployed heads of families. The situation after the last gasp of the program in 1964 was all the worse.[6]

The dilemma in Tijuana was exacerbated by problems in San Diego's economy which forced record numbers of Mexicans back across the border. Convair Aircraft Company, the city's largest employer, laid off thousands of workers due to the failure of its jet transport program. Other layoffs in the city's aerospace industry followed, along with cutbacks in the federal defense budget. The city's business fell by as much as forty percent, creating an 8.9 percent unemployment rate and a local depression. San Diego tried to readjust by drawing in still more tourists. In 1964 the San Diego Cultural Center and the new 1,000-acre campus of the University of California at San Diego opened. That same year, Sea World Aquatic Park arose on Mission Bay and did its part by drawing in one million nonresident visitors a year. Also in that momentous year, Mission Bay saw the addition of beach, marina, and fishing dock developments. The Balboa Park aerospace museum, a civic theater, and a cultural center were launched in 1965. The fame of the San Diego Zoo brought in more visitors than any other California attraction except Disneyland. The San Diego Padres baseball team was founded in 1969.[7]

Yet the tourist industry proved to be no replacement for the lost military contracts and industrial jobs. In August 1965, San Diego was shaken by race riots sparked by massive unemployment. The *Free Press*, an underground paper, stirred such unrest with its attacks on the alleged corruption of local business leaders and on the local Copley Press (with its two city newspapers) that in 1969 the *Free*

Press offices were broken into and its presses destroyed. A subsequent underground paper, the *Street Press*, ran into harassment as well, as one of its fundraising parties in 1970 was disrupted by the city police. The papers' allegations of local shenanigans were borne out, however, when in 1970 Mayor Curran and eight fellow members of the city council were charged with bribery and conspiracy in planning a taxi rate increase. In 1976 city management was also accused by the U.S. Justice Department of racist bias in its hiring.[8]

The Mexican Response to the Border Dilemma

The Mexican government tried two major programs to lift the Mexican border towns out of their dilemma. The first program, PRONAF, failed in its goals, while the second, the *maquiladora* program, exerted a major impact.

The Programa Nacional Fronterizo, or PRONAF, introduced in 1961, was an attempt to boost the economies of the Mexican border towns by drawing in more tourism. Changes included modernization, the construction of hotels, museums, and arts and crafts centers, and the attachment of tax and freight subsidies to articles sold along the border. The results were generally disappointing. Stores in the American border towns continued to enjoy a more thriving business. Success in this period was greatest in Tijuana and Nuevo Laredo, thanks to their location on major crossing points close to American population centers. The success was least in Cd. Juárez, which was too remote from American centers of population, despite the pouring of thirty percent of the PRONAF budget into the latter city compared to a little over ten percent going to Tijuana. Juárez was graced with a new PRONAF complex complete with a convention center, stores, an arts and crafts center, an art gallery and history museum, restaurants and hotels, as well as a bull ring, racetrack, and country club not far away. Unfortunately for the program, the American tourist masses headed elsewhere, while Mexican tourists continued to enjoy shopping in the American border towns.[9]

The second main period of nightlife tourist industry which had started with World War II now also came to an end, as the United States relaxed its morality laws. Beginning in 1970, Texas again permitted liquor to be sold by the drink, and topless and bottomless bars were again allowed to stay open to late hours. Drugs, prostitutes, and X-rated movies became easily accessible in the American towns. The American soldiers who had until recently spearheaded patronage of the Mexican sin industry were, at the end of the Vietnam War, mainly relocated from the border, which began to resemble the demilitarized U.S.-Canadian border over much of its extent.[10] The Mexican border town quickie divorce service was also halted by a new ease of divorce in the United States and by a Mexican law of 1971 which limited divorces to Mexican citizens and permanent residents.[11]

In 1971 these original measures were supplemented by the program of *artículos ganchos*, which allowed Mexican border towns to bring in certain U.S. commodities duty-free for local sales. The idea was to make Mexican stores competitive with their American counterparts for these key products. It was intended that this would act as a "hook" (*gancho*) to catch the Mexican buyer, who would then be lured into also buying the more expensive Mexican goods (which had to represent at least half of all goods in each store). Special efforts continued to be made to help Cd. Juárez, including the building of the Rio Grande Mall, the largest such shopping center on the Mexican side of the border, stocked with "hook" items. Nowhere did the scheme function as hoped; most Mexican buyers refused to be hooked, swimming right past the bait to the yummier feeding-grounds on the other side. Indeed, business in the Mexican towns was hurt that same year by a rise in Mexican gas prices, discouraging those Americans who had been crossing the border to buy gas and, coincidentally, other items. Store owners in Cd. Juárez were so exasperated that they managed to block streetcar service between the two cities, in the desperate hope that this would discourage Mexican shoppers from crossing the bridge.[12]

Yet, as is so typical in border town history, the darkest hour of hostility preceded a new dawn of closer relations. The following period was to draw the twin cities closer together than had hitherto been thought possible.

The *Maquiladora* Program

By the time that PRONAF, along with the *artículos ganchos* program, had clearly failed, another plan of the Mexican government was beginning to catch hold, with much greater promise for the future of the Mexican border towns. The *maquiladora*, or twin plant, system had been started as the Border Industrialization Program in 1965. This plan induced American factories to set up a small American-dominated management plant on the U.S. side of the border, controlling a large assembly plant with at least ninety percent Mexican workers on the south side of the border. Components and nonprecious metals were allowed to cross to the assembly plants free of duty. The manufactured parts were permitted back into the United States for final assembly and processing, with nothing more than a ten percent value-added tax imposed. This program attracted so much American industry that by 1975, thirty-seven percent of American foreign-assembled goods were being put together in Mexico. Tijuana, with Cd. Juárez right behind it, attracted the lion's share of the new twin plants. A significant number of Mexicans also continued to cross the border to work in American agriculture, industry, sales and services, authorized by green cards granted by the U.S. border authorities. Mexican maids in American households generally came in by holding the so-called "mica," a seventy-two-hour permit designed for shoppers, not for workers. When U.S. border guards tried to crack down on dishonest entries of this sort in the mid-1970s, feelings soured, causing repeated attacks on border guards.[13]

The devaluations of the peso, starting with its fall in 1976-1977 and again in 1982, greatly decreased the cost of Mexican labor, giving a further incentive to American industries for relocation on the border. The devaluation also accomplished what the *gancho* program had failed to do—to attract a surge of buying to the Mexican border towns. The Mexican consumer now lacked purchasing power to shop in the U.S., while American buyers were drawn by the cheap rates to shop on the Mexican side. At the same time, the devaluation dealt the coup de grâce to the old *gancho* scheme by making American goods too expensive to sell in Mexico, even without duties added. Business, hard-hit in the American border towns, shifted to their Mexican twin towns.[14]

Impact of the *Maquiladoras* on Key Towns

Almost two-thirds of all border plants were located in the western cities of Tijuana (with 530 plants), Cd. Juárez (with 320), and Mexicali (with 154).[15] Tijuana specialized in food packing and construction *maquiladoras*, where Cd. Juárez emphasized electronics plants. Juárez experienced the worst pollution problem, although Matamoros gained its own unenviable reputation for the pollution from its Química Fluor plant.[16] A major new infusion of capital into the Mexican border towns resulted. Cd. Juárez's budding electronics plants were set up by such companies as RCA, General Electric, and Sylvania.[17] Juárez held the position of the second-largest city on the border, after San Diego, and the largest Mexican border city, with 567,365 people in 1980. Mexicali was right behind, with 510,664 inhabitants, followed by Tijuana with 461,257.[18] Cd. Juárez had become Mexico's sixth largest city in 1970, with Mexicali its seventh and Tijuana its eleventh largest. By 1990, Tijuana had passed up Mexicali, with Cd. Juárez holding 797,679 inhabitants, Tijuana 742,686, and Mexicali 602,390.[19]

Maquiladoras were not so dominant in the growth of Tijuana as in the cases of Cd. Juárez and Mexicali. In 1983 the *maquiladoras* were still providing only ten percent of Tijuana's jobs. The main money-maker there remained tourism. Californians were lured across the border by the cultivation of the Mexican border's mystique in popular songs romanticizing the wasting effect of tequila consumption and other border pastimes. Branches of big-name stores were built, and flood control construction started in 1972. The worst of the local slums was resettled in a housing development by 1976.[20] In contrast, tourism in Mexicali was little developed, due to the tiny size of its twin town Calexico, which was a mere one-fiftieth its size, and due to tourists being drawn away to the magnet of Tijuana.[21]

Tijuana now joined San Diego in becoming a cultural center, with the founding in the 1960s of associations of writers, of composers, of geographers, and of historians. Theaters and dance groups sprang up on all sides, while local art, including mural painting, flourished. It is remarkable how fast this development occurred, considering that Tijuana's first daily newspaper had started only in 1941. Among the new cultural institutions were the Casa de la Cultura in 1977 and the Instituto de Cultura y Arte Latinoamericano in 1981.[22] In 1983 a new Centro Cultural was completed, called La Bola for its ball-like appearance. The complex included an omnitheater, a performing arts center, an anthropological museum, and a restaurant, alongside other features.[23] A literary review, *Juventud*, was started, and a series of local radio broadcasts inspired the founding in 1960 of an annual drama contest. Local writing that addressed border themes began to receive national recognition. Tijuana is described as it was in the 1920s in Dashiell Hammett's detective story "The Golden Horseshoe" and as it was in the 1960s in Rosina Conde's "Revolutionary Vignettes," while the plight of illegal border crossers is dramatized in Hugo Salcido's play "The Journey of the Minstrels." The town's first art studio opened in 1962, followed by an exhibit of the work of local painters the next year.

Tijuana's transformation in higher education was part of this cultural emergence. The Universidad Autónoma de Baja California, which had been established in 1957, grew to over 8,000 students. The transformation of the Hotel Agua Caliente into the local Instituto Tecnológico was completed in 1971, followed in 1978 by the start of a teachers' university. In 1980 appeared the Centro de Estudios Fronterizos, which spun off various Colegios de la Frontera del Norte through the other Mexican border cities all the way to Matamoros. The next year, the Universidad Iberoamericana, emphasizing graphics, architecture, and law, opened its doors.[24]

Tijuana's emphasis on winning the tourist dollar was shared by Nogales, Sonora, which attracted visitors from burgeoning Tucson and Phoenix. The city reached a population of 107,000 in 1990, dwarfing Nogales, Arizona, with its population of 15,000. Little Sonoita, Sonora, also drew in its share of American tourists, thanks to the neighboring Organ Pipe Cactus National Monument and to the growing popularity of the beach at Puerto Peñasco on the Gulf of California to the south.[25]

The cities of the eastern end of the border were not so far behind their western counterparts in number of workers employed in the *maquiladoras* as they were in number of plants. While Cd. Juárez accounted for the majority of *maquiladoras* workers, with 134,838 employees, and Tijuana came next with 58,590, Matamoros came in third with 38,268 and Reynosa fourth with 30,000. The most elaborate of the industrial parks were also located in Cd. Juárez, Tijuana, and Matamoros.[26] Matamoros, chosen as pilot city for the *maquiladora* program, had begun to be affected already by 1965. Almost every couple of years brought Matamoros new developments. That same year of 1965, a major street paving program was completed, a bigger customs building arose, and tourist shops and stores proliferated. Two years later, air service was opened to Mexico City and La Paz. In 1969 the local Academia de Bellas Artes was founded.[27] In 1972 the Instituto Tecnológico and a medical school of the University of Tamaulipas were both founded.[28] Matamoros in 1990 was still the largest city on the eastern end of the border, with 303,392 inhabitants, closely followed by Reynosa with 281,618 and by Nuevo Laredo with 217,912. It had also become the largest city in Tamaulipas.[29]

Some of the smaller Mexican border towns likewise enjoyed a new impetus from the *maquiladoras*. By 1967, Nogales, Sonora, was experiencing a population explosion under the impact of various new *maquiladoras*, including a Motorola plant, in addition to the tourist trade discussed earlier. In 1972, Nogales was enabled to found the Instituto Tecnológico, and subsequently a teachers' university and an Association for Cultural Advancement.[30] From 1968, Reynosa brought in a wide variety of factories. The Zenith plant alone employed several thousand workers.[31] The resulting wealth found expression in a new cultural institution, the Ateneo de Reynosa, to promote the arts and education.[32]

The American twin towns also benefited from the *maquiladora* industry. San Diego in 1980 held the first position for size among border towns, with 875,538 residents, making it the only large American border city which was larger than its Mexican twin. By 1990, San Diego had grown to over one million people, making it California's second-largest city.[33] It was also the fastest growing city in the United States, with a gross annual product larger than that of Greece. Except for sewage contaminating the river coming from Tijuana, in contrast to some of the other cities on the border San Diego has had little problem with pollution. This blessing is the result of the type of industry that has taken root there, such as high tech, aerospace, medical research, and electronics. The quality of life has been further enhanced by its many parks, good health care, a good urban transportation system, and acclaimed university and research centers (including the Salk Institute, founded in 1963).[34]

El Paso grew from 276,000 residents in 1960 to 425,259 in 1980, making it the fifth largest city on either side of the border. The concept of the motel sprang up locally to accommodate the growing numbers of visitors coming by car, Camp Grande on El Paso's Alameda being one of the earliest of the type. The year 1969 saw the founding of both El Paso Community College and of the Texas Tech Regional Academic Health Center. A highway which was opened in 1970 over Mount Franklin facilitated contact between the two sides of town. The city's new Exhibition Hall and civic center opened in 1972. Whereas Tijuana's center was built in the shape of a ball, El Paso's took the form of a sombrero. In 1979 the nearby Franklin Range was converted into a state park, with a museum, nature trail, and replicas of early Indian dwellings. The Association of Borderland Scholars was founded in 1976, followed by the Center for Inter-American and Border Studies. Endowed by 1980 with libraries, museums, a symphony orchestra, ballet, theaters, and a zoo, El Paso joined San Diego as the second cultural center on the border.[35]

The combined impact of *maquiladoras* and tourism allowed Laredo to continue growing despite the closing of Laredo Air Force Base in 1973. Local manufacturing emphasized the production of Levis, shoes, hats, electronic wares, plastics, and metals, including the only antimony smelter in the United States. In 1974 Laredo enjoyed the status of being America's largest inland port on the basis of dollar value of imports (three-fourths of the worth of its goods in transit coming into the United States) and exports (into Mexico).[36]

Brownsville became one of the fastest-developing Texas cities, and its port began a new period of growth in the late 1980s.[37] In 1980 Brownsville was in second place for population among the American cities of the eastern end of the border, behind Laredo's 91,449 inhabitants, with its own 84,997 residents. McAllen followed with 67,042.[38] Much of the building spurt (especially in houses and condominiums, but including modern shopping malls) in Brownsville and nearby Padre Island were stimulated by newly affluent Mexican middle-class investors and shoppers.[39] American tourists and winter visitors also brought in wealth.[40] In 1971 the Gladys Porter Zoo was added to the attractions.[41] In 1973 upper-division and graduate courses became available on the local campus of Texas Southmost College. This cooperative effort would lead to the merger of the two institutions in 1991 to form the University of Texas at Brownsville.[42]

The *maquiladora* era created three giant agglomerations toward the western end of the border: San Diego/Tijuana with 1,337,000 residents in 1980, Cd. Juárez/El Paso with 992,000 residents, and Mexicali/Calexico with 524,000.[43] The western part of the border grew much more than the eastern portion due to the pull of the Californian economy, which was much stronger than its Texan counterpart.[44] The three more modest leading urban clusters of the eastern end of the border in 1980 were Matamoros/Brownsville, with 324,000 residents, Nuevo Laredo/Laredo, with 294,000, and Reynosa/McAllen, with 278,000.[45]

New Problems Created by the *Maquiladoras*

As in the case of earlier programs, the success of the *maquiladora* system, while bringing major new employment to alleviate the existing local poverty, attracted huge numbers of job-seekers from the exploding population of interior Mexico, Central America, and even the Caribbean. The border became one of the world's fastest-growing areas.[46] Many of the immigrants, failing to find work locally, pushed their way into the interior of the United States. By the 1980s, the number of Mexican immigrants had swelled to far beyond what the U.S. could handle. Attempts by the Immigration and Naturalization Services to harass the illegal immigrants to the point where they would lose heart failed, due to a distaste for such methods in the United States. The organization of undocumented workers by the Texas Farm Workers Union and the recognition by a U.S. federal district court of the rights to an education of undocumented children further stiffened the determination of many to cross into the United States.[47]

As the border towns swelled with people, the traditional problems of unemployment, lack of sanitary conditions, absence of basic services, and the existence of sprawling slums intensified. The situation was made all the more difficult by the preference of the *maquiladora* industry for hiring women, due to their greater passivity in union matters and patience in the tedious assembly work. Most men were left unemployed, often turning, in their humiliation, to liquor, drugs, extramarital sex, or fatal efforts to cross the border illegally to find work in the United States. The result was to throw many families into a crisis regarding the roles of the man and woman of the house, causing widespread divorce and single-parent families.[48]

The social structure was further undermined by the spread of the use of illegal drugs, which were easily available due to their growing role in the traditional border smuggling. Tijuana gained a reputation for being the Medellín of Mexico.[49] The 1991 film *Mariachi*, by Texas college student Robert Rodriguez, provided a poignant reminder of how life on the border was dehumanizing the Mexican resident with its drug-related violence and its industrialization. The resulting malaise even produced a spate of witchcraft sacrifices.

Politics and Government since 1960

Although dramatic, episodic growth had occurred previously along the border, the *maquiladora* boom was unprecedented in scope. The problems presented by the erratic demographic and economic expansion strained the infrastructure of the region's cities and stimulated political conflict. On the American side, the occasional challenges to elite power now became more general, and included an ethnic transformation in office-holding in Texas as Mexican-Americans achieved political equality through the civil rights movement. On the Mexican side, the stresses of growth and proximity to American democracy and prosperity stimulated increasingly successful elec-

toral challenges to domination by the Partido Revolucionario
Institucional. By the 1990s, states as well as municipalities in the
border region had fallen to the political opposition, particularly the
conservative Partido Accion Nacional.

Politics in the American Border Cities

The ethnic transformation in local United States office-holding
was particularly evident in the Lower Rio Grande Valley. In Cameron
County, the fifty-year tenure of County Judge Oscar Dancy termi-
nated with his retirement in 1970. Dancy's chosen successor was a
Mexican-American, Ray Ramon. By 1986, nearly eighty percent of
the county commissioners, constables, and justices of the peace were
Mexican-Americans. A recent development has been the reemergence
of partisan competition in Cameron County politics, resulting in
the election of Republican lawyer Antonio Garza as county judge in
1988. A second Republican was elected to the county commission in
1992.[50]

The city of Brownsville has had a long history of Mexican-
American participation in its government, although normally in a
numerically inferior position. The early 1940s saw a Mexican-American majority on the city commission, but politics and government
underwent little change. When the Populist mayor M. M. Vicars was
defeated in 1959, Antonio (Tony) Gonzalez was a member of the
victorious establishment commission slate. Gonzalez was elected
mayor in 1963, as the first Mexican-American to hold that office,
and was reelected three times. As commissioner and mayor, Gonzalez
focused on the creation and operation of the Public Utilities Board,
which provided electricity and water to city residents.

Mayor Gonzalez' preoccupation with nuts-and-bolts governmental activity during the era of national civil rights activism was
indicative of the low level of ethnic conflict in Brownsville, although
there was ample evidence of subtle forms of discrimination. Much
of the discrimination, however, was in the nature of class bias, as
many Mexican-Americans of the elite and middle classes participated
fully in the social, economic, and political life of the city. Elections
reflected class divisions to a much greater extent than ethnic divisions. Both Anglo and Mexican-American candidates on an establishment slate received strong support in prosperous neighborhoods
and low totals in poorer areas.[51]

Even the success of an anti-elite candidate in the tradition of

Robert Runyon and Vicars did little to change the status quo. Emilio Hernandez, whose family had backed Vicars in the 1950s, was elected mayor in 1979 by promising to represent "all the people," which was a slogan aimed at working-class Mexican-Americans. Hernandez may have had the interests of the poor in his heart, but he and his associates had become successful businessmen with little interest in socioeconomic upheaval. After two terms, Mayor Hernandez left office under a cloud of investigations into possible corruption at city hall. Hernandez' subsequent exoneration seemed to confirm the suspicions of his supporters that he was the victim of an elite plot, and his political influence continued to be felt in later elections.[52]

Hernandez was succeeded as mayor by Ygnacio "Nacho" Garza, son of Reynaldo Garza, senior federal appeals court judge and one of the Mexican-American city commission majority in the 1940s. Garza's election seemed to signal a return to elite control of the government, but the political situation proved to be much too fluid. Garza, who became a successful spokesman for the city, did not seek reelection, and Brownsville faced the 1990s with divided leadership and no clear sense of direction.[53]

Political developments in Hidalgo County paralleled those in Cameron County as Mexican-Americans gained control of county offices during the 1970s and 1980s through the dominant Democratic Party. That partisan dominance remained unchallenged into the 1990s.

The political story in McAllen in recent decades has been the story of the charismatic and domineering Othal Brand. A Georgia native, Brand began building an agricultural empire in the Rio Grande Valley in the 1940s. After three terms on the school board in the 1960s, Brand was elected to the city commission in 1973. In 1977 Brand defeated the establishment candidate to become mayor of McAllen, and he has held that post continuously ever since, including reelection to a presumably final four-year term in 1993.[54]

The structure of city government in McAllen provided scope for Mayor Brand's "hands-on" approach. City Manager Don Sisson observed that while he was the chief administrator, the mayor was the chief executive officer; this led to conflict between the two and political involvement in management. Sisson called for a true city manager form of government and the elimination of the mayor's veto power, but no such changes occurred, and the mayor was able to implement his businessman's approach to governing. In his first term, Brand pushed through massive public works programs aimed at improving conditions in the poverty stricken *colonias* of south McAllen, sought airport expansion and a new international bridge, and solidified the city's financial standing.[55]

In many ways Brand seemed a reincarnation of the turn-of-the-century Valley political bosses. In the classic *patrón* tradition, the mayor provided thousands of dollars for scholarships for poor Mexican-Americans, financed construction of a Boys' Club on the south side, and provided generous support to loyalists. By the end of his first term, however, two issues had arisen which threatened his reelection. The first was the decision of the city commission to sell the aging city hospital to a private corporation. The plan was defeated in a city referendum, prompting a minority coalition headed by Dr. Ramiro Casso to challenge Brand at the polls. The second was the shocking taped evidence of McAllen police brutality, which received national news coverage and came to light just prior to the elections. Casso led in the election for mayor, but failed to obtain a majority. In the runoff, Brand's attempts to associate Casso with Cesar Chavez and radical politics helped bring out eighty-three percent of the north side (primarily Anglo) vote, and Brand was victorious.[56]

Mayor Brand has remained a controversial figure. Many associate his aggressive leadership with the extensive economic and population growth of McAllen. Over the years, however, Brand's prickly and confrontational style made him many enemies as he gained fame from such bizarre behavior as shooting at grackles from his car. By 1993, Brand was opposed by all city councilmen, but still managed to convince voters that his leadership was essential for continued growth. Just before the 1993 election, one Brand critic acknowledged that "Win or lose, Brand's conservative legacy will survive for years to come."[57]

Coinciding with the rise of Othal Brand in McAllen was the collapse of the political machine in Laredo. Mayor J. C. "Pepe" Martin and the Old Party were in complete control at the beginning of this era, and local government, both city and county, had strong authoritarian overtones. By 1978, however, Martin had been in office for twenty-four years and he seemed less able, or willing, to utilize the political skills and power that had served him so well earlier. Martin openly acknowledged the existence of a *patrón* system of loyalty and rewards and claimed that he could deliver 8,000–10,000 votes.[58]

Although Mayor Martin faced occasional challenges in the 1950s and 1960s, these were brushed aside with little difficulty. During the sixties, however, the first of the factors that would undermine Martin's control made its appearance. The War on Poverty programs, which delivered various forms of economic assistance to Laredo's numerous poor, were administered independently of local government. Mayor Martin maneuvered to keep these programs from providing a base for independent political power, but the concept of the Old Party as the source of all benefits had been destroyed.[59]

As the seventies advanced, other factors arose to threaten the Martin regime. Corruption had siphoned off funds for public services, such as street-paving, leaving half of the streets in Laredo unpaved. Such conditions provoked concerned citizens like Larry Berry to form Taxpayers Organized for Public Service (TOPS), and development-oriented entrepreneur Tony Sanchez to found the *Laredo News* as a rival to the pro-Martin *Laredo Times*. Most crucial was the role of Aldo Tatangelo, an Italian-American "outsider" and businessman who became active in one of the local War on Poverty programs. Tatangelo began to attend city council meetings and to openly question the rubber stamp process.[60]

In 1977 Tatangelo and TOPS began checking city financial records and calling for an independent audit. A Texas Ranger investigation and the public exposure of corruption prompted the resignation of numerous officials, as well as Mayor Martin's decision not to seek reelection. Aldo Tatangelo was elected to replace Martin, and a month later Martin was indicted by a federal grand jury. Martin was convicted, and eventually was forced to repay $500,000 to the city. A charter reform referendum in 1979 resulted in the establishment of a city manager system. City council meetings were often raucous, but demonstrated that democracy had come to Laredo.[61]

The governance of Laredo changed dramatically when Tatangelo became mayor. Public services became a priority, especially the paving of Laredo streets that had remained unpaved as of 1978. The reformers also enacted a new city charter, which provided for term limits for elected officials. Mayor Tatangelo served three terms, and when his eligibility expired, he unsuccessfully sought the county judgeship. In a highly competitive election, Saul Ramirez was chosen to succeed Tatangelo in 1990.[62]

During the 1960s, El Paso was the fastest growing city in Texas, providing a major challenge for city government and city services.

Despite the election of Mayor Raymond Telles in the late 1950s, the social, economic, and political structure was dominated by an Anglo business community led by the older established families. A study of El Paso influentials conducted for the *El Paso Times* in 1978 failed to list even one Mexican-American among the top thirty of the economic elite that constituted the city's power structure. The Chicano rights movement on the University of Texas at El Paso campus caused an upheaval in the academic community but had limited impact on the greater El Paso community.[63]

City fathers moved to meet the challenges of the great expansion on a variety of fronts. Housing, highways, and a wilderness park received attention, and a charter commission recommended changes designed to strengthen city government. The commission proposals made the mayor's office more powerful and reduced the responsibilities of the aldermen. The most controversial of the major projects, however, began with strong support. The need for a civic center was apparent, and in 1968 Mayor Judson Williams declared, "Now is the time for action to provide for our City's greatest needs."[64] A successful bond issue, involving no increase in property taxes, enabled construction which was completed by 1972. The controversy arose over structural defects, and the debate resulted in political conflict and lawsuits.[65]

Housing proved to be a major political bone of contention during the 1970s and 1980s. Mayor Don Henderson, who took office in 1975, was determined to step up slum clearance in the barrios, but was opposed by La Campaña por la Conservación del Barrio, whose members feared displacement of the residents. Ethnic overtones were apparent when the mayor declared that he would "not be intimidated by any minority." Henderson also suggested, "If you don't like us, vote us out."[66] La Campaña followed his advice in the next election, electing Ray Salazar as mayor, but when the new mayor would not support rent controls, he, too, found himself at odds with La Campaña. Conditions in the barrios remained appalling, and Salazar was defeated for reelection by a well-organized Anglo vote.[67]

El Paso city government in the 1980s and early 1990s faced common big city and border city problems. Water scarcity resulted in conflict with New Mexico over drilling in the aquifer. Growing air and water pollution problems due in part to the rapid industrialization of Ciudad Juárez required international solutions which were slow in coming. Confrontations erupted between the administrations of the twin cities over intercity transportation. Committees, commissions, and new programs sought elusive solutions, but the problems could not negate the economic success of the city.[68]

A somewhat oblique factor on the political scene in both El Paso and the Rio Grande Valley beginning in the early 1980s was the establishment of community organizations by Saul Alinsky's Industrial Area Foundation. Valley Interfaith and the El Paso Interreligious Sponsoring Organization (EPISO), both closely allied with the Catholic church, did not directly participate in elections or endorse candidates. They did, however, hold "accountability sessions" to pressure state and local officials to take action on local problems affecting poor and working-class Mexican-Americans. In El Paso, for example, EPISO persuaded Mayor Jonathan Rogers in 1988 to reverse his policy and make arrangements to provide city water services to surrounding *colonias*.[69]

While El Paso was in the process of becoming a metropolis, San Diego had already achieved that status by the beginning of this era. One consequence of its size was the realignment of the power structure from control by a small elite group, composed of old families, to groups tied to property development and construction. The old battles over heavy industry development were long over as San Diego welcomed high technology industry and continued to focus on the military, trade, and tourism. City government also continued its obsession with urban planning for everything from parks to public buildings to various master plans.[70]

The internal struggle for power within the city government continued as well. By 1961, Mayor Charles Dail was frustrated by his lack of power under the city manager system, while City Manager George Bean accused the city council of "operating almost daily on the basis of expediency, with few members who understand basic principles." The result was the firing of Bean, but not the end of the controversy. A charter review committee recommended, and the voters approved, expansion of the mayor's appointment power and the addition of two members to the council. Dail failed, however, to obtain a strong mayor system and did not seek reelection.[71]

The prevailing political ideology in the San Diego power structure was staunch conservatism. Political power was exercised in a significant way by C. Arnholt Smith, banker and developer, who was highly influential in the state Republican Party. The conservative influence opposed the external controls that "urban renewal" funds would bring to efforts to revitalize downtown. Frank Curran was elected mayor with the backing of an establishment which wanted continuity of direction. In 1967 Curran and incumbent council members were reelected, and voters approved a General Plan which contained some elements of the distrusted urban renewal. San Diego's clean image received a blow in 1970, when Mayor Curran and eight members of the council were indicted on charges of bribery and conspiracy. Curran was acquitted, but failed in his bid for another term.[72]

To replace Curran, voters chose future Governor Pete Wilson, who "emerged as a vital, dominant factor in controlling economic policy and determining patterns of growth."[73] Wilson and the city council established the Centre City Development Corporation in 1975 to revitalize the downtown through the development of Horton Plaza. The establishment of a park at Old Town and the national bicentennial called attention to the city's Hispanic heritage, but Hispanic political influence has been minuscule despite recent growth to more than twenty percent of the population.[74]

In recent years, the conservative image of San Diego has undergone some modification. By 1992, the city had adopted a policy prohibiting anti-gay discrimination and was threatening to evict the Boy Scouts from city property for violating that policy. The influence of women expanded as Maureen O'Connor became mayor, Helen Copley took control of the newspaper, and Joan Kroc inherited a fortune that enabled her to influence social policy through philanthropy. Following the lead of Pete Wilson, city policy evolved from maximizing growth to controlled development.[75]

Politics in the Mexican Border Cities

While the Mexican border cities derived definite economic benefits from the *maquiladora* industrial growth, that growth has placed considerable stress on local government services and resources, with consequent political repercussions. The federal government attempted, with declining success, to maintain political control over the border cities. Federal officials did, however, make one significant concession to local authority. In 1980 President José López Portillo issued, through Congress, a decree ending the Juntas Federales de Mejoras Materiales and turned over the income from customs duties to the respective municipal governments.[76]

As Mexican borderlands inhabitants began to develop a regional identity, they depicted "their cultural norms as nurturing individualism, openness, optimism, and energetic hard work, creating a climate for the pursuit of free enterprise in a business context dominated by the private sector."[77] These cultural values influenced the ideology, policies, and programs of the PAN, which consequently received steadily increasing support in the border cities. During the 1980s and early 1990s, PAN controlled several major cities and also such smaller cities as Piedras Negras, Agua Prieta, and San Luis del Rio Colorado. Purported fraud during elections resulted in violent demonstrations against the PRI government in those same three cities.[78] The cultural values of Mexicans in the border cities, support for the PAN, and the demands for honest elections manifested the influence of American ideology and mores.

A major problem for several border cities during this era has been the existence of a rival power structure composed of organized criminal syndicates. Certainly this has been the case in Matamoros, where the Juan N. Guerra organization exercised extra-legal power for decades until President Carlos Salinas de Gortari began his campaign to eradicate such entities. The existence of these groups in border cities was the result of the profitability of illegal vices including smuggling, narcotics traffic, and prostitution. Local public officials were sometimes affiliated with the criminal organizations and at a minimum were intimidated by the willingness of the vice lords to use violence.[79]

In Matamoros, as in the other border cities, the monolithic political control by the PRI continued well into this period. Matamoros was fortunate during the 1960s to have an influential patron, Dr. Emilio Martínez Manatou, secretary of the presidency of the Republic. Martínez Manatou influenced the appointment of the local director of *mejoras materiales* and prompted the construction of the new Mercado Juárez as well as a hospital, schools, playgrounds, and streets. Problems of political complacency became apparent during the 1970s as the collusion between the police department and auto-theft rings came to light and a destructive riot broke out over police brutality.[80]

The most significant political development of recent decades was the emergence of a serious challenge to PRI hegemony in the person of the charismatic Jorge Cárdenas Gonzales. A native of Ciudad Victoria, Cárdenas established a radio station in Matamoros in 1951, then moved into agriculture and other business enterprises. Long active in the local Red Cross, he became its president in 1968. Accepted by the PRI, Cárdenas was appointed to head the local

mejoras materiales in 1975. He had hoped to receive PRI endorse-
ment for mayor, but was passed over more than once.[81]

In 1980 Jorge Cárdenas decided to run for mayor as the candidate of a minor party, the PARM. Cárdenas' campaign slogan was
"Por un Cambio total en los sistemas," and he promised to break the
corruption in the PRI government. Cárdenas had independent media
outlets to reach the public, and his campaign received enthusiastic
response. The establishment responded with violence and fraud, but
a massive turnout, followed by public pressure, forced the state (and
probably national) government to acknowledge Cárdenas' victory,
as announced by Dr. Emilio Martínez Manatou.[82]

Mayor Cárdenas acted on his promises and Matamoros became
the Ciudad del Cambio, despite efforts to cut off funds for the city
from the state and national governments. Cárdenas provided open
access to himself and his government and spent available local funds
on projects ranging from paving seventy-two miles of streets to the
establishment of Expofiesta, an annual fair for entertainment and
commerce. His reform efforts won such respect that he was chosen
as Brownsville's "Mr. Amigo" in 1982 and was honored at the Charro
Days celebration. Cárdenas retained strong popular support, and the
PRI found succeeding elections for many offices closely contested.
Cárdenas was elected in 1990 to a second term, further weakening
the power of the PRI.[83]

In 1992 Mayor Cárdenas launched a campaign for governor of
Tamaulipas with the support of the two major left- and right-wing
parties, PAN and PRD. His municipal administration was subjected
to investigations and allegations of malfeasance. When the government declared that Cárdenas had lost the election, protesters burned
the electoral office in Matamoros. In the same election, Cárdenas'
son was elected mayor of Ciudad Victoria and soon claimed that he,
too, had been cut off from state funds in the same manner as his
father.[84]

Government financial resources continued to flow uninterrupted
to Reynosa, which remained in PRI hands. A major sewage treatment plant was constructed and infrastructure development supported commercial and industrial growth. PRI control of Reynosa
did not go unchallenged, however, as a disputed election in 1977
resulted in state appointment of a civil administrative council headed
by Ernesto Gómez Lira to run the city. Ironically, Gómez Lira ran a
successful race for mayor in 1987 as candidate of the PARM.[85] Gómez

Lira's return to the PRI at the end of his term indicated the use of PARM as a vehicle for frustrated but popular PRI politicians, as was the case with Jorge Cárdenas Gonzáles in Matamoros. Both PARM mayors stressed electoral opportunity and local issues, rather than ideological concepts, in their campaigns.

As in other cities, Reynosa experienced problems concerning drugs and labor. Mayor Efrain Martínez negotiated a truce in a serious and highly publicized labor dispute over the transportation of *maquiladora* workers, and at least one mayor was engaged in smuggling while holding office. Another local challenge to the PRI appeared in November of 1992, in the adjacent municipality of Rio Bravo, which overwhelmingly elected PAN mayoral candidate Marco Antonio Buentello. Like Mayor Cárdenas of Ciudad Victoria, Buentello was soon complaining of unfair treatment in funding from the state government.[86]

The tremendous *maquiladora* growth in the border cities greatly enhanced another component of the local political power structure, the labor bosses or *caciques*. Since labor unions constituted a major element of the PRI, labor *caciques* wielded great political influence. For decades, Agapito Gonzáles dictated labor-industry relations in Matamoros, but when he proved intractable in the early 1990s, the Salinas de Gortari government had him arrested, imprisoned in Mexico City, and eventually deposed. In Reynosa in 1989, labor warfare erupted in a contest for power between a weakening *cacique* and his rival. Investors began to shy away from the Tamaulipas border cities and their labor problems.[87]

For decades, Nuevo Laredo was firmly in the grasp of the most powerful of the border *caciques*, Pedro Pérez Ibarra, a former teacher known as "El Profe." As in the other border cities, Pérez's power base was his control of local unions. A former president of the Nuevo Laredo Chamber of Commerce, Eloy Vega described Perez's power in the mid-1980s: "Like a viceroy, the cacique gets his control from the federal government. In exchange for votes, it lets him steal federal money destined for the city. It supports him against challenges. The people fear him because he can ostracize them, take away their jobs, see that they get no contracts. So they become apathetic. Complainers are marked men—unless, of course, they are purchased. If someone is a car dealer, the government might buy his cars in gratitude for his loyalty. The cacique can do physical harm or make people disappear. This happens in Mexico. I don't discard the possibility here in Nuevo

Laredo. We've had much violence and assassination in the past thirty years."[88]

The graft and other abuses in Nuevo Laredo contributed to an apparent 1983 PAN election victory, but El Profe reversed the results. The PRI mayoral candidate had distanced himself from the scandalous El Profe and was rewarded by a series of strikes when he took office. The public responded by rioting against El Profe and burning his newspaper, cars, and home. El Profe adopted a lower profile and proved adept at adjusting to the modernization policies of the Salinas regime. By agreeing to cut red tape in the customs office, the *cacique* managed to preserve his rule. Investment free from labor strife would be welcomed in Nuevo Laredo, even at some cost to El Profe's prerogatives.[89]

Labor strife continued in Nuevo Laredo even after El Profe departed the political scene in 1992. In April 1994 striking *maquiladora* workers protesting the length of the work-week and manipulation of union representation demonstrated outside the Sony plant. Mayor Horacio Garza, viewing the problem as a conflict between competing union factions, sent police in riot gear to disperse the protesters.[90]

The economic and political elite of Ciudad Juárez began this era by pushing for means of development which would provide funds to meet public services needs. The 1961 PRONAF program of the Mexican government to promote the sale of Mexican products along the border brought a major investment to Ciudad Juárez and improved its appearance. Former Mayor Antonio J. Bermúdez was appointed to head the Border Development Program. The Chamizal settlement, which awarded disputed territory from El Paso to Ciudad Juárez, further demonstrated federal interest in the long-neglected border cities. By the 1970s, however, intercity commerce still worked to the disadvantage of Ciudad Juárez.[91]

Despite the rapid growth of the *maquiladora* program in the seventies, Juárez leaders were frustrated by such federal actions as the refusal to reopen the streetcar line to El Paso. Juárez Mayors Mario Jacquez and Raúl Lezama appealed and negotiated without success. Such frustrations, coupled with disorienting peso devaluations and the beginning of the national economic crisis in 1982, set the stage for political revolt. In 1983 the dynamic Francisco Barrio Terrazas ran for mayor on the PAN ticket and achieved such a substantial victory that the government felt compelled to acknowledge it.[92]

Mayor Barrio was a charismatic leader in the mold of Matamoros' Jorge Cárdenas. Given to informal dress, Barrio maintained an open-door policy as Cárdenas had done. His hands-on approach to citizen problems instilled hope that his larger projects would improve life in Juárez. As an opposition mayor, of course, Barrio was short-changed on funding by the state and federal governments. Barrio ran unsuccessfully for governor in 1986, while PRI recaptured city hall by endorsing the independent-minded but highly respected industrialist Jaime Bermudez. The PRI victories were met with a campaign of civil disobedience which included the blocking of the international bridges.[93]

Although the PRI responded to the political revolt by providing more competent and less corrupt candidates, heavy-handed election tactics continued to take their toll in public credibility and support. In 1992 Barrio Terrazas again sought the governorship as the PAN candidate and achieved a clear victory, helping to carry a PAN mayoral candidate to victory in Ciudad Juárez. Another border city had become truly politically competitive, but major infrastructure problems resulting from rapid growth remained. Former Mayor Bermudez nevertheless maintained that the quality of life was superior to what it had been before the *maquiladora* development.[94]

Municipal governance and politics in the Baja California border cities during this era continued to reflect their isolation from the rest of Mexico, the strong influence of American political culture, and the very brevity of their existence. These were metropolises whose entire experiences were limited to the twentieth century. Also unique among the border cities was the status of Mexicali as a state capital. In the early years, PRI political dominance was uncontested and PRI leaders in 1965 engaged in an abortive experiment to allow democratic selection of PRI candidates for local office.[95]

Power sources in the Baja California del Norte border cities were either outside the structure of local government institutions or outside the community. Power within the communities existed in the informal and personal liaisons among businessmen; external control emanated from state and national governments and the PRI, which determined who would hold office. Local officials lacked revenue sources that would enable them to cope with public service needs and were unable to control budgets subject to state approval. At least part of the problem of scarcity of local public resources in Baja California del Norte cities, as well as the other border cities, has been attributed to "the inefficiencies of uncoordinated bureaucratic machinery and the diversion of public funds to the private use of bureaucratic functionaries."[96]

The Mexican practice of arbitrary imposition of PRI candidates for local office resulted in a political revolt in 1968 in both Mexicali and Tijuana. PAN claimed mayoral victories in both cities amidst charges of government election fraud and demonstrations by PAN supporters. Unwilling to accept opposition victories, the governor annulled the election for mayor. Beginning a practice that would be employed where significant opposition appeared, the PRI ran a respected local businessman in the special election of 1970 rather than a party hack. The government also attempted to pacify the opposition with a 1979 provision for political minority representation on the city councils of both Mexicali and Tijuana.[97]

Mexicali and Tijuana suffered from a deficit of public services even before the phenomenal population growth of the seventies and eighties. While the cities made a few feeble attempts at limiting growth, the local governments failed to develop master plans and instead focused on development of infrastructure for economic growth as encouraged by federal funding policies. Highways, river control, and beautification projects were aimed at *maquiladora* and trade growth in both cities, with the addition of tourism for Tijuana.[98]

Despite its rapid growth, Mexicali has developed a relatively stable society and "exudes a civic confidence unknown in border cities in places like Tamaulipas."[99] Tijuana, which still holds notoriety for seedy tourist vice and transients, has been modernized and its tourist district sanitized. Both cities have encountered problems of water supply, sewage disposal, and river pollution resulting in friction with American authorities. The Baja California Norte border cities' problems have been somewhat complicated by the election of Governor Ernesto Ruffo Appel in 1989. The first non-PRI governor since the Revolution, Ruffo faced not only the urban problems of infrastructure development and political corruption, but also lack of cooperation and hostility from PRI officials at all levels. In Tijuana, for example, recent flood relief efforts were hampered by political disputes between the governor and federal officials.[100]

Political tension between the state and federal governments doubtless contributed to a shootout between federal and state police in Tijuana in March 1994. In April, Tijuana police chief José Federico Benitez López was ambushed and killed. Both incidents were related to drug traffic, and rumors of the involvement of local lords circulated widely. According to Tonatiuh Guillén López of the Colegio de la Frontera Norte, "The logic of local politics doesn't explain these events."[101]

The two Baja California Norte border cities figured prominently in national politics in 1994, as the presidential nominee of the PRI, Luis Donaldo Colosio, was assassinated in Tijuana and replaced by Mexicali native Ernesto Zedillo, who was chosen as president in a reasonably honest election.

The *maquiladora* system had brought growth, but had also intensified many of the border town problems. As if in response, in the 1990s a fresh hope blew in to hover over the border — the suggestion that a solution might be found in a free trade zone of North America.

CHAPTER TWELVE

Family Reunion:
North American Free Trade Zone

What family saga should not have a happy ending? The latest development to affect the border towns is the formation of NAFTA, the North American Free Trade Agreement, between the United States, Mexico, and Canada, starting 1 January 1994. The emergence of a strong European Union has provided the incentive and the model, and as Europe moves from economic toward political unity, the desirability of a comparable political unification of North America will doubtless occur to some American leaders as well. Such a possibility may seem extremely unlikely, but then the prediction of a North American free trade zone was considered absurd only a few years ago. In that case, the border towns will have served as a historical foreshadowing of the bilingual and bicultural Englanish-speaking Spanglo society which could spread through most of North America. The whole continent could settle into the flip-flop culture already common along the border. Such a development could recapitulate the cultural and linguistic syncretism that marked the ancient Mediterranean under the leadership of Rome, whose elite was bilingual in Greek and Latin. The recent passage of Proposition 187 in California, however, demonstrates the strength of resistance to such developments.

Will the American and Mexican eagles agree to spread their wings as boldly as the eagle of ancient Rome? Some factors seem to indicate that sooner or later they will. For one, the United States has an interest in Mexican oil, Mexico being its leading foreign supplier of that resource. Mexico's natural gas, coal, and geothermal energy are all being utilized by American consumers. California buys geothermal power from the Mexicali region, and Texas receives a gas pipeline from south of its border.[1] Furthermore, U.S. manufacturers feel a need to find a viable source of cheap labor closer to home than the Orient in order to allay the threat to their investments which could be posed by a resurgent Asia. China's generals are talking about China's need to secure the Straits of Malacca — China's entryway to the Indian Ocean, along with the wealth and power it commands.[2]

What are the prospects for the border's twin sister towns under NAFTA? First of all, from the sociological standpoint, there would seem to be a chance of ending the historical alternation of cooperation and rivalry between the twin towns of each set. The see-sawing of border town relations made the 1850s a decade of rivalry, the early 1860s a moment of partisan bonds, Reconstruction a period of hostility, the Porfiriato an era of mutual benefits, the 1910s a time of strain, the 1920s a decade of mutual growth, the 1930s a term of troubled symbiosis, the 1940s and 1950s a season of ups and downs, and since the 1960s an age of tentative rapprochement. New clouds on the horizon include competition for increasingly scarce water sources, bitterness over uncontrolled pollution spreading from one town to another, and the losing fight to hold Mexicans from seeking residence and employment in the United States.[3] If no adequate solution is found to any one of these problems, another period of hard feelings could set in. The North American free trade zone could bring a more lasting cooperation between border towns in tackling such issues.

Secondly, the economic advantage has hitherto shifted back and forth across the border from generation to generation. The prosperity that set in with the early 1850s on the American side of the border shifted back in the late 1850s to the Mexican side, to remain there until the Porfiriato. There is nothing inevitable about the present pattern of rich American towns paired with poorer Mexican twins; this relationship has been and can again be reversed. The North American free trade zone holds out a hope for ending such vagaries. It could also open up a natural border trade that has long been retarded by lack of cooperation between the two nations, lifting towns on both sides out of their long-standing poverty relative to towns in other regions.[4] However, major changes would be required if the economic benefits were to be reasonably distributed, given the traditional monopoly of local wealth by a small elite.[5] The move into a common economic fate could also be bumpy for the residents of the American side, whose per capita income is presently so very much higher than that in the Mexican towns.[6]

The border security enforcement and related military issues are clearly compelling considerations for the twin towns. For two giant nations to coexist on a crowded continent with unresolved resentments stemming from the Mexican-American War is a situation fraught with dangers for both. The rapid growth in numbers of American residents of Mexican ancestry makes a policy of goodwill between the United States and Mexico imperative. The wounds of the past must be healed; they are so deep that cheap band-aids will not suffice, but only the strongest medicine. The border towns have been swept up repeatedly in the shifting relations between their two parent nations. Mexico's French connection in the 1860s and its German connection in the 1910s point to patterns of Old World intervention that could one day be used to bring the worst sort of military disaster to the border towns.

NAFTA, whether or not it grows into a larger North American political block, will surely bring an enhanced importance to the border towns by placing them at the nexus of a continental power rather than at the back door of two neglectful nations. The three main twin clusters of the eastern border, consisting of the two Laredos, Reynosa/McAllen, and Matamoros/Brownsville, stand a chance to narrow the gap with the larger and more modern twin cities of the west — San Diego/Tijuana, Mexicali/ Calexico, and Cd. Juárez/El Paso. The two Laredos, perched on the San Antonio-Monterrey-Cd. Mexico route, have much to gain. The newly augmented importance of the western end of the border is suggested by the assassination in Tijuana on 23 March 1994 of the PRI candidate for president of Mexico, Luis Donaldo Colosio, and by the choice of a native of Mexicali, Ernesto Zendillo Ponce de León, to replace him.

However, opportunity can also become a curse, as witnesses the present blighted state of life in New York City, located on one of the continent's prime pieces of real estate. Richard Gephardt, former majority leader of the U.S. House of Representatives, expressed concern regarding NAFTA's impact on environment and labor.[7] Some of the town sets likely to see major industrial growth are already suffering from the effects of pollution.[8] Some employees of General Motors and Zenith *maquiladora* plants are living at subhuman levels with inadequate wages, poor benefits, and sweat-shop hours. In 1992, when concern was rising that the slightly higher wages paid plant workers in Matamoros compared to Reynosa might discourage *maquiladora* settlement in the former town, the director of Matamoros' CTM labor union, Agapito González, was arrested and held for nine months in Cd. México. A popular feeling was that the charges of corruption leveled against him were contrived to undercut his effectiveness as a labor leader.[9] This development was followed in the summer of 1993 by a challenge to the position of union workers among the stevedores at the key Port of Brownsville on the American side.[10] If the environment is not protected, basic worker rights not guaranteed, growth not controlled, and the social fiber not held strong, progress will be bought at too high a price.

In the fairy tale of Snow White and Rose Red, the sisters are lifted from their humble abode to a royal lifestyle compliments of a bear who turns into a Prince Charming. Hopes are high that the North American free trade zone is opening a period of cooperation which will lift the twin cities into a grand new life. The question is, will free trade prove to be a magical Prince Charming or just another beastly upset? Whichever proves to be the case, may the sister cities of the border always hold closely to one another.

Notes

CHAPTER ONE

1. "Schneeweisschen und Rosenrot," *Die Märchen der Brüder Grimm* (München: Der Goldmann Verlag, 1988), 488–493.

2. Raúl Fernández, *The Mexican–American Border Region: Issues and Trends* (Notre Dame, IN: University of Notre Dame Press, 1989), 33.

3. Fernández, 36 and 40.

CHAPTER TWO

1. Oscar J. Martínez, *Border Boom Town: Ciudad Juárez since 1848* (Austin: University of Texas Press, 1978), 3.

2. W. H. Timmons, *El Paso: A Borderlands History* (El Paso: Texas Western Press of The University of Texas at El Paso, 1990), 7, 9–10, and 12–14.

3. Timmons, 15.

4. Martínez, *Border Boom Town*, 9 and 17; Timmons, 15 and 17.

5. Timmons, 4 and 5.

6. C. L. Sonnichsen, *Pass of the North: Four Centuries on the Rio Grande*, Vol. I (El Paso: Texas Western Press, 1968), 19.

7. Sonnichsen, Vol. I, 76–77.

8. Martínez, *Border Boom Town*, 9, 17; Timmons, 15, 17, 19.

9. Fernández, 13 and 31.

10. Martínez, *Border Boom Town*, 9; Timmons, xviii, 18 and 45.

11. Sonnichsen, Vol. I, 56–57; Timmons, 20–21.

12. Donald E. Chipman, *Spanish Texas, 1519–1821* (Austin: University of Texas Press, 1992); Timmons, 20–21.

13. Sonnichsen, Vol. I, 88–89; Timmons, 20–21, 23, 25–27, 34 and 36.

14. Timmons, 31–34; Sonnichsen, Vol. I, 91.

15. Daniel D. Arreola and James R. Curtis, *The Mexican Border Cities: Landscape Anatomy and Place Personality* (Tucson: The University of Arizona Press, 1993), 15–16.

16. Arreola and Curtis, 16.
17. Timmons, 41 and 58.
18. Luis Benedicto, *Historia de Nuevo Laredo* (Nuevo Laredo: n.p., 1956), 7.
19. Gilberto Miguel Hinojosa, *A Borderlands Town in Transition: Laredo, 1755–1870* (College Station: Texas A & M University Press, 1983), 4–5.
20. J. Lee and Lilian J. Stambaugh, *The Lower Rio Grande Valley of Texas* (Austin: The Jenkins Publishing Co., 1974), 30.
21. Rosa Salinas de Villarreal, *Reynosa, Nuestra Ciudad* (Reynosa: R. Ayuntamiento de Reynosa, 1990), 13–14 and 17–18; Antonio María Guerra, *Mier en la Historia* (Mier: n.p., 1953), 30; Hinojosa, 19, 21, 23, 34, 40; *Brownsville Saturday Plus*, 12 September 1992, 1; Benedicto, 105–106.
22. Stambaugh, 31.
23. Richard T. Marcum, "Fort Brown, Texas: The History of a Border Post," Ph.D. dissertation, Texas Technological College, August 1964, 90; Milo Kearney, "Brownsville's Santanderino Strain," in Milo Kearney (ed.), *Studies in Brownsville History* (Brownsville: Pan American University at Brownsville, 1986), 67; Milo Kearney, "De la Garzas, Ballís, and the Political History of the Region that would later become Cameron County," in Milo Kearney (ed.), *More Studies in Brownsville History* (Brownsville: Pan American University at Brownsville, 1989), 40.
24. Hinojosa, 8; *The Brownsville Herald, Saturday Plus*, 12 September 1992, 1.
25. Ismael Villarreal Peña, *Seis Villas del Norte: Antecedentes históricos de Nuevo Laredo, Dolores, Guerrero, Mier, Camargo y Reynosa* (Ciudad Victoria, Tamaulipas: Universidad Autónoma de Tamaulipas, Instituto de Investigaciones Históricas, 1986), 41–44; Benedicto, 106; Hinojosa, 5.
26. Villarreal Peña, 53–57; Salinas de Villareal, 13–19, 29; Benedicto, 105–106.
27. Villarreal Peña, 25–29; Guerra, 14.
28. Villarreal Peña, 35–37; *The Brownsville Herald, Saturday Plus*, 12 September 1992, 8; Guerra, 6, 12–16, 18, 23, 52.
29. Villarreal Peña, 5–6; Hinojosa, 4, 6, 8, 41; Benedicto, 11.
30. Hinojosa, 9.
31. Chipman, 180.
32. Benedicto, 11–12.
33. Eliseo Paredes Manzano, *Homenaje a los Fundadores de la Heróica, Leal e Invicta Matamoros en el Sesquicentenario de su Nuevo Nombre* (H. Matamoros: Imprenta "El Norte," 1976), 77–78, 89; Mario T. García, *Desert Immigrants: The Mexicans of El Paso, 1880–1920* (New Haven: Yale University Press, 1981), 15–16; José Raúl Canseco, *Historia de Matamoros* (H. Matamoros: Litografíca Jardín, 1981), 17.
34. Canseco, 17; Paredes Manzano, *Homenaje*, 29 and 90.
35. Canseco, 18; Paredes Manzano, *Homenaje*, 45.
36. Minnie Gilbert, "Texas' First Cattle Queen," in Valley By–Liners, *Roots by the River* (Mission, TX: Border Kingdom Press, 1978), 22.
37. Robert Mayer (ed.), *San Diego: A Chronological and Documentary History, 1535–1976* (Dobbs Ferry, NY: Oceana Publications, Inc., 1978), 4; and Richard F. Pourade, *The Explorers, Volume I of The History of San Diego* (San Diego: The Union–Tribune Publishing Company, 1960), 35, 42, 45–51.
38. Leon C. Metz, *Border: The U.S.–Mexican Line* (El Paso: Mangan Books, 1989), 15; Mayer, 3, 5, 49; Charles J. G. Maximin Piette, O.F.M., *Évocation de Junípero Serra, Fondateur de la Californie* (Bruxelles: Lecture au Foyer, 1946), 115.

39. Philip R. Pryde, *San Diego: An Introduction to the Region* (Dubuque, IA: Kendall/Hunt Publishing Company, 1976), 49; Mayer, 79.

40. Elizabeth A. H. John, *Storms Brewed in Other Men's Worlds: The Confrontation of Indians, Spanish, and French in the Southwest, 1540–1795* (Lincoln: University of Nebraska Press, 1975), 559.

41. Mayer, 7.

42. David Piñera Ramírez (ed.), *Historia de Tijuana: Semblanza General* (Tijuana: Centro de Investigaciones Históricas UNAM–UABC, 1985, 23–25.

43. Dorothy Krell (ed.), *The California Missions: A Pictorial History* (Menlo Park, CA: Lane Publishing Company, 1979), 73–74; Metz, 15; Mayer, 3; and Pourade, *The Explorers*, 150.

44. Mayer, 5–6 and 8; and Pourade, *The Explorers*, 123.

CHAPTER THREE

1. W. H. Timmons, *El Paso: A Borderlands History* (El Paso: Texas Western Press, 1990), 37 and 75.

2. Gilberto Miguel Hinojosa, *A Borderlands Town in Transition: Laredo, 1755–1870* (College Station: Texas A&M University Press, 1983), 6–7.

3. Rosa Salinas de Villareal, *Reynosa Nuestra Ciudad* (Reynosa: R. Ayuntamiento de Reynosa, 1990), 32–33.

4. Salinas de Villarreal, 33; Timmons, 79.

5. Raul Fernández *The Mexican-American Border Region* (Notre Dame, IN: University of Notre Dame Press, 1989), 13.

6. Hinojosa, 17–18.

7. Florence Johnson Scott, *Historical Heritage of the Lower Rio Grande Valley of Texas* (Waco, TX: Texian Press, 1965), 101–102.

8. Hinojosa, 8, 11, 17 and 22.

9. Donald E. Chipman, *Texas en la Epoca Colonial* (Madrid: Editorial Mapfre, 1992), 260, 286; Timmons, xvii and 45–50; Hinojosa, 13–15.

10. Eliseo Paredes Manzano, *Homenaje a los Fundadores de la Heróica* (H. Matamoros: Imprenta "El Norte," 1976), 34–36.

11. David J. Weber, *La Frontera Norte de México, 1821–1846: El sudoeste norteamericano en su época mexicana*, trans. by Agustín Bárcena (México: Fondo de Cultura Económica, 1988), 120.

12. Rodriguez Brayda, "O Todo O Nada," in Milo Kearney (ed.), *More Studies in Brownsville History* (Brownsville: Pan American University at Brownsville, 1989), 82–84.

13. Clotilde P. García, *Padre José Nicolás Ballí and Padre Island* (Corpus Christi: Grunwald Publishing Co., 1979), 2 and 4; Minnie Gilbert, "Texas' First Cattle Queen," in Valley By-Liners, *Roots by the River* (Mission, TX: Border Kingdom Press, 1978), 22–23.

14. Walter W. Hildebrand, "The History of Cameron County, Texas," master's thesis, North Texas State College, August 1950, 16 and 41; Minnie Gilbert, "Valley Place Names: Signposts Rooted in History," in Valley By–Liners, *Roots by the River* (Mission, TX: Border Kingdom Press, 1978), 9; Gilbert, "Texas' First Cattle Queen," in Valley By-Liners, *Roots by the River*, 17–20; and Kearney, "De la Garzas," 40–41, 44.

15. José Raúl Canseco, *História de Matamoros* (H. Matamoros: Litografíca Jardín, 1981), 17.

16. Paredes Manzano, *Homenaje*, 45, 56 and 90.

17. Gilbert, "Texas' First Cattle Queen," 21; Canseco, 18; Paredes Manzano, *Homenaje*, 91.

18. Gilbert, "Texas' First Cattle Queen," 23.

19. Paredes Manzano, *Homenaje*, 45.

20. Gilbert, "Texas' First Cattle Queen," 15.

21. *The Brownsville Herald, Saturday Plus*, 12 September 1992, 8; Ismael Villarreal Peña, *Seis Villas del Norte* (Ciudad Victoria, Tamaulipas: Universidád Autónoma de Tamaulipas, 1986), 19 and 21.

22. Virgil N. Lott, *Story of Reynosa, Mexico* (N.p.: Complimentary Souvenir Edition, 1920(?)), 1.

23. Lott, 1; Villarreal Peña, 37, 45–47.

24. Hinojosa, 23.

25. Timmons, 68–69.

26. Robert Mayer (ed.), *San Diego: A Chronological and Documentary History, 1535–1976* (Dobbs Ferry, NY: Oceana Publications, Inc., 1978), 12–13.

27. LeRoy P. Graf, "The Economic History of the Lower Rio Grande Valley, 1820–1875," Ph.D. dissertation, Harvard University, February 1942, 26.

28. Graf, 20.

29. John G. Clark, *New Orleans, 1718–1812: An Economic History* (Baton Rouge: Louisiana State University Press, 1970), 195–196, 204–210.

30. Hildebrand, 16; Vernon Smylie, *Conquistadores and Cannibals: The Early History of Padre Island (1519–1845)* (Corpus Christi: Texas News Syndicate Press, 1964), 22.

31. Canseco, 71.

32. Antonio N. Zavaleta, "The Twin Cities: A Historical Synthesis of the Socio–Economic Interdependence of the Brownsville–Matamoros Border Community," in Milo Kearney (ed.), *Studies in Brownsville History* (Brownsville: Pan American University at Brownsville, 1986), 134.

33. Timmons, 59–60.

34. Mayer, 8–9.

35. Mayer, 10.

36. Mayer, 11.

37. Mayer, 9–10.

38. Hinojosa, 28.

39. Rie Jarratt, *Gutiérrez de Lara, Mexican–Texan: The Story of a Creole Hero* (Austin: Creole Texana, 1949), 1–3, 7; Vidal Covián Martínez, *Don José Bernardo Maximiliano Gutiérrez de Lara* (Ciudad Victoria: Ediciones Siglo XX, 1967), 6–7; Félix D. Almaraz, Jr., *Tragic Cavalier: Governor Manuel Salcedo of Texas, 1808–1813* (Austin: University of Texas Press, 1982), 142; Antonio María Guerra, *Mier en la História* (Mier: n.p., 1953), 30.

40. Jarratt, 3–4.

41. Jarratt, 5; Guerra, 30; Hinojosa, 25.

42. Gilbert, "Texas' First Cattle Queen," 23.

43. Jarratt, 7; Covián Martínez, 6–7 and 13; Almaraz, 142; Guerra, 30.

44. Covián Martínez, 13; Guerra, 31; Almaraz, 176–181; Jarratt, 45–46; Villarreal Peña, 50 and 113.

45. Jarratt, 55–56; David Piñera Ramírez (ed.), *Visión Histórica de la Frontera*

Norte de México, Tomo II (Tijuana: Universidad Autónoma de Baja California, 1987), 36.

46. Hinojosa, 26–28.

47. Almaraz, 175–181; Jarratt, 45–46.

48. Paredes Manzano, *Homenaje,* 92.

49. Canseco, 20–21; *Bautismos Matamoros, Cuaderno Número 2* (1810–1812) and *Cuaderno Número 3* (1812–1820), in the Frank Cushman Pierce Collection, the Stillman House Museum, Brownsville, Texas.

50. Canseco, 18; Clotilde García, *Captain Blas María de la Garza Falcón* (Austin: San Felipe Press of The Jenkins Publishing Co., 1984), 28–29; Almaraz, 172.

51. Canseco, 21.

52. *Family Trees,* manuscript book in the Frank Cushman Pierce Collection, the Stillman House Museum, Brownsville, Texas; *Libro de Matrimonios, Número 1* (1816–1863), in the Frank Cushman Pierce Collection, the Stillman House Museum, Brownsville, Texas; *Bautismos Matamoros, Cuaderno Número 3* (1812–1820), in the Frank Cushman Pierce Collection, the Stillman House Museum, Brownsville, Texas; and *Soliseño, Blancas, Tigre, Palma* (late nineteenth-century manuscript record book of data pertaining to the ownership of these four ranches, including wills, genealogical records, and plot descriptions), in the Archivos del Museo Histórico de Casa Mata, Matamoros, Tamaulipas, Mexico, in the section on La Palma estate, no page numbers given; Paredes Manzano, *Homenaje,* 62.

53. Smylie, 19.

54. Canseco, 18.

55. Timmons, 61, 63–64.

56. George G. Daniels (ed.), *The Spanish West* (Alexandria, VA: Time–Life Books, 1976), 164–168.

57. Mayer, 12.

58. Smylie, 20.

59. Eliseo Paredes Manzano, *La Casa Mata y Fortificaciones de la Heróica Matamoros, Tamaulipas* (H. Matamoros: Imprenta "El Norte," 1974), 4.

60. Canseco, 21; Paredes Manzano, *Homenaje,* 49–50.

61. Timmons, 65–66 and 71.

62. Mayer, 13.

63. Hinojosa, 28–30.

64. Villarreal Peña, 50–51.

65. Hinojosa, 28–31.

CHAPTER FOUR

1. Jerry Thompson, *Warm Weather and Bad Whiskey: The 1886 Laredo Election Riot* (El Paso: Texas Western Press, The University of Texas at El Paso, 1991), 40; LeRoy P. Graf, "The Economic History of the Lower Rio Grande Valley, 1820–1875," Ph.D. dissertation, Harvard University, February 1942, 52–56.

2. Charles Daniel Dillman, "The Functions of Brownsville, Texas and Matamoros, Tamaulipas: Twin Cities of the Lower Rio Grande," Ph.D. dissertation, University of Michigan, 1968, 60.

3. Eliseo Paredes Manzano, *Homenaje a los Fundadores de la Heróica* (H. Matamoros: Imprenta "El Norte," 1976), 59–60; José Raúl Canseco, *Historia de Matamoros* (H. Matamoros: Litográfica Jardín, 1981), 21, 24, 26–27.

4. Minnie Gilbert, "Mexico's First Ambassador," in Valley By–Liners, *Roots by the River*, 31.

5. Graf, 26–29; Paredes Manzano, *Homenaje*, 30.

6. Walter W. Hildebrand, "The History of Cameron County, Texas," master's thesis, North Texas State College, August 1950, 38; Kearney, "De la Garzas," 50.

7. W. H. Timmons, *El Paso: A Borderlands History* (El Paso: Texas Western Press, 1990), 71, 76.

8. Richard F. Pourade, *The Silver Dons: Volume III of The History of San Diego* (San Diego: The Union–Tribune Publishing Company, 1963), 12–13; Robert Mayer (ed.), *San Diego: A Chronological and Documentary History, 1535–1976* (Dobbs Ferry, NY: Oceana Publications, Inc., 1978), 13–14.

9. Gilberto Miguel Hinojosa, *A Borderlands Town in Transition: Laredo, 1755–1870* (College Station: Texas A&M University Press, 1983), 39–40.

10. Hinojosa, 37.

11. Timmons, 73.

12. Graf, 39 and 44.

13. David Martell Vigness, "Indian Raids on the Lower Rio Grande, 1836–1837," *The Southwestern Historical Quarterly*, 59, no. 1 (July 1955): 6.

14. James Heaven Thompson, "A Nineteenth Century History of Cameron County, Texas," master's thesis, University of Texas at Austin, 1965, 17.

15. Gilbert, "Valley Place–Names," 10.

16. A. B. J. Hammett, *The Empresario: Don Martín De León, The Richest Man in Texas* (Kerrville, TX: Braswell Printing Co., 1971), 8–9, 13–14, and 46; Charles W. Goldfinch, "Juan N. Cortina, 1824–1892: A Reappraisal," master's thesis, University of Chicago, June 1949, 19; Graf, 81, 117, 157–158, and 286.

17. Canseco, 21 and 71; Graf, 45–46.

18. A. A. Champion with Mary Champion Henggler, Consuelo Champion, and Vivian Kearney, "Papers and Personalities of Frontier Journalism (1830's to 1890's)," in Milo Kearney (ed.), *More Studies in Brownsville History* (Brownsville: Pan American University at Brownsville, 1989), 113; Graf, 76–78; Canseco, 24.

19. C. L. Sonnichsen, *Pass of the North, Vol. 1* (El Paso: Texas Western Press, 1968), 91–92 and 106; Timmons, 79.

20. David Piñera Ramírez (ed.), *Historia de Tijuana*, 28–30; Mayer, 15–16.

21. Piñera Ramírez, *Historia de Tijuana*, 30; Mayer, 16.

22. Pourade, *The Silver Dons*, 16; Mayer, 16; Piñera Ramírez, *Historia de Tijuana*, 30–33.

23. Pourade, *The Silver Dons*, 23; Mayer, 100; Piñera Ramírez, *Historia de Tijuana*, 26–28, 31.

24. Pourade, *The Silver Dons*, 12–13; Mayer, 100; Piñera Ramírez, *Historia de Tijuana*, 26–28 and 30–32.

25. Leon C. Metz, *Border: The U.S.-Mexican Line* (El Paso: Mangan Books, 1989), 15; Piñera Ramírez, *Historia de Tijuana*, 31–32; Mayer, 15–17 and 100.

26. Hinojosa, 64.

27. Graf 21, 48–49, 50; Paredes Manzano, *Homenaje*, 29–30 and 43.

28. Paul Horgan, *Great River: The Rio Grande in North American History* (New York: Holt, Rinehart and Winston, 1971), 470; J. Lee and Lilian J. Stambaugh, *The Lower Rio Grande Valley* (Austin: Jenkins Publishing Co., 1974), 72–73; Graf, 63–67; Goldfinch, 21; Jerry Thompson, 75 and 84.

29. Sonnichsen, Vol. I, 105; Timmons, 76–77, 79, and 84.

30. Mayer, 15–17, 100; Piñera Ramírez, *Historia de Tijuana*, 31 and 38.

31. Ed Davidson and Eddy Orcutt, *The Country of Joyous Aspect: A Short History of San Diego, California (1542 to 1888)* (San Diego: San Diego Trust and Savings Bank, 1929), no page numbers.

32. Hinojosa, 50 and 64.

33. Clotilde García, *Captain Blas*, 29, 41–42, 49; Jerry Thompson, 46; "Family Trees," manuscript in the Pierce Collection, under "T," in the Stillman House Museum, Brownsville, Texas.

34. Sonnichsen, Vol. I, 105; Timmons, 84.

35. Theodore W. Fuller, *San Diego Originals: Profiles of the Movers and Shakers of California's First Community* (Pleasant Hill, CA: California Profiles Publications, 1987), 198; George C. Daniels (ed.), *The Spanish West* (Alexandria, VA: Time-Life Books, 1976), 185; and Pourade, *The Silver Dons*, 62 and 64.

36. Pourade, *The Silver Dons*, 11 and 18; Fuller, 157–160.

37. Canseco, 21 and 31.

38. Clotilde García, *Captain Blas*, 41–42 and 49.

39. Hammett, *The Empresario*, 8–13, 44, 46.

40. Piñera Ramírez, *Visión*, Tomo I, 85.

41. Hammett, 8–9, 13–14, and 46; Goldfinch, 19.

42. Kearney, "Brownsville's Santanderino Strain," 67; Smylie, 24.

43. Horgan, 488 and 493.

44. Hinojosa, 44.

45. Graf, 82, 91, and 117–118; Horgan, 492.

46. Sonnichsen, Vol. I, 92.

47. Mayer, 17.

48. Piñera Ramírez, *Historia de Tijuana*, 33–34; and Richard Pourade, *Time of the Bells: Volume II of The History of San Diego* (San Diego: The Union–Tribune Publishing Company, 1961), 201.

49. David J. Weber, *La Frontera Norte de México, 1821–1846* (México: Fondo de Cultura Económica, 1988), 105.

50. Eliseo Paredes Manzano, *La Casa Mata* (H. Matamoros: Imprenta "El Norte," 1974), 15–16, 27; Canseco, 27, 31; Horgan, 507–508; Graf, 79 and 91–92.

51. Timmons, 80–81 and 83–84.

52. Pourade, *The Silver Dons*, 18; Mayer, 17–18, 20; Piñera Ramírez, *Historia de Tijuana*, 33–35.

53. Pourade, *The Silver Dons*, 14, 18, 33, 49–50, 52, 77, 268; Mayer, 15–18, 20; Piñera Ramírez, *Historia de Tijuana*, 33–34.

54. Pourade, *The Silver Dons*, 14 and 18; Mayer, 17–18, 20; Piñera Ramírez, *Historia de Tijuana*, 33–34.

55. Pourade, *The Silver Dons*, 23.

56. Champion, "Papers," 114.

57. José T. Canales, *Bits of Texas History* (San Antonio: Artes Gráficas, 1950), 68; Virgil N. Lott, *Story of Reynosa, Mexico* (N.p.: Complimentary Souvenir Edition, 1920(?)), 55.

58. Stambaugh, 49.

59. Graf, 121–122.

60. Horgan, 518.

61. Canseco, 70; Horgan, 527; Paredes Manzano, *Casa Mata*, 19; Hildebrand, 21.

62. Timmons, 84; Pourade, *The Silver Dons*, 23–24; Piñera Ramírez, *Historia de Tijuana*, 35 and 38.

63. Rosa Salinas de Villarreal, *Reynosa, Nuestra Ciudad* (Reynosa: R. Ayuntamiento de Reynosa, 1990), 57.

64. Hinojosa, 44.

65. Pourade, *The Silver Dons*, 25–40; Mayer, 19; Piñera Ramírez, *Historia de Tijuana*, 35–36.

66. Pourade, *The Silver Dons*, 38–39.

67. Pourade, *The Silver Dons*, 43–45.

68. Stambaugh, 45–48.

69. Graf, 121.

70. Vigness, 11–12, 20–23.

71. Hinojosa, 49–50.

72. Paredes Manzano, *Casa Mata*, 22; Graf, 126–128.

73. Stambaugh, 48–49.

74. Graf, 134–136.

75. Hinojosa, 49 and 51–53.

76. Paredes Manzano, *Casa Mata*, 19 and 21.

77. Timmons, 80.

78. Sonnichsen, Vol. I, 94.

79. Pourade, *The Silver Dons*, 33–34; Mayer, 18–19; Piñera Ramírez, *Historia de Tijuana*, 31.

80. Graf, 124 and 126–128.

81. Pourade, *The Silver Dons*, 53–54; Mayer, 18–20; Piñera Ramírez, *Historia de Tijuana*, 31.

82. Vigness, 54; Paredes Manzano, *Casa Mata*, 22; Canales, 69–70.

83. Lott, 53, 56; Horgan, 560–562.

84. Paredes Manzano, *Casa Mata*, 22–23; Graf, 139.

85. Horgan, 562–568.

86. Hinojosa, 53; Horgan, 562–568, and 589–597; Graf, 139.

87. Hinojosa, 54.

88. Graf, 143.

89. Timmons, 88–89.

90. Canseco, 104.

91. Graf, 457; Smylie, 24.

92. John C. Rayburn and Virginia Kemp Rayburn, *Century of Conflict, 1821–1913: Incidents in the Lives of William Neale and William A. Neale, Early Settlers in South Texas* (Waco, TX: Texian Press, 1966), 23 and 52.

93. Canseco, 40.

94. Rupert Norval Richardson, Ernest Wallace, and Adrian N. Anderson, *Texas: The Lone Star State* (Englewood Cliffs, NJ: Prentice–Hall, Inc., 1981), 156.

95. Guerra, 38–42; Hinojosa, 54.

96. Rayburn and Rayburn, 7–10; Guerra, 41–43; James Heaven Thompson, 18–19.

97. Pourade, *The Silver Dons*, 54–56; Mayer, 20–21; Piñera Ramírez, *Historia de Tijuana*, 36.

98. Pourade, *The Silver Dons*, 56–58 and 61–74; Mayer, 21–23.

99. Michael C. Meyer and William L. Sherman, *The Course of Mexican History* (New York: Oxford University Press, 1991), 345; Lieutenant W. H. Chatfield, *The Twin Cities: Brownsville, Texas, Matamoros, Mexico* (New Orleans: E. P. Brandao, 1893), 23; Richard Marcum, "Fort Brown, Texas: The History of a Border Post," Ph.D. dissertation, Texas Technological College, August 1964, 18 and 24.

100. Canseco, 150.

101. Marcum, 31–36; Chatfield, 13 and 28.

102. Ruby A. Wooldridge and Robert B. Vezzetti, *Brownsville: A Pictorial History* (Norfolk, VA: The Donning Company, 1982), 27; James Heaven Thompson, 21; Chatfield, 28; Stambaugh, 76–77.

103. James Heaven Thompson, 21–22; Paredes Manzano, *Casa Mata*, 27–28.

104. Hinojosa, 55–56; Jerry Thompson, *Warm Weather*, 1–2.

105. Stambaugh, 80, 82; James Heaven Thompson, 22–23; Salinas de Villarreal, 62–63; Hinojosa, 55.

106. Pourade, *The Silver Dons*, 90–93; Mayer, 23–24.

107. Timmons, 95.

108. Graf, 157.

109. "Epic of Twin Border Cities Had Beginning in Mid–1700's," in the Vertical File on Brownsville in the Hunter Room of the Arnulfo Oliveira Library of The University of Texas at Brownsville; Stambaugh, 91.

110. Rayburn, vii–viii, 1–6; Chatfield, 12.

111. John F. Schunk (ed.), *1850 U.S. Census: Cameron, Starr and Webb Counties, Texas*, no page numbers given; Chatfield, 23; Hildebrand, 38.

112. Shirley Brooks Greene, *When Rio Grande City Was Young: Buildings of Old Rio Grande City* (Edinburg, TX: Pan American University, 1987), 1; Brian Robertson, *Wild Horse Desert: The Heritage of South Texas* (Edinburg, TX: New Santander Press, 1985), 86–87.

113. Nancy O'Malley, Lynn Osborne Bobbitt, and Dan Scurlock, *A Historical and Archeological Investigation of Roma, Texas* (Austin: Office of the State Archeologist, Texas Historical Commission, October 1976), 4.

114. Sonnichsen, Vol. I, 105; Timmons, 84, 86–87, 105, 109; Oscar J. Martínez, *Border Boom Town* (Austin: University of Texas Press, 1978), 10.

115. Stambaugh, 91.

116. James Robert Crews, "Reconstruction in Brownsville," master's thesis, Texas Tech University, December 1969, 28; Stambaugh, 91 and 104; Schunk, no page given; Chatfield, 23.

117. Eliseo Paredes Manzano, *Conmemoración del CXXV Aniversario de los Honrosos Títulos, de Heróica, Leal e Invicta* (H. Matamoros: Imprenta "El Norte," 1976), 4; David Montejano, *Anglos and Mexicans in the Making of Texas, 1836–1986* (Austin: University of Texas Press, 1987), 42.

118. James Heaven Thompson, 41; Chatfield, 21.

119. Graf, 152–153, 162–163, 169–170, 176, 182, 210; Horgan, 702.

120. Timmons, 91–93 and 95.

121. James Heaven Thompson, 45; Marcum, 15, 91; Horgan, 712, 842; Lott, 57–59.

122. Interview with Claudio Ortiz, Jr., a descendant of José Miguel Ramírez, on 29 September 1985; Paredes Manzano, *Casa Mata*, 26.

123. Horgan, 701, 703.

124. Hinojosa, 55–56; Jerry Thompson, *Warm Weather*, 1–2.

125. Timmons, 95–97.

126. Pourade, *The Silver Dons*, 92 and 267; Davidson and Orcutt, no page numbers given; Mayer, 23–24.

127. Davidson and Orcutt, no page numbers given.

128. Hinojosa, 56–57.

CHAPTER FIVE

1. Antonio María Guerra, *Mier en la Historia* (Mier: n.p., 1953), 44.

2. Gilberto Miguel Hinojosa, *A Borderlands Town in Transition: Laredo, 1755–1870* (College Station: Texas A&M University Press, 1983), 65–66; Oscar J. Martínez, *Border Boom Town* (Austin: University of Texas Press, 1978), 14.

3. Guerra 44; Martínez, *Border Boom Town*, 14.

4. Hinojosa, 65–66.

5. T. R. Fehrenbach, *Lone Star: A History of Texas and the Texans* (New York: Macmillan Company, 1968), 508.

6. Reverend P. F. Parisot, *The Reminiscences of a Texas Missionary* (San Antonio: St. Mary's Church, 1899), 85–89; Gilbert Rafael Cruz and Martha Oppert, *A Century of Service* (Harlingen, TX: United Printers and Publishers, Inc., 1979), 17–18.

7. Lucy H. Wallace, "Father Keralum's Gift," in Valley By–Liners, *Roots by the River* (Mission, TX: Border Kingdom Press, 1978), 58–59; Nancy O'Malley, Lynn Osborne Bobbitt, and Dan Scurlock, *A Historical and Archeological Investigation of Roma, Texas* (Austin: Office of the State Archeologist, October 1976), 4–6.

8. Minnie Gilbert, "Caravans to the Rio Grande," in Valley By–Liners, *Roots by the River* (Mission, TX: Border Kingdom Press, 1978), 7; James Robert Crews, "Reconstruction in Brownsville," master's thesis, Texas Tech University, December 1969, 27; Lieutenant W. H. Chatfield, *The Twin Cities: Brownsville, Texas, Matamoros, Mexico* (New Orleans: E. P. Brandao, 1893), 5, 8; O'Malley, et al., 4–6.

9. Milo Kearney, Alfonso Gómez Arguelles, and Yolanda Z. González, *A Brief History of Education in Brownsville and Matamoros* (Brownsville: The University of Texas–Pan American, 1989), 5–6; Cruz and Oppert, 25.

10. Chatfield, 17.

11. Robert B. Vezzetti, "Steamboats on the Lower Rio Grande in the Nineteenth Century," in Milo Kearney (ed.), *Studies in Brownsville History* (Brownsville: Pan American University at Brownsville, 1986), 77; Minnie Gilbert, "A Petticoat Missionary," in Valley By–Liners, *Roots by the River* (Mission, TX: Border Kingdom Press, 1978), 62, 64; Walter W. Hildebrand, "The History of Cameron County, Texas," master's thesis, North Texas State College, August 1950, 92–93; Ruby A. Wooldridge and Robert B. Vezzetti, *Brownsville: A Pictorial History* (Norfolk, VA: The Donning Company, 1982), 33, 44; Stambaugh, 292; James Heaven Thompson, "A Nineteenth Century History of Cameron County, Texas," master's thesis, University of Texas at Austin, 1965, 63; Crews, 23.

12. Gilbert, "Petticoat," 62, 64; Hildebrand, 92–93; Crews, 23.

13. LeRoy P. Graf, "The Economic History of the Lower Rio Grande Valley," Ph.D. dissertation, Harvard, February 1942, 246.

14. James Heaven Thompson, 32–33.

15. John C. Rayburn and Virginia Kemp Rayburn, *Century of Conflict, 1821–1913: Incidents in the Lives of William Neale and William A. Neale, Early Settlers in South Texas* (Waco, TX: Texian Press, 1966), 53–54; Graf, 229–231; Kearney, "De la Garzas," 55.

16. Rayburn and Rayburn, 53–54; Chatfield, 14; James Heaven Thompson, 78; Crews, 3, 37.

17. Crews, 34, 36, 42; James Heaven Thompson, 77, 79, 80–81; Chatfield, 14.

18. Charles Daniel Dillman, "The Functions of Brownsville, Texas and Matamoros, Tamaulipas," Ph.D. dissertation, University of Michigan, 1968, 65.

19. Wooldridge, *Brownsville*, 86.

20. Crews, 36; Graf, 215–216.

21. Richard Marcum, "Fort Brown, Texas," Ph.D. dissertation, Texas Technological College, August 1964, 67–68.

22. Vezzetti, "Steamboats," 78; Graf, 291; James Heaven Thompson, 55.

23. Graf, 233–235, 246–247; Crews, 4–5.

24. James Heaven Thompson, 39, 75–76.

25. Chatfield, 13, 21.

26. Marjorie Johnson, "Steamboat Captain and Rancher Captain Richard M. King (1824–1885)," in Valley By–Liners, *Roots by the River* (Mission, TX: Border Kingdom Press, 1978), 46–48; Graf, 360; James Heaven Thompson, 39–40.

27. Graf, 470.

28. Chatfield, 18.

29. Milo Kearney and Anthony Knopp, *Boom and Bust: The Historical Cycles of Matamoros and Brownsville* (Austin: Eakin Press, 1991), 74.

30. Crews, 6.

31. James Heaven Thompson, 73.

32. Virgil N. Lott, *Story of Reynosa, Mexico* (N.p.: Complimentary Souvenir Edition, 1920(?)), 57–59; Kearney, "De la Garzas," 55.

33. Ann Reed Washington, "Three Restless Men of Violent Times: Carbajal, Cortina and Ford," in Valley By–Liners, *Roots by the River* (Mission, TX: Border Kingdom Press, 1978), 42; Marcum, 96; James Heaven Thompson, 36.

34. Kearney, "De la Garzas," 54–55.

35. Kearney, *Santanderinos*, 68–69; James Heaven Thompson, 84; Betty Bay, *Historic Brownsville: Original Townsite Guide* (Brownsville: Brownsville Historical Association, 1980), 119, 160.

36. Lilia García, "Francisco Yturria," in Milo Kearney (ed.), *Studies in Matamoros and Brownsville History* (Brownsville: The University of Texas at Brownsville, 1993), no page number assigned yet; Wooldridge, *Brownsville*, 39.

37. Marcum, 47, 77; Graf, 182–184, 226; James Heaven Thompson, 34.

38. A. A. Champion, "The Miller Hotel in the Antebellum Period," in Milo Kearney (ed.), *More Studies in Brownsville History* (Brownsville: Pan American University at Brownsville, 1989), 163–166; Milo D. Kearney, *A Brief History* (Brownsville: University of Texas-Pan American, 1989), 5; James Heaven Thompson 55, 61–62; Wooldridge, *Brownsville*, 39, 58, 60.

39. Lucy Wallace, "McAllen–Father–Son Team," in Valley By-Liners, *Roots by the River* (Mission, TX: Border Kingdom Press, 1978), 78; Brian Robertson, *Wild Horse Desert* (Edinburg, TX: New Santander Press, 1985), 89, 234; Stambaugh, 96.

40. Rosa Salinas de Villarreal, *Reynosa, Nuestra Ciudad* (Reynosa: R.

Ayuntamiento de Reynosa, 1990), 66, 68–71.

41. Thomas E. Simmons, *Fort Ringgold: A Brief Tour* (Edinburg, TX: University of Texas–Pan American Press, 1991), vii; Brian Robertson, *Rio Grande Heritage: A Pictorial History* (Norfolk/Virginia Beach: The Donning Company, 1985), 48; Robertson, *Wild Horse Desert*, 87; Shirley Brooks Greene, *When Rio Grande City was Young* (Edinburg, TX: Pan American University, 1987), 1–3.

42. Robertson, *Rio Grande Heritage*, 49–50; Stambaugh, 160–161.

43. O'Malley, 4–6.

44. Robertson, *Wild Horse Desert*, 86–87.

45. O'Malley, et al., 4.

46. Guerra, 45.

47. James Heaven Thompson, 37, 56; Graf, 240, 255, 266, 297–298; Crews, 20–22, 30–31; Marcum, 54, 57–58; David Montejano, *Anglos and Mexicans in the Making of Texas, 1836–1986* (Austin: University of Texas Press, 1987), 96.

48. Eliseo Paredes Manzano, *Conmemoración* (H. Matamoros: Imprenta "El Norte," 1976), 12; Washington, "Three Restless Men," 40; James Heaven Thompson, 43.

49. Canseco, 123; Washington, "Three Restless Men," 40–41.

50. Margaret Wentworth Petrovich, "The Civil War Career of Colonel John Salmon 'RIP' Ford," master's thesis, Stephen F. Austin State College, August 1961, 1–14, 27; Washington, "Three Restless Men," 40; Paredes Manzano, *Conmemoración*, 8–12, 15; Graf, 321, 326–327, 329.

51. Champion, "Journalism," 131; Washington, "Three Restless Men," 40; Graf, 321, 326–327, 329; Marcum, 70–72; Paredes Manzano, *Conmemoración*, 3–4, 6–7, 8–15, 21–24, 32; James Heaven Thompson, 31, 55; Petrovich, 1–14, 27, 29.

52. Canseco, 127, 130, 132–134; Paredes Manzano, *Casa Mata*, 31; Chatfield, 33; Graf, 660.

53. Martínez, *Border Boom Town*, 15; Paredes Manzano, *Casa Mata*, 31.

54. Kearney, *Brief History*, 3–4; Salinas de Villarreal, 1–4; Canseco, 134, 138.

55. Graf, 663–664.

56. Marcum, 82–83.

57. Crews, 17.

58. Lyman L. Woodman, *Cortina: Rogue of the Rio Grande* (San Antonio: The Naylor Company, 1950); Marcum, 85–88; Fehrenbach, *Lone Star*, 512; Graf, 381; Chatfield, 15, 23; Stambaugh, 105.

59. Graf, 386; Marcum, 92–95, 97–98, 107–112; James Heaven Thompson, 53, 119; Chatfield, 15.

60. Petrovich, 37–47; James Heaven Thompson, 50–51; Stambaugh, 107; Marcum, 122, 129, 131.

61. Salinas de Villarreal, 73.

62. Ben E. Pingenot, *Historical Highlights of Eagle Pass and Maverick County* (Eagle Pass, TX: Eagle Pass Chamber of Commerce, 1971), 1–3, 6.

63. Pingenot 1, 3–6.

64. Pingenot, 4–5, 7.

65. Martínez, *Border Boom Town*, 10; W. H. Timmons, *El Paso: A Borderlands History* (El Paso: Texas Western Press, 1990), 105–106, 109, 118–119.

66. Timmons, 157; Martínez, *Border Boom Town*, 12–13.

67. Sonnichsen, Vol. I, 127, 149; Timmons, 51; Martínez, *Border Boom Town*, 10.

68. Sonnichsen, Vol. I, 122–123, 147–149; Timmons, 105, 109.

69. Sonnichsen, Vol. I, 122–123, 147–149.

70. Sonnichsen, Vol. I, 143–145; Timmons, 107–108, 110–112, 128, 136–137.

71. Timmons, 129, 131; Martínez, *Border Boom Town*, 10.

72. Timmons, 115; Martínez, *Border Boom Town*, 11, 12.

73. Hinojosa, 59; Luis Benedicto, *Historia de Nuevo Laredo* (Nuevo Laredo: n.p., 1956), 13, 15–17, 20, 84.

74. Hinojosa, 56–59, 60–62; Jerry Thompson, *Warm Weather and Bad Whiskey: The 1886 Laredo Election Riot* (El Paso: Texas Western Press, 1991), 3–4, 7–9, 11–12, 14.

75. Jerry Thompson, *Warm Weather*, 7–9, 14–18; Hinojosa, 71.

76. Benedicto, 1920.

77. Frank Love, *From Brothel to Boom Town* (Colorado Springs: Little London Press, 1981), 7, 11–12, 31.

78. Love, 5, 7–9, 31.

79. Pourade, *The Silver Dons*, 162, 166, 196; Mayer, 24–27, 29, 95–96.

80. David Piñera Ramírez (ed.), *Visión Histórica de la Frontera Norte de México* (Tijuana: Universidad Autónoma de Baja California, 1987), Tomo II, 269.

81. Mayer, 24–31.

82. Pourade, *The Silver Dons*, 159–160; Ed Scott, 29; Davidson and Orcutt, no page numbers.

83. Davidson and Orcutt, no page numbers; Pourade, *The Silver Dons*, 178–185.

84. Davidson and Orcutt, no page numbers.

85. David Piñera Ramírez (ed.), *Historia de Tijuana* (Tijuana: Centro de Investigaciones Históricas, 1985), 25, 39.

86. Piñera Ramírez, *Historia de Tijuana*, 53; Piñera Ramírez, *Visión*, Tomo II, 275.

87. Davidson and Orcutt, no page numbers; Mayer, 27.

CHAPTER SIX

1. Richard Pourade, *The Silver Dons* (San Diego: The Union-Tribune Publishing Company, 1963), 246–247; Robert Mayer (ed.), *San Diego: A Chronological and Documentary History* (Dobbs Ferry, NY: Oceana Publications, Inc., 1978), 31–32.

2. David Piñera Ramírez (ed.), *Historia de Tijuana* (Tijuana: Centro de Investigaciones Históricas, 1985), 61–62.

3. Oscar J. Martínez, *Border Boom Town* (Austin: University of Texas Press, 1978), 10; W. H. Timmons, *El Paso: A Borderlands History*, 146–147; Sonnichsen, Vol. I, 144, 153.

4. Timmons, 148–151.

5. Timmons, 154–155.

6. Walter W. Hildebrand, "The History of Cameron County," master's thesis, North Texas State College, August 1950, 46–47; Crews, 1, 5, 9, 13–14, 43.

7. W. H. Chatfield, *The Twin Cities*, 13; James Heaven Thompson, "A Nineteenth Century History of Cameron County," master's thesis, University of Texas at Austin, 1965, 58, 89; Petrovich, 59, 62.

8. Jerry Thompson, *Warm Weather* (El Paso: University of Texas at El Paso, 1991), 21–22.

9. Luis Benedicto, *Historia de Nuevo Laredo* (Nuevo Laredo, Tamaulipas: n.p., 1956), 22.

10. Eliseo Paredes Manzano, *La Casa Mata y Fortificaciones de la Heróica Matamoros* (H. Matamoros: Imprenta "El Norte," 1974), 33–34, 93.

11. Rosa Salinas de Villarreal, *Reynosa, Nuestra Ciudad* (Reynosa: R. Ayuntamiento de Reynosa, 1990), 87–88.

12. Benedicto, 21–22, 25–26, 31.

13. Milo Kearney and Anthony Knopp, *Boom and Bust: The Historical Cycles of Matamoros and Brownsville* (Austin: Eakin Press, 1991), 161–162.

14. Petrovich, 50–62; Richard Marcum, "Fort Brown, Texas," Ph.D. dissertation, Texas Technological College, August 1964, 86; Hildebrand, 46–47; Chatfield, 28.

15. Ruby A. Wooldridge and Robert B.Vezzetti, *Brownsville: A Pictorial History* (Norfolk, VA: The Dunning Company, 1982), 38–39; Crews, 44; James Heaven Thompson, 87, 91.

16. Jerry Thompson, *Warm Weather*, 23, 25.

17. Jerry Thompson, *Warm Weather*, 25.

18. Hildebrand, 48; Charles Dillman, "The Functions of Brownsville, Texas, and Matamoros, Tamaulipas," Ph.D. dissertation, University of Michigan, 1968, 66; Fehrenbach, *Lone Star*, 359; Petrovich, 59–60, 64.

19. Tom Carroll, "Heróica Matamoros, Tamaulipas: Where Were the Fortifications of the Walled City?" in Milo Kearney (ed.), *Studies in Brownsville and Matamoros History* (Brownsville: The University of Texas at Brownsville, 1995), 75–121.

20. José Raúl Canseco, *Historia de Matamoros* (H. Matamoros: Litográfica Jardín, 1981), 145–146; LeRoy P. Graf, "The Economic History of the Lower Rio Grande Valley," Ph.D. dissertation, Harvard, February 1942, 494; Paredes Manzano, *Casa Mata*, 33–34; Eliseo Paredes Manzano, *Conmemoración* (H. Matamoros: Imprenta "El Norte," 1976), 9.

21. John Warren Hunter, "The Fall of Brownsville, 1863," in Milo Kearney (ed.), *More Studies in Brownsville History*, 220, 227; Petrovich, 76; Crews, 55; Graf, 527; Hildebrand, 48–49; Jerry Thompson, *Warm Weather*, 27–28.

22. Marcum, 166–167; Chatfield, 13.

23. Salinas de Villarreal, 89.

24. Fehrenbach, *Lone Star*, 388; Graf, 529.

25. Benedicto, 26–27.

26. Graf, 595; Crews, 60; Canseco, 147; Petrovich, 123–126, 129, 132; Marcum, 171–173; Paredes Manzano, *Casa Mata*, 36–40; Fehrenbach, *Lone Star*, 386–387.

27. Piñera Ramírez, *Visión*, Tomo II, 234.

28. Benedicto, 26–27.

29. Salinas de Villarreal, 89.

30. Crews, 61–64.

31. Canseco, 152; Paredes Manzano, *Casa Mata*, 45–48.

32. Paredes Manzano, *Casa Mata*, 47; James Heaven Thompson, 100.

33. Rev. P. F. Parisot, *The Reminiscences of a Texas Missionary* (San Antonio: St. Mary's Church, 1899), 56–58.

34. Salinas de Villarreal, 89; Paredes Manzano, *Casa Mata*, 50–51; Graf, 606–608; Canseco, 153.

35. Paredes Manzano, *Casa Mata*, 50–51; Graf, 606–608; Canseco, 153.

36. Paredes Manzano, *Casa Mata*, 51–55, 57; Canseco, 153.

37. Graf, 594.

38. Crews, 60.

39. Minnie Gilbert, "Safe in No–Man's Land," in Valley By–Liners, *Roots by the River* (Mission, TX: Border Kingdom Press, 1978), 71; Kearney, *A Brief History*, 3; Parisot, 55; James Heaven Thompson, 94; Marcum, 156–159; Champion, "Journalism," 137; Graf, 494–495; Oscar J. Martínez, *Border Boom Town*, 15.

40. Jaime Mendoza Martínez, *Historia del Teatro de la Reforma* (Matamoros: El Colegio de la Frontera Norte, 1992), 19.

41. James Heaven Thompson, 76, 90, 92, 94; Marcum, 150; Petrovich, 64; Crews, 50.

42. Graf, 572–573.

43. Crews, 48, 50, 60, 72; James Heaven Thompson, 90; Hildebrand, 46–47.

44. Chatfield, 21; James Heaven Thompson, 114.

45. Salinas de Villarreal, 89.

46. Antonio María Guerra, *Mier en la Historia* (Mier: n.p., 1953), 45; Nancy O'Malley, Lynn Osborne Bobbitt, and Dan Scurlock, *A Historical and Archeological Investigation of Roma, Texas* (Austin: Office of the State Archeologist, October 1976), 5.

47. Jerry Thompson, *Warm Weather*, 20–28.

48. Ben E. Pingenot, *Historical Highlights of Eagle Pass* (Eagle Pass, TX: Eagle Pass Chamber of Commerce, 1971), 5–7.

49. Oscar J. Martínez, *Border Boom Town*, 16–17.

50. Crews, 68–76, 115; Champion, "Journalism," 143–144; Petrovich, 158.

51. Graf, 666–668, 670, 719; Chatfield, 24.

52. James Heaven Thompson, 76, 106; Wooldridge, *Brownsville*, 35.

53. Paul Horgan, *Great River* (New York: Holt, Rinehart, and Winston, 1971), 855–856; Marcum, 181, 185–186; Crews, 83–84; Stambaugh, 152.

54. Rayburn, 116, 120; Stambaugh, 151; Paredes Manzano, *Casa Mata*, 60; Marcum, 201; Chatfield, 32.

55. James Heaven Thompson, 105–110; David Montejano, *Anglos and Mexicans in the Making of Texas* (Austin: University of Texas Press, 1987), 96; Cruz and Oppert, 22; Crews, 104–107.

56. Jerry Thompson, *Warm Weather*, 33–34.

57. Jerry Thompson, *Warm Weather*, 18, 31, 37.

58. Ovie Clark Fisher, *King Fisher* (Norman, OK: The University of Oklahoma Press, 1966), passim; Pingenot, 7.

59. Timmons, 150–151, 156–157, 162; Sonnichsen, Vol. I, 168–171.

60. Timmons, 158–159, 161.

61. Timmons, 151–152, 165–166.

62. Parisot, 66–74.

63. Guerra, 45.

64. Martínez, *Border Boom Town*, 16–17.

65. Parisot, 56; Canseco, 165.

66. Canseco, 76.

67. Canseco, 182; Graf, 619; Paredes Manzano, *Casa Mata*, 59–60.

68. Canseco, 161–162.

69. Guerra, 46.

70. O'Malley, Bobbitt, and Scurlock, 5.

71. Benedicto, 31, 35.

72. Graf, 674.

73. Manuel Cantú Olvera, *Narraciones* (N.p.: Canales Herrán, no date), 40, 93–96; Piñera Ramírez, *Visión*, Tomo III, 48–49.

74. Timmons, 162–163.

75. Mayer, 32.

76. Pourade, *The Glory Years*, *Vol. IV of the History of San Diego* (San Diego: The Union-Tribune Publishing Company, 1963), 10–11.

77. Pourade, *The Glory Years*, 12; Mayer, 101.

78. Mayer, 101–102.

79. Mayer, 103–104.

80. Mayer, 33–34, 104.

81. Ed Davidson and Eddy Orcutt, *The Country of Joyous Aspect* (San Diego: San Diego Trust and Savings Bank, 1929), no p.n.; Mayer, 34–39.

82. Mayer, 33–41.

CHAPTER SEVEN

1. Luis Benedicto, *Historia de Nuevo Laredo* (Nuevo Laredo, Tamaulipas: n.p., 1956), 31–33, 36, 89; LeRoy P. Graf, "The Economic History of the Lower Rio Grande Valley," Ph.D. dissertation, Harvard, February 1942, 619–620; Bruce Aiken, "Telephone Plays Role in Cross–border History," *The Brownsville Herald Plus*, 4 August 1993, 2; Ovie Clark Fisher, *King Fisher* (Norman, OK: University of Oklahoma Press, 1966), 46.

2. Eliseo Paredes Manzano, *La Casa Mata* (H. Matamoros: Imprenta "El Norte," 1974), 60–62; Angel Taracena, *Porfirio Díaz* (México: Editorial Jus, S.A., 1960), 103.

3. José Raúl Canseco, *Historia de Matamoros* (H. Matamoros: Litográfica Jardín, 1981), 148, 174.

4. Rosa Salinas de Villarreal, *Reynosa, Nuestra Ciudad* (Reynosa: R. Ayuntamiento de Reynosa, 1990), 93–94.

5. Luis Benedicto, *Historia de Nuevo Laredo* (Nuevo Laredo, Tamaulipas: N.p., 1956), 36.

6. Frank Cushman Pierce, *Texas' Last Frontier: A Brief History of the Lower Rio Grande Valley* (Menasha, WI: The Collegiate Press, George Banta Publishing Company, 1917, republished in 1962, 72; Manuel F. Rodríguez Brayda, "Así paga el Diablo," in Milo Kearney (ed.), *More Studies in Brownsville History* (Brownsville: Pan American University at Brownsville, 1989), 86–88; Taracena, 104; Paredes Manzano, *Casa Mata*, 61–62; Rayburn, 113; Canseco, 172.

7. Salinas de Villarreal, 93–94.

8. Taracena, 104–106.

9. Oscar J. Martínez, *Border Boom Town* (Austin: University of Texas Press, 1978), 17.

10. Martínez, *Border Boom Town*, 16, 25–27; Salinas de Villarreal, 85.

11. Martínez, *Border Boom Town*, 19–20, 28–30; Piñera Ramírez, *Visión*, Tomo II, 350.

12. Martínez, *Border Boom Town*, 19–20, Salinas de Villarreal, 95, 97; *The Brownsville Herald*, 6 Dec 1942, 1–2D; Walter W. Hildebrand, "The History of Cameron County," master's thesis, North Texas State College, August 1950, 74–75; Brian Robertson, *Wild Horse Desert*, 148–149.

13. Martínez, *Border Boom Town*, 35.

14. Timmons, 166–168; Martínez, *Border Boom Town*, 20–23.

15. C. L. Sonnichsen, *Pass of the North* (El Paso: Texas Western Press, 1968), Vol. I, 249; Timmons, 176.

16. Martínez, *Border Boom Town*, 33.

17. Martínez, *Border Boom Town*, 21, 32–33.

18. Sonnichsen, Vol. I, 233, 252, 258; Timmons, 171–179, 193–194.

19. Timmons, 172–173, 190–192.

20. Sonnichsen, Vol. I, 233, 252, 258; Timmons, 171–179, 193–194; Brian Robertson, *Rio Grande Heritage: A Pictorial History* (Norfolk/ Virginia Beach: The Donning Co., 1985), 105.

21. Timmons, 174–175, 185; Martínez, *Border Boom Town*, 34.

22. Piñera Ramírez, *Visión*, Tomo II, 345, 349; Martínez, *Border Boom Town*, 17, 21, 23–25, 29–30.

23. Luis Benedicto, *Historia de Nuevo Laredo* (Nuevo Laredo, Tamaulipas: n.p., 1956), 40, 46, 59; Jerry Thompson, *Warm Weather and Bad Whiskey* (El Paso: Texas Western Press, 1991), 45–46.

24. Benedicto, 40, 48–51.

25. Piñera Ramírez, *Historia de Tijuana*, 62; Mayer, 40–42.

26. Robert Mayer (ed.), *San Diego: A Chronological and Documentary History* (Dobbs Ferry, NY: Oceana Publications, Inc., 1978), 42–44.

27. Mayer, 47, 53.

28. Piñera Ramírez, *Historia de Tijuana*, 76; Mayer, 45–48, 50.

29. Piñera Ramírez, *Historia de Tijuana*, 25–26, 55–56, 59.

30. Piñera Ramírez, *Historia de Tijuana*, 62, 64, 66–67.

31. Ben E. Pingenot, *Historical Highlights of Eagle Pass* (Eagle Pass, TX: Eagle Pass Chamber of Commerce, 1971), 7–8, 10–11, 16, 18; Oscar J. Martínez, *Border Boom Town*, 21, 24, 30.

32. Fisher, passim.

33. Tom Miller, *On the Border: Portraits of America's Southwestern Frontier* (Tucson: The University of Arizona Press, 1981), 65; Leon C. Metz, *Border: The U.S.-Mexican Line* (El Paso: Mangan Books, 1989), 161–164.

34. Raúl A. Fernández, *The Mexican-American Border Region* (Notre Dame, IN: University of Notre Dame Press, 1989), 11; Metz, 164, 177–178.

35. Pingenot, 10–11.

36. Frank Love, *From Brothel to Boom Town: Yuma's Naughty Past* (Colorado Springs: Little London Press, 1981), 18, 29, 30–31, 47.

37. Celso Aguirre Bernal, *Compendio Histórico-Biográfico de Mexicali, 1539–1966* (Mexicali: n.p., 1966), 53.

38. Siliva Raquel Flores García, *Nogales: Un Siglo en la Historia* (Hermosillo, Sonora: Editorial Reprográfica, S.A., 1987), 9–10, 13–14.

39. Flores García, 21, 27–28, 31, 33–34, 36, 45; Metz, 109–110.

40. Martínez, *Border Boom Town*, 20.

41. Flores García, 27–28, 31, 33, 40, 45, 67; Metz, 109–110.

42. Flores García, 27–46; Metz, 102–103.

43. Metz, 110–111.

44. Flores García, 27–46.

45. Daniel D. Arreola and James R. Curtis, *The Mexican Border Cities* (Tucson: University of Arizona Press, 1993), 15, 20–21.

46. Metz, 246–247, 258–263; Celso Aguirre Bernal, *Compendio Histórico-Biográfico de Mexicali* (Mexicali: n.p., 1966), 55.

47. Mayer, 48.

48. Aguirre, 55.

49. Aguirre, 21, 42–43.

50. Fernández, 86; Aguirre, 45–46, 66–67, 75, 77.

51. Aguirre, 66–67; Metz, 252, 265.

52. Hildebrand, 73–74; James Heaven Thompson, 113; Canseco, 178–179.

53. Lieutenant W. H. Chatfield, *The Twin Cities: Brownsville, Texas, Matamoros, Mexico* (New Orleans: E. P. Brandao, 1893), 20, 27; Kearney, *A Brief History*, 9; James Heaven Thompson, 80, 114–115, 119–121; Minnie Gilbert, "Caravans to the Rio Grande," 6.

54. Chatfield, 32–33.

55. Canseco, 33, 76, 97, 174, 176, 178–179; Richard Marcum, "Fort Brown, Texas," Ph.D. dissertation, Texas Technological College, August 1964, 238–240.

56. Marcum, 217; Canseco, 184.

57. Guerra, 47.

58. Kearney, *A Brief History*, 7; Canseco, 184.

59. *The Brownsville Herald*, 6 December 1942, 1–2D; Hildebrand, 74–76; Brian Robertson, *Wild Horse Desert* (Edinburg, TX: New Santander Press, 1985), 148–149.

60. Hildebrand, 77.

61. Canseco, 186.

62. James Heaven Thompson, 107.

63. Piñera Ramírez, *Visión*, Tomo II, 400.

64. Graf, 438; Charles Daniel Dillman, "The Functions of Brownsville, Texas and Matamoros, Tamaulipas," Ph.D. dissertation, University of Michigan, 1968, 76–77.

65. Fehrenbach, *Lone Star*, 687–688.

66. Wooldridge, *Brownsville*, 84.

67. Dillman, 30, 71, 74; Hildebrand, 41–42.

68. J. Lee and Lilian J. Stambaugh, *The Lower Rio Grande Valley of Texas* (Austin: Jenkins Publishing Co., 1974), 266; *Herald*, 6 December 1942, 7D and 4 July 1967, 15B.

69. Ruby A. Wooldridge and Robert B. Vezzetti, *Brownsville: A Pictorial History* (Norfolk, VA: The Donning Company, 1982), 86.

70. *Herald*, 6 December 1942, 7D and 8G.

71. Minnie Gilbert, "Joseph Kleiber of Alsace-Lorraine," in Valley By-Liners, *Rio Grande Roundup: Story of Texas' Tropical Borderland* (Mission, TX: Border Kingdom Press, 1980), 128; Wooldridge, *Brownsville*, 86, 123; *Herald*, 6 December 1942, 4E, and 4 July 1967, 7C.

72. Dillman, 70; Stambaugh, 319.

73. *Herald*, 6 December 1942, 3D.

74. Canseco, 198.

75. William V. Wilkinson, "Lawlessness in Cameron County and the City of Brownsville: 1900 to 1912," in Milo Kearney (ed.), *More Studies in Brownsville History* (Brownsville: Pan American University at Brownsville, 1989), 297–300; Rodolfo Rocha, "Background to Banditry in the Lower Rio Grande Valley of Texas: 1900 to 1912," master's thesis, Pan American University, 1974, 37–38; Rodolfo Rocha, "The Influence of the Mexican Revolution on the Mexican-Texan Border, 1910–1916," Ph.D. dissertation, Texas Tech University, May 1981, 41; Robertson, *Wild Horse Desert*, 203–207; Frank Pierce, 113–114; Stambaugh, 207.

76. Américo Paredes, "El Corrido de Gregorio Cortez: A Ballad of Border Conflict," Ph.D. dissertation, University of Texas, 1956, 25; Rocha, "Background," 72, 100.

77. Lucy H. Wallace, "McAllen—Father-Son Team," in Valley By-Liners, *Roots by the River* (Mission, TX: Border Kingdom Press, 1978), 77; Stambaugh, 175; Robertson, *Rio Grande Heritage*, 115.

78. Robertson, *Rio Grande Heritage*, 115.

79. Stambaugh, 175–177.

80. Stambaugh, 184–186, 232–233, 236, 266, 303.

81. Virgil N. Lott, *Story of Reynosa, Mexico* (N.p.: Complimentary Souvenir Edition, 1920(?)), 1.

82. Piñera Ramírez, *Visión*, Tomo II, 425–426.

83. Arreola and Curtis, 20, 81.

84. David M. Pletcher, *Rails, Mines, and Progress: Seven American Promoters in Mexico, 1867–1911* (Port Washington, NY: Kennikat Press, 1958), 290; Arreola and Curtis, 16, 81.

85. Arreola and Curtis, 20.

86. Metz, 164–165, 168.

87. Salinas de Villarreal, 96–97.

88. Metz, 165–167.

89. Metz, 153.

90. Charles M. Robinson III, *Bad Hand: A Biography of General Ranald S. Mackenzie* (Austin: State House Press, 1993), 43.

91. Eldon Cagle, Jr., *The History of Fort Sam Houston*, no page numbers.

92. Timmons, 173–174, 188–190.

93. Walter Pierce, "The Brownsville Raid: A Historical Assessment," in Milo Kearney (ed.), *Studies in Brownsville History* (Brownsville: Pan American University at Brownsville, 1989), 220–227; Albert Bigelow Paine, *Captain Bill McDonald: Texas Ranger* (New York: J. J. Little and Ives Co., 1909); Marcum, 265–273; Robertson, *Wild Horse Desert*, 207–211, 213; Rayburn, 139; Wooldridge, *Brownsville*, 87, 92–93; Frank Pierce, 121; *Herald* 14 August 1906, 1.

94. Cagle, no page number.

95. Flores García, 55.

96. Flores García, 56–58.

97. Evan Anders, *Boss Rule in South Texas* (Austin: University of Texas Press, 1982), 13–14.

98. Ozzie G. Simmons, *Anglo Americans and Mexican Americans in South Texas*

(New York: Arno Press, 1974), 272–292; Jerry Thompson, *Laredo: A Pictorial History* (Norfolk, VA: The Donning Company, 1986), 180–194.

99. Anders, 4–23; Russell C. Richardson and Anthony K. Knopp, *A Citizens' Guide to Government and Politics in Brownsville* (Valencia, CA: Blue Moon Publishing Co., 1987), 9.

100. Anders, 13.

101. Anders, 12, 143–144.

102. Stambaugh, 175; Robertson, *Wild Horse Desert*, 195–196.

103. Robertson, *Wild Horse Desert*, 224.

104. *Herald*, 20 October 1908, 1.

105. Robertson, *Wild Horse Desert*, 234–237.

106. Jerry Thompson, *Laredo*, 114.

107. Jerry Thompson, *Warm Weather*, 40.

108. Jerry Thompson, *Warm Weather*, 43–44, 55.

109. Jerry Thompson, *Warm Weather*, 66–67.

110. Jerry Thompson, *Warm Weather*, 85–99.

111. Jerry Thompson, *Warm Weather*, 130–134, 143–144.

112. Jerry Thompson, *Laredo*, 123, 194, 214–216, 234.

113. Jerry Thompson, *Laredo*, 184; Wilkinson, 374–375.

114. Timmons, 165–166; Metz 170–172.

115. Timmons, 172–175.

116. Sonnichsen, Vol. I, 350–353.

117. Timmons, 192–193.

118. Mayer, 33–45.

119. Stephen Birmingham, *California Rich* (New York: Simon and Schuster, 1980), 64–65; Richard F. Pourade, *Gold in the Sun, Vol. V of The History of San Diego* (San Diego: The Union-Tribune Publishing Company, 1965), 15–17, 29, 34.

120. Michael C. Meyer and William L. Sherman, *The Course of Mexican History* (New York: Oxford University Press, 1991), 454–456; Juan Fidel Zorrilla, Maribel Mir Flaguer, y Octavio Herrera-Pérez (ed.), *Tamaulipas: textos de su historia, 1810–1921* (Mexico City: Instituto de Investigaciones Dr. José María Luis Mora, 1990), Vol. II, 59–61.

121. Adaljiza Sosa Riddell, "Who Cares Who Governs? A Historical Analysis of Local Governing Elites in Mexicali, Mexico," Ph.D. dissertation, University of California, Riverside, 1974, 49, 56–57; William P. Tucker, *The Mexican Government Today* (Minneapolis: University of Minnesota Press, 1957), 399.

122. Kearney and Knopp, *Boom and Bust*, 155–156, 171; Zorrilla, Mir Flaguer y Herrera, II, 61–62.

123. Kearney and Knopp, *Boom and Bust*, 182–183.

124. *Reynosa, nuestra ciudad* (Reynosa, Tamaulipas: Ateneo de Reynosa, 1987), 94–97.

125. Benedicto, 36–41, 86–87.

126. Benedicto, 41–49, 85–86, 90.

127. Piñera Ramírez, *Historia de Tijuana*, 62–66; John A. Price, *Tijuana: Urbanization in a Border Culture* (Notre Dame, IN: University of Notre Dame Press, 1973), 46.

128. Piñera Ramírez, *Historia de Tijuana*, 67.

129. Martínez, *Border Boom Town*, 35–36.

Notes

CHAPTER EIGHT

1. Luis Benedicto, *Historia de Nuevo Laredo* (Nuevo Laredo, Tamaulipas: n.p., 1956), 59.

2. Rosa Salinas de Villarreal, *Reynosa, Nuestra Ciudad* (Reynosa: R. Ayuntamiento de Reynosa, 1990), 99.

3. Manuel Cantú Olvera, *Narraciones Monográficas de Cd. Acuña* (N.p.: Canales Herrán, no date given), 95.

4. Benedicto, 59.

5. Silvia Raquel Flores García, *Nogales: Un Síglo en la Historia* (Hermosillo, Sonora: Editorial Reprográfica, S.A., 1987), 51.

6. Ben E. Pingenot, *Historical Highlights of Eagle Pass and Maverick County* (Eagle Pass, TX: Eagle Pass Chamber of Commerce, 1971), 12.

7. Leon C. Metz, *Border: The U.S.-Mexican Line* (El Paso: Mangan Books, 1989), 206–208.

8. David Piñera Ramírez (ed.), *Historia de Tijuana*, 73–74, 76.

9. Celso Aguirre Bernal, *Compendio Histórico-Biográfico de Mexicali* (Mexicali: N.p., 1966), 91; David Piñera Ramírez (ed.), *Visión Histórica de la Frontera Norte de Mexico* (Tijuana: Universidad Autónoma de Baja California, 1987), Tomo III, 146.

10. Piñera Ramírez, *Historia de Tijuana*, 76–77.

11. Piñera Ramírez, *Historia de Tijuana*, 77–80.

12. Piñera Ramírez, *Historia de Tijuana*, 76, 80–83; Oscar J. Martínez, *Troublesome Border* (Tucson: University of Arizona Press, 1988), 48.

13. W. H. Timmons, *El Paso: A Borderlands History* (El Paso: Texas Western Press, 1990), 211–212.

14. Don M. Coerver and Linda B. Hall, *Texas y la Revolución Mexicana: Un Estudio sobre la Política froneriza nacional y estatal, 1910–1920*, trans. by Carlos Valdés (México: Fondo de Cultura Económica, 1988), 38–39; Oscar J. Martínez, *Border Boom Town* (Austin: University of Texas Press, 1978), 39; Timmons, 213.

15. Timmons, 214.

16. Benedicto, 59, 91.

17. Jerry Thompson, *Warm Weather and Bad Whiskey* (El Paso: Texas Western Press, 1991), 143–144.

18. Robert Mayer (ed.), *San Diego: A Chronological and Documentary History, 1535–1976* (Dobbs Ferry, NY: Oceana Publications, Inc., 1978), 50–53; Piñera Ramírez, *Historia de Tijuana*, 70, 72, 76.

19. Mayer, 51–52, 120–122.

20. Coerver and Hall, 59; Timmons, 214; Piñera Ramírez, *Visión*, Tomo III, 7.

21. Coerver and Hall, 60–62; Martínez, *Border Boom Town*, 39.

22. Timmons, 215–216.

23. Michael C. Meyer and William L. Sherman, *The Course of Mexican History* (New York: Oxford University Press, 1991), 518–521.

24. Flores García, 52.

25. Timmons, 216–217.

26. Salinas de Villarreal, 100–101.

27. Eliseo Paredes Manzano, *La Casa Mata y Fortificaciones de la Heróica Matamoros, Tamaulipas* (H. Matamoros: Imprenta "El Norte," 1974), 62, 65; José

Raúl Canseco, *Historia de Matamoros*, 202–205; *The Brownsville Herald*, 6 December 1942, 3E and 12 May 1913, 1 and 4.

28. Paredes Manzano, *Casa Mata*, 65–66; Canseco, 202–205; Ruby A. Wooldridge and Robert B. Vezzetti, *Brownsville: A Pictorial History* (Norfolk, VA: The Donning Company, 1982), 87, 90; *The Brownsville Herald* 4 June 1913, 1, and 4 July 1967, 20.

29. Armando Hugo Ortiz Guerrero, *Vida y Muerte en la Frontera: Cancionero del Corrido Norestense* (Cd. Victoria: Hensa Editores, S.A., 1992), 128–129.

30. Paredes Manzano, *Casa Mata*, 66–67, 90; Canseco, 202–208; J. Lee and Lilian Stambaugh, *The Lower Rio Grande Valley of Texas* (Austin: Jenkins Publishing Co., 1974), 209.

31. Paredes Manzano, *Casa Mata*, 65, 90; Canseco, 202–208; Frank Pierce, *Texas' Last Frontier* (Menasha, WI: Collegiate Press, 1917, republished 1962), 77–78, 80–81; Robertson, *Wild Horse Desert*, 241; Stambaugh, 209; *The Brownsville Herald*, 17 February 1913, 1 and 6 December 1942, 4H.

32. Timmons, 217.

33. Martínez, *Border Boom Town*, 42–43; Timmons, 219.

34. Mayer, 52.

35. Timmons, 220.

36. Canseco, 212–215; Paredes Manzano, *Casa Mata*, 69–70; Pierce, 89.

37. Canseco, 212–218; Paredes Manzano, *Casa Mata*, 69–70.

38. Jake Watts, "The Plan of San Diego and the Lower Rio Grande Valley," in Milo Kearney (ed.), *More Studies in Brownsville History* (Brownsville: Pan American University at Brownsville, 1989), 323–329, 333–334; Richard Marcum, "Fort Brown, Texas," Ph.D. dissertation, Texas Technological College, August 1964, 289–290; T. R. Fehrenbach, *Lone Star: A History of Texas and the Texans* (New York: Macmillan, 1968), 691.

39. Coerver and Hall, 104–106, 110; Watts, 323–329, 334; Fehrenbach, *Lone Star*, 691; Marcum, 289–291; Timmons, 220.

40. Pierce, 96–97; Robertson, *Wild Horse Desert*, 257–258.

41. *The Brownsville Herald*, 4 July 1967, 2C; Evan Anders, *Boss Rule in South Texas* (Austin: University of Texas Press, 1982), 220–221; Pierce, 96–97; Robertson, *Wild Horse Desert*, 257–258; Marcum, 284–286.

42. Coerver and Hall, 110.

43. Martínez, *Border Boom Town*, 45–46; Timmons, 221.

44. Metz, 224–225; Raúl A. Fernández, *The Mexican-American Border Regions: Issues and Trends* (Notre Dame, IN: University of Notre Dame Press, 1989), 29.

45. Metz, 224–225; Pingenot, 12, 14–15.

46. Martínez, *Border Boom Town*, 40

47. Martínez, *Border Boom Town*, 43–44.

48. Flores García, 54.

49. Coerver and Hall, 124, 127–129.

50. Fehrenbach, *Lone Star*, 691.

51. Coerver and Hall, 145; Martínez, *Border Boom Town*, 40; Timmons, 222.

52. Martínez, *Border Boom Town*, 40–41.

53. Anders, 235; Wooldridge, *Brownsville*, 101.

54. Martínez, *Border Boom Town*, 45.

55. Piñera Ramírez, 98.

56. Edilmiro Villarreal, *Antiguo Instituto Científico y Literario de San Juan: Año de 1864* (Matamoros: n.p., 1962), 6, 7, 12, 13, 15.

57. Canseco, 176.

58. Zavaleta, "The Twin Cities," 162.

59. Martínez, *Border Boom Town*, 40–41.

60. Virgil N. Lott, *Story of Reynosa, Mexico* (N.p.: Complimentary Souvenir Edition, 1920(?)), 1.

61. Pingenot, 12, 14; Martínez, *Border Boom Town*, 41.

62. Benedicto, 61–62.

63. Martínez, *Border Boom Town*, 40, 46–47, 49–50.

64. Piñera Ramírez, *Visión*, Tomo III, 44.

65. Charles Daniel Dillman, "The Functions of Brownsville, Texas," Ph.D. dissertation, University of Michigan, 1968, 78–79; Watts, 332–333.

66. Wooldridge, *Brownsville*, 87; Pierce, 89–91, 93; Stambaugh, 211–213; Hildebrand, 43.

67. Zavaleta, "The Twin Cities," 162.

68. Anders, 217; *The Brownsville Herald*, 4 July 1967, 20; Marcum, 284–286.

69. Anders, 232–233.

70. Pingenot, 12.

71. Wooldridge, *Brownsville*, 101.

72. Timmons, 198, 200, 218.

73. Martínez, *Border Boom Town*, 49.

74. Timmons, 205.

75. Flores García, 44–46.

76. Piñera Ramírez, *Visión*, Tomo III, 138.

77. Aguirre, 243.

78. Daniel D. Arreola and James R. Curtis, *The Mexican Border Cities: Landscape and Anatomy and Place Personality* (Tucson: University of Arizona Press, 1993), 21.

79. Aguirre, 167, 170–171, 179–180, 183–184, 186–188.

80. Mayer, 53–55.

81. Timmons, 239–240; Flores García, 58–59.

82. Metz, 237.

83. Anders, 12; Rupert N. Richardson, Ernest Wallace, and Adrian N. Anderson, *Texas: The Lone Star State* (Englewood Cliffs, NJ: Prentice-Hall, Inc., 1981), 10–11.

84. Anders, 148–149.

85. Kearney and Knopp, *Boom and Bust*, 202–204; Ralph Schmeling, "The Murder of Joe Crixell," in Milo Kearney (ed.), *More Studies in Brownsville History* (Brownsville: Pan American University at Brownsville, 1989), 318–319.

86. Anders, 163–165.

87. Anders, 278–279.

88. Norman Binder and Frank García, "Winning Political Office in Cameron County, 1876–1988: The Mexican-American Case," in Milo Kearney (ed.), *More Studies in Brownsville History* (Brownsville: Pan American University at Brownsville, 1989), 430–437.

89. Anders, 168–170.

90. Anders, 147–148, 170; Simmons, 272–273.

91. Jerry Thompson, *Laredo: A Pictorial History* (Norfolk, VA: The Donning Company, 1986), 123; J. B. Wilkinson, *Laredo and the Rio Grande Frontier* (Austin: Jenkins Publishing Co., 1975), 383.

92. Jerry Thompson, *Laredo*, 194.

93. Flores García, 158–64.

94. Timmons, 215.

95. Flores García, 168–69.

96. Timmons, 224.

97. Richard F. Pourade, *Gold in the Sun, Vol. V of the History of San Diego* (San Diego: The Union-Tribune Publishing Co., 1965), 41–43.

98. Pourade, *Gold in the Sun*, 86–87, 90.

99. Pourade, *Gold in the Sun*, 112–173.

100. Iris H. W. Engstrand, *San Diego: California's Cornerstone* (Tulsa: Continental Heritage Press, 1980), 91; Pourade, *Gold in the Sun*, 171–173, 223–224, 235.

101. *The Brownsville Herald*, 17 February 1913, 1.

102. Kearney and Knopp, *Boom and Bust*, 208–211; Piñera Ramírez, *Historia de Tijuana*, 89.

103. *Reynosa, nuestra ciudad* (Reynosa: Tamaulipas: Ateneo de Reynosa, 1987), 99–102.

104. Benedicto, 59–61.

105. Benedicto, 61–65.

106. Flores García, 173–178; C. L. Sonnichsen, *Pass of the North* (El Paso: Texas Western Press, 1968), Vol. I, 399.

107. William H. Beezley, *Insurgent Governor: Abraham Gonzales and the Mexican Revolution in Chihuahua* (Lincoln: University of Nebraska Press, 1973), 97–104, 109; Flores García, 172–178; Piñera Ramírez, *Historia de Tijuana*, 15; Martínez, *Border Boom Town*, 53.

108. Timmons, 227–228; Martínez, *Border Boom Town* 45, 53; Piñera Ramírez, *Historia de Tijuana*, 25, 34.

109. Piñera Ramírez, *Historia de Tijuana*, 93–94.

110. Adaljiza Sosa Riddell, "Who Cares Who Governs?" Ph.D. dissertation, University of California, Riverside, 1974, 50–53.

111. Sosa, 52–53; Piñera Ramírez, *Tijuana*, 95–98; John A. Price, *Tijuana: Urbanization in a Border Culture* (Notre Dame, IN: University of Notre Dame Press, 1973), 48–51.

CHAPTER NINE

1. Oscar J. Martínez, *Border Boom Town* (Austin: University of Texas Press, 1978), 75.

2. Antonio N. Zavaleta, "The Twin Cities: A Historical Synthesis of the Socio-Economic Interdependence of the Brownsville-Matamoros Border Community," in Milo Kearney, ed., *Studies in Brownsville History*, 125–173.

3. Milo Kearney and Anthony Knopp, *Boom and Bust: The Historical Cycles of Matamoros and Brownsville* (Austin: Eakin Press, 1991), 224.

4. *The Brownsville Herald*, 24 April 1924, 1.

5. Martínez, *Border Boom Town*, 75.

6. W. H. Timmons, *El Paso: A Borderlands History* (El Paso: Texas Western Press, 1990), 292.

7. Martínez, *Border Boom Town*, 62–63.

8. Timmons, 235–237.

9. Martínez, *Border Boom Town*, 62–63.

10. Charles Daniel Dillman, "The Functions of Brownsville, Texas and Matamoros, Tamaulipas," Ph.D. dissertation, University of Michigan, 1968, 79; Walter W. Hildebrand, "The History of Cameron County, Texas," master's thesis, North Texas State College, August 1950, 57.

11. Dillman, 94; J. Lee and Lilian Stambaugh, *The Lower Rio Grande Valley of Texas* (Austin: Jenkins Publishing Co., 1974), 254.

12. Peter Gawenda, "Cameron County's Public Schools in 1935," in Milo Kearney (ed.), *More Studies in Brownsville History* (Brownsville: Pan American University at Brownsville, 1989), 382; Dillman, 75, 79; Ruby A. Wooldridge and Robert B. Vezzetti, *Brownsville: A Pictorial History* (Norfolk, VA: The Donning Company, 1982), 128; *The Brownsville Herald*, 28 December 1927, 1, 29 December 1927, 1, 6 December 1942, 4F, and 4 July 1967, 7c; José Raúl Canseco, *Historia de Matamoros* (H. Matamoros: Litográfica Jardín, 1981), 240–243; Gilbert Rafael Cruz and Martha Oppert, *A Century of Service* (Harlingen, TX: United Printers and Publishers, 1979), 26.

13. Kearney, *A Brief History*, 12–13; Kearney, "The Creation of the University of Texas at Brownsville," in Milo Kearney (ed.), *Still More Studies in Brownsville History* (Brownsville: The University of Texas at Brownsville, 1991), 297.

14. Manuel Olvera Cantú, *Narraciones Monográficas de Cd. Acuña* (N.p.: Canáles Herrán, no date), 40–41; Martínez, *Border Boom Town*, 61.

15. Mario Margulis and Rodofo Tuirán, *Desarrollo y población en la frontera norte* (México: El Colegio de México, 1986), 64; Virgil N. Lott, *Story of Reynosa, Mexico* (N.p.: Complimentary Souvenir Edition, 1920(?)), 2.

16. Dillman, 84–85, 94; Canseco, 228.

17. Martínez, *Border Boom Town*, 61.

18. Daniel D. Arreola and James R. Curtis, *The Mexican Border Cities* (Tucson: University of Arizona Press, 1993), 15, 21–22.

19. Martínez, *Border Boom Town*, 53–54.

20. Timmons, 225–226; Martínez, *Border Boom Town*, 57, 61.

21. *The Brownsville Herald*, 6 December 1942, 3F; Martínez, *Border Boom Town*, 57–58.

22. Timmons, 227–228, 230; Martínez, *Border Boom Town*, 30–31.

23. Lott, 2; Rosa Salinas de Villarreal, *Reynosa, Nuestra Ciudad* (Reynosa: R. Ayuntamiento de Reynosa, 1990), 109, 112.

24. Silvia Raquel Flores García, *Nogales: Un Siglo en la Historia* (Hermosillo: Editorial Reprográfica, S.A., 1987), 37–39.

25. Raúl Fernández, *The Mexican-American Border Regions* (Notre Dame, IN: University of Notre Dame, 1989), 18.

26. David Piñera Ramirez, *Historia de Tijuana*, 93, 95–96, 98–99, 104, 115–116.

27. Frank Love, *From Brothel to Boom Town* (Colorado Springs: Little London Press, 1981), 48.

28. Timmons, 227–229; Martínez, *Border Boom Town*, 30–31, 59.

29. Martínez, *Border Boom Town*, 52; Piñera Ramírez, *Historia de Tijuana*, 93, 93–99; Aguirre, 292.

30. Timmons, 227; Martínez, *Border Boom Town*, 30–31.

31. Piñera Ramírez, *Historia de Tijuana*, 104, 115–116.

32. Aguirre, 216, 298–299, 306–307.

33. Piñera Ramírez, *Historia de Tijuana*, 93–98, 104, 115–116.

34. Arreola and Curtis, 100.

35. Martínez, *Border Boom Town*, 30–31; Timmons, 227–228.

36. Martínez, *Border Boom Town*, 62, 64; Piñera Ramírez, *Historia de Tijuana*, 95; Aguirre, 159, 198, 229, 250, 257, 263, 278, 282, 296, 300.

37. Aguirre, 159, 198, 229, 250, 257, 263, 278, 282, 296, 300; Piñera Ramírez, *Historia de Tijuana*, 101–103, 106, 276.

38. Martínez, *Border Boom Town*, 60.

39. Lott, 2; Salinas de Villarreal, 109, 112.

40. Canseco, 245, 261.

41. Canseco, 229–230, 314.

42. Stambaugh, 269.

43. Timmons, 227.

44. Timmons, 227; Martínez, *Border Boom Town*, 30–31, 53, 57–58.

45. Piñera Ramírez, *Historia de Tijuana*, 93–100.

46. Martínez, *Border Boom Town*, 68–69, 71.

47. John R. Peavey, *Echoes from the Rio Grande* (Brownsville: Springman-King Company, 1963), 181–182; Canseco, 235–236.

48. Martínez, *Border Boom Town*, 73, 92–93.

49. Aguirre, 298.

50. Martínez, *Border Boom Town*, 66–67.

51. Antonio María Guerra, *Mier en la Historia* (Mier: n.p., 1953), 50.

52. Luis Benedicto, *Historia de Nuevo Laredo* (Nuevo Laredo, Tamaulipas: n.p., 1956), 69, 72.

53. Martínez, *Border Boom Town*, 62.

54. Robert Mayer (ed.), *San Diego: A Chronological and Documentary History* (Dobbs Ferry, NY: Oceana Publications, Inc., 1978), 55–57, 59.

55. Zavaleta, "The Twin Cities," 154–155; Martínez, *Border Boom Town*, 83–86, 89; Timmons, 238–239; Piñera Ramírez, *Historia de Tijuana*, 117.

56. Mayer, 59–60.

57. Martínez, *Border Boom Town*, 83–84; Piñera Ramírez, *Historia de Tijuana*, 117, 129–130, 137, 148.

58. Martínez, *Border Boom Town*, 87–88; Piñera Ramírez, *Historia de Tijuana*, 129–130, 133–135, 205.

59. Zavaleta, "The Twin Cities," 153–154; Dillman, 80; Wooldridge, *Brownsville*, 128.

60. Richard Marcum, "Fort Brown, Texas," Ph.D. dissertation, Texas Technological College, August 1964, 295; Dillman, 80; Wooldridge, *Brownsville*, 130.

61. Hildebrand, 79; Ida Morris, "Where the Magic Valley Meets the Sea," in Valley By-Liners, *Roots by the River* (Mission, TX: Border Kingdom Press, 1978), 329; Wooldridge, *Brownsville*, 130.

62. Ruby Wooldridge and Robert B. Vezzetti, "The Founding of Charro Days,"

in Milo Kearney (ed.), *More Studies in Brownsville History* (Brownsville: Pan American University at Brownsville, 1989), 390–391.

63. Salinas de Villarreal, 125, 127.

64. Dillman, 84; Zavaleta, "The Twin Cities," 155–156.

65. Kearney, *A Brief History*, 10–11; Canseco, 267.

66. Benedicto, 72–73.

67. C. L. Sonnichsen, *Pass of the North* (El Paso: Texas Western Press, 1968), Vol. II, 42–43.

68. Martínez, *Border Boom Town*, 78–82, 84–85, 90–91.

69. Flores García, 45, 62.

70. Arreola and Curtis, 80.

71. Aguirre, 316–317, 321, 323–326, 330, 337, 341, 356–359.

72. Leon C. Metz, *Border: The U.S.-Mexican Line* (El Paso: Mangan Books, 1989), 265.

73. Ben E. Pingenot, *Historical Highlights of Eagle Pass and Maverick County* (Eagle Pass, TX: Eagle Pass Chamber of Commerce, 1971), 12.

74. Timmons, 238, 240.

75. Michael C. Meyer and William L. Sherman, *The Course of Mexican History* (New York: Oxford University Press, 1991), 590; William P. Tucker, *The Mexican Government Today* (Minneapolis: University of Minnesota Press, 1957), 394–396.

76. John W. House, *Frontier on the Rio Grande* (Oxford: Clarendon Press, 1982), 240–241.

77. Kearney and Knopp, *Boom and Bust*, 225.

78. Kearney and Knopp, *Boom and Bust*, 232–233.

79. *The Brownsville Herald*, 25 July 1932, 1 and 6.

80. Kearney and Knopp, *Boom and Bust*, 233.

81. Kearney and Knopp, *Boom and Bust*, 233–234.

82. *The Brownsville Herald*, 22 July 1942, 1.

83. Kearney and Knopp, *Boom and Bust*, 235.

84. Ozzie G. Simmons, *Anglo Americans and Mexican Americans in South Texas* (New York: Arno Press, 1974), 273.

85. Evan Anders, *Boss Rule in South Texas* (Austin: University of Texas Press, 1982), 238–239; Simmons, 272–273.

86. Owen P. White, "High-handed and Hell-bent," *Collier's*, 22 June 1929, 8–9.

87. Marie Jones, "Hidalgo County, Ed Couch, and the Good Government League," in Valley By-Liners, *Roots by the River* (Mission, TX: Border Kingdom Press, 1978), 263–264; Spence, passim.

88. Simmons, 280–281.

89. *American Studies Class, McAllen: A Bicentennial Reflection* (McAllen, TX: 1975), no page numbers, 21–22, 49–50, 57–58; *Valley Evening Monitor*, 1 March 1961, 10E.

90. Simmons, 226, 284, 288; *American Studies Class*, 61–62, 108–109.

91. Jerry Thompson, *Warm Weather*, 148–149.

92. Jerry Thompson, *Laredo*, 281.

93. Sonnichsen, Vol. II, 11–12; Timmons, 231–232.

94. Sonnichsen, Vol. II, 12–14; Timmons, 232–235.

95. Shawn Lay, *War, Revolution and the Ku Klux Klan* (El Paso: Texas Western Press, 1985), 155–159.

96. Sonnichsen, Vol. II, 20–24.

97. Sonnichsen, Vol. II, 44–45.

98. Sonnichsen, Vol. II, 36–39.

99. Sonnichsen, Vol. II, 45–48.

100. Richard F. Pourade, *The Rising Tide: Volume VI of The History of San Diego* (San Diego: The Union-Tribune Publishing Company, 1967), 11–12.

101. Pourade, *The Rising Tide*, 21–23.

102. Iris H. W. Engstrand, *San Diego: California's Cornerstone* (Tulsa: Continental Heritage Press, 1980), 98.

103. Pourade, *The Rising Tide*, 67.

104. Pourade, *The Rising Tide*, 181–182, 229–233, 235.

105. Kearney and Knopp, *Boom and Bust*, 229–230.

106. Kearney and Knopp, *Boom and Bust*, 236–237.

107. *Reynosa, nuestra ciudad* (Reynosa: Tamaulipas: Ateneo de Reynosa, 1987), 107–110.

108. Benedicto, 67–71.

109. Benedicto, 72–74.

110. Martínez, *Border Boom Town*, 60–61.

111. Martínez, *Border Boom Town*, 65.

112. Piñera Ramírez, *Historia de Tijuana*, 175; Sonnichsen, Vol. II, 41–42; Martínez, *Border Boom Town*, 83–84, 86–91.

113. Martínez, *Border Boom Town*, 96–97.

114. Adaljiza Sosa Riddell, "Who Cares Who Governs?" Ph.D. dissertation, University of California, Riverside, 1974, 60–62.

115. Piñera Ramírez, *Historia de Tijuana*, 100–102.

116. Piñera Ramírez, *Historia de Tijuana*, 104–105, 117, 130–131; John A. Price, *Tijuana: Urbanization in a Border Culture* (Notre Dame, IN: University of Notre Dame Press, 1973), 57.

CHAPTER TEN

1. David Piñera Ramírez (ed.), *Historia de Tijuana* (Tijuana: Centro de Investigaciones Históricas, 1985), 140–141.

2. Brian Robertson, "World War II Era Authorities Urged Brownsville to Stay Vigilant," in Milo Kearney (ed.), *Still More Studies in Brownsville History* (Brownsville: Pan American University at Brownsville, 1989), 271–272.

3. Piñera Ramírez, *Historia de Tijuana*, 140–141.

4. Oscar J. Martínez, *Border Boom Town* (Austin: University of Texas Press, 1978), 96–97; Silvia Raquel Flores García, *Nogales: Un Siglo en la Historia* (Hermosillo: Editorial Reprográfica, S.A., 1987), 62.

5. Raúl A. Fernández, *The Mexican-American Border Region* (Notre Dame, IN: University of Notre Dame Press, 1989), 61.

6. Martínez, *Border Boom Town*, 95, 110.

7. Martínez, *Border Boom Town*, 110.

8. *Time*, 12 July 1993, 15.

9. Neil Morgan, "Where Two Californias Meet," *National Geographic*, vol. 176, no. 2 (August 1989): 182, 200.

10. Fernández, 86.

11. Martínez, *Border Boom Town*, 108–110.

12. Martínez, *Border Boom Town*, 96–97.

13. Mario Margulis y Rodolfo Tuirán, *Desarrollo y población en la frontera norte: el caso de Reynosa* (México: El Colegio de México, 1986), 50, 65.

14. Martínez, *Border Boom Town*, 112–113.

15. Martínez, *Border Boom Town*, 112–113.

16. W. H. Timmons, *El Paso: A Borderlands History* (El Paso: Texas Western Press, 1990), 246.

17. J. Lee and Lilian Stambaugh, *The Lower Rio Grande Valley of Texas* (Austin: Jenkins Publishing Co., 1974), 248–250; Antonio N. Zavaleta, "The Twin Cities: A Historical Synthesis of the Socio-Economic Interdependence of the Brownsville-Matamoros Border Community," in Milo Kearney, ed., *Studies in Brownsville History*, 156.

18. Martínez, *Border Boom Town*, 110–113; Timmons, 246.

19. Luis Benedicto, *Historia de Nuevo Laredo* (Nuevo Laredo: n.p., 1956), 78; Manuel Cantú Olvera, *Narraciones Monográficas de Cd. Acuña* (N.p.: Canales Herrán, no date), 132.

20. Richard Marcum, "Fort Brown, Texas," Ph.D. dissertation, Texas Technological College, August 1964, 297–298; Charles Daniel Dillman, "The Functions of Brownsville, Texas and Matamoros, Tamaulipas," Ph.D. dissertation, University of Michigan, 1968, 139.

21. Walter W. Hildebrand, "The History of Cameron County," master's thesis, North Texas State, 1950, 81.

22. Dillman, 136–137.

23. Ann Reed Washington, "Cameron County's Judge of the Half-Century," in Valley By-Liners, *Roots by the River* (Mission, TX: Border Kingdom Press, 1978), 245.

24. Dillman, 167; Wooldridge, *Brownsville*, 170.

25. Dillman, 81.

26. Dillman, 56, 86–90, 95, 142, 161, 179; José Raúl Canseco, *Historia de Matamoros* (H. Matamoros: Litográfica Jardín, 1981), 249, 266, 314–315.

27. Dillman, 88, 182; Stambaugh, 246–247.

28. Martínez, *Border Boom Town*, 99.

29. Piñera Ramírez, *Historia de Tijuana*, 171.

30. Celso Aguirre Bernal, *Compendio* (Mexicali: n.p., 1966), 372, 381.

31. Piñera Ramírez, *Historia de Tijuana*, 224.

32. Fernández, 81.

33. Aguirre, 428, 431–434, 444–445, 453, 455, 457, 459; Leon C. Metz, *Border: The U.S.-Mexican Line* (El Paso: Mangan, 1989), 278–279, 281, 285–286, 289–290.

34. Robert Mayer (ed.), *San Diego: A Chronological and Documentary History* (Dobbs Ferry, NY: Oceana, 1978), 61–65.

35. Fernández, 36.

36. Martínez, *Border Boom Town*, 96; Timmons, 245.

37. C. L. Sonnichsen, *Pass of the North* (El Paso: Texas Western Press, 1980), Vol. II, 58–59; Timmons, 241, 244.

38. Timmons, 242, 245–246.

39. Martínez, *Border Boom Town*, 96.

40. Rosa Salinas de Villarreal, *Reynosa, Nuestra Ciudad* (Reynosa: R. Ayuntamiento de Reynosa, 1990), 128.

41. Ben Pingenot, *Historical Highlights of Eagle Pass and Maverick County* (Eagle Pass, TX: Eagle Pass Chamber of Commerce, 1971), 20.

42. Flores García, 62–63.

43. Frank Love, *From Brothel to Boom Town* (Colorado Springs: Little London Press, 1981), 48.

44. Dillman, 56, 86–88, 142, 161, 179; Canseco, 266, 314–315.

45. Benedicto, 75–76, 80.

46. Dillman, 185–186.

47. Piñera Ramírez, *Historia de Tijuana*, 139.

48. Fernández, 44.

49. Piñera Ramírez, *Historia de Tijuana*, 142, 171–173, 185, 187–188, 192, 210, 261.

50. Timmons, 242.

51. Martínez, *Border Boom Town*, 96, 98–99, 111, 126.

52. Martínez, *Border Boom Town*, 106–107.

53. Anthony Keith Knopp, "The Populist Revolt of M. M. Vicars," in Milo Kearney (ed.), *More Studies in Brownsville History* (Brownsville: Pan American University at Brownsville, 1989), 405.

54. *The Brownsville Herald*, 2 November 1955, 4.

55. Knopp, 405–406.

56. Knopp, 407–409.

57. Simmons, 183; *Valley Evening Monitor*, 1 March 1961, 10E.

58. Simmons, 284–285, 291–292.

59. *American Studies Class*, 23–25, 31.

60. Hinojosa, 121; Jerry Thompson, *Warm Weather and Bad Whiskey* (El Paso: Texas Western Press, 1991), 148–149.

61. William V. D'Antonio and William H. Form, *Influentials in Two Border Cities* (Notre Dame, IN: University of Notre Dame Press, 1965), 132–135; Sonnichsen, Vol. II, 55–56.

62. Sonnichsen, Vol. II, 56; D'Antonio and Form, 23, 139–140.

63. D'Antonio and Form, 140–146; Timmons, 253; Sonnichsen, Vol. II, 56.

64. Richard F. Pourade, *City of the Dream, Vol. VII of The History of San Diego* (La Jolla, CA: Copley Books, 1977), 22, 67.

65. Pourade, *City of the Dream*, 34.

66. Pourade, *City of the Dream*, 40–50, 73; Engstrand, 116.

67. Pourade, *City of the Dream*, 58–60, 70–71, 78, 93–94.

68. Pourade, *City of the Dream*, 78–79, 101, 139.

69. Kearney and Knopp, *Boom and Bust*, 243–244.

70. Kearney and Knopp, *Boom and Bust*, 244, 246.

71. Benedicto, 75; Piñera Ramírez, *Historia de Tijuana*, 333.

72. Benedicto, 76–77.

73. Benedicto, 78.

74. Martínez, *Border Boom Town*, 103–104, 108–109; Sonnichsen, Vol. II, 79.

75. Martínez, *Border Boom Town*, 107.

76. Martínez, *Border Boom Town*, 109–110.

77. D'Antonio and Form, 162–178.

78. Piñera Ramírez, *Visión*, 352–353; Adaljiza Sosa Riddell, "Who Cares Who Governs?" Ph.D. dissertation, University of California, Riverside, 1974, 97.

79. Sosa, 97, 101–102, 106, 113, 136–137.

80. Piñera Ramírez, *Historia de Tijuana*, 173; Price, 71–73; Jonathan P. West, "Public Administration and Local Coordination," in Ellwyn R. Stoddard, Richard L. Nostrand and Jonathan P. West, *Borderlands Sourcebook: A Guide to the Literature on Northern Mexico and the American Southwest* (Norman, OK: University of Oklahoma Press, 1983), 197.

81. Dillman, 162–163; Canseco, 315; T. R. Fehrenbach, *Lone Star* (New York: Macmillan, 1968), 666.

82. Martínez, *Border Boom Town*, 108–109.

CHAPTER ELEVEN

1. W. H. Timmons, *El Paso: A Borderlands History* (El Paso: Texas Western Press, 1990), 251–252.

2. Raúl Fernández, *The Mexican-American Border Region: Issues and Trends* (Notre Dame, IN: University of Notre Dame Press, 1989), 2.

3. Timmons, 254–257, 265–266, 269.

4. Timmons, 201, 278–281.

5. Oscar J. Martínez, *Border Boom Town* (Austin: University of Texas Press, 1978), 116.

6. Martínez, *Border Boom Town*, 132.

7. Robert Mayer (ed.), *San Diego: A Chronological and Documentary History* (Dobbs Ferry, NY: Oceana Publications, Inc., 1978), 66–69.

8. Mayer, 67–71.

9. Martínez, *Border Boom Town*, 117–124; David Piñera Ramírez (ed.), *Historia de Tijuana* (Tijuana: Centro de Investigaciones Históricas, 1985), 208.

10. Fernández, 21.

11. Martínez, *Border Boom Town*, 126.

12. Martínez, *Border Boom Town*, 124–125, 127, 129–130.

13. Martínez, *Border Boom Town*, 131–132, 139, 146; Timmons, 285–286, 288.

14. Martínez, *Border Boom Town*, 127–128, 131; Zavaleta, "The Twin Cities," 160; *The Economist*, 16 September 1989, 82; Gilberto De los Santos and Jerry Prock, "International Trade: A Timely Opportunity for Border Business," *The Borderlands Journal*, vol. 8, no. 2 (Spring 1985): 7–8; María Guadalupe Oropesa Kérlegan, *El Despertar de un Pueblo* (Monterrey: Grafo Print Editores, S.A., 1985), 32–33.

15. Daniel D. Arreola and James R. Curtis, *The Mexican Border Cities: Landscape Anatomy and Place Personality* (Tucson: University of Arizona Press, 1993), 203.

16. *El Bravo*, Matamoros, 19 March 1990, B-1; *The Economist*, 16 September 1989.

17. Timmons, 268.

18. Oscar J. Martínez, *Troublesome Border* (Tucson: The University of Arizona Press, 1988), 127.

19. Arreola and Curtis, 13, 24.

20. Piñera Ramírez, *Historia de Tijuana*, 192–193, 207, 209, 211, 215–216.

21. Arreola and Curtis, 80.

22. Piñera Ramírez, *Historia de Tijuana*, 261, 271–272.

23. Arreola and Curtis, 94–95.

24. Sebastian Rotella, "Tijuana Battles for Respect," *Los Angeles Times*, 22

April 1994, A1 and A26; Piñera Ramírez, *Historia de Tijuana*, 192–193, 207, 209, 215–216, 244, 256–258, 265–266.

25. Arreola and Curtis, 81–82, 187, 208.

26. Arreola and Curtis, 203–204.

27. Charles Daniel Dillman, "The Functions of Brownsville, Texas and Matamoros, Tamaulipas," Ph.D. dissertation, University of Michigan, 1968, 199–200; José Raúl Canseco, *Historia de Matamoros* (H. Matamoros: Litográfica Jardín, 1981), 335, 341, 348–349.

28. Milo Kearney, et al., *A Brief History* (Brownsville: University of Texas-Pan American, 1989), 16.

29. Arreola and Curtis, 25, 70.

30. Silvia Raquel Flores García, *Nogales: Un Siglo en la Historia* (Hermosillo: Editional Reprográfica, S.A., 1987), 64–67.

31. Mario Margulis y Rodolfo Tuirán, *Desarrollo y población en la frontera norte* (México: El Colegio de México, 1986), 50.

32. Rosa Salinas de Villarreal, *Reynosa, Nuestra Ciudad* (Reynosa: R. Ayuntamiento de Reynosa, 1990), 135, 142–143.

33. Martínez, *Troublesome Border*, 127; Arreola, 81.

34. Neil Morgan, "Where Two Californias Meet: San Diego," *National Geographic*, vol. 176, no. 2 (August 1989): 178–179, 183, 185, 196.

35. C. L. Sonnichsen, *Pass of the North* (El Paso: Texas Western Press, 1980), Vol. II, 65, 73; Timmons, 243, 263–266, 270, 302.

36. Keith Elliott, "Laredo: Border Boomtown," *Texas Parade*, vol. 34, no. 11 (April 1974): 35, 41.

37. Kearney, *A Brief History*, 16; *The Brownsville Herald* 30 July 1989, 1D.

38. Martínez, *Troublesome Border*, 127.

39. Zavaleta, "The Twin Cities," 160; Dillman, 123–124.

40. Dillman, 128.

41. Ruby A. Wooldridge and Robert B. Vezzetti, *Brownsville: A Pictorial History* (Norfolk, VA: The Donning Co., 1982), 201, 203.

42. Kearney, *A Brief History*, 18–19, 23; Kearney, "The Creation of The University of Texas at Brownsville," 291–299.

43. Martínez, *Troublesome Border*, 127.

44. Arreola and Curtis, 29–30.

45. Martínez, *Troublesome Border*, 127.

46. Lawrence A. Herzog, *Where North Meets South* (Austin: Center for Mexican American Studies at The University of Texas at Austin, 1990), 9–10, 30.

47. Fernández, 70–72; Zavaleta, "The Twin Cities," 163.

48. Zavaleta, "The Twin Cities," 163; Martínez, *Border Boom Town*, 132–134; Timmons, 286.

49. Flores García, 66; Susana Hayward, "Gobierno panista de B. C. N. sometido a prueba," *El Heraldo de Brownsville*, 25 April 1994, 1.

50. Milo Kearney and Anthony Knopp, *Boom and Bust* (Austin: Eakin Press, 1991), 260–263; Norman Binder and Frank J. García, "Winning Political Office in Cameron County, 1876–1988: The Mexican-American Case," in Milo Kearney (ed.), *More Studies in Brownsville History* (Brownsville: Pan American University at Brownsville, 1989), 427–431.

51. *Brownsville Herald*, 8 December 1971, 1A; Kearney and Knopp, *Boom*

and Bust, 261–262.

52. Kearney and Knopp, *Boom and Bust*, 263.

53. Kearney and Knopp, *Boom and Bust*, 263–264.

54. Susan Duffy, "The Last Patrón," *Texas Monthly*, July 1981, 85.

55. *The Monitor*, McAllen, Texas, 23 August 1983, 1A; Duffy, 85.

56. *The Monitor*, 5 April 1981, 1A; *The Monitor*, 9 April 1981, 4A; Duffy, 84–85, 88.

57. Gary Mounce, "NOTHAL," *The Texas Observer*, 7 May 1993, 21.

58. Bill Moyers, personal interview, CBS Reports "You Can Fight City Hall," 1979.

59. Fernando Piñón, *Patrón Democracy* (Mexico: Ediciones "Contraste," 1985), 138–150.

60. Piñón, 23–28, 133–136, 154–157, 166–170; Peter Applebome, "The Sheets of Laredo," *Texas Monthly*, November 1984, 136; Moyers interview.

61. Applebome, 136; *The Laredo Times*, 28 March 1978, 1; *The Laredo Times*, 26 March 1978, 1; *The Laredo Times*, 5 April 1978, 1; Piñón, 176–189; Alan Weisman, *La Frontera: The United States Border with Mexico* (Tucson: The University of Arizona Press, 1986), 34.

62. Steve Lewis, Laredo Junior College, personal interview, 16 August 1993.

63. Timmons, 252–260; Sonnichsen, Vol. II, 62–63.

64. Sonnichsen, Vol. II, 99.

65. Sonnichsen, Vol. II, 75, 98–100; Timmons, 262–264.

66. Sonnichsen, Vol. II, 110.

67. Sonnichsen, Vol. 109–111; Timmons, 251.

68. Timmons, 272–276; Sonnichsen, Vol. II, 102–103, 114–117.

69. Weisman, 20–21; Alison Cook, "Just Add Water," *Texas Monthly*, May 1988, 70, 72.

70. Herzog, 230–231; Richard F. Pourade, *City of the Dream, Vol. VII of The History of San Diego* (La Jolla, CA: Copley Books, 1977), 154, 167–180.

71. Pourade, *City of the Dream*, 189–190, 203–204.

72. Mayer, 70–71; *The San Diego Union*, 8 November 1967, A1–A2; Pourade, *City of the Dream*, 204–206, 215–216, 220, 225, 229–230.

73. Iris H. W. Engstrand, *San Diego: California's Cornerstone* (Tulsa: Continental Heritage Press, 1980), 142.

74. Engstrand, 142; Patrick Seslar, "Where Hispanicity Thrives," *Vista*, 6 September 1992, 10, 12.

75. John Gallagher, "San Diego Mulls Scout Eviction," *The Advocate*, 20 October 1992, 21; Jordan Bonfante, "Lady power in the Sunbelt," *Time*, 19 March 1990, 21.

76. Canseco, 306; E. V. Niemeyer, Jr., "Texas Discovers Its Mexican Neighbors: Border-State Governmental Relations, 1978–1991," *Rio Bravo*, vol. II, no. 1 (Fall 1992): 79–80.

77. Edward J. Williams, "Culture and Politics in the Mexican-United States Borderlands: National and Binational Perspectives," paper presented to an international workshop on the U.S.-Mexican Borderlands, El Colegio de Sonora, Hermosillo, March 1991, revised April 1991.

78. Williams, 5–7.

79. *The Brownsville Herald*, 1991–92; Kearney and Knopp, *Boom and Bust*, 255–256.

80. Kearney and Knopp, *Boom and Bust*, 253–256.

81. Kearney and Knopp, *Boom and Bust*, 257; María Guadalupe Oropesa Kérlegan, *El despertar de un Pueblo* (Monterrey: Grafo Print Editores, S.A., 1985), 17–23.

82. Kearney and Knopp, *Boom and Bust*, 257.

83. Kearney and Knopp, *Boom and Bust*, 257–258.

84. *The Brownsville Herald*, 11 June 1993, 3B.

85. Prof. Joel Garcia Cruz, Reynosa, Tamaulipas, letter to Prof. Elia Garcia, 5 September 1994.

86. Weisman, 18–19; *The Brownsville Herald*, 30 June 1993, 11A.

87. Stephen Baker, "An Old-Time Boss — And a City of the Future," *Business Week*, 5 February 1990, 18D, 18F.

88. Weisman, 38.

89. Weisman, 38–39; Baker, "An Old Time Boss," 18D, 18F.

90. *Texas Observer*, 6 May 1994, 24.

91. Martínez, *Border Boom Town*, 116–124; Timmons, 277–285.

92. Manuel A. Machado, *Barbarians of the North: Modern Chihuahua and the Mexican Political System* (Austin: Eakin Press, 1992), 80–87; Martínez, *Troublesome Border*, 108, 110; Martínez, *Border Boom Town*, 124–125; Timmons, 290.

93. Machado, 92–122.

94. Machado, 187–193; *The Brownsville Herald*, 13 June 1993, 18A.

95. Adaljiza Sosa Riddell, "Who Cares Who Governs? A Historical Analysis of Local Governing Elites in Mexicali, Mexico," Ph.D. dissertation, The University of California at Riverside, 1974, 159.

96. Jonathan P. West, "Public Administration and Local Coordination," in Ellwyn R. Stoddard, Richard L. Nostrand, and Jonathan P. West, *Borderland Sourcebook: A Guide to the Literature on Northern Mexico and the American Southwest* (Norman, OK: University of Oklahoma Press, 1983), 196–197; Leon C. Metz, *Border: The U.S.-Mexican Line* (El Paso: Mangan Books, 1989), 405.

97. Sosa, 104, 114; Piñera Ramírez, *Historia de Tijuana*, 176–177.

98. Herzog, 217–219; Piñera Ramírez, *Historia de Tijuana*, 173.

99. Weisman, 168.

100. Weisman, 168, 173; Stephen Baker, "Can Ernesto Ruffo Bounce From Baja to Mexico City?" *Business Week*, 8 January 1990, 44H; *New York Times*, 22 January 1993, A6, A8.

101. *Brownsville Herald*, 29 May 1994, 1A.

CHAPTER TWELVE

1. Raúl A. Fernández, *The Mexican-American Border Region* (Notre Dame, IN: University of Notre Dame Press, 1989), 78 and 105.

2. "Asia Unleashed," *The Economist*, 3 April 1993, 15.

3. Lawrence A. Herzog, *Where North Meets South: Cities, Space, and Politics on the U.S.-Mexico Border* (Austin: Center for Mexican American Studies at The University of Texas at Austin, 1990), 11; W. H. Timmons, *El Paso: A Borderlands History* (El Paso: Texas Western Press, 1990), 197, 292–293, 296–297.

4. Oscar J. Martínez, *Border Boom Town* (Austin: University of Texas Press, 1978), 4–7.

5. Fernández, 93, 95.

6. Martínez, *Border Boom Town*, 4–7.

7. Louis Dubose, "Free Trade: Boil the Water," *The Texas Observer*, 7 May 1993, 12.

8. Fernández, 108–109.

9. Dubose, 10–12.

10. Hector F. Garza-Trejo, "Longshoremen losing battle for local jobs," *The Brownsville Herald*, 24 July 1993, 1.

Bibliography

General

Almaraz, Félix D., Jr. *Tragic Cavalier: Governor Manuel Salcedo of Texas, 1808–1813.* Austin: University of Texas Press, 1982.

Anders, Evan. *Boss Rule in South Texas.* Austin: University of Texas Press, 1982.

Arreola, Daniel D., and James R. Curtis. *The Mexican Border Cities: Landscape Anatomy and Place Personality.* Tucson: The University of Arizona Press, 1993.

Bancroft, Hubert Howe. *History of Texas and the North Mexican States.* San Francisco: The History Company, Publishers, 1890.

Cagle, Eldon, Jr. *The History of Fort Sam Houston.* N.p.: n.d.

Canales, José T. *Bits of Texas History.* San Antonio: Artes Gráficas, 1950.

Chipman, Donald E. *Spanish Texas, 1519–1821.* Austin: University of Texas Press, 1992.

———. *Texas en la Epoca Colonial.* Madrid: Editorial Mapfre, 1992.

Clark, John G. *New Orleans, 1718–1812: An Economic History.* Baton Rouge: Louisiana State University Press, 1970.

Coerver, Don M., and Linda B. Hall. *Texas y la Revolución Mexicana: Un Estudio sobre la política fronteriza nacional y estatal, 1910–1920.* Trans. by Carlos Valdés. México: Fondo de Cultura Económica, 1988.

Covián Martínez, Vidal. *Don José Bernardo Maximiliano Gutiérrez de Lara.* Ciudad Victoria, Tamaulipas: Ediciones Siglo XX, 1967.

Cruz, Gilbert Rafael, and Martha Oppert. *A Century of Service: The History of the Catholic Church in the Lower Rio Grande Valley.* Harlingen, TX: United Printers and Publishers, Inc., 1979.

Daniels, George G. (ed.). *The Spanish West.* Alexandria, VA: Time-Life Books, 1976.

D'Antonio, William V., and William H Form. *Influentials in Two Border Cities.* Notre Dame, IN: University of Notre Dame Press, 1965.

305

Dubose, Louis. "Free Trade: Boil the Water," *The Texas Observer*, 7 May 1993, 10–12.

Fehrenbach, T. R. *Fire and Blood: A History of Mexico*. New York: Bonanza Books, 1973.

_____. *Lone Star: A History of Texas and the Texans*. New York: Macmillan Company, 1968.

Fernández, Raúl A. *The Mexican-American Border Region: Issues and Trends*. Notre Dame, IN: University of Notre Dame Press, 1989.

García, Clotilde. *Captain Blas María de la Garza Falcón*. Austin: San Felipe Press of The Jenkins Publishing Co., 1984.

Goldfinch, Charles W. "Juan N. Cortina, 1824–1892: A Reappraisal." Master's thesis, University of Chicago, June 1949.

Graf, LeRoy P. "The Economic History of the Lower Rio Grande Valley, 1820–1875." Ph.D. dissertation, Harvard University, February 1942.

Hammett, A. B. J. *The Empresario: Don Martín DeLeón, The Richest Man in Texas*. Kerrville, TX: Braswell Printing, 1971.

Herzog, Lawrence A. *Where North Meets South: Cities, Space, and Politics on the U.S.-Mexico Border*. Austin: Center for Mexican American Studies at The University of Texas at Austin, 1990.

Horgan, Paul. *Great River: The Rio Grande in North American History*. New York: Holt, Rinehart and Winston, 1971.

House, John W. *Frontier on the Rio Grande*. Oxford: Clarendon Press, 1982.

Jarratt, Rie. *Gutiérrez de Lara, Mexican-Texan: The Story of a Creole Hero*. Austin: Creole Texana, 1949.

John, Elizabeth A. H. *Storms Brewed in Other Men's Worlds: The Confrontation of Indians, Spanish, and French in the Southwest, 1540–1795*. Lincoln: University of Nebraska Press, 1975.

Lay, Shawn. *War, Revolution and the Ku Klux Klan*. El Paso: Texas Western Press, 1985.

Maril, Robert Lee. *Poorest of Americans*. Notre Dame, IN: University of Notre Dame Press, 1989.

Martínez, Oscar J. *Troublesome Border*. Tucson: The University of Arizona Press, 1988.

Mendoza Martínez, Jaime. *Historia del Teatro de la Reforma*. Matamoros: El Colegio de la Frontera Norte, 1992.

Metz, Leon C. *Border: The U.S.-Mexican Line*. El Paso: Mangan Books, 1989.

Meyer, Michael C., and William L. Sherman. *The Course of Mexican History*. New York: Oxford University Press, 1991.

Miller, Hubert J. *José de Escandón: Colonizer of Nuevo Santander*. Edinburg, TX: The New Santander Press, 1980.

Miller, Tom. *On the Border: Portraits of America's Southwestern Frontier*. Tucson: The University of Arizona Press, 1981.

Montejano, David. *Anglos and Mexicans in the Making of Texas, 1836–1986*. Austin: University of Texas Press, 1987.

Ortiz Guerrero, Armando Hugo. *Vida y Muerte en la Frontera: Cancionero del Corrido Norestense*. Cd. Victoria: Hensa Editores, S.A., 1992.

Paredes, Américo. "El Corrido de Gregorio Cortez: A Ballad of Border Conflict." Ph.D. dissertation, University of Texas, 1956.

Parisot, Rev. P. F. *The Reminiscences of a Texas Missionary.* San Antonio: St. Mary's Church, 1899.

Piñera Ramírez, David (ed.). *Visión Histórica de la Frontera Norte de México.* Tijuana: Universidad Autónoma de Baja California, 1987.

Piñon, Fernando. *Patrón Democracy.* México: Ediciones "Contraste," 1985.

Pletcher, David M. *Rails, Mines, and Progress: Seven American Promoters in Mexico, 1867–1911.* Port Washington, NY: Kennikat Press, 1958.

Rayburn, John C., and Virginia Kemp Rayburn. *Century of Conflict, 1821–1913: Incidents in the Lives of William Neale and William A. Neale, Early Settlers in South Texas.* Waco: Texian Press, 1966.

Richardson, Rupert Norval, Ernest Wallace, and Adrian N. Anderson. *Texas: The Lone Star State.* Englewood Cliffs, NJ: Prentice-Hall, Inc., 1981.

Robinson, Charles M. III. *Bad Hand: A Biography of General Ranald S. Mackenzie.* Austin: State House Press, 1993.

Schunk, John F. (ed.). *1850 U.S. Census: Cameron, Starr and Webb Counties, Texas.* Wichita, KS: S-K Publications, 1987.

Scott, Florence Johnson. *Historical Heritage of the Lower Rio Grande Valley of Texas.* Waco: Texian Press, 1965.

Simmons, Ozzie G. *Anglo Americans and Mexican Americans in South Texas.* New York: Arno Press, 1974.

Smylie, Vernon. *Conquistadores and Cannibals: The Early History of Padre Island* (1519–1845). Corpus Christi, TX: Texas News Syndicate Press, 1964.

Spence, Ruth Griffin. *The Nickel Plated Highway to Hell.* Unpublished manuscript, 1986.

Taracena, Angel. *Porfirio Díaz.* México: Editorial Jus, S.A., 1960.

Tucker, William P. *The Mexican Government Today.* Minneapolis: University of Minnesota Press, 1957.

Weber, David J. *La Frontera Norte de México, 1821–1846: El sudoeste norteamericano en su época mexicana.* Trans. by Agustín Bárcena. México: Fondo de Cultura Económica, 1988.

Weisman, Alan. *La Frontera: The United States Border with Mexico.* Tucson: The University of Arizona Press, 1986.

West, Jonathan P. "Public Administration and Local Coordination," in Ellwyn R. Stoddard, Richard L. Nostrand and Jonathan P. West, *Borderlands Sourcebook: A Guide to the Literature on Northern Mexico and the American Southwest.* Norman, OK: University of Oklahoma Press, 1983.

White, Owen P. "High-handed and Hell-bent." *Collier's,* 22 June 1929, 8–9, 47–48.

Zorrilla, Juan Fidel, Maribel Mir Flaguer, and Octavio Herrera-Perez (eds.). *Tamaulipas: textos de su historia 1810–1921.* Mexico City: Instituto de Investigaciones Dr. José María Luis Mora, 1990.

San Diego/Tijuana

Birmingham, Stephen. *California Rich.* New York: Simon and Schuster, 1980.

Davidson, Ed, and Eddy Orcutt. *The Country of Joyous Aspect: A Short History of San Diego, California (1542 to 1888).* San Diego: San Diego Trust and Savings Bank, 1929.

Engstrand, Iris H. W. *San Diego: California's Cornerstone.* Tulsa: Continental Heritage Press, 1980.

Fuller, Theodore W. *San Diego Originals: Profiles of the Movers and Shakers of California's First Community.* Pleasant Hill, CA: California Profiles Publications, 1987.

Krell, Dorothy (ed.). *The California Missions: A Pictorial History.* Menlo Park, CA: Lane Publishing Company, 1979.

Mayer, Robert (ed.). *San Diego: A Chronological and Documentary History, 1535–1976.* Dobbs Ferry, NY: Oceana Publications, Inc., 1978.

Morgan, Neil. "Where Two Californias Meet: San Diego," *National Geographic,* vol. 176, no. 2 (August 1989): 176-205.

Piette, Charles J. G. Maximin, O. F. M. *Évocation de Junípero Serra, Fondateur de la Californie.* Bruxelles: Lecture au Foyer, 1946.

Piñera Ramírez, David (ed.). *Historia de Tijuana: Semblanza General.* Tijuana: Centro de Investigaciones Históricas UNAM- UABC, 1985.

Pourade, Richard F. *The Explorers, Vol. I of The History of San Diego.* San Diego: The Union-Tribune Publishing Company, 1960.

———. *Time of the Bells, Vol. II of The History of San Diego.* San Diego: The Union-Tribune Publishing Company, 1961.

———. *The Silver Dons, Vol. III of The History of San Diego.* San Diego: The Union-Tribune Publishing Company, 1963.

———. *The Glory Years, Vol. IV of The History of San Diego.* San Diego: The Union-Tribune Publishing Company, 1964.

———. *Gold in the Sun, Vol. V of The History of San Diego.* San Diego: The Union-Tribune Publishing Company, 1965.

———. *The Rising Tide, Vol. VI of The History of San Diego.* San Diego: The Union-Tribune Publishing Company, 1967.

———. *City of the Dream, Vol. VII of The History of San Diego.* La Jolla, CA: Copley Books, 1977.

Price, John A. *Tijuana: Urbanization in a Border Culture.* Notre Dame, IN: University of Notre Dame Press, 1973.

Pryde, Philip R. *San Diego: An Introduction to the Region.* Dubuque, IA: Kendall/ Hunt Publishing Company, 1976.

Scott, Ed. *San Diego County Soldier-Pioneers, 1846–1866.* National City, CA: Crest Printing Company, 1976.

Mexicali/Calexico

Aguirre Bernal, Celso. *Compendio Histórico-Biográfico de Mexicali, 1539–1966.* Mexicali: N.p., 1966.

Sosa Riddell, Adaljiza. "Who Cares Who Governs? A Historical Analysis of Local Governing Elites in Mexicali, Mexico." Ph.D. dissertation, University of California, Riverside, 1974.

Cd. Juárez/El Paso

Beezley, William H. *Insurgent Governor: Abraham Gonzales and the Mexican Revolution in Chihuahua.* Lincoln: University of Nebraska Press, 1973.

García, Mario T. *Desert Immigrants: The Mexicans of El Paso, 1880–1920.* New Haven: Yale University Press, 1981.

Machado, Manual A. *Barbarians of the North: Modern Chihuahua and the Mexican Political System*. Austin: Eakin Press, 1992.

Martínez, Oscar J. *Border Boom Town: Ciudad Juárez since 1848*. Austin: University of Texas Press, 1978.

Sonnichsen, C. L. *Pass of the North: Four Centuries on the Rio Grande, Vol. I*. El Paso: Texas Western Press, 1968.

———. *Pass of the North: Four Centuries on the Rio Grande, Vol. II*. El Paso: Texas Western Press, 1980.

Timmons, W. H. *El Paso: A Borderlands History*. El Paso: Texas Western Press, The University of Texas at El Paso, 1990.

Nuevo Laredo/Laredo

Applebome, Peter. "The Sheets of Laredo," *Texas Monthly*, November 1984, 134, 136, 138.

Benedicto, Luis. *Historia de Nuevo Laredo*. Nuevo Laredo, Tamaulipas: n.p., 1956.

Elliott, Keith. "Laredo: Border Boomtown," *Texas Parade*, vol. 34, no. 11 (April 1974): 35–43.

Hinojosa, Gilberto Miguel. *A Borderlands Town in Transition: Laredo, 1755–1870*. College Station: Texas A&M University Press, 1983.

Thompson, Jerry. *Laredo: A Pictorial History*. Norfolk, VA: The Donning Company, 1986.

———. *Warm Weather and Bad Whiskey: The 1886 Laredo Election Riot*. El Paso: Texas Western Press, The University of Texas at El Paso, 1991.

Wilkinson, J. B. *Laredo and the Rio Grande Frontier*. Austin: Jenkins Publishing Co., 1975.

Reynosa/McAllen

American Studies Class, McAllen: A Bicentennial Reflection. McAllen, TX: N.p., 1975.

Herrera-Perez, Octavio. *Monografia de Reynosa*. Cd. Victoria, Tamaulipas: Instituto Tamaulipeco de Cultura, 1989.

Lott, Virgil N. *Story of Reynosa, Mexico*. N.p.: Complimentary Souvenir Edition, 1920(?).

Margulis, Mario, y Rodolfo Tuirán. *Desarrollo y población en la frontera norte: el caso de Reynosa*. México: El Colegio de México, 1986.

Pierce, Frank Cushman. *Texas' Last Frontier: A Brief History of the Lower Rio Grande Valley*. Menasha, WI: The Collegiate Press, George Banta Publishing Company, 1917, republished in 1962.

Reynosa, nuestra ciudad. Reynosa, Tamaulipas: Ateneo de Reynosa, 1987.

Robertson, Brian. *Rio Grande Heritage: A Pictorial History*. Norfolk/Virginia Beach: The Donning Company, 1985.

———. *Wild Horse Desert: The Heritage of South Texas*. Edinburg, TX: New Santander Press, 1985.

Salinas de Villarreal, Rosa. *Reynosa, Nuestra Ciudad*. Reynosa: R. Ayuntamiento de Reynosa, 1990.

Scott, Florence Johnson. *Historical Heritage of the Lower Rio Grande*. Waco, TX: Texian Press, 1965.

Stambaugh, J. Lee, and Lilian J. Stambaugh. *The Lower Rio Grande Valley of Texas.* Austin: The Jenkins Publishing Co., 1974.

Valley By-Liners. *Gift of the Rio: The Story of Texas' Tropical Borderland.* Mission, TX: Border Kingdom Press, 1975.

———. *Rio Grande Roundup: Story of Texas' Tropical Borderland.* Mission, TX: Border Kingdom Press, 1980.

———. *Roots by the River.* Mission, TX: Border Kingdom Press, 1978.

Matamoros/Brownsville

Bay, Betty. *Historic Brownsville: Original Townsite Guide.* Brownsville: Brownsville Historical Association, 1980.

Canseco, José Raúl. *Historia de Matamoros.* H. Matamoros: Litográfica Jardín, 1981.

Chatfield, Lieutenant W. H. *The Twin Cities: Brownsville, Texas, Matamoros, Mexico.* New Orleans: E. P. Brandao, 1893.

Crews, James Robert. "Reconstruction in Brownsville." Master's thesis, Texas Tech University, December 1969.

Dillman, Charles Daniel. "The Functions of Brownsville, Texas and Matamoros, Tamaulipas: Twin Cities of the Lower Rio Grande." Ph.D. dissertation, University of Michigan, 1968.

García, Clotilde. *Padre José Nicolás Ballí and Padre Island.* Corpus Christi: Grunwald Publishing Co., 1979.

Hildebrand, Walter W. "The History of Cameron County, Texas." Master's thesis, North Texas State College, August 1950.

Kearney, Milo (ed.). *More Studies in Brownsville History.* Brownsville: Pan American University at Brownsville, 1989.

——— (ed.). *Still More Studies in Brownsville History.* Brownsville: The University of Texas at Brownsville, 1991.

——— (ed.). *Studies in Brownsville History.* Brownsville: Pan American University at Brownsville, 1986.

Kearney, Milo, Alfonso Gómez Arguelles, and Yolanda Z. González. *A Brief History of Education in Brownsville and Matamoros.* Brownsville: The University of Texas-Pan American, 1989.

Kearney, Milo, and Anthony Knopp. *Boom and Bust: The Historical Cycles of Matamoros and Brownsville.* Austin: Eakin Press, 1991.

——— (ed.). *Studies in Browsville and Matamoros History.* Brownsville: The University of Texas at Brownsville, 1995.

Marcum, Richard. "Fort Brown, Texas: The History of a Border Post." Ph.D. dissertation, Texas Technological College, August 1964.

Oropesa Kérlegan, María Guadalupe. *El Despertar de un Pueblo.* Monterrey: Grafo Print Editores, S.A., 1985.

Paredes Manzano, Eliseo. *Conmemoración del CXXV Aniversario de los Honrosos Títulos, de Heróica, Leal e Invicta.* H. Matamoros: Imprenta "El Norte," 1976.

———. *Homenaje a los Fundadores de la Heróica, Leal e Invicta Matamoros en el Sesquicentenario de su Nuevo Nombre.* H. Matamoros: Imprenta "El Norte," 1976.

———. *La Casa Mata y Fortificaciones de la Heróica Matamoros, Tamaulipas.* H. Matamoros: Imprenta "El Norte," 1974.

Richardson, Russell C., and Anthony K. Knopp. *A Citizens' Guide to Government and Politics in Brownsville*. Valencia, CA: Blue Moon Publishing Co., 1987.

Thompson, James Heaven. "A Nineteenth Century History of Cameron County, Texas." Master's thesis, The University of Texas at Austin, 1965.

Wooldridge, Ruby A., and Robert B. Vezzetti. *Brownsville: A Pictorial History*. Norfolk, VA: The Donning Company, 1982.

Zavaleta, Antonio N. "The Twin Cities: A Historical Synthesis of the Socio-Economic Interdependence of the Brownsville-Matamoros Border Community," in Milo Kearney, ed., *Studies in Brownsville History*, 125–173.

The Smaller Twin Towns

Cantú Olvera, Manuel. *Narraciones Monográficas de Cd. Acuña*. N.p.: Canales Herrán, no date.

Fisher, Ovie Clark. *King Fisher*. Norman, OK: The University of Oklahoma Press, 1966.

Flores García, Silvia Raquel. *Nogales: Un Siglo en la Historia*. Hermosillo, Sonora: Editorial Reprográfica, S. A., 1987.

Greene, Shirley Brooks. *When Rio Grande City Was Young: Buildings of Old Rio Grande City*. Edinburg, TX: Pan American University, 1987.

Guerra, Antonio María. *Mier en la Historia*. Mier: N.p.: 1953.

Love, Frank. *From Brothel to Boom Town: Yuma's Naughty Past*. Colorado Springs: Little London Press, 1981.

O'Malley, Nancy, Lynn Osborne Bobbitt, and Dan Scurlock. *A Historical and Archeological Investigation of Roma, Texas*. Austin: Office of the State Archeologist, Texas Historical Commission, October 1976.

Pingenot, Ben E. *Historical Highlights of Eagle Pass and Maverick County*. Eagle Pass, TX: Eagle Pass Chamber of Commerce, 1971.

Simmons, Thomas E. *Fort Ringgold: A Brief Tour*. Edinburg, TX: The University of Texas-Pan American Press, 1991.

Villarreal Peña, Ismael. *Seis Villas del Norte: Antecedentes históricos de Nuevo Laredo, Dolores, Guerrero, Mier, Camargo y Reynosa*. Ciudad Victoria, Tamaulipas: Universidad Autónoma de Tamaulipas, Instituto de Investigaciones Históricas, 1986.

Additional Articles

Baker, Stephen. "An Old-Time Boss—And a City of the Future." *Business Week*, 5 February 1990, 18D, 18F.

Baker, Stephen. "Can Ernesto Ruffo Bounce From Baja to Mexico City?" *Business Week*, 8 January 1990, 44H.

Binder, Norman, and Frank J. Garcia. "Winning Political Office in Cameron County, 1876–1988: The Mexican-American Case" in *More Studies in Brownsville History* by Milo Kearney, ed. (Brownsville: Pan American University at Brownsville, 1989), 423–437.

Bonfante, Jordan. "Lady Power in the Sunbelt." *Time*, 19 March 1990, 21.

Cook, Alison. "Just Add Water." *Texas Monthly*, May 1988, 70, 72.

Duffy, Susan. "The Last Patrón." *Texas Monthly*, July 1981, 84–85, 88.

Gallagher, John. "San Diego Mulls Scout Eviction." *The Advocate*, 20 October 1992, 21.

Gilbert, Minnie. "R. Runyon and His 'Little Hunk of the World'," in *Roots by the River* by Valley By-Liners. (Mission, TX: Border Kingdom Press, 1978).

Jones, Marie. "Hidalgo County, Ed Couch, and the Good Government League," in *Roots by the River* by Valley By-Liners (Mission, TX: Border Kingdom Press, 1978), 263–265.

Knopp, Anthony Keith. "The Populist Revolt of M. M. Vicars," in Milo Kearney, ed., *More Studies in Brownsville History*. (Brownsville: Pan American University at Brownsville, 1989).

Lewis, Steve. Personal interview. Laredo Junior College, 16 August 1993.

Mounce, Gary. "NOTHAL." *The Texas Observer*, 7 May 1993, 21.

Moyers, Bill. Personal interview. CBS Reports "You Can Fight City Hall," 1979.

Niemeyer, Jr., E. V. "Texas Discovers Its Mexican Neighbors: Border-State Governmental Relations, 1978–1991," *Rio Bravo*, vol. II, no. 1 (Fall 1992): 76–102.

Seslar, Patrick. "Where Hispanicity Thrives." *Vista*, 6 September 1992, 10, 12.

White, Owen P. "High-handed and Hell-bent." *Collier's*, 22 June 1929, 8–9, 47–48.

The Brownsville Herald
The Laredo Times
The Monitor (McAllen)
The New York Times
The San Diego Union

Index